6

7

8

9

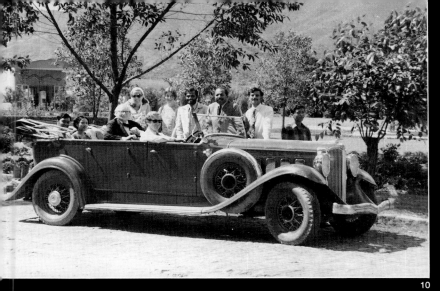

10

1

14

15

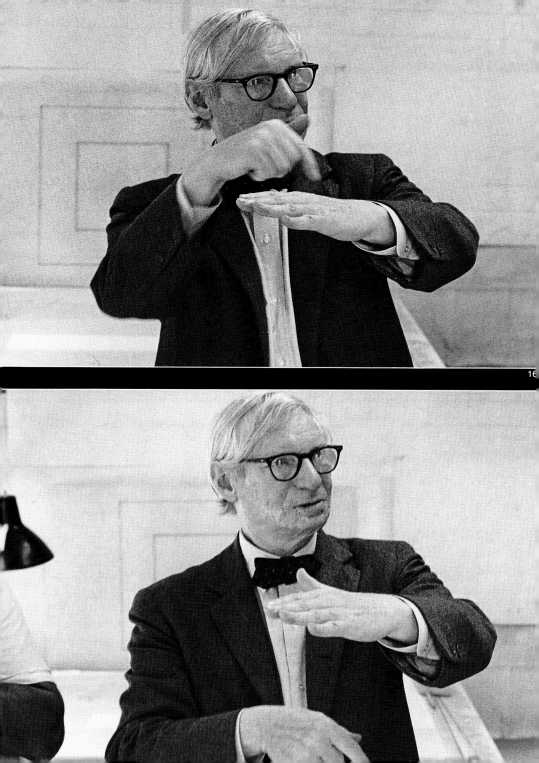

18

19

34

35

36

37

March 16, 1974

What Will Be Has Always Been The Words of Louis I. Kahn

Richard Saul Wurman

This volume is published with the approval of the Louis I. Kahn Collection, a unique resource for research and information, owned by the Pennsylvania Historical and Museum Commission and administered by the Trustees of the University of Pennsylvania.

ACCESS and
RIZZOLI New York

Editing and Design
Richard Saul Wurman

Editorial
Alexandra Tyng, *Senior*
Joy Aiken
Linda Lenhoff
Devorah Rosen

Design and Production
Michael Everitt, *Senior*
Jerry Abbott Miller
Lisa Victor
Mayling Braun
Hugh Enockson

Typesetting
George Quioan, *Senior*
Robin Carr
Linda Lenhoff
Typeset in the USA

Generous contributions from the following helped make this project possible:

The National Endowment for the Arts, Design Arts Program.
Bill N. Lacy
Michael Pittas

The Graham Foundation.

Sui Dynasty Inc.

Photos were graciously contributed by many.
Our thanks to:
Martin E. Rich (1,2,3)
Henri Cartier-Bresson (4,5)
Phillippe Brouste (6)
Charles Madden (7)
Karen M. Rasmussen (8)
Itzhak Amit (13)
George Krause (14-17, 30)
Berko, Aspen CO (18-21)
Marvin Lyons (22)
Oreste Cagnato (23)
Cameraphoto di Celio Scapino (24)
Hans Namuth (26-28, 37)
Stanley M. Feurstein (31)
Robert C. Lautman (32)
Eric Kroll (33)
William Turner (34-37)
Beverly Pabst (40-42)
Bill Eppidge (39)
Ada Karmi-Melamede (43)
B.V. Doshi (44,45)
Esther I. Kahn Collection (10, 12, 25)
Credits not available (9, 11, 29)

Published in the United States of America in 1986 by
ACCESSPRESS Ltd. and
RIZZOLI International Publications, Inc.
300 Park Avenue South, New York, NY 10010

Copyright © 1986 by **ACCESS**PRESS Ltd.

Reprinted 1990

Library of Congress Cataloging-in-Publication Data

Kahn, Louis I., 1901-1974.
  What will be has always been.

  1. Kahn, Louis I., 1901-1974—Quotations. I. Wurman,
Richard Saul, 1935- . II. Title.
NA 737.K32A35 1986   720′.92′4   85-71359
ISBN 0-8478-0606-5
ISBN 0-8478-0607-3 (pbk.)

Printed in Hong Kong

*Our thanks to the following for the speeches, interviews and
conversations transcribed here which were were graciously
contributed by many:*

VIA magazine, Graduate School of Architecture, University
of Pennsylvania, Philadelphia, Pennsylvania.

domus magazine

Institute for the History and Theory of Architecture, Swiss
Federal Institute of Technology, Zurich/Heinz Rommer,
Sharad Jhaveri, Alessandro Vasella

College of Design, Architecture, Art and Planning,
University of Cincinnati, Cincinnati, Ohio

Progressive Architecture magazine

First International Congress of Architects, Isfahan, Iran

Arnold J. Aho, Architect, AIA

Thursday's Drummer magazine

Renzo Salvadori

Robert S. Wemischner

Journal of the American Institute of Architects

Peter Blake

University of Virginia, Charlottesville, Virginia

Temple Beth El of Northern Westchester, New York

Jonas Salk, Founding Director, Salk Institute for Biological
Studies, San Diego, California

International Design Conference at Aspen, Aspen, Colorado

House & Garden magazine

The Pennsylvania Gazette alumni magazine, University
of Pennsylvania

Kimbell Museum, Fort Worth, Texas

Phillips Exeter Academy, Exeter, New Hampshire

John W. Cook

Heinrich Klotz

Arnold Garfinkel

Jaime Mehta

David Rothstein

Jim Hatch

Samuel S. Fleisher Art Memorial, Philadelphia Museum of
Modern Art, Philadelphia, Pennsylvania

Third World Congress, Association of Engineers and
Architects in Israel

Balkrishna V. Doshi

Interior Design magazine

Perspecta 3, The Yale Architecture Journal, Yale University,
New Haven, Connecticut

Alumnae Bulletin, Bryn Mawr College, Bryn Mawr, Pennsylvania

H.P. Daniel van Ginkel

Arts Canada magazine, Canadian Arts Council

Voice of America

Fort Wayne Fine Arts Foundation, Fort Wayne, Indiana

David Slovic

William Jordy

Carl W. Hauser, Jr.

School of Architecture, Princeton University,
Princeton, New Jersey

Drexel Architecture Society, Department of Architecture,
Drexel University, Philadelphia, Pennsylvania

Towne School of Civil and Mechanical Engineering,
University of Pennsylvania, Philadelphia, Pennsylvania

He was the youngest person I ever knew.

His fundamental belief in the fairy tale and a country called *Zero* were the filaments of his fabric of beginnings.

Beginnings, beginnings, beginnings, beginnings were frequently the words that started one of his talks.

Gene Feldman said to me just after Lou died, *We can now all try to copy Lou, because none of us will be able to.*

Somehow Lou managed to totally consume a grapefruit, drink aquavit, follow football, fail to drive a car, play the piano and serve Architecture (with a capital A) all from a single page in his own thought-bound book of principles. Architecture the thoughtful making of place and space.

He had, similarly, a single agenda whose format mirrored an Asimovian world where spoons, buildings and learning were continuously becoming yet never designed.

He was proud of his physical strengths—in his 70's running up five flights of stairs to his office—and he held memories of wrestling people in his youth. He had the charismatic strength that comes to those who are plagued with the rejection that befalls those who serve a single purpose.

His words conjured up images sometimes more exciting than his buildings and yet needing his work to prove their validity and their qualities. He gave new meaning to words: dumb, servant space, river and threshold. His face was said to be half demonic and half angelic and those extremes were felt by many.

I believe I have seen all of his buildings, yet Lou lives for me in his words and in the continuing conversations about him with others. In fact, there is a real and mystical bond that one has with others who knew him independent of knowing each other.

When Gene and I published *The Notebooks and Drawings of Louis I. Kahn* in 1962, Lou allowed me, 26 years old, to choose the drawings and words, and my choice, different from his, fascinated him. In that same way he felt that everything said was the truth although not necessarily factual. Lou's truth as well as the reminiscences of others give a charcoal-like rendition of the collective memory.

Lou was drawn in vine charcoal: scarred, hesitant features, high-pitched voice so direct in its comments yet struggling always to find a simpler phrasing. Once he was asked why he didn't move to New York City where obviously fame and fortune would more readily be his and Lou answered quickly *why would he want to be a Philadelphian living in New York City?*

Perhaps there was no better teacher, as he allowed us to be more of ourselves.

He evolved plans in charcoal, erasing and replacing.

He modeled buildings and landscape in never-hardening plasticine.

He developed ideas in words over words, scratching out phrases and in speeches with refrains containing only minor variations.

This book also is meant to be repetitive and non-hardening. It is to be read at moments, opened at random and read a passage at a sitting.

Six months before he died I taped him as we flew to San Francisco and he spoke of his distrust of facility and how the gift of facility, by easing struggle, hindered the creative depth of work. The cover of this book and the repetition of certain passages give evidence of his struggles.

He was the most extraordinary person I will know, childlike, clear, yet most obscure. His incisive conversations with bricks, steel and concrete will last as long as Architecture itself.

Lou said of Luis Barragan's house that it had no time; it could have been built a hundred years ago or a hundred years from now, and I think his description of that wonderful house in Mexico City is my memory of Lou himself.

Richard Saul Wurman

We are all born with a sense of what to do. Within our own singular limits we know instinctively that, given a sufficient opportunity to put this instinct into practice, we know what to do almost instantaneously, if what we do is true to our singularity.

But *how* to do it we are not born with. We must learn to speak, we must learn to use tools. If you make a great virtue out of just how you do things, it is the least important of all.

Everyone is, in some way or another, an artist.

The only language of man is art.

Science, all knowledge, only serves art. Because we live with only one purpose, and that is to express. This urge to express I try to give an aura, rather than trying to describe. The aura is silence, voiceless, wordless, but still a kind of voice you hear when you pass the Pyramids.

The Pyramids try to say to you, *Let me tell you how I was made.*

It must be considered nothing short of a human miracle to have thought of a building which doesn't in any way resemble what is in nature and which could not have been done if nature hadn't approved its making.

Nature is the maker. It is the giver of presences.

You can have a thought, but a thought has no presence until you call on nature to exercise its powers of order, to make it manifest.

What you saw just now is the truth, because the truth is anything that happens whether you like it or not. The fact that man can think of it makes it the truth. But does it indicate the nature of man? I don't think it does. However, it does involve comparison, criticism, lasting criticism cannot be employed but to take stock in the things we do.

When Burke spoke in Parliament in favor of Americans, he said something beautiful, that surely the Americans got their sense of liberty from England, but the chapel of liberty is in America. He read the frontiers as giving an American the greatest possible courage. He also realized that if America lost any engagement with the English they would simply go west. They had somewhere to go.

We are still living on that sense of freedom. A sense of freedom is still evident in the number of the great, vast institutions that we have in this country.

I like to call those institutions *availabilities*. It is a better word than institutions.

There is no country that can match ours. There is no country that gives availability as freely as America.

We hear a lot about planning, but no one mentions that the real measure of a city is the nature and the character of its availabilities. It is not the traffic system, nor the services. It is the availabilities which a city gives. All other things only serve those availabilities.

I have seen a great deal of the order in city building, and there must be considerations for the services not to be isolated from each other. We need an order of services. You don't consider a traffic system without considering the order of movement.

Because these orders are not considered, we have great destructiveness in our cities: values that have been plowed under, streets that have become roads. All cities now have only roads, hardly any streets.

The street is one of the first institutions of a city, where the buildings opposite each other talk to each other.

Now they are apart from each other.

The order of movement would tell us that the airport is really a wound-up street, an extension of the street. Its architecture should be that of road architecture.

At the intersection, great turnarounds for intersecting traffic could be the recipient of many public services. There could be reservoirs where those intersections are. Certainly they would be places for the fire department and the police department. They shouldn't be buildings at all—they should simply be station points from which you are immediately on the road to where you have to go.

Garages should not be buildings, or be stacked underneath buildings, giving the first stories of buildings as garages. What a hapless thing it is to see those buildings which destroy the continuity of a street association! Garages should also be wound-up streets and should be part of the order of movement, not interfering with the flow of the commerical environment.

Gandhinagar, Gujarat, India 1963-64

I was assigned to do a city near Ahmedabad, to be named *Gandhinagar,* city of Gandhi. All the water goes down the riverbeds during the monsoons. It is wasted, good water coming right from the skies. I proposed bridges or stations across the river which were really reservoirs for the capturing of this water as if it were a crop harvested every year. The water would be distributed in aqueducts through the areas of Gandhinagar. There, with a central air conditioning plant, the center of city services, were various stations. Police and fire department were there, integrated as civic buildings. The mango tree was the point of departure for the laying out of all the houses. The mango tree is a sacred tree. You cannot destroy such a tree in India. It was a respect for the order of water.

There must be an order of movement, an order of winds, an order of light.

The order of light was respected in the buildings I did in India and Pakistan, now Bangladesh, by giving the outside building to the sun and the interior building to habitation.

We blindly follow programs given to us by various boards. We build schools without windows to save air conditioning costs.

What teacher deserves priority over a bird in the tree, the movements of leaves in the tree, the passing cloud, or the passing person fighting the rain? All these are tremendous lessons as you sit within. What teacher deserves that much attention?

Salk Institute
La Jolla, California 1959-65

While working on the Salk Insititute, I designed the first garden, and was struggling with the second. Dr. Salk said, *How are you going to design the second garden?* and I said, *I've got to think of other plants. I wouldn't think of designing it the way the first garden was designed.* But he said, *The buildings are quite the same.* I said, *You're right,* and I came to the realization that one garden is much greater than two.

Then, having struggled for two years trying to find out what I should do with the one garden, I called Luis Barragan of Mexico City. He had done wonderful things with gardens.

The buildings were up, the garden was left unmade. He looked at the space, and he said, *There should be no garden. It should be a plaza.*

I looked at Salk, he looked at me. and we both agreed that a garden was not what we wanted; it should be a plaza. Barragan said, *If you make it a plaza, it will give you a facade to the sky,* and it killed me, because it was a wonderful idea. I could only counter it by saying, *That's right, then I would get all these blue mosaics for nothing,* meaning, of course, the Pacific (Ocean).
Then he proceeded to suggest what design should be applied. At that moment I realized that I had better take over because my sense of what a plaza is was completely different from his.

How delicate then is singularity!

Reprinted from *Perspecta 3: The Yale Architectural Journal,* "Louis I. Kahn: Order and Form," pp. 46-63, Yale University, 1955.

The Architect and the Building
Bryn Mawr College
Bryn Mawr, Pennsylvania
Spring 1962

Erdman Hall Dormitories
Bryn Mawr, PA—1960-65

It is a most interesting thing how the mind has to be stimulated by circumstantial things—let us say by knowledge or by the specific knowledge that is necessary to understand the function of a building such as a dormitory. One must not assume that he knows anything about such a building when he begins to conceive its design, but must think about what is the nature of such a building. What is the nature of a girls' dormitory as compared with a hotel or an apartment building or even, say, a men's dormitory. A dormitory for girls is not the same as a dormitory for men. In a women's dormitory one must feel the presence of *house* much more than in a men's dormitory.

The three larger spaces—the entrance hall, the dining hall, and the living hall—I thought had to be constructed in an entirely different way than the dormitory room. I thought they should be different rooms, larger and higher. They could be built of a different construction than the smaller rooms, could even be placed apart from the smaller rooms, so that when you saw the building from the outside you felt that you could distinguish the halls and, somewhere in the background in association with these rooms, the sleeping quarters or living quarters of the girls. I wouldn't want to confuse the construction of the one with the other, one being of rather powerful and the other of smaller scale construction.

But what constantly remained a problem was the kind of connection one made between the larger and the smaller spaces. The connecting building always complicated the shapes, and one had to be clever but not necessarily successful in the meeting of the two kinds of spaces. This interconnection between the larger spaces and the living quarters gave a third consideration: an architecture of connection, one which was never satisfactory, mostly very costly, and one which had more light in it than was necessary. The connecting architecture became the most difficult. The problem was not how you made an efficient plan for a dormitory room, or how you made a good-looking or imposing hall, but how the buildings would be connected to give an uncomplicated image and positioned to have an effective and sympathetic relationship with the other campus halls. It became a major problem to find the coming together of the larger hall and the sleeping quarters without the use of connectors.

After trying many schemes, it was found that three square buildings, each containing one of the larger spaces and dormitory rooms, could satisfy the requirements of light and area and that by the way they were placed together could join to form one building without the use of connectors. This was now without question the scheme, considering all the requirements, the demands of space, and the position on the site.

The image then became strong, so strong that one could not break away from it. You felt it could withstand criticism. Unlike other schemes which had been developed over a long period of time, this composition could not be dismembered. It had its own resourcefulness to adapt itself to whatever were the requirements of the spaces. Only hard work was necessary to bring all the many requirements into harness within the simple statement of the image. One immediately saw the variations of theme which were possible without destroying the singleness of the image.

And so the building is composed of three square buildings which are joined to form their own connectors. The sides of each square give light to dormitory rooms around the periphery, and the number of rooms required determines the size of the squares. The interior areas of the squares become the three big spaces—the entrance hall, the living hall, and the dining hall—and these interior spaces which have no light from the outside are given light by clerestories. The plan can be compared to that of a Scottish castle, in which the thick walls of the castle contain small rooms serving the center hall. Here you have a kind of hollow wall of rooms around the sides of the squares, freeing the interiors for the larger rooms. The building is on three levels with the middle level [being] the entrance and social level. On this level are the three larger halls which are two stories high. From this level, one travels upward to dormitory rooms or down to dormitory rooms.

The building is placed on the site in the position suggested by Douglas Orr, Architectural Consultant for Bryn Mawr College, facing Pembroke Hall and about midway between Pembroke and Morris Avenue. The center square building of the composition of squares is the entrance building and is in direct axis with Pembroke Hall. Also, as suggested by Douglas Orr, Lambaert Avenue will be closed and become a mall connecting the new dormitory with the rest of the campus. The building fits the natural slope of the ground and forms a two-story building on the entrance side and a three-story building facing Morris Avenue. Along the entrance side and touching the corners of the three squares is a wide brick walk between two walls. The one near the building is a bicycle wall and forms two triangular gardens with the walls of the squares. The other is a low sitting wall which holds back the slope of the earth. The little exedra near Wyndham is brought into the composition of the wide walk and becomes an arabesque against the squares.

The effect of the building as one approaches from the arch of Pembroke Hall will be that of diagonal walls facing east and west. When the sun is rising, three walls will appear in light and three walls will be in shadow; and when the sun is setting, the walls previously in light will be in shadow.

The clerestories of the center halls and the chimneys of the fireplaces of these halls make a crown of rising forms which give a soaring quality to the building. Their silhouette against the sky serves to give harmony with the sloping roofs and chimneys of the existing buildings and makes the new building find its place among the other buildings.

Speaking again of the geometry of the building which is based on the interlocking of squares, one corner of each square is interlocked to form the connectors. These points serve as lounges or as the entries to the dining and living halls. The two end corners of the composition of squares harbor the stairways, while the other corners serve as the double rooms where the geometry of the single rooms comes together.

When the three halls found their position on the interior and got their light from clerestories, it was further desired to let these rooms open to the outside so they would have their position on the campus. Again the corners become the point of opening up of these interior spaces. And so the corners of the squares are always serving to make the connections, the entrance, the stairs, the double rooms, or points of opening. They naturally become adaptable for these purposes. They are not forced into being; they simply work out as though the rooms make themselves out of the characteristic of the square.

It is always the hope on the part of the designer that the building, in a way, makes itself rather than be composed with devices that tend to please the eye. It is a happy moment when a geometry is found which tends to make spaces naturally, so that the composition geometry in the plan serves to construct, to give light, and to make spaces.

Reprinted by permission of the
Alumnae Bulletin, Bryn Mawr College

The Animal World
from an interview with H.P. Daniel van Ginkel
Cambridge, Massachusetts
Spring 1961

Think in terms of light, air, the sounds that you hear, water, the green world, the animal world. If I take the last, the animal world, I see the cheetah, running at great speed; and this humiliates man. It makes him inferior to the cheetah—the cheetah you haven't got. In your mind you become conscious of this and you dream of greater locomotion. You dream of being able to move through space with speed—at the ground—speed of such as the cheetah. The cheetah is sort of an out and out jealousy of the animal. And the same is so with birds—how could you ever not think of flying if you see a bird.

The mere fact that there are things in nature that do fly, and that there are animals in creation that run faster than you, makes that part of your brain and your motivation (which are really the same thing) want to do so. Therefore, I consider the automobile, like any means of locomotion, as being something which is definite progress, and we are just as much responsible for the design as the designer himself. It's something which belongs to man's aspirations.

Another thing, the forest wants the city and the city wants the forest. The green world isn't just simply that you like flowers, or that you like trees. Deep down in our experience we lived off such foliage. There must have been something which we deeply venerated and is still part of us. We can't divorce the city from the green world in any way. We could see urbanism completely without trees, but the trees must be made part of our life. You can extend it to water as being something which makes a fountain a necessity, and not just a decoration in a city—something which you must be close to. To command water, as the Romans did when they brought the water from the mountains and into the form of the fountain is something which gives you a command over that thing which is very much part of you deep down. When you see a moving stream you feel as though you have caught sight of what life really is, because you, yourself, have a record of this in you in some way—and your response to it is as something which is very much part of life and you want to make it part of your living.

And there you can make a distinction between living and life if you wish. Life is something that is. It's the nature, really, of our existence—where living is just the exercise of it. And life is the part I'm talking about. Living—like design—concerns me very little. What does concern me is that which makes design an understandable thing. And if you don't understand the sense of life, it is very hard to sense whether you are satisfying this life through living. It is the same if you stand in a square and see a number of windows. These give you the first trace of light. You're not so much conscious of light until you see windows. You know that these windows light the interior of things.

You can't talk about the motorcar in isolation, without realizing that it is one of the items only—one of the ones which we ourselves have created. And you can't even take the attitude that you can kick it around because you don't like the looks of it, or because you don't like the design of it, or because you think it destroys the city. It is a force which has to do with our life, and the living must be patterned so that you include it in what you call the force of life—of which this is an instrument of its expression. Therefore, if the car is ugly now, you must strive to make it beautiful. By beautiful, I mean that it must have no redundancies. Nothing in nature can tolerate an instrument that is full of redundancies. It's bound to be either pared down or destroyed by its own weight.

Therefore, the fight must be to make the car as efficient as it wants to be with the least materials, and the least space occupancy (and yet the largest you can make it). This is all very natural. Otherwise it would weigh too much, cost too much, take up too much room and be uneconomical to operate. So, therefore, we must strive to make it more beautiful, and that means more true to itself.

Motion—movement—is such an important part of our dreams. I don't know of anybody who doesn't dream of flying through space (you've got to move your arms a little bit) and this is speed to equal any kind of speed—or to swim marvellously, without much effort at all. From this, I feel that the making of a positive architecture of movement, which I like to call a viaduct architecture—which takes into account all the aspects of movement and separates them into identities which don't inhibit—has free exercise of one characteristic or the other. So, a viaduct that requires speed cannot be mixed up with a viaduct that is designed to have frequent intervals of interchange. And it must all terminate in a kind of stopping point, because after all it is the nature of movement to stop, when it comes to the city. So, therfore, the architecture of movement.

Now the viaduct architecture in the open country is one form of architecture, with one form of material use, and one form of design, because it is moving at great speeds and also has no immediate objective but to move. This architecture is different; it doesn't require so much integration with other things. But when it reaches town, it becomes a much more respectable kind of viaduct than it was on the open road. In other words, that viaduct in the city becomes a very strategic thing. It is using valuable land and the city can't waste land. The concentration is too great. And therefore the viaduct, when it reaches town, must consider what you can use underneath the viaduct, the materials you use for the viaduct—and that it is made of a tough material, not just a fragile material so that it can withstand the relentless natural forces on it. And as it reaches the centre of town it must be strength highly used in every sense—as storage places (underneath the viaduct or associated with it), for incoming utility of sorts, and even being the centre for the control of utilities. Until it gets to the very core at the entrance to important places in the city—at which point the viaduct must terminate in service areas—service areas which are very close to the centre, and which, because they must be placed in the most strategic and expensive places must not become for one use, but for many, because the storage of a car must cost the city nothing, must cost even the building that you construct for its use, nothing—because nothing is more expensive than a car that's not moving. So therefore, this building must be large, in order to develop a value on the periphery of the building. It can itself be a hotel, or a motel, and the lower stories must be for shopping or some other service that the city needs at that point, (probably in connection with the use around it). The very core of this central shopping building, could possibly be the central air-conditioning station for the core of the city instead of having everybody scrambling for their particular air-conditioning system. Air-conditioning and the control of atmosphere could be a city function. And so you can sense that an architecture can grow out of movement which can be of terrific service to the centre of the city.

When you are going on the open road no speed will satisfy the motorist. He becomes less conscious of the landscape than one might think. How much you see—what way you see isn't a question of speed. Because he is in a car, it becomes something which he has no control over. He can't go at twenty miles an hour because he's a sensitive man, against the other man who goes sixty because he's a less sensitive man. He becomes equally as insensitive. And looking at it the other way, it disregards the difference between one man and another. The motorcar has a way of demanding of you that it become a cheetah. It's completely on its own. You can't read any sentimentality into the fact. You can't make out what you think is good for another person because it's good for you. It must be thought of in that sense.

And there's no reason that you should not find the range of speeds much less as you enter the centre of the city. Someone could even design roads that change accordingly. There's no sense in trying to speed when you're in the city. There's no necessity for speed when one is in the city. So therefore one can slow down. What I'm trying to say is that you can't let your car be stopped at a certain point in the city and adopt another mode of transportation to get the centre. This I don't believe in. I believe that there can even be two or three centres that you come to instead of one. But my belief is that you cannot set an arbitrary line around the center city unless that line is a great line. In other words that line is so great—the city is so great—that everything you touch beyond that line destroys the greatness of the city. Then you can make a man stop behind one very close line if the city itself is great.

But once the man has gone through what might be considered building landscape, and not any important part of the city—no place which is the citadel—that man will not rest until he reaches the citadel—to stop at the gates of the citadel. And so, for that reason, my belief is that the man should come as close as possible to what you'd call the centre, where everything is. And this centre must be protected from all cars and be made completely a walking place, and not have any cars in it. You can of course, incidentally say that there's taxi service and that certain cars enter in order to have that kind of service.

But whether that is so doesn't make much difference. You have taken the major problem and solved it in terms of the cheetah. If you don't mind I'll take that analogy, because I think that is fundamentally what it is. It distinguishes you from the elephant, you see, because the elephant doesn't have any dreams of imitating the cheetah. And so, this being man, he might even destroy the city because of his dreams. But hold no reverence for the city as it is in the hope that you might save it—so as not to destroy its wonderful values. No, you must defend these values in another way—by the interjection of new forms from which a whole realm of new designs can come about and which can make the city what you never saw before—only because you recognize that man is taken as a measure (in other words to satisfy his desires).

But I believe that many cities won't stand up against the demands of this, and that cities will actually be destroyed (or wither away by inaction), in this light, or because the city itself cannot extend its greatness, or really capture a greatness by reason of its position—and so forth. The circumstantial demands of the car, of the parking and so forth, will eat away all the spaces that exist now and pretty soon you have no identifying traces of what I call loyalties—the landmarks. Remember, when you think of your city, you think immediately of certain places which identify the city, as you enter it. If they're gone, your feeling for the city is lost and gone. But new landmarks can be created, new confidences, new loyalties. These need not be financial loyalties—they can be any kind of loyalties—faith in something. But in looking ahead we must sense the form which the city may take. If, because of the demands of the motorcar, we stiffen and harden the city—omitting water, omitting the green world—the city will be destroyed. Therefore the car, because of its destructive value, must start us rethinking the city in terms of the green world, in terms of the world of water, and of air, and of locomotion—and that is really the animal world.

United States Consulate
Luanda, Angola 1959-61,

I am doing a building in Africa, which is very close to the equator. The glare is killing, everybody looks black against the sunlight. Light is a needed thing, but still an enemy. The relentless sun above, the siesta comes over you like thunder.

I saw many huts that the natives made.

There were no architects there.

I came back with multiple impressions of how clever was the man who solved the problems of sun, rain, and wind.

I came to the realization that every window should have a free wall to face. This wall receiving the light of day would have a bold opening to the sky. The glare is modified by the lighted wall, and the view is not shut off. In this way the contrast made by separated patterns of glare which skylight grilles close to the window make is avoided. Another realization came from the effectiveness of the use of breeze for insulation by the making of a loose sun roof independently supported and separated from the rain roof by a head room of six feet. These designs of the window and wall and of the sun and rain roofs would tell the man on the street the way of life in Angola.

Salk Institute
La Jolla, CA 1959-65

I am designing a unique research laboratory in San Diego, California.

This is how the program started.

Richards Research Building
Philadelphia, PA 1957-64

The director, a famous man, heard me speak in Pittsburgh. He came to Philadelphia to see the building I had designed for the University of Pennsylvania. We went out together on a rainy day. He said, *How nice, a beautiful building. I didn't know a building that went up in the air could be nice. How many square feet do you have in this building?* I said, *One hundred and nine thousand square feet.* He said, *That's about what we need.*

Reprinted Courtesy Voice of America

Board Meeting, Fort Wayne Fine Arts Foundation
Fort Wayne, Indiana
1965

Fine Arts Center
Fort Wayne, IN 1961-65

The entrance to a building need not have car entrances buried in the ground. Make it something that becomes the door to the entire project.

A door cannot be considered a door, per se, always remaining the way it was. Styles will change because of circumstantial developments. A door could become a more important thing, something which invites the car as well.

The car wants to drive right into the lobby.

It won't admit it, but it wants to do precisely that. And you must serve this, even if you can't solve it exactly.

Piranesi made beautiful drawings of Rome as it never could have been. He made drawings of visionary prisms and great spaces where art can be displayed. He envisioned things like Jules Verne. He envisioned things that later turned out to be not at all fantastic. His visions of entering great spaces were always an inspiration to architects.

And I envision them.

This area will have a very high roof. To one side will be a garage, which will really be a wound-up street. It will be a ramp system varied so gradually that you would not know you were going from level to level. It will not be round. It is going to be sort of level so that you drive in and find yourself a place to park, and then you come down a central avenue to the actual complex of buildings.

The entrance will be as high as the garage itself and as high as some of these buildings here, a great looped area, outside of a tunnel you come through, on either side of which there will be the appearance of a building and the appearance of another building.

What you will see of the garage will only be the walkways that people take after they get out of the car. It will be a matter of crossing the carways so that you are in danger. When you get out of the car, you simply take a little walkway and you go to a stairway or elevator down to the point where you can get into the building.

A great opening here and a great opening on the other side will be the entrance and exits by car. At no point will a person be disappointed in where to park for the activities that come here.

Reprinted courtesy of the
Fort Wayne Fine Arts Foundation

On the death of Le Corbusier
28 August 1965

Yesterday Le Corbusier died.

Death felt like a great door that fell between here and somewhere. Everything that led the spirit in one *to make* is from there, that the combined treasury of minds cannot sense, yet every mind alone seeks its nearest lumen to live, to fill life and give one's life to express it.

Yesterday something died in me in the loss of the someday when I could have met Le Corbusier with the feeling of right to give him my reverence.

Contributed by David Slovic

Comments on the Fort Wayne Fine Arts Center
Fort Wayne, IN 1961-65

I want to talk off the cuff, because I've nothing prepared for this.

I was born into the consideration of art as a part of life, not something that's attached to life in a peripheral way.

My parents were in the middle of it. My mother had been a harpist and my father a stained glass worker, and we knew that art was in everybody's life. Even a man who walks gracefully is conscious of the art of walking. He's thinking of how graceful he is, his prowess, all-important to a man. The grace in a woman, even in the light of pain, is art.

Art is the expression of the soul.

It is the only language of the soul.

I hold it above a religion because I know that a religion is answerable to religion itself. Religion has to do with the language of the soul.

Art should not be denied anyone in the presence of the expressions of man which have to do with form. Goethe was always reflecting on whether life was form or form was life. From that he means you are cognizant of the characteristics of something.

When I was doing this building, I was looking for the characteristics of the building as distinct from any other building. The fact that various organizations come together to be a single center doesn't mean that they'll all be together but separated. Or will something new come out of the idea of them being together? Is a new thing being born, or is it just an organization of various centers? The entire work so far has been to look for the nature of this combination of art concerns and how it becomes a new thing by being together rather than apart.

Last year, when some of your important people were here, I made one remark which I was very proud of.

I said there were two realities, one the reality of belief and the other the reality of the means.

Most of the realities of the means are employed and the reality of belief is absent. Many buildings are built without belief. They are built merely for profit. They are built to make things more convenient, more modern. But they don't have the belief in the back of them which has to do with the establishment of a new institution. The same kind of belief that made the first monastery, that made the first schools, that made the first bureau of health. That's the kind of belief which, when established, becomes an inseparable part of the way of life.

Every building that an architect builds is answerable to an institution.

It could be the institution of the home, the institution of learning. His first duty is not to look at the way things are done today, but to see in what way new strength, new vitality can be given to an already existing institution—which, once it establishes itself in man, never is changed, never dies.

Man will not accept that which is not part of eternity.

An institution may have its moments when it doesn't act as well as it might, but it always will be there once man establishes it. It will not even last a moment if it doesn't answer all aspects of the inner part of man's existence. This part of man distinguishes itself from a rock in that the soul is present.

From nature man gets the brain, but the soul is in the mind.

I've used this mind to try to capture the meaning of it.

My concern wasn't just the combination, to make a nice, beautiful arrangement. I was trying to find the essence of the belief. The belief which is your belief, not mine. What was it that must be there from which designs can come?

Design is only a means.

It is a way of saying something specifically.

But when you talk about belief, you are not talking about anything specifically. You're talking about the existence of an aura, which must be answerable to all the unmeasurable parts of man, vibrating with the desire to have it, to need it, which comes from wanting it.

This plan is in the archaic period of its attainment.

I have much work to do to iron it out and to satisfy the various details which every organization here would need to have something to say about. But I believe I can now point to that which holds it together, which makes it a belief out of which design is possible.

It isn't worth it to build the wrong thing.

Never spend a dime on the wrong thing.

It is not worth it to use marble for what you don't believe in, but it is worth it to use cinder blocks for that which you believe in.

I urge you to think in those terms.

Reprinted courtesy of the Fort Wayne
Fine Arts Foundation

Yale University

Fine Arts Center
Fort Wayne, IN, 1961-65

I am scared stiff of people who look at things from the money angle.

I had to meet some of them the other day at Fort Wayne in connection with an art center that I am doing there—a small Lincoln Center.

The project is to locate separate organizations. Fort Wayne, for example, has a full-fledged philharmonic orchestra (that's pretty remarkable for a population of a hundred and eighty thousand), a civic theater, and distinguished from it, a theater in the round, an art school, a school of music, a school of dance, a dormitory, and an art museum and historical exhibit.

All this is to be one bundle on one piece of land, and I had to say what it costs. This was a very ticklish question for me because I wanted them to want the project first, then to talk about cost.

I was armed with just one fact: that the square foot area which they required, which of course had nothing to do with the cubage, was equal to the area I developed in the design.

This was nothing short of a miracle. Most architects, not excluding me, exceed these square foot areas and have various reasons for justifying it.

In this case, however, all the member organizations had written their program individually. They had a reasonable cushion in there for contingent areas. Such realism, to begin with, made it possible for me in the composing to equal the required area. And I was armed then with accepted areas, though not the cost.

Except, yes, I had the cost. I knew it exceeded very much the cost that this committee had in mind.

I presented the plans to them in as inviting a way as I possibly could. I described the new philharmonic especially so that they could never refuse its existence, and did the same with the other buildings.

Then, when they asked me how much it would cost, I said, *Well, gentlemen, I must first introduce the fact that the area which you have asked me to have is the same as the area on my plans.* They said, *All right, but how much does it cost?* I said, *It will cost twenty million dollars.* They had in mind something like two and one-half million dollars as the initial expenditure. But the way buildings become interdependent made it seem quite impossible to begin making meaningful choices with such a low amount.

I waited for a reaction.

I felt the quiet shock of the new figure, which caused one man to say, *Well, Mr. Kahn, we only expected to spend two and one-half million dollars. What can we get for two and one-half million?*

I said, *Nothing. If you had asked me six months ago what you could get for two and one-half million, I'd have said you could have gotten two and one-half million dollars' worth. But as you see it presented now, there is an entity present. Something which was impossible before. The philharmonic is dependent upon the art school, the art school on the civic theater, the civic theater on the ballet, and so forth.*

And it is so. The plan is so made that you feel one building is dependent on the other. After all, what was the purpose of coming here? Was it to make a convenient arrangement or to make something with an extra quality?

I have found the extra quality, I said, *which makes the coming together more than what they are when the buildings are separated from each other. Therefore, for two and one-half million dollars you would probably get the hind leg of a donkey and his tail, but you wouldn't get the whole donkey.*

After a little bit of wait, one man asked me, *Suppose we simply said to you, 'We want an art school built. It's part of our other buildings which are going to be built. But now we want to build only the art school.' Could you have done it without an elaborate program including all the buildings?*

I said, *Yes, I could have done that. But you would have a mosquito and not a donkey.*

They had a donkey in their minds—half a donkey, not even half a donkey. And the mosquito, the whole thing, which they didn't want of course. And that was it.

Finally one said, because they did like the entity and they realized that there was something about the entity which was not the same as having each organization represented in its own way, *Well, Mr. Kahn, I can see spending ten million dollars, but I can't see spending twenty million.*

Of course, at that point, I realized that I was having an easier time than I had anticipated. Then it was the time to be generous, and I said, *I will try everything possible to pare down expenses, and pare down costs, but you realize that you have to give up something in order to do this. And for the moment I can't promise anything, because I myself think that this entity is now hard to destroy.*

Form is of that nature.

Form is that which deals with inseparable parts. If you take one thing away, you can't have the whole thing.

Nothing is ever fully answerable to that which man wants to accept as part of his way of life unless all its parts are together.

From a conversation at Yale University
about the Fort Wayne Fine Arts Center.

I expect that what I'm going to say will be highly edited. I'm not used to speaking that which could be recorded, and published as recorded.

I may speak about the second lecture as well as the first. I have no orderly way of making my point clear. But I imagine with three attempts I should be able to come out all right.

The three titles which were asked for I had a difficult time determining. I delayed as much as I could until I got a desperation call and then I really had to do something about it. I gave myself a deadline, which I didn't keep.

But finally I found the three titles as a result of a visit I had from one of my students, whose concern is the word. The word to him is equal to a sculpture by Phidias. He realized that the word has both unmeasurable qualities and measurable qualities. To make it practical, the word is measurable. But that which inspires it, that which gives it the quality of something which only man can make, is certainly the unmeasurable quality of the word.

He asked me a question—this was about two o'clock in the morning, about the time I'm thinking of going home. But this young gentleman who works in my office thinks nothing of time. He asked me, *How would you describe this epoch?*

That's the kind of question that deserves a quick answer—one that says, *Well now, it's late;* and, *One shouldn't talk about such questions at this hour;* and, *I don't know the answer* and we could brush things off.

But I was tremendously interested in what this could mean—this epoch. And I thought, in silence, about an article I had just read in the *New York Times* about doings in California. I had been to Berkeley just a few weeks before. I read this article about men who were inspired to write poetry without words. And this impressed me very much.

I know how impractical it is, but I also know its meaning.

I thought of men I know working to express the way of life now. Nothing in the way of *happenings* impressed me very much.

Then I went back to more primitive considerations, and I thought of light. I thought of how I was trained to think in terms of the yellow light and the blue shadow.

I asked this man who was sitting in front of me, also thinking, *Gabor, what is the shadow of white light?*

He has a way of thinking out loud as well as internally, and he said, *White light, white light, the shadow of white light...white light...shadow...I don't know.* I said, *Black.*

White light is not in nature.

There is no white light, nor is there black shadow.

But somehow I thought it expressed the epoch, that we are living in a time when the sun is temporarily suspended from serving man. Somehow even the sun was under suspicion. All our institutions were to be reviewed. Nothing that existed was taken with any reverence. This can be thought to be a catastrophic thing.

And it could have been a catastrophic thing in my mind, if I hadn't thought of this. The white light and the black shadow filled my mind with great possibility.

I knew the sun was still shining.

I also knew that it wasn't death, nor harmful, but something truly inspiring.

I also knew that the white light would turn yellow, only a brighter yellow; that the black shadow would turn blue, a brighter blue. Because people will not take things as they are, and in the deepest sense they distrust everything until it filters through the mind as being true.

Therefore those who want to write poetry without words....

When I first was introduced to modern architecture, the books were being burned. The books that I care for a great deal somehow did not look as bright as the pages of Le Corbusier's explorations, his drawings, his speculations, his point of view. I even learned that a simple house, which was never a consideration in my training, became something of importance.

I had no idea that I would ever practice architecture because I didn't know people who had lots of money.

I suddenly realized that it wasn't the enormity of the commission which was important, but that in every crevice of architectural thinking there was the opportunity to express.

With the present atmosphere of the white light and the black shadow, new institutions will come about. They will strike new attitudes which will also create a new sense of wonder.

This is not an age of wonder.

I see no wonder in what's being done, but the apparent lack of reverence is only a sign of the seeking of reverence, something to revere and fight for.

One day in the rain, in rain like this, I was dressed to the teeth to combat it, waiting for a taxi, when out of the house ran two young people in their bare feet, dressed most casually. They ran joyously across the street, completely free, and I felt like an ass. I could just as well have taken a different attitude towards them, that they were slovenly, disrespectful, militant. But, no, they were right—and inspiring.

I believe I have this same revolution in my way of thinking, because I believe that architecture doesn't exist.

Only the spirit of architecture exists.

What has presence is a work of architecture, which should be made in a way that is worthy of an offering to architecture.

When I speak about the emergence of new institutions, I am also thinking of the review of present institutions. The institutions of man come from the inspirations of man.

The inspiration to learn stems from the way we were made. Everything that nature makes, it records in what it makes how it is made. In the rock is the record of the rock. In man is the record of man.

Through our gift of consciousness, in the hierarchy of consciousness in which every living thing, even the rose, has consciousness of its kind, there is this affinity for the great history of how we are made. Some are endowed with the ability to reconstruct the entire universe just by knowing a blade of grass.

The inspiration to learn is the source of all institutions of learning: it inspires the institutions of learning.

The inspiration to live brings about its institutions.

The inspiration to express is all art.

Art is the language of God.

Art is the making of life.

The works today have great permissiveness. Any era can tolerate a classroom without light, commission it, build it, and allow another architect to disregard what was considered the economic move in building a classroom without light—saving fuel, giving wall space, arguing concentration—is certainly an era on trial.

Is it to be condemned? No.

Is it to be thought adventurous? Of course.

The mere fact that it is permitted is something that will settle down to new values entirely.

In a commission which I just received in New Haven to do a redevelopment project, I was asked to do a school. A school built by one of the architects in New Haven which had no light for classrooms was shown to me as an example of the classroom of the future.

I said if I had to do a classroom without light, I would give up the commission very readily, because I don't believe in it whatsoever.

I said, *How do you know how much power the teacher has to hold his students to the point of being non-conscious of light? How important is distraction, actually, to get always the sense of the bird outside and of people hurrying out of the rain to class, and the wind playing in the trees? The distraction is as important as the lecture.*

We are born out of light, and you can't take these things away for any isolated practical reasons.

So it is with structures that, because of their fascination and newness, have an effect on us. We want eagerly to make them, and we forget many other equally important aspects.

But it's a time when one can think in the broadest terms, and not be any more responsible than the man who wants to write poetry without words.

There was a time when I visited (Louis) Barragan of Mexico, and he asked me how one would define tradition. My mind went to the Globe Theater in London, Shakespeare had just written *Much Ado About Nothing.* The play was on: the actors were onstage in full regalia, the audience was ready for the play. At the first gestures of the actor, he fell in a heap of dust under his costume. The same thing happened to the second actor, and so it was with the rest. The audience, reacting to the actors, also fell into a heap of dust. And here I was peering through a little opening in the Globe Theater.

I realized that everything that has happened can never be recaptured.

I saw a picture of the Battle of Waterloo, and every horse, every man was glued to the position in which he was painted. I couldn't make a horse of action.

But if you dug up a tarnished mirror of periods thousands of years ago, you could re-enact the use of this mirror.

The play of Shakespeare exists; all previous actions do not.

I saw the future—not in act, but in anticipation—very clearly. I could see a horse running in the future, but I couldn't see it run in the past.

I tried to tie this in my mind to the meaning of the white light and the black shadow, only to know that the black is life and the white shadow is death.

The white light and the black shadow is life, life without certitude, life where the sun gives no reflected light.

I remember when we used to draw shadows and light. It was important that in the shadow you read the details freely, but the light obliterated much detail. We knew that red light gave a green shadow, and we knew that green light gave a red shadow. We trusted color as given by the sun. Local color was incidental.

Men today can paint with the same reverence for painting—which I also say does not exist except for a work of painting which is offered to the spirit of painting, hoping that it will come to the treasury of painting, the treasury that knows no style, knows no method, always ready to receive that which is true to painting, that which is true to sculpture, that which is true to architecture.

The black shadow obliterates, is possessive.

It is something within itself.

It is punishment, but punishment for the emergence of purer considerations rather than just the unraveling or the extension of things known now, the play of modifications that have long lost their original inspirations.

I know it is not the only age of wonder.

What about the Greeks?

What about all ages, for that matter? They had their wonder.

In no sense do I think what's happening today is condemning, as some people think. It is only a primitive time of new wonder.

No one knows what this wonder is; no one can invent it.

Can you think of the music of Bach without the existence of Bach? The machine thinks it can do it.

How silly is the machine.

The machine will never take the place of the mind, but it will prove itself as being a marvelous brain.

There is a great difference between a mind and a brain. A brain is merely an instrument, but the mind is the sole instrument. What the mind brings is unmeasurable, and what the brain can do can become measurable.

The difference is like day and night—like black and white.

How close music is to architecture. If you read a musical score and read a plan architectural, the plan architectural is the structure of the space in its light. To a musician the sheet is sound, time. To architecture, this plan must be the clue to all that it is the order of the architect's instructions, in the same way that a sheet of music is an instrument to play.

The plan is also an instruction to build. It is not like sculpture, because sculpture should show the thumb marks of every decision, as painting also must show every decision that was made. But architecture resembles sculpture in that it modifies space. Sculpture does not make space, it modifies it.

Architecture is the thoughtful making of spaces which, as an entity, is sculptural in the sense that it modifies space, orders space.

I trust very much the implied meanings of the white light and the black shadow.

Thank you.

I was asked whether questions were in order and I said yes, because I can do better with questions than I can with trying to read my mind out of something which has yet not been written down. It is something new in my mind and I have a long way to go before it emerges into a freer, easier understanding. I welcome questions.

You spoke of the sun as being never the reflected light. Would you then compare the sun to the white of the light, and the black shadow to intuition, inspiration anew and all-inspired?

Yes.

Maybe our time lacks, in some way, inspiration for the new. We aren't quite open to the newness of thought because we are drenched in tradition or in meeting requirements that are put upon us.

To give an example which belongs more to the second lecture—it amazes me that I'll ever do more than one lecture—I gave a problem to the students of a new Catholic church requiring a school and a community building, besides the other elements of the place of the Word: the sanctuary, the sacristy, the narthex, the nave. I noticed that the community building and the school were sometimes placed opposite to the church. In others there was an attempt to get in out of the rain, to bring it to the church so you have circulation.

But at no time was it thought that the narthex was the place of commonness, and that actually the narthex gave the right for the community building to exist, and also to the school to exist. The school in a church had to be equal to the name, and the community building had to be equal to the church. Otherwise it had no place in the composition of that Catholic church which could receive the school and the auditorium in its way.

By thinking of it that way, the auditorium changes the design, the school also changes the design. One knows less about a school and therefore the school's plan becomes more general. You don't know how many students, but you really know more about it because you know it's giving its right not by ordinary means. You don't apply less cost to the auditorium and school than you do to the rest of the church.

It's a reconsideration of values. Even the old institutions now receiving new expression, or new powers, are brought into the full consideration of the church in a way different from the very same thing in another context.

The white light and the black shadow is a mental thing, and it is to me a source of inspiration because it is uncondemning of anybody's work.

Previously, I could have picked on anybody's work and said, *I don't like this, I don't like that. I think he's wrong, I think he's right.*

But when one can devote all his life to something—even die for it—he is right and you have something to learn.

The white light and the black shadow has changed my attitude, though I know it doesn't exist.

Attitude doesn't exist; it is an unmeasurable word.

We know that a building has both site requirements or external requirements, and program requirements or internal requirements. Would you say that one or the other is more easily seen in the white light, or are they both equally easily interpreted through the white light?

In the white light, what you call a site plan is yet unnamed.

In the white light, a column is not a column.

In the white light, there is no plan.

It's through mental revolution, though its existence is a kind of freedom. It's a freedom which is not in everyone's control, in the same way as you must wait to know what Bach is like by waiting for Bach.

There will be leaders, and they will be the creative people. There will be artists who will sense the meaning of this towards the future.

Picasso said something very wonderfully, that everything that is created must be ugly. It must be ugly because the artist doesn't know what he's doing.

Once it is made, the artists around him will work towards its beauty. They will know what to do because the image is created, like the creation of an attitude or a point of view.

I, not having read Picasso until just recently in a booklet by Gertrude Stein, tried to say it by saying that a thing must be archaic. But it has historical connotations which are not as good as Mr. Picasso's harsh word, *ugly*.

How many buildings today attempt to be shatteringly beautiful? They are irrefutable, but are they right? Have they really emerged?

If I want to sense the full message to me of the meaning of the white light and the black shadow, I must not judge.

I must simply question and hopefully sense wonder.

You said that architecture doesn't exist. From there you developed the thought that there is a basic underlying set of principles which centuries have lived by to establish or to move toward some architecture. What generation can determine what the prior generation has done that has begun to achieve architecture, if it does not have a value of the white light and the black shadow?

The white light and the black shadow don't exist.

I did not speak about any rules or regulations. I did say that architecture itself has no rule, no regulation, no style, no method. It simply waits for something that is made which it receives without judgment.

It receives that which is true to itself.

It doesn't go through a jury. It simply establishes itself in the minds of all as being something which inspires you.

This is true of Le Corbusier's work. It's highly criticized for being non-functional, and the materials don't hold up, and the program is disregarded. But it has immense inspirational value. That doesn't mean that after many years it shall have the same effect; one doesn't know this.

Architecture of old, or just architecture, is felt deeply in the Pantheon, certainly in the Parthenon. But the Pantheon, more to our understanding, was ordered as a place for any religion to worship. How beautifully it was stated in its round shape, which did not have a directional position for a set ritual. Its shape can inspire any ritual. Even the window in the dome gives no concession to anything directional. That is highly inspiring as an expression of an institution of man.

The building in the Renaissance that gave shade to the street with its porticoes, out of the street invented the court.

Those elements make it a living thing.

It's received by the spirit of architecture, and even if some things don't work as well as they might, they still belong to architecture.

It mustn't be the function. Function is implied.

You could make the mistake of it not being functional, but you can't make the mistake of it not being architecture.

It doesn't have to function if it tends to inspire those that can give it function.

When you criticize the Marseilles apartments for minor faults or even greater faults, you do not condemn them as non-architecture.

Do you feel that the ability to conceive of architecture in the white light is a gift, or something that can be learned?

Architecture is received in the white light as though you are reviewing everything in your mind.

The white light means that you're not ready yet to make that which deserves the yellow light.

It's merely an attitude.

It's an acceptance of the broad revolt against our institutions, against wearing ties to lectures.

It's the same kind of thing as a man who can paint as well as Giotto—which is difficult to conceive—who because of his reverence for Giotto doesn't paint like him, but paints purely a red canvas. And paints something that's not figurative, not easily recognizable. He's going through a kind of penance. This I would consider the white light and the black shadow.

It isn't a gift.

It's a point of realizing that condemnation is only honored by the presence of a work so great that the other fades and doesn't exist any more. The period is now a period of servitude to the idea which yet doesn't exist.

The Institutions of Man
Lecture at Princeton University
Princeton, New Jersey
13 March 1968

Last week I spoke in a large auditorium, far from everyone, and it was difficult. I was like a boy reaching into his pocket for something and out rolls a marble, in the wrong place at the wrong time.

Somehow it felt as awkward as that, mostly because what I was talking about was fresh in my mind. It was on the surface of my mind rather than deeply ingrained. It hadn't yet found its position in the other things I have been thinking about, although I do believe that there is content in the thought of the white light and the black shadow.

It is an indication of the tentative nature of things, the question of the institutions. One still doesn't want to have the real sun appear and the blue shadow that would result from it. You want not to accept this because you want it to shine on good things, and the questioning of the institutions will bring about a much purer translation of our institutions, and even bring about those we yet can't see or feel.

My own work is in search for just that, because the best work of the architect is how he reviews the program he receives from the client and translates into spaces what he gets in areas.

In a recent problem I gave at the university, of a monastery, I assumed the role of a hermit.

There was yet no name *monastery*.

For two weeks the students tried to extricate themselves from the knowledge they had of monasteries as they are known. One young Indian girl ventured, *I believe the cell is the nucleus of the monastery. The chapel earns its right to exist because of the cell, the refectory has a right to exist because of the cell. The retreat is the same, the place of work is the same.*

This made the class thoughtful about the subject. Another Indian student who had never been in a monastery said, *I agree completely with Nina, but I have this to add: Once the cell gives the right for the chapel to exist, the chapel becomes equal to the cell. The school becomes equal to the cell, and the school becomes equal to the chapel. The refectory becomes equal to the cell and to the chapel. Nothing is more important than the other.*

The refectory was not a restaurant; it wasn't just a place of eating, it had special significance. The Indian students weren't the best designers in the class, but they were certainly feeling-filled people.

The feeling of their beautifully thoughtful statements inspired one of the students, who is by far the best designer, to make a design in which he placed the refectory half a mile away from the center of the monastery and put the monastery near the retreat, saying that it was such a great honor for the retreat to be next to the monastery that one of the important arms of the monastery should be given to the retreat. He also had a very large fireplace, larger than what is practical, symbolic of fire—never to lose the beginning, the wonder of fire. We were very excited.

The program becomes a ragged thing waiting for something to appear.

Constantly the question *What is a monastery? What inspired the first monastery?*

You needn't know the truth of the circumstantial fact because that is not a guide at all. Anything in history which happens circumstantially is of little worth.

What in history is a sign of the inevitable is of tremendous worth.

We invited a monk from Pittsburgh to come and review our designs. We showed him our little cells, weighing them carefully so they did not become pretentious. He said, *It's all right for some monks. But I'm a painter and I have a large studio in my monastery, and when I come to my cell I feel claustrophobic.* And he said, *The design is beautiful—I love the way the trees are rendered—but I wouldn't want to walk half a mile to the refectory. I would rather have my meals served in bed.*

There were other merry criticisms, and I thought he was amusing, but we felt something against him.

The fact that he was a monk of course meant that we respected him greatly for his beliefs. He left us with a weight of responsibility which we didn't expect.

We thought he would be terribly overwhelmed, but it wasn't so.

We worked on, and it was one of the most exciting experiences I had in teaching, to see the unraveling of thoughts that were not bound by any tradition other than a spirit, which is really what tradition is.

Not the acts of tradition, but the spirit of it.

We invited him for the jury. We sure were bold to do this. And when he appeared, he was the staunchest defender of the most exploratory schemes. It was a great lesson for me. I'm eternally grateful for the experience.

A recent problem was the design of a Greek Orthodox church. The position of the school and the community center was a matter of question.

We were taught by a priest all about the functions of the church. We visited churches that functioned in the ritual of the religion. The tendency was to place the school and community center on another side of a court.

After some talk about the meaning of anything that may enter the realm of religious environment, everyone accepted the idea that the narthex had to take another shape than it always had. It was the entrance to the community hall and also the school.

Every part has to be answerable to every other.

Not that it cannot be translated many ways, that it cannot be across the court. Of course it can. But when you begin with such freedom, then you lose a sense of what in history we know as an archaic beginning. You haven't the right to be quite so free when you haven't tested the strength of its singularity in the environment, which in itself is singular.

Salk Institute
La Jolla, CA 1959-65

The Salk Institute of Biological Sciences stands in my mind as a realization in the coming of new institutions.

Salk asked me to design a research building for scientists. He needed a hundred thousand square feet because there were ten scientists, each wanting ten thousand square feet—whether they needed it or not.

He added that he wanted to be able to invite Picasso to the laboratory. He felt that the belief which makes a painter paint must be constantly felt by the scientist so that he never forgets, in his measurable work, that the unmeasurable desires, somehow has come together.

He felt that the artist dealing with the unmeasurable and the scientist dealing with the measurable, though motivated by unmeasurable desires, somehow has come together.

If he hadn't said that, I would have given him the medical research laboratories which I had just finished.

They contained things I thoroughly believed in. I felt that such a building should be built around the idea that the air you breathe and the air you throw away must be in different channels. That the service of the building had to be designed for the success of the experiment.

But the sense that Picasso might be invited formulated in my mind three inseparable parts for the Salk Institute.

The laboratory was the center of the measurable, beginning with nature. Physical nature lends itself to measurement. Whether we ever reach ultimate measurement isn't of real concern.

But everything that has to do with man defies measurement.

I thought of the meeting place, the true address of the Institute. Every part was conceived in the character of unmeasurable qualities. There was no great dining room, but small dining rooms.

I didn't know of a more natural seminar room than a dining room.

Certainly seminar rooms designated *Seminar One, Seminar Two, Seminar Three* can never be seminar rooms.

The bar was probably bigger than any one of those dining rooms, and that was all right. That suited everybody.

The library, too, was made a small room, not a large reading room.

There was a gymnasium, which should be in every building.

There was an apartment of hospitality—someone would live there. Also living quarters for fellows, invited guests.

Picasso would live here.

There was a large room, not named, in the center, which was purely a place of entrance.

I learned from previous deliberations what a program means coming to the architect. He reads in the program the lobby, which is measured by so many square feet per person. The corridor is the recipient of air-conditioning ducts and return grilles.

The lobby had to be turned into the place of entrance.

The corridors had to become galleries and corridors relegated to little sneak places, which go from one room to another privately.

The budget had to be turned to a point of economy, which meant that the wrong thing was not worth building.

The unnamed place of entrance was immediately recognized as a place where one could have a banquet or an exhibition. If you start a building with the idea of anticipating this banquet where you dine every day—a banquet not happening every day—you ruin the potentiality which a small dining room can give you: the most beautiful, the most natural seminar room.

I mean in that sense the institutions of man, that a certain environment of spaces—friendly, inspiring to the activities of man—be sensed by the architect and presented to the client as his best contribution.

How he does it should not concern the client at all.

An architect who does not retranslate the program in relation to the sense of the emergence of the new institution, of the modification of strengthening of one that exists, is serving the client very little.

City Hall is now nothing more than an office building.

How wrong that is.

The Department of Zoning has the same lobby as the Department of Licenses and Inspections.

Zoning should be a great hall which shows all the aspirations of the city, the models of the City Planning Commission, the lively in-touchness with all the problems that could make the city great.

It isn't one floor after another, it is an aggravated three-dimensional contour.

It could be the most exciting building. One comes to such a building and feels the aspirations of the city, the duties of the city. It comes from a consciousness of creating a translation of an institution of man.

Sher-E-Banglanagar
Dacca, Bangladesh 1962-74

In Dacca, where I am building the Second Capital of Pakistan, I was given a long and wordy program. Some parts were not quite as developed as others. For instance, I was told that I was to build a Supreme Court and the program amounted to *Allow so many square feet*. There was also a prayer room asked for, with a closet for prayer rugs. Other places were elaborately specified, even to the number of toilet fixtures.

One needs very little instruction.

If one could write what he aspired to have, he could find the answer to the needs even better than if he were told, word for word, what was needed.

On the third night I thought of a devil of an idea. A house of legislation is a religious place. No matter how much of a rogue you are as a legislator, when you enter the assembly, there is something transcendent about your view.

The prayer room changed to a mosque in my mind. And the three thousand square feet of space which was allocated for this prayer room turned into thirty thousand square feet.

I went with excitement to Ahmed to tell him about my view. He called several people on the phone, he turned to me and said, *I think you have an idea there.*

The mosque was an absolute necessity for the assembly, because the way of life involved the mosque five times a day. I extended the idea, trying to get great chunks of position in my plan mentally, realizing that the place of assembly was really the maker of the institutions.

It was virtually the institution.

It gave the right for the school to exist, for the place of health to exist, and even for the house of legislation to exist—all the institutions of man.

I immediately grouped in my mind the positions of all the other parts of the program, those that are associated with the institutions of man and those that are associated with the sense of legislation.

I had also this idea that the Supreme Court had to be part of the Assembly. Subsequently I changed my mind about the necessity of that because I realized that the assembly dealt with everyday problems. It was full of a sensitivity to circumstance, whereas the Supreme Court could be miles away just thinking of law and its relation to man in a general way. Its position had to be on axis with the assembly.

When I saw the Chief Justice, he warned me that he didn't want to be anywhere near the assembly. He went through delicate formalities of tea and very nice talk—but I felt I was losing my argument. When I explained to him that I had changed the hotels which were contemplated for the members of the assembly, the ministers, the judges, and the secretaries to studies in their gardens on a lake facing the assembly, he liked that idea. I told him about my idea of the mosques which was an entrance to the assembly, and he took the pencil out of my hand as I made this little sketch, and put the Supreme Court where I would have put it, right opposite the mosque. He said, *I believe the mosque is insulation enough for me.*

It was a primitive idea.

In our way of life we can be far away and still feel the connection.

It's not true there. It has to be much more literal, and in that sense that naivete is strong.

You give more by thinking not in terms of how you know it to be, but in the terms of how you sense it might be somewhere else.

You discover wonderful things about the nature of beginnings.

You can learn even from the sense of connection, that there is an architecture of connection, whether it be the avenue which is in sympathy with the rhythm of trees, or the place of stopping where the sound of water is heard, or the establishment of an order of squares so that you can feel that there are centers around which things can generate.

The connections of the institutions of man—and I'm not thinking of it as being *city beautiful*—are a sense of belonging, a sense of wanting to contribute, a sense of being inspired by the very giving of that which you don't have to give in the making of a city.

The art gallery should belong next to a bank.

I hold no truck for cultural centers. They don't make any sense.

A bank is also culture. So is a factory, so is everything else.

Last time I spoke about the inspirations of man, that the sense of the institutions of man stems from the inspirations of man. Though I spoke about several facets of inspiration, I can boil them down to two:

The inspiration to live—I see no reason for living unless it is to express.

The inspiration to express is truly a thing of wonder.

And the inspiration to learn, which is really to learn to express, but isolates itself sufficiently to be an urge of its own.

Silence is power, too.

And maybe you do express yourself in silence as well as you do in word or in act.

These inspirations give the material for the institutions of man. All the institutions of learning stem from the inspiration to learn. They are drawn from the sense that every living thing has of how it was made. Every living thing, be it a microbe or a rose, has a sense of wanting to be what it is.

I was wondering about a direct explanation of the composite order of the concrete and the brickwork. I can't quite understand why you use concrete, a material that is best in compression, in a tension role.

This is a good question. The concrete is a way of capturing the tension members. Things rust very badly in India; you couldn't use metal. You'd have to use a masonry material. You use a composite of metal and concrete. Concrete can be just as much in tension as not. You can use tension members in concrete, acting not in compression. It's not foreign to concrete.

But your question is good and one that should worry you—and for that reason never use this design.

How much did the Salk building cost?

Well, let me say I don't know. I really don't.

You spoke last week of a *treasure house* of the art of the past, some sort of storehouse in which various objects of the past were arriving. I wondered to what extent you find it valuable to dig into this *treasure house* of the past, in search of essential values for your institutions of today.

First of all, this *treasure house* doesn't exist.

It has nothing to do with anything in the past that lies there.

One doesn't dip into it to find out what it is because it's verboten to do so. It's there because of spirit. It pulls at you, it tells you certain things.

You would be a fool if you drew from it.

If you recognized the fact that I use a square or a circle as dipping into the past, then I'm afraid we're pretty much licked. Everything is valid. But there is such a thing as a feeling for its position in the treasury—I didn't say *treasure house*—the treasury, which means it's guarded. It's guarded by the spirit of architecture, and the recognition that architecture per se doesn't exist.

Everything is an offering to architecture.

In the formulation of your structural concept, would you talk about how you interact with your structural engineer, how you and Dr. Komendant totally bring out a structural concept for a building?

Komendant is very sensitive to the nature of structures. The fact that he's an actor and a great performer is of no importance. Every time he approaches the problem, he has a very great manner about it. Though your problems are burning ones, he looks at them as though they just came out of an icebox. But he is a wonderful sensor of the validity of certain structures.

He has a weakness, like all men have, of thinking that he's an architect. But he has a lot to give to architecture.

I don't live in concrete, I don't live in steel, I just sense their potentialities.

But he lives in them. He feels the strain of every member. He knows when a thing is pulling away, or when it's staying at rest. He knows repose very well. He's not worried about symmetry, he's just a great balancer. He feels that the thing is out of balance without analyzing it.

His suggestions, when they are referring to the architectural field, are to be disregarded. But when they are purely from an engineering standpoint, they're completely regarded.

Lecture
Drexel (University) Architectural Society
Philadelphia, PA
5 November 1968

I was asked by one of the students to play down my talk architecturally and play up what it means to be a man in architecture, someone who completes himself or aspires to complete himself in preparation for the expressions which he is called on to make. Drawings are, designs are *expressions* of—and in all instances, expressions of—his striving to reach the spirit of architecture.

Architecture has no presence

Only a work of architecture has presence, and that at its best is an offering of architecture itself.

Architecture has little to do with solving problems.

Problems are run-of-the-mill. To be able to solve a problem is almost a drudgery of architecture. Though it is tremendously delightful, there is nothing equal to the delight of coming to realizations about architecture itself.

There's something that pulls on you as though you were reaching out to something primordial, something that existed much before yourself. You realize when you are in the realm of architecture that you are touching the basic feelings of man and that architecture would never have been part of humanity if it weren't the truth to begin with.

Man will reject that which is not the truth. Many attempts that have been made in earlier times to make things exist and perpetuate themselves have failed because they weren't the truth.

Architecture is the reaching out for the truth.

I read an article in the *Encyclopaedia Brittanica*, an old edition printed when the *Encyclopaedia Brittanica* was still in English hands. It had very good writers, and no such thing as extraneous subject matter. The unimportant stuff was left out in pure disdain. One writer was writing about Bach, trying to explain the nature of so great a man as Bach, and he explained it beautifully. I've tried to find out who wrote this thing, and he has so many degrees that I couldn't recognize his name for the number of letters that followed his name. But besides his great distinction, he had a sense of what art was when he said that Bach couldn't have cared less whether he was original or contemporary.

All Bach cared about was the truth. Undefinable, unmeasurable truth.

And so it is with architecture. It's a search for the truth.

The expression of it is personal. And when one finds in his personal expression the quality that does not belong to the one who creates it, then he has made the greatest work.

In the offering there must be such a degree of commonness that the offering is gladly made as though it were given without a feeling for reward, because its generalness, its commonness is so self-rewarding that no reward is necessary.

I was asked by this young student to speak about current things, and to derive something out of dilemmas about our course of existence and living. Nothing could be more delightful to me than to speak about just such a thing, because nothing interests me more than the nature of something.

The process of architecture is a bore. I know of nothing so insignificant in my mind as learning about method. Method is not important.

But the spirit of method is tremendously important. It's the true measure of architecture.

Another thing that's unimportant is solving problems. Solving problems is run-of-the-mill. If my office is engaged in solving problems, I can hear the tears flowing, because it is completely insignificant. It's the part that is the drudgery of architecture.

All circumstance, including the current circumstance, is of no significance whatsoever unless you can extract from it the nature of man. The date of a battle, the occurring of a battle, has to result in something that falls as a golden dust, which is the extract of what happened. What happened is the primer of the realization of man, the search for what he is. If you have the sense of what man is from what happened, then this golden dust that forms—if you try to pick it up, if it falls through your fingers, if you can touch this golden dust—then you have the powers of anticipation.

An architect must have tremendous power of anticipation.

When he builds a building, he is building it today.

There's no such thing as building a building for the future.

It's impossible to anticipate the future, but it is possible to anticipate the lasting quality in what you do today!

That is why buildings that have been done in a certain era last; they simply reverberate. There isn't a time when a great building isn't felt to be a great building. It's a manifestation of what is a miracle in man's realm of expression.

It must be considered so marvelous that the Parthenon was built. Out of what? Out of inspiration. Can anybody define inspiration? Can you eat it? Can you feel it? Can you hold it? You can't.

It's a quality which comes out of a *desire to be to express*.

It comes out of the soul. It comes out of the essence soul which only has one surge, one force, one energy.

I cross out the word *energy*. It doesn't apply because everything that has to do with soul has nothing to do with material. But if for a moment you may borrow a word from science, it is a kind of nonmaterial energy.

A desire to be to express—*it simply is prevailing. One cannot say it has presence. Prevailing, only looking for a fiddle or a violin upon which to play this feeling.*

This prevailing desire to be to express *is in the realm of eternity.*

To dare talk about eternity, one can think of it as being of two brothers, one who wanted to be to express, and one—not saying the other because there weren't two brothers, there was just one—*to be to make.* The brother *to be to make* became light, luminous. *To be to make* was a prevalence of luminosity, non-material. The desire *to be to express* was light, nonluminous.

Light, luminous hoped to ignite into flame, raising flame, a dance of fire which subsided into material.

Material is spent light.

You're spent light, the mountains are spent light, the trees are spent light, the atmosphere is spent light, water is spent light. All material is spent light.

If you know the orders, the reverse may be equally true, that material can turn to light. One does not know.

When spent light was in the image of the desire to be to express, there was the presence of the inspiration. The desire to be to express meeting the means to express which was the material.

It was a moment when the desire to express met the possible.

The violin is spent light. It is the expression, it is the instrument upon which the song of the soul is played.

The temple, the rock, the mountain, the desire to be to express goes to the mountain, sees the rock. In the mind of the will to express is the temple, yet not made.

A manifestation of desire, not need.

Need is so many bananas. Need is a ham sandwich.

But desire is insatiable and you cannot ever know what it is. It is renewed all the time.

The desire to be to express comes to the mountain and tells the mountain about its aspirations to build a temple: *Look, I won't hurt you, I'm going to take you and treat you beautifully. I'm going to cut your edges, I'm going to put stone upon stone and I'm going to build an enclosure, a place where I can try to express the greatness of eternity of which I am a part.*

When you're dealing with materials, you deal with them as though you want to know the nature of concrete.

Not know *about* it. Knowing it means nothing, absolutely nothing.

In fact, it's audacious! In fact, it's pretentious!

Knowledge isn't, but knowing certainly is pretentious. There's a great difference between the two.

From knowing the nature of stone comes the respect for every stone which sits—in the realization of what you are doing and its sense of perfection, the sense of producing that which honors the original inspiration to express.

We are far from it.

The old building which started without any courses in architecture was far greater than our philosophizing about it. Because you can't begin to teach the practical application of the original beginnings.

I cannot in any way practice what I just preached.

However, not to aspire to it would be like living no life at all. So you live with the feeling that you will create one good thing, the one thing that harkens back to the original inspiration.

When the astronauts went up into space I followed them. I went with them every single mile of it, and I saw this great marble, blue and green in space, and I felt that knowing things was the least important thing. But one aspect came back. The feeling of wonder. Suddenly Paris meant nothing. I looked at it and said, *Well, so what?* Rome meant nothing. Philadelphia certainly didn't. But somehow the strains of the Fifth Symphony were still important. They were the most abstract. The Greek temple that stood up like that, right as it ever was.

It was the manifestation of the beginning, a manifestation so close to wonder that you could feel it again.

So it is with the great abstractions, the works which do not have to answer to me. They don't have to answer to anything but simply give vent to spirit in you, which is as old as anything could be.

You can't measure it by age or by scientific approximation.

It began when everything else began, even though it wasn't noticeable. There's no such thing as something starting later and something coming before. Potentially it's the same thing from the very beginning, otherwise it couldn't have been.

Just think of the scientist calculating that the beginning must be twenty billion years ago instead of fifteen billion years ago. In the years that follow, the number of years in the calculation of beginnings will go more and more into the billions and billions.

They don't have to calculate. It all began at the same time.

It couldn't be anything else. If one senses order, one knows that it must be simultaneous, even though it was not material.

Wonder, then, is what you feel at this great distance, and only the most abstract seems to be indestructible.

If you think of the book of knowledge, you can say readily that the book has never been written. It's a single word in an endless volume of what we know now.

I was thinking about all this controversy that exists in the schools of architecture as to what they should do about the courses in architecture. They now have divided architecture into about twenty equal parts, all of them unworthy of each other unless they are together: urban design, urban planning, ecology, landscape architecture—each one having its own degree.

What is planning? What is architecture? If it isn't one, then it's nothing. It's not divided, it's one.

They could for operational reasons have two courses, one called *architecture and land,* and the other called *land and architecture.* One may be called *landscape architecture* because the emphasis is on land, and the other may be called *architecture* because the emphasis is on architecture.

But should an architect have to call in a consultant when the problem has to do with the land?

It should not be called *landscape architecture* because you are not making pictures, you're treating land as though it were a great conservation, as though you're taking a piece out of the whole, as though you really appreciate the nature of things.

Land isn't just a hunk of real estate. Even a little square inch of it has many worms. Something's going on. You can go as microscopic as you like.

It's a recognition of oneness, not division.

Not degrees, not multiple degrees. I had one student recently who finagled the degree in landscape and architecture, both Masters Degrees, by convincing the dean of the School of Architecture that she was smart enough to absorb both subjects at the same time, whereas others have to take four times the number of courses in order to do so. This is all part of the sense of allowance to make everything open and understanding. She actually was home all the time, submitting some scratches on paper and thought it was enough. Her absence from class was considered to be the order of the day.

I did a foolish thing by announcing in my class before anybody got any strokes on paper that everyone would pass. I said, *Nobody is going to flunk this class. Everybody is going to pass. But I do require attendance. That's all, just attendance.*

Because one shouldn't judge in a school of architecture.

One should criticize, but not judge.

It's this atmosphere of criticism, not to take any subject which has to do with the development of the mind, which has nothing to do with process or measurement.

Just being present, in the presence of others, is sufficient to be the mark which you give yourself in the courses which have to do with our work.

But it's taken advantage of. What should be the result? Should you get sore? Should you change your system? Of course not.

What should you do about the planning department that now wants to have all the specialties in it? They give degrees in planning to lawyers and to economists and to social scientists.

I never understood social science. I don't understand what kind of science has to do with people.

Because everyone is different, everyone is an individuality.

What science can you get out of the massive considerations? None at all. They don't apply to science.

It's just as architecture is no science, and planning is no science. You may use some scientific method, but it is a matter of feeling, it is a matter of knowing the whole, and it is usually vested in an individual and not in a committee.

Group action has nothing to do with making a wonderful plan.

You can find groups getting together, but the one man finds the wonderful plan.

The group never does. You've heard the old story that a giraffe is a horse made by a committee.

If you want to make this division between a course in land and architecture, and architecture and land, the dean should be the philosopher of the meaning of the expression of the way of life. He should have lawyers and scientists and men in various fields as his advisors. But never should they be the composition of a department which has to do with creative sense.

If you do not have all of them, you do not have any of them. It must be so complete that you just can't have a few.

Out of all that you represent, you may have three quarters that are unworthy of teaching altogether. Who are you fooling? They can be advisors. Easily dispensible. The traveling advisor might be a better one than the one that keeps you in school all the time. Just to be there constantly looking for the sense of the whole thing.

The dean should be the custodian of the school, which is within the school. The school which is actually the pure school, studying only the nature of the course in architecture, the nature of the course on land.

He should not be concerned with solving of problems but only with saying what is such school.

He should be custodian of this nucleus, a man particularly engaged in knowing the nature of what to study.

In the same way, there should be a school next to the Supreme Court whose only concern is: What is a Supreme Court? If a judge were to go up the steps of his place of justice, and this little school sits there with a few fellows in it concerned only with the nature of the Supreme Court, that judge would nod to that place and consider *I must be a very good judge because these fellows really know what it's all about, because their study is in the nature.*

Reprinted Courtesy of
Drexel Architectural Society
Department of Architecture
Drexel University
Philadelphia, Pennsylvania

Lecture to Towne School of Civil and Mechanical Engineering,
University of Pennsylvania
Philadelphia, Pennsylvania
19 November 1968

33

I said to Professor Le Ricolais a little while ago, *How dare I speak; this is not my subject.*

He said to just present my thoughts, and that is right, because thought does not preclude knowing.

I feel I have a few things to say which may have been already said by Professor Unger, but I see it from the point of view of span, not cable structures per se.

Span is an exciting and challenging thing.

When a realization comes to mind it does so through a sense of validity, and an idea comes from a sense of order in which knowledge of the particular is only a humble crumb of all that can be known. Hence, cable structures to me must fit an order realization in which everything about it takes its place as though it were always there and never not there.

Order is the embodiment of all the laws of nature, the giver of presences.

In design of a realization of a structure or space container, the suborders are to be considered.

The order of material is like knowing concrete immediately, as though you talked to every grain of it, knowing it in that way.

In the order of structure, when considering concrete, the forms which make the concrete and contain it in creation must be intimately and equally designed, not left to the constructor, but designed for its installation, handling and removal.

There is also an order of time which connects you with structure. When we specify a building, and then we drive to the job and we are surprised and say, *Hey, look! They are going to use the crane!*—this should not happen to the man who is designing. He should know that a crane will be present because he has already accounted in the design for the presence of the crane. A lack of cautiousness on the part of architects and, to a great degree, engineers has led them to say they can easily use a crane or not use a crane. This truly would result in an inferior design.

It should be exciting to know that a crane can lift twenty-five tons. What it lifts must be part of the design.

Cable structures come closer and closer to the wishes of fairy tales.

The wish of a fairy tale is our inheritance of first desires. When you have desire but you have no means, all you can do is wish, and it is still a fairy tale.

It is the wish which drives us forward, not know-how, not technology. What drives us is the yet unmade thing. The whole basis of this century is only to satisfy the yet-not-expressed, the yet-not-produced.

Not that which is available. That is not exciting at all.

When I think of cable structures and the capability of spanning great distances, I cannot think of columns any more. Columns disappear. Somehow, stations come to my mind, places of generation where things can happen around the column.

I hate to see the column disappear, it is such a marvelous creation.

The column meets with a constant urge to dematerialize and to cut weight. We are able now to weigh a building and know its price. I had an estimator who played with the idea, and he was miraculously accurate. Before he went into the great thrills of finding material and labor estimates, he would sit down and say, *Let me weigh this building*. He weighed it and it came out just right.

In speaking of cable structures, I sense that the consideration of the elements is different from the consideration of the elements we all talk about. In fact, another name should be used for columns. *Stations* appears to be a better name.

Columns to me is a rhythm of darkness and light, darkness and light, darkness and light. The columns are dark and the release of light is the distance between two columns. When you think of cable structures, you cannot think this way. I haven't thought of a name for the new verbal images which must accompany it. But a name must be found; otherwise communications get muddled.

Accompanying a cable structure there is a kind of conical design, like an insect, where the events happen in the path of the cable. This cannot be considered as just a design item. It must, in the architect's mind, be an event, because the joint is the beginning of ornament.

The joint should not be something which the engineer picks out of the catalogue which will do.

It should be an event in the structure as though he were punctuating the structure.

The designing of this should be a department type of thing. Something that in the order is an element and not just an adjustment. Distinguishing every element should be just as important as calling Saturn *Saturn* and Mars *Mars*. It is just as important not just to make it a strand of such and such a thickness, when the consciousness should be made from an optical standpoint.

The immediate rapport would be between the engineer and the architect if those distinctions are made.

We may call it poetic, for that is the only way of saying that you have found a word for it.

If you have great spans, I don't care how you make them. In design you have distances of three hundred, four hundred, five hundred or more. These points become stations and not columns. Because they are servants of the entire construction, they might become a generating plant, they become structures, buildings. It does not matter what the individual elements look like, only the entire structure.

A column is important in space-making because it must serve the space itself. There is no other rule to serve, because structure should encase a space with such clarity as to have its own will to be such a space, using any system to make it. If I were in the space, I should be able to read the space itself.

It is possible to make any enclosure and in it be able to place many things. This is a different kind of consideration. You may need to do it, but you do it after you have considered the reason for making the span: that you are making a space which is readable within the span.

An interesting thing about a span is that the facade is absent—and I am speaking about an enclosure, not a bridge. The facade you have tells you that you can have any facade you like around the columns and there is no difference. The facade is merely the skin on the outside.

Inside you can build a Renaissance building if you want to, of stone, brick, concrete, paper or anything.

How interesting our architecture could become if urban design were called urban architecture, which is merely architecture in a greater sense, a more ordered sense, in which the orders of wind, of water, of transportation, of movement come into play. The orders here are more comprehensive, but still they are orders.

The employment of order must be distinguished from conception. Order belongs to design, it does not belong to realization.

Realization is a sense of potentiality and desires.

Design is the part you do in making it exist, it is the part which makes presence possible. As long as the idea is in the mind, it is still not design.

Design is to bring order into whatever you do. In the order of structure, the beam of brick is an arch. When you use the concrete beam with a brick wall you have a composite order of concrete and brick. The same distinction will have to be made in the developing of cable structure. Each contributing part has its name, just as it has its radiance.

The column seems to be more and more the enemy of structure.

In building a factory, a column is the enemy of a factory. The factory becomes a building which can be good for many operations. In a way it is a field, a football field within which you work. It is an enclosure.

From one realization comes another realization, but you must come to one.

You cannot consider how much money to use when building a factory. If you give me the job of building the factory, I will tell you what you will need to build the factory.

Only then will I tell you how much it will cost.

If you do not start off with the premise that you are building a characteristic building, then it will just retard your march to beauty.

I am building a factory. I could only get sixty-foot spans. My argument was not big enough, and I gave it to a good company. They were also hamstrung by the consideration of what a building like this would cost, because they have their economic order which they must meet, too, and I don't disregard it. But as long as we are unable to solve this problem, our building won't reach any high point.

Economy is building the right thing; financing is building the wrong thing.

Office Building
Kansas City, KS 1966-73

The office building I am designing in Kansas City is built on the split form construction. Columns rise to the tension structure above. The cable construction is the entire structure after it has reached that point, because all the floors hang from it. The multicolumn of the hanging devices, which are really the little columns that come down, cut the depth of the floors considerably, and thereby reduce the weight.

The rising up to the high point takes many days of lingering above to make the supporting structure, but coming down you are aided by the gravitational forces. In this there is time order.

There is an economy of materials of which I am appreciative, which can be a design factor.

Buildings must look different if the principles behind them are different.

Often you see buildings which look alike, but the principles are different. Design is the bringing out of the nature of things, as far as material goes, as far as the laws of nature go. In the course of building, when you come to a realization about something, it is something of which nature does not have any part. But in design, nature plays the greatest part, because the building must be made to stand.

Reprinted courtesy of Towne School of
Civil and Mechanical Engineering
University of Pennsylvania

An Interview, *VIA* magazine
Philadelphia, Pennsylvania
11 January 69

...The shelter...*found*...is an inspiration to something which you cannot find, something you make. If it were all able to be found, if man only was a creature who found the cave and could not have the resourcefulness to learn from it to make that which really he desires—which is something yet not made but, we know, is inspired—but what does it inspire, but that which is incredible because there's nothing that had any precedent [was a forerunner] other than that which is made by nature. When you think [in terms] of a building, you can't but think almost immediately of a poem, because a poem to one mind is the same as the building is to another mind. They are both incredible. So is the painting. So is the piece of sculpture. So, not so much, is the tool because there it's self-protection; it has a different quality. The tool has a different quality than that which has to do with shelter growing to be that which man makes, which inspires man to make. When you think of very old structures like the ones in Minoa and the walls that are decorated, the scale, though small, is still larger than was easy to make.

I was speaking of Minoa. It just came to me as something very, very old, and you sort of feel that it is very old and that the things that preceeded it could not have been grander, were probably more modest. And it is already very modest, compared to what you're able to do. You see, it's sort of like you visualize yourself living then, which is a very familiar engagement that we have. We often think of how well we could have fitted into ages before and how our sense of even love for people, you see, would be different, having the feeling that you have now, as if there are revelations which could not have been then or which at that time would have been tremendously revealing, knowing what you know now. But it also can go back to your own sense of how you would relate yourself to the world—I mean to say that at that point I think people who are naturally kind would be kinder. And people who are despotic would be more despotic. They'd be more themselves, having found the instruments of their expression. *Be more themselves.* How important is that? I don't know.

When I think of myself as a teacher, you see, I could think of myself as a very poor teacher if I were very frustrated and I was unable to also back up what I say with things that I am working on, things I believe in. But I would be a very poor teacher indeed if I had to refer to other people's work, and yet that is supposed to establish my authority. This is the question. I would be respected probably as a historian, but I wouldn't be respected as an architect. So, you can see in this that the people who were there in the environment of something which was revealed to them, how it became a primer of their own mind which couldn't have been done with knowledge but could have been done only with a certain completeness, a sort of satisfaction that is to say desire, completeness, or—desire is not the word, but something that has to do with having opened a door which cannot be opened in any other way but, I mean, could not be revealed in any other ways as being the seat of the incredible which you might say is filled with the sense of desire. That it opens up more and more of the incredible, something which is not manifest in nature, with that which is manifest in man. Now what is this wonderful thing that could be made by nature which can embody that which nature cannot make? So why doesn't it lead you then to a counter or rather a contrasting characteristic other than nature, which has in it the generative powers which direct nature in the making of itself (something of that nature, the making of itself)? Vincent Scully, in his book on the Greek temples, draws much on the stone, and he is criticized as a historian because he has no documentation, he follows no documents which he refers to. He looks at the stone and rebuilds the temple. He gets some sketchy information on temples, he's got a good mind, terribly retentive, and he's really, you might say, an intuitive scholar.

Well, I haven't said anything yet. I'm just trying to find something which I haven't found. I was speaking of Scully and of his stone, yes, and I have this feeling that the inheritance is what we inherit in the way of the psychological, is that which...you know, we speak about children being terribly smart today, as if they weren't smart before or they were smarter now than they were then—it really is true but it isn't a tangible smartness. It's a kind of undefineable thing which if the evidence or the appearance of things is there, there's a response to it. Because I feel that in the undefineable aspects—let's say what made the Greeks make a temple and the fact that you see a picture of the temple though it isn't the temple you see anyway—there's a feeling of the sense of *man as man*, which I think is absorbed. It's a different thing from knowledge—it's a kind of human confidence or human in-touchness with something which really belongs to all humans, like you might say commonness. It actually touches the commonness in that you see something made by man and though you don't understand it, it's just there. I just believe in it as a kind of inheritance.

I may speak about something else because I can't continue this. I don't know what to say really. I was speaking to two men who just came to the office this morning. One was black and you couldn't find a person who doesn't immediately give you [more of] a sense of great beauty, you know, a man of great beauty. His manner was full of the will to live and his conduct, that is, his presence was one in which you could tell that he was conducting himself the way he'd like to have somebody treat him, as though he were respectful of this thing. I was very attracted to him because immediately I saw this man who, well....

Another client came, a little later, and they were talking about landscape architecture. They wanted to know what was the system that one should use in employing his mind and just what does landscape architecture mean? What does it do to you? Should it take on the responsibility of city planning? In what way can it serve an architect? They were all good questions. And I said that I thought that the profession is one thing and the man is another, that if you think of serving the profession then you must think of serving the marketplace. And if you think of serving the man then you are serving that which can set an example and be an interpretation *in completeness*, from all angles, meaning to say that an architect cannot really entrust the land which belongs to his project to anyone at all but himself. If he must divide it, if he must say that this belongs to landscape architecture, this belongs to the planner, this belongs to the engineer, then he is not in touch. He is not offering anything really. It cannot be good what he is offering as an individual; it cannot be.

So therefore I'm not an advocate of collaboration. I told him that he must work for the change of what the profession is called, *landscape architect*, to that of *land architect*. If he were to change it to land architect, then I would say even the President of the United States would understand his role in the affairs of the world. As *landscape architect* he cannot, as *land architect* he can, and as *land architect* I showed him so many ways how nature can be the great partner of his work. And he must consider it, but he must also consider that, when he is called in, it has to do with not nature in the broadest sense but nature as it applies to a place which has been chosen by man and is being developed for man's use in a certain way. And the architect is called in as the advocate of nature, and makes everything in the deepest respect for nature by not imitating it at all, and not allowing himself to think that he's a designer if he imitates how the bird plants the tree. He must plant the tree as he is a man, a choosing individual, and conscious man, which nature, not being conscious, makes.

And then I took him, you see, from the garden to conservation, or ecology, from the garden to ecology in its broadest sense, and how he thinks of the garden as being the interpreter of a personal thing (the garden belongs to a person, you see) and that it is not a place of invitation—if it is an invitation, it's a very intimate one—and that he must make a drawing for the garden with the idea that things will grow and that his drawing is only really an instruction for something that starts. And that even every balustrade or every fountain or the choice of stone is something that belongs so much to this garden that his next garden must begin over again. So therefore he *must* destroy his drawing of the garden once it is instructed to be built, put it into the fireplace. All details, all ideas of the garden must go into the fireplace because it really belongs to no other garden. Therefore he keeps no record of it; he must begin again as though it were the most intimate act.

Now of course, you go to the universities and they're going away being so obsessed, so fascinated by the idea that they can spread their wings over planning that they lose sight of the garden, and therefore they also lose sight of their particular talents, which can make some plan really very effective.... How rich planning—which should be considered an open field, not one in which it is a particular prerogative of a man called a planner—could be. The whole field would be enriched by not trying to make ordained degrees which divide the architect from the planner, the landscape or rather the land architect must be so conscious of his work that the architect is very close to him because he knows the extent of his prerogatives. So that the architect, then, looks at land from his point of view. He does not mimic the landscape architect, he looks at land from his point of view. He is in that sense a land architect, as the land architect must be also a building architect, in a sense, that the bridges and the highways and the interchanges are all just part of his consciousness. He must know it from his point of view.

So if the landscape architect cannot criticize the building then he is not a good landscape architect, and if the architect cannot understand, cannot criticize the landscape architect, he is not a good architect, because the fullness of his work is that attitude which through certain activities, through certain beliefs and so forth can add much to the broader aspects of planning. And that it will not be this way I think, I know, because all the attempts at the present time for hyphenated degrees and the setting up of new fields is really a marketplace condition, and it isn't truly out of the discovery of man realizing what man really is, it isn't this. It's sort of a marketplace thing.

I see [the marketplace] as the place of the opportunity of expression. The marketplace is different from the mind to the mind. The mind to the mind is yet an unexercised thing. There's no place for it. For one, it's not recognized nor even thought about as a *place* or environment of spaces, or you could shamelessly say, *I'm going to the place of the mind.* Do you go to the place of the mind? You don't, you see. How wonderful a thing would be if there *was* a place of the mind. And also how wonderful it would be if it were a place of a free expression, which is very much in the mind, like a place of happening. And you go to a place where you are introduced to many ways of making sound, making drawings for that matter, I don't care what it is, anything like this. You go there and you say, *The hell with it, or Gee, I got an idea.* That sense, like there's the potentiality of collaboration even. But you know your position in the collaboration as one would know if he's a land architect concerned with architecture and an architect concerned with land architecture. That's another thing.

The university should never teach practical things because practical things are a running condition, it is not a set condition. In the marketplace it's free and dispersed by opportunity and opportunism, but in the place—which you call the planning or the considerations of the worths, that which does not disdain need but does not disdain desire.... In the university there should be desire; in the marketplace there's need; and the place between, the forum, should be the place where need and desire are both considered.

Now those who get little out of this because their minds don't take it should not also block those who get a tremendous amount out of consideration of this *medium*, within which desire and need both are present. So I think it needs this thing. Now it is also, somehow, the place of representation too. You see, it isn't really here because here it is the opportunity, the roads of opportunity. The paths of particular advantages of opportunities are here, crisscrossed in many, many ways, making the picture very unclear. Here there are hardly any paths. They are not paths, they're sort of like clear lines, diagonals, you know, very clear, geometric things, round things, square things, oblong things, and everything is quite clear and unobstructed. That which is the conditional is left out of it because the conditional thing is so circumstantial that you never see the clear path, the clear ray except reflected in so many ways as it is in the marketplace.

Representation is an undeniable position of an individual in regard to his right to express, so the blacksmith becomes a Republican because his work seems to be less curtailed. That he is able to express himself as a blacksmith more easily if he is a Democrat at the moment or a Republican, and he votes accordingly, his interest very much based on the freedom. His work may be making money, his work may be a blacksmith, his work may be something else, a preacher, but his representation, in the village green, is somehow tempered, the moment he is in the village green, with the desires of others, realizing that if he only wanted something himself he would not get it.

So he needs the place where what he wants is also what other people want, allows him to have what he wants, and allows others also to have. So the place of representation, where representation really is felt for its particular directions in entrusting, let's say, the governing of a nation, which has to do with the release of funds and the release of law for the establishing of the institutions, and the regulations that come with a place where you know you're going to get authentic paint and not get something which has a fancy name and is beclouded with all kinds of devious virtues—you have the sense that you're being protected, that the government is that kind of thing, and that representation is understood.

I'm very concerned about this, with representation, because I feel as though the village green has been lost to us. And during the traffic of things, and thinking always of the new institutions of man, I cannot but think of a new place of representation, and it constantly goes to a new kind of green, village green, which is, after all, not a village green but is the place where the plan, you might say, the horse sense of the day—which is not the marketplace because the marketplace is not really horse sense, it is absolutely opportunism—but the horse sense is here. Desire and need is horse sense.

But the marketplace is advantage, it's exchange: you give me this, I'll give you that. Here there's nothing transacted except mind to mind. And the mind of things that you need and the mind of something that you desire comes there. Now the desire part of it, I believe, will never be able to really be an exchange. It is something so vested in the individual that it cannot be exchanged. The need though is full of exchange. There one can really say, *There's so many.* If you like marble and the other fellow doesn't like marble, it's quite clear that this can be discussed. But the desire is inspired here because things are not beclouded by a statement which is meant to mislead, as it is in the marketplace. You say this is wonderful, well just feel it. The guy knows nothing about cloth, and he feels it and he says, *That's nice.* You say, *Well, why don't you buy it?* But this wouldn't be true in this place where you come in and you're not selling anything.

Speaking of the Centennial, I was thinking very much of a space which in the end would become, when the dust is cleared and the thing is used and it becomes a residue of this space, something that belongs to all the schools of the city. There is no University of Pennsylvania, there is no Drexel. Other places have sort of gotten themselves up and the University has done nothing but bargain on its name to do very mean things, its building being one of the meanest of all to have done. And the buildings are such terrible, terrible examples.

So in any case, it would be then a place of meeting. But it must be also a place of *coming to* by everyone, which means that it is full of wonderful restaurants. I would say that you can buy things there. It is a place where you come to. It becomes a landmark. It is the same thing I'm trying to do in Venice: produce a place which takes the inevitable focus of the tourist off St. Mark into something which belongs to Venice in another sense in that it is a place where the automobile isn't, you see. It's a place that is rich with art and restaurants and things of that nature. You come and the automobile is not there, which is wonderful; it's quiet. And you're induced to walk. You're in an environment which you might say, *If you go to a hotel you go to another hotel*—you go for one reason. You go to Venice because it's a beautiful kind of historic living thing breathing from age to age, and you establish in this place, like you could find in any other location, a place of meeting. And in this case it happens to be one where the Asiatics, Africans, and Europeans—that's the way they put it—come together. They sort of feel historically that they're trying to recapture something that already happened. I don't know how successful that will be. But they have confidence in it. And it's a place somewhat similar, a place which has a place of meeting, and a place of, let's say, of distinguishing the difference between performance and event. And so you have exhibitions there, but you also have stages which have no exhibitions, within which an exhibition could be made as inspired. It is constantly in the possession of students and young people, you see, or anybody, during the time of its waiting for the second year, for the Bienniale, and then it's turned over to the Bienniale. And this place turned over to the Bienniale represents a place of learning or environment where I would say no marks are given—taken or given—and that you could go there like you do at the Academy. You don't grade the person who's there until the two years are over and then they say, *Well now, how was it?* Locked in you is the kind of thing that's either worthy or not. Nobody judging you and that sort of thing. Now I'm thinking about it all the time and I mustn't tell you quickly about it because I haven't got it clear in my mind, but before the drawings are made, I know I will have it clear.

I think that in Jerusalem, in the Biennale, or the Centennial, it is, let's say, reviving the validity of, the constant validity of, that which is fundamentally incredible. The place of worship is in this case not a meeting of the mind, but it is that part of the mind which is spirit, because the mind is a spirit in the rain. So it is spirit. But school is the meeting of the mind and when I said that, you went through a precessional of the schools of the prophets to the synagogue of the wall, you see, which is an outside synagogue. It was the recognition again that in school there probably is the generator of religion, that is to say *a* religion, not religion. Religion itself sits there as constantly unanswered, inspiring. It's the undefined intouchness from which man came as distinguished from what Nature makes. And I have a feeling that that same feeling exists in a flower as it does in man. And you wouldn't understand religion if it is really something that man himself has and the flower doesn't have. But it is *a* religion which is the practice of a philosophy based on that which is completely intangible that you cannot really touch. And so, the Hurva, or the synagogue itself, the place, is made *to be*, which happens to be in the Hebrew religions, there's no one who preaches, it's simply the words that have best expressed the spirit of that which is completely undefinable and to which all things are answerable to....you call it God. But actually it is all things answerable too because actually man would never resist it if it hadn't been for that character which in man can be expressed consciously and in other living things cannot be expressed consciously. It's a motivator of that which somehow, somewhere needed an instrument to express whatever it is. And a religion is somewhat an involvement of dedications and loyalty—not loyalty, a feeling of the intouchness with that which began all living things. And the prophet, the teacher, had a sense of how he could make others in touch with it by some instrument, being the voice, being the word, how you look at things, how you observe things, from which you can get higher and higher expressions. Then the schools of the prophets would also teach science. It isn't a question of their teaching religious teachings because that is probably the lowest, I would say, in my opinion, the least worthy to express religion, like a religious learning. But not poetry or a painter's brushes. In it sits much more religion. In the scientist is much more religion, when he knows that he is offering his particular predilections to discover that which could raise the level of expression.

So when you go to the moon, you see, it's interesting that, when they saw the moon and described it the way they did, I felt that all poetry of the moon, at that point, was destroyed. And all the planetary references were destroyed. And was this, of course, a great loss? Yes it's a great loss, only because you're left in this wonderful state of not knowing and feeling you can draw on and here you're left with something which was unreachable, which became certainly just powder, and because it's powder you have nothing to hold on to. But you must find it because if you don't have that you can never reach the incredible.

Hurva Synagogue
Jerusalem, Israel—1968-74

So therefore you must find something else now. What a wonderful adventure it is to find these others, the substitutions for this. I said I want to write the new fairy tale. It's precisely that. And I feel the power of it, the need of it, very much, even more so now than before because having gone to the moon or seen it as a kind of dirty gray green mat, as being something which threw Pope out of the window for a moment, and Shakespeare somehow had to rethink the thing, you see, and I just felt this way. The references to it were not enough, they were too easy if they can be dispelled so easily. It must be something much more unreachable...than the moon, or Venus, or those places. They're simply objects now. What is beyond this, you see what I mean, that one must find now, go beyond it. Like my little things about Silence, you know, which is just a touch in that direction. And I would not think of the moon because I already felt it was too accessible. So now I think man feels that at least (not man but I mean certain men, which means man really because one man expresses for all others what they couldn't express).... So if you had discovered that a thing can be suspended, you have found out a secret of nature in the making, which had as much power as making you. Because to make you, to make man have the instrumentations around in which you could sense the spirit of man, which he does, that it...let us say, that man creates something living because he's living. And, like a great engineer, I think he discovers a new validity. He doesn't discover just a way of making something, but he's discovering a new validity.

Maillart's bridges, beautiful example, of which is not structurally accounted for each department as being the most economical concrete, the most economical steel, the most economical one thing or another, but the validity lies in this sense: If I were to bridge, go across, let's say the Delaware River with 20 posts and I said this was the most economical way of bridging the river, I would be absolutely at fault. You know. And then *No*, I'd say. *Correction, correction please. It's the cheapest,* you see. But not the most economical. So therefore he's got to account for the fact that he got to bridge this river. Why? Because the river is billions of years old. Running down there, it's found its path. It's like a contour that you change. That contour says, *You know who I am?* And the man says, *I don't know, but I've got a bulldozer here. I'm sorry, I've got to go to work. I'm being paid 25 dollars an hour, and they'll be very upset if I don't use up my time properly.* This is the way the conversation goes here, where actually the contour says, to me, *You know how long I've been here?* You know the weak voice? It's all there, and so the river has to do this and do that and the river has to change its course in a sense. It doesn't mind changing its course, you know, like when I was reading a little bit about Audubon at the time when he was making his drawings, and he described the Mississippi River and how it had the ability of changing its contours by reason of its force. Now man has actually dammed things up and made the river behave. But at that time it didn't have any sense of behavior. It just naturally took, because of the course and strength of the river, it just took a path like this and just simply took this piece of land and threw it into the water with all the trees and everything else, and they clogged the river down the way and changed another course because of these trees.

And he said, *You never saw the beauty of these trees which were just tumbling in Nature's ways, into new sorts of patterns of equilibria. And they were just blocking the thing, producing new sorts of designs, surfaces.* You know how it is...words. But he was blinded to how this was changing, how beautiful it was.... I've forgotten the train of my thought...the bridge, yes....

So Maillart says the economical thing to do is, of course, to bridge from land to land. That's more expensive, so now I must find the economy of this. In other words, to find out of Nature a validity. He knows how poetic it is to use less material, but he wouldn't just count the lessness of the material, but feel it. You know, actually measuring it cup for cup in concrete is not nature's way...like man is man, let's say, to run to a distant tree because he hasn't got the patience to walk to it—it makes the bones hollow. And so he becomes lighter. And then Nature says, *Yes, it's hollow, then I must fill it. I make marrow here.* I mean it just manufactures things this way. And so structure as I see it tends also towards lightness, not towards heaviness. The Romans, though they made elephantine structures, when they made their bridges, and the other people like Roebling made spider-like things which by far weigh much, much less because the span was greater, and that sort of thing.

And the Romans just had to put the legs in the water—they had no choice when they were bridging something—and changed the course of the river. It's charming to see it, these things. Today it wouldn't be so. And the striving that today it wouldn't be so, because people are aware again of the beauty of the river being unobstructed. Of course, the boats became higher too and need and desire sort of came together at this point.

But why? Why does man do all this?

Inside is this striving to satisfy, to answer the demands which are desire, demands within him. And then the structure. Like Le Ricolais' structures, for instance. He is more concerned about putting things, let us say, on three legs instead of four. And that kind of thing is really a great desire to get from Nature its most guarded secrets. And this is what he keeps in his mind, I'm sure. And Nature's secrets lead him to be able to put before those who have yet not found ways of expressing their desires, something which can inspire them to spark up and find the desires, and so the ways of doing it meet. Both meeting.

And how beautiful a sense of man and nature. And going back to the Hurva and going back to Jerusalem, the thought was that the school in all its shades of being able to be the environment of revelation, that new intouchness with the spirit and, I was going to say, religion—that to be able to express the feelings of religion philosophically will not come from the man who is a professional priest, it will come from the teacher. Not from the professional priest who, in many instances, is a peddler of good things said. It comes from the teacher.

Desire is irresponsible. You can't say that desire is a sense of purity. It has its own purity, but in the making of things great impurities can happen, if it is in itself the serving of a realm of expression. The more in his mind it's an offering, the more he wants to seek that which in his poetry has a kind of eternal validity. So that what is presented before him that could influence him most beautifully are undeniable validities. So that, if sensing this validity, he cannot but choose that which has this character. For instance, if the desire of a poet and then his will to express, before him were a consciousness...bringing before him was that the word gave him the power, the sense that he could invent. Like if you read Shakespeare you can't help but think that the language is his opinion, you see, because Shakespeare certainly broke all the rules. But this gave tremendous courage and in it was a tremendous validity because it has nothing to do with fact, it had to do with truth. And truth is in a sense the very essence of validity. It has nothing to do with fact. So if he's presented truth—if structure then is not just an interesting thing (which is not so easily recognizable, because it's a great conglomeration of things which looks damn interesting), he can be thoroughly misled and never have the instrument before him, which can make the expression of what sits in him as a desire to express. Never would he derive from it the courage of the inventiveness or the rights which would come to him unless before him are validities. So structure is very important. It is almost the first clue to validities. Because if it is personal desire words or personal desire ways which do not already belong to the archives of validities, than he cannot use it without being a plagiarist. Whereas the validity is outside the veil of plagiarism. It cannot be plagiarized. It's valid. So when Le Ricolais finds the validity around the tripod of support, he is giving the poet the courage of his language.

You see my point? It's a remote point, but I think there is something to that.

So that what also gives the poet the validity—and it doesn't have to be new, but one thing that he can be very, very attracted to, you see? For instance, a man today can build a stone wall just the way it was built a long, long time ago.

But as long as he is using veneer to look like stone, in back of which is cinderblock and all kinds of things of crap, and it looks all the world as if it were really a stone wall in all its integrity, that does not have validity. It has validity more in the marketplace validity. But it doesn't bring out the sense of the order that makes the stone appear as though you have actually built it from the interior out, as a stone wall. You can build it; it would be terribly expensive, but it would be completely valid, provided he uses all.

The incredible is only the way one describes that which does not conform to the laws. And I would also say what laws in themselves non-conscious can make. In other words, it's credible because you can describe it, you can weigh it, you can see it. It's incredible when you can not really measure it, but you feel it as being valid. But it is not something you can measure. You see the incredible as the unmeasurable you might say, and the credible is something you can measure.

It's like if you thought that the first house that was ever made is incredible…that would truly be described as incredible. Because it was built not from any examples of Nature, but made out of the will. Made out of will, it's incredible. There, you see, you can't measure the will.

There are physical validities and there are psychological validities. You see the validity of a man who bridges the river in one stroke is a psychological validity, but not necessarily a validity of cost. In this sense there are all kinds of attitudes in which you add to nature what nature cannot make, or give presence to that which nature cannot make, but which at the same time respects nature. To the extent that it is more and more validity, the more all the laws of nature are absolutely adhered to. But at the same time, all the desires of man to make what nature cannot make are also adhered to. So that is called a psychological validity. In the making it must obey the laws most strictly because if you do, the greatest economy comes out of it, the greatest poetry. You see, if you add weight, you add cost. There's something about it which meets beautifully. So the person who tries to hang his bridge, he is finding these ways in which lightness—and truly lightness, in the case of the bridge I'm talking about now—is manifest. Realizing that unless he makes it light also it would fall. Nature will say, *Alright, boy, you do what you want. But if you make it too heavy it will just fall. And I don't give a damn about you at all, you can just start over again as far as I'm concerned. But if you obey the laws, you're OK; if you didn't obey the laws you're not OK.* And there's another law which says, *That's very nice Mr. Komendant, that you have this great idea, but how much does it cost?*

So the city father says, *Well that's fine, but if you put one post in there, how much would it cost?* And then, Komendant of course will sidestep it seven different ways, but he'd have to admit that it would cost less money. At which point he would have to find a way in which it costs less money to do it *his* way. Therein also lie the points of validity. Since everybody wants to destroy it for you, they do not sense the same desire as you. So psychological validities are really what man makes. He's not discovering a dam… He can claim no ownership that belongs to man, and his work, and his feelings, and his right to express, and his right to live, and the right to sleep with women, and anything you want to talk about—unless he is fundamentally satisfying that which no one else can satisfy but man. So, if he discovers oxygen, it's very nice. But oxygen just says to him, *Well, I was there before. It took you a helluva long time, you know, I was there before….* So it's nothing really! it's to be praised, but he can't own it. But he can own the bridge. He can give rise to, access to new expressions out of desire. You might say the word incredible can also be applied to nature when you say, *Isn't it incredible that Nature could make this damned thing? That it could do all this?* And Nature says, *Ok, I can do that.* You knew it could, it's incredible only to have demanded it.

Now I was thinking about the fairy tales and about...architecture. I was just thinking of the invention of unknown characters or unknown go-betweens in the travel of the mind, nature, desire, need, that kind of thing...and the invention of the revelation that the stone can bring to someone, which could rise eventually to a temple. So that one sort of feels the right or the power of imagination, that he trusts imagination, recognizes imagination, and recognizes that it is, though intangible, a tremendous instrument that has no weight but still has the power to lift stones out of mountains and has some medium which gives the confidence to do what is almost impossible to do, and opens possibilities by the act of one man, saying, *Oh yes, that's the way it's done,* to the other. But then if you think in terms of what could happen instead of what has already happened, you realize that although a man may make something which has never been seen before, never been heard before, he really wants to be compensated by nothing else but recognition and recognition is the same thing as a king who only can be king.

I have a feeling that everybody wants to be a king in his own way. And, well, you could say that man *is* a king and woman's a queen. I think it's true, that it is in their own way to want to be this. Which politically became possible in history...and in his own way which could mean that you go threadbare to the desert like what's true of some people, some of us, who could express their religious fervor this way. Give up, as many Muslims have done in history, to go back to that which was a feeling of worthlessness of all things possessed, and there was something that was far more than this...so how could it be but desire to express that which—I'm never able to define what it is. If I did put my mind to it, maybe I could say few really worthless words, but I do feel it is this without mentioning it. Not expressed by words, expressed somehow to yourself, something which is more rewarding, that you live with more, that you don't want to die for but to live for. It's true of the Muslim because he doesn't want to die at all. There's nothing that ever enters the Muslim's mind about dying for something. He's living for it, you see, meaning to say, when he's in the battlefield, he's living the battle, and that is the big thing.

[Goethe] is a good man to read, in a sense...Thoreau is another very wonderful man in the sense of feeling for all living things. He truly felt the tree, felt the bird, and he was beautiful to read.... I discovered him just a half a year ago; I never read him. I heard of Thoreau and never read it until I got a little pocket book. *Walden* I think it was called....

[The new fairy tale] would have to be...more speculation of what you really do not see. As long as you can see Venus through a telescope it is already a point of accessibility. To speculate on whether there are people on Venus or not and to visualize the kind of people they are is not enough. Because you feel through the moon flight that it's only just tomorrow when you have the other. And the fact that you're able to go up and come back, there is this sense of being accessible.

When a scientist views things, he's not considering the incredible at all.

So you go up there with the idea that you are taking into account all things which physically you are satisfying; it's the same as an engineer. The satisfaction, the curiosity of not having seen it before, that's...in other words, when you talk about these photographs as being incredible, it's not the real meaning of the word incredible. It's amazing...

It's beautiful because the mountain is beautiful. It means there is something about that which made you which can also make other things...and it is the mountain. Beautiful also because you are small and the mountain is big.

I see [the incredible, the inaccessible] as the search for that environment which can bring to us more of what nature itself cannot make. Like Giotto's painting is still incredible. The moon now isn't. Nor is it incredible to speak of the moon as being something which is a great secret, and you impinge on that because no one knows anything about it. And as long as speculation on it is different in three scientists, three opinions, the incredible still cannot be. But to rely on something as convenient as the moon—convenient to say the moon is out, for instance, when two lovers are secretly together. The moon looks, but it doesn't really have any right to criticize. And so tremendous a friend is the moon. There it is, you see, and it's a tremendous understanding that exists between man and the moon, because the moon looks and is completely uncritical. Now the moon doesn't look down in the same way to these two lovers. Yes? It doesn't. Now man must therefore respect Giotto more than he ever did because this is really the essence of the incredible. Because you'll find Giotto in no part of the world before man. So the incredible could really be the new school, where man is recognized as a marvelous being which has locked in it secrets, or rather capabilities, which are yet not known. And there must be in the seeking of the avenues, the auras, the passages of desire; in these lie the incredible—where incredible is! So it is really closer to you, not relying on things distant, spatial, measurement; all these things are out.

Again the non-measurable becomes the source of the fairy tale. It becomes, you might say... everything is now to begin all over again. And that which was considered great must now wait for new greatness.

Oh, I think I'm exaggerating when I say that which lies beyond, things to explore, fields unknown—I mean I'm being not necessarily cut off. I'm counting for how the mind can bring new adventures of the mind. Certainly even this could throw away the minor mind to one who can really speculate on things physically beyond our real world that would be equally as captivating and inspiring to the mind.... To me it isn't incredible that the airplane was invented because it is something which must answer to all the laws of nature. It was inspired from the bird, it has to do with the relentless desire on the part of man to not in any way take an inferior position to anything that exists, anything that's present.

So the bird is wonderful but you wouldn't be like the bird, because you want to really have the freedom of being able to look down and look above, and fly away. How many times do you dream of flying freely over a city? And being completely weightless?

Structure gives the backbone upon which you can place the...I was trying to find the right word...but when you say that structure is the ever giver of light, structure must be seeing the space you create. It isn't something that is made and then you have to find out how the structure is. If you say that, structure is the beginning of presences. It is the first learning. If you learn something before structure, it rattles all over the place. But if structure is there, it begins to be something on which you can hold something. It's a kind of realization of the beginning of containment.

In a way it's like the scientist who has been given the formula which is a structure. It's a structure; in other words, it's like form. It's a structure of an equilibrium of some kind, like as if it becomes something because the combinations are right, and it is there and so from *it* he builds other structures. So when the stones are found to hold together and rise through bonding, you see, one stone into another, this is structure. It isn't structure when it is simply the material per se, but when it is bonded together it knows it can go higher and higher. And so it is in the nature of the material, but it has structure. We talk about the structure of a sentence as well, and if one knows it you can break all the rules but without the structure you really have no powers. Without the structure you don't think of breaking the rules because there would be nothing there from which you can work. But you recognize that what has inspired you is a structure, you see, which had its validity, within the meaning of language and everything else.

You get the power from that, break the rules. And you see new strengths which lie in...for instance, if you know about bonding in a stone wall, then your whole sense of wanting to not be subservient to what, you say, comes about. Man's funny this way. He will not really be held down because, since desire in each is a particular selection, to present man with structure is to present him with instruments of personal expression. Because if structure is valid then it's a rung on the ladder of his expression. Structure in another sense—I think one can talk about structure in many senses.

For instance, you might say that Le Ricolais finds a kind of validity in the combination of certain materials. I'm not sure about a building of his as the most economical or whether it proves itself engineering-wise, but his mind begins to feel in what way it's occupied. I'm quite sure that he doesn't begin by saying, *I shall now build a bridge across which traffic will go.* That's remote in his mind, I think it's remote in his mind. But having made this validity, he realizes in what way it's felt, how it becomes filled. It is the same way as nature makes physical validities and does not care, rather is completely unconscious of the fact that the bear will occupy a cave. It makes its decision unconsciously. Now man makes it consciously. He's inspired by the cave the same way, as a hollow, a place you can go—a log falls and you can walk across a river. In other words, he doesn't think of it as a bridge. Now the first boats were never thought of as beams, but actually they *were* really hollow beams, because they must sometimes rest upon a wave that's doing this (gesture) in which the whole boat is in suspension.

Let's say the first man who thought of it this way, though of all these things that are happening which made it possible for him to think of the damnedest boats that were a thousand feet long. Why? Because he realized the validity. As long as a thing was, the validity was more and more meager; it wasn't full enough. The validity became fuller, and the boat became bigger. It's this kind of thing. The smallest thing can open the mind in the biggest way. That's why the validity is so important—he hooks on to that. And if it is a man who says, *If he can paint, I can paint,* then it's nothing, it's nothing. He's deriving it out of the way he expresses it, which is not his prerogative.

What the painter has left in the way of what is true to painting is tremendously important to the other painter—but not the way he did it. It is the same with the engineer who leaves what is valid in structure, not the way he constructed something but that which is valid in structure. It becomes a definite inspiration for someone else. Like the finding of the catenary, for instance— that doesn't belong to the man who invented it, it belongs really to the sense of structure, which opens the minds of many. It is not in the completed thing but the interpretation. Now there is an interpretation, then the reverence for the man who can but say and still express so beautifully. That's why you must admire Maillart—because if the bridge is beautiful, it is out of the validity he has expressed in beautiful words, concrete words. He has also given you a vision of this validity—not only a sense of it but a vision of it, the way it's made. Now of course, not knowing really the real calculation behind Maillart; I'm sure that many engineers will say, *Oh that thing, man alive, he doesn't need all this material, he has this material, he has too much.*

But that's why it's great, because though he did not follow the unexpressed characteristics, by expressing them he has, because it doesn't say that it's valid for a span like this and not valid for a span like this—this would impress nobody. The fact that it can span makes the mind want to make it valid for other things that it spans, because of a certain beauty it has of expression that's possible. This man, in other words, can live better with himself if he's able to make this possible. So he may extend the validity beyond what is capable, and you may condemn him for this, and if you're very true also to validity. But as long as you copy him, then you know nothing of the validity, because you must start from the validity, not from the example of how it is made, but constantly from what it actually is, in its truest sense. And I'm sure Maillart broke many rules....

Man must recognize the validity of something which remains unexpressed in its purest form. Because even the material often isn't right for the validity. If the validity is such that it depends on a certain material that is now made, then it's hardly a validity. It must be true of all structure, you see, to be valid. Not just true of material on hand, or something like this. The validity says that if you're using brick you have such characteristics to work with. I mentioned that the arch is the *beam* of brick, you see, is the beam of brick. And if you talk to brick, he'll talk to you about it: *I have my own beam, I have my own beam.* And then you say, *Well now I know a fellow out there who knows a lot about beams, and he can put this up for only twenty dollars, and the way things are now, your arch which is your beam is costing me sixty dollars.* So what is the answer to this? Brick, protecting his rights, says, *But look how beautiful is my arch. And the beam is like an unwelcome guest in the beauty of the brick.* The brick, you know, which I know so well—he's my friend, sure he has faults, he's too expensive, but he is.... It belongs to brick, to the realm of brick, and I don't know how the arch feels or how it ends, but you see that there is, if one wants to look at it as though one were making a work of art, then one says, *Well, you like painting and I like sculpture as a form of expression.* So therefore this man who has this beam that can span [so far] must be made of that order which calls for the beams which already calls for the column. And so the whole arch system goes because the beam calling for a column does not call for brick at all. You see, it's a different arrangement of things.

Giotto, who, if you look, if you study his things, would symbolize a castle with a castle but never think anything of making the man in the castle just about one half the height of the castle. He brings out the validity of painting this way, because he can paint it that way. It wouldn't be true to the architect who built the castle upon which a person is. It's true of the painter who can make that person half the height of a castle, so he brings out the validity, you see, within painting, the prerogatives of painting, by making such a statement, and that inspires a painter enormously. How do you think Chagall got his courage [to make] his great people float in the air? But from Giotto you see this proportion which is within the prerogative of a painter. Therein it lies, it's incredible....

The beauty of [the arch] lies in how decisions which mount during the development of all other employments of this are made. As long as it holds to satisfy the desires, the needs you have of small openings, large openings, the desire is never let down, then the beauty is very deep. Because what's the sense of using paint? What's the sense of making a piece of sculpture? And you see, what's the sense of making a building? It lies also in the fact that the instruction to the other man is there.

Decision is automatic, as though it were a nature in itself, as though you were not really a human but nature has given to you something which the brick has, which can be conveyable to someone else. And the other one becomes a craftsman who is thinking in terms of making even greater arches, more beautiful arches, where willfully, you see, you wanted to put a beam across it any old way because you know it can span as the other can span. So the instruction to the other man is a confused instruction. So that beauty is symphonic. It's symphonic beauty. That wherever you go, the evidence of its nature is felt—that's the beauty of it, it lies in instruction. I think that's rather an important point—it's very important. You walk through it and you have produced something which has its answerableness to every part of itself, to its inside and out. It lies in the decision, and how it is received by the other man is there.

If you think of the society of man, it's beautifully expressed by the consistency that lies in the exercise of a material throughout the entire thing. And the fact that the other man builds it with a sense of contribution, by saying, *Well, why can't we do it this way?* Already he's part and parcel of the thing because he's willing to think. That architect would say, *Gee, that's a swell idea.* He wouldn't say it if—he couldn't say it, as a matter of fact—if he had one type of beam here, one type of beam here...*I'll think it over.* He'll think it over, he can't decide.

When I'm in Pakistan and dealing with these arches, I have no question of deciding anything. The fellow comes to me and says, *No, I can't. I can't span this. You gave me a jack-arch which is ten feet long and I know the thing will fall. It won't work. My experience says that eight feet is all it can take.* I learned from that point—my mind only has to say, *Yes, all of them now become eight instead of ten.* And I don't say he's wrong at all. Nor do I want an arch like this, because I know I have to put a window in it. So therefore the order which would cause tremendous design problems of lunar windows and other windows—the decisions easy I said, *All right, make 'em all eight.* Not, *Here, make it ten.* I musn't want ten, I must want eight. The man builds it, he becomes part of it, and immediately he says, *Gee, this fellow's okay.* He agrees with me. Actually, if he didn't agree with us, he would fall apart, you see, it's just self-protection.

You could build the entire idea of the society of man by just thinking of the brick structure which can be built. Or a painting that's true of painting. You see, it allows the prerogative of a painting to exercise it so. And it would be true of a piece of legislation, and would be true of the way you sell a banana. Everything would sort of work together.

As an institution the space is felt. The spaces which you are satisfying of an institution, has in it, in the way it's made, what the institution is involved in constantly. And it finds its spaces through it; the character of the spaces is felt in the enclosure which satisfies an institution of man.

I think the institution is rather a less known thing.

I think the social structure and the physical structure is not on one side or the other.... I think that physical structure and social structure is all in this threshold, at no point is it anywhere else really. It's just in the physical aspect, it's constantly the means of presenting itself, where the other is always the inspiration of making something; the making of the incredible is released as possible at the point of the threshold. Because you see *here* the possibility of making it. So the scientist who sort of goes in here, travels, is showing some signs before you, H_2O, C_5, whatever it is, and you are reflecting that it gives you the courage to make things. But the threshold is the place where the inspirations are, because the inspirations are not there unless also the possibility of making is there. Whereas, see, here it is the spirit which somehow meets at this point and things are possible....

I think next time, what would be a very good thing, I'd open some of these books, and open it up to, say, capitals, stair sections, to churches, and just peer into it. Peer into it and I see these things here. On the one side I see the mountains; I see air, the clouds, the birds flying, the roll of the ground, the hollow, the cave, all these things here. Here is man, you might say, in limbo, and he's full of unknown things. And then he finds himself in the presence of presences. There it is, there it is, it is all there. Now whatever is here, which you'd call the embodiment of the reason to be here, he can sense that; he can sense that what is there was what made him.

Here is the will to be—it's not the reason—and there is what made him. Now of course, he's at the threshold, because he is not there, he is not there, and he's just at the threshold, constantly at the threshold, between that which is his will to be to express that which has made him, given him the means. The experience in the making of him, in the making of man, already is recorded, all the truths of this are there, because they were in the process, and you can say it's a process. There were many things discarded, many things were accepted in this thing. So there is where the arch is born, here. Not here nor there, because it is actually a means which was a raison d'etre for existing—to express is certainly crossed at this point and something happens at this point you see, right in there, everything that is represented—man's realizations, you, everything else, sits right in here. It doesn't sit in here, you see, nor does it sit over there. It's the making of something.

Now you can see that Giotto knew that man won't fly, he knows also that a castle is much greater than a man, he knows he's little. But he's expressing something and he's got to find the medium of expression and he's found this marvelous thing in the validity of what he is doing because he's a painter and not an architect, who's a different animal. And his presentation really is not representation because he is representing much more, the architect, than the painter does.

But he realizes, through a kind of talent. The talent is only that power to express what he has a predilection for and that predilection of expression gives him tremendous power to even refute things which to the other mind would be true of the representation. So once he realizes he can go into a cave because somehow over him, you see, what has been eaten out by water or wind, he feels that it is over him and that he can go in it and that the weight is locked and cannot go anywhere. Certainly he learns something from this and brings it back here. He must find a way which is not the way it is made, but he recognizes that there is something about going in somewhere which is a different feeling, and when the rain falls, and when the snow falls, and the wind blows, and he does not have to guard himself against it, his desire for this is very great. And he finds a means, which probably is discovered by even a casual rock, let's say, which has been left by the way things tumbled, bridged over other rocks, and becomes a passage for a chipmunk. He finds in this the validities—the physical validities. And then he makes the psychological validity, because he wants a house and he will not accept a cave, as such. So he makes the incredible because nature can't make it—but must follow nature's rules, laws in every sense, to make it.

Now if one discovers this nature of an arch, his mind becomes completely obsessed with the arch. In fact he wants to test its validity all the way through. His natural sense is not to just say, *Now I discovered this, I want to do something else.* On the contrary. It's the very thing that makes Beethoven Beethoven, because he discovered things within a very narrow kind of realization, but his mind said that anything I wanted to express, I have found the pencil for it. You see, I like crayon instead of liking pastels, or I like oil paints instead of something—he doesn't fool around because he is so full of what this can satisfy at that point that all the means of whatever he wants to express is already in it. It's why a man chooses music, and the next one does something else. In the music lies all his desire for expression. It lies in this form because he sees through certain characteristics all the means he needs to express the tremendous variety of things yet unsaid.

Sher-E-Banglanagar
Dacca, Bangladesh—1968-74

So it isn't in the knowing of many things like I could really, up to a point, build all buildings in brick, you see, and I would not be jealous a bit of concrete, of whether I was using it or not, or precast, or prestressing, or anything of that nature. I got into doing brick merely because I could not use any other material. So I had to use it, it was self-protection to use brick in Dacca. I knew concrete would be a complete failure. But still my love for concrete couldn't be denied, so I tried to make these people make a purse, let's say, out of a sow's ear. I still suffered from that bad decision, because I had made so many buildings in the form of brick and no other material but brick. The large assembly room—I said, *Well it's no bigger than Santa Sophia, you see.* And it isn't, you see; that central chamber, that's the big problem after all. I could have ruled to proceed by making brick, but it was because I myself had so much more experience and had this feeling of a big span which is made with a little finger in concrete and made with all the thousands and hundreds of everything else you could possibly imagine in brick. I felt as though I didn't satisfy something in me. So I vested the central building in concrete and the other buildings in brick. Now if I had decided on brick as the validity of the moment and I could express symphonically everything that I wanted to do in brick, that building would have been finished, instead of being about one third up or one fourth up. It would have been finished. And, by the way, I would have been paid furthermore, you see. It would have lasted so long, you see, therefore I wouldn't lose so much money. You see, it is this sense, it possesses you with a sense that like a great musician who finds in that which he easily recognizes as his selection of the way of expressing constantly, always the same, the greater is the man.

The dangers of misunderstanding how one can use or represent structures is only to go where angels fear to tread, that's all... like, as he also said, Pope, that a little knowledge is a dangerous thing. Drink deep or taste not bare in the spring....The danger lies in thinking of that as an experiment. The danger is not even recognizing your natural talents, you see, and sort of being jealous. It's very natural, and so the danger is in that. To employ a means that more and more becomes part of you and that's it, and I think that even musicians try to compose for the violin and then their real understading is somewhat different from that—let's say, the piano. I think they try to make the piano the violin. Chopin is a beautiful example of one who really did not. Well, I don't mean he composed for the violin but he did because he did some symphonic music, but the piano is truly the piano in Chopin—it's really brought under the instrument, and he fought with it so much he made the piano do what others couldn't do, but it's still piano, piano.

I think the danger is in being so surrounded, especially in so resourceful a country as ours, to be surrounded by so many means and ways—you imagine you can choose freely, but actually you can't because you don't have a true command of what you choose.

I myself am not engineering minded, and I really don't understand structure in a knowledgeable way. I know it in the way I respect it. I know it more through music than I do through engineering or architecture. In the music the structure is so—you might say, it's given to you and still you are able to bring out of it your personality as compared to someone else's. The same fundamental rules apply to Beethoven as they do to Brahms. But Brahms is still able to be Brahms and Beethoven Beethoven. So if you think of a brick structure as being something that makes old buildings recognizable only for their material, then of course in back of it is nothing. It must be something that recognizes the expression of an individual, out of the order of brick. There can be no danger, provided the order of brick itself is understood, not just shapes which have been made by someone else as his expression through the use of brick. The danger is in copying the way it's done, not what sits behind the truth of the nature of a material—in this case the orders of the material which tell you that things must be heavy below and light above. Now when you start to reinforce in which you make the wall rise in the same thickness, then it becomes not in the order of the brick, but in the order of the composite construction of metal and brick, which is completely as valid as any other material. But it doesn't lend itself as well to showing, which is a tendency of the artist, of how a thing is made, because the material in it is secretively there and does not really bring out the order at all of that material. So then the more extreme artist would try and find ways in which the nature of this composite order is again visible. And this tendency would be to want to use stainless steel threads because if he were to really employ it properly, the stainless steel threads could really do much to make it even more elegant by bringing it out in the open. Certain stages in the development of this reinforcing, when brought out in the open, actually strengthens it more than if you were to conceal it entirely on the interior.

This would be the tendency: to make how it's made visible. And there in a sense each building becomes a lesson to the other man. The man itself is tremendously rewarded because from it he can make any number of compositions, and that which doesn't belong to him, which is the truth of this composite order, he must surrender to someone else. The danger is only in the copying of the outward manifestation or the way a man does it, which really truly belongs to him only. What is the point, let's say, of composing like Mozart, too? What is the point of it? There isn't any.

Reprinted from *VIA* magazine
Graduate School of Architecture,
University of Pennsylvania

I visualized the Congress Hall as a place of the meeting of minds.

Palace of Congress
Venice, Italy—1968-74

I can see the Congress Hall as if it were a theatre in the round—where people look at people. It is not like a movie theatre where people look at a performance.

My first idea, regardless of the shape of the site, was to make so many concentric circles with a nucleus in the middle. Because the site is long and narrow, I simply sliced the theatre in the round with two parallel cuts and it would still retain good visibility from everywhere. Therefore the impression in the hall will be of people seeing people. The curve of the meeting hall is slight in order to retain the sense that it is really a street-like piazza gently sloping. One could be reminded of the Palio Square in Siena which was also created to give it a character of a civic theatre.

To each side of the hall there are two streets (fifteen feet wide) which lead to the seating place. These two streets are actually in the inside of the beams which carry the structure. These two side streets communicate throughout the entire length of the auditorium and are also connected to the reception hall on the second floor. The hall will hold twenty-five hundred people, but it can be divided into two separate sections for a seating capacity of fifteen hundred people. Finally the central section could be separated from the rest of the auditorium as a theatre in the round for five hundred people. The side streets, which lead to the seats, are provided with niches where people can go away from the congress and discuss things separately.

The reception hall on the second floor is also like a long plaza which is crowned with three domes. The domes are made up of rings of stainless metal and of solid glass, the exterior being covered with lead just as those of St. Mark. The domes also imply that the hall could be divided into three rooms, their size being related to the diameter of the dome above (seventy feet). To the sides of this hall, there are series of rooms which again are part of the supporting beams.

The third floor is the roof where the sky is the ceiling. Here you are in the presence of the three domes which again tend to divide this terrace into three parts. The parapet which encloses the roof is open to the view of Venice and the lagoon through three crescent openings. On the terrace you will again have, on the sides, covered niches where one can shelter.

The ground floor is a piazza covered by the underside of the auditorium where you can sense the sweep of the structure.

The whole structure, reinforced concrete with marble details, is conceived like a hanging bridge supported on the two ends by two columns on each end, where also the stairs and elevators reach the various levels. In these two supporting sections there are other rooms for different purposes.

The Conference Hall is four hundred sixty feet long, seventy-eight feet high and one hundred feet wide.

A place given over not so much to performances as to events: essentially it is given over to the youth. As a teacher and practicer I am very inspired by the unrest of students....

The Biennale building is made of two sections facing each other, divided by a square. Both ends of the square are open: one to the widening of the canal, offering a broad water entrance to the Biennale, and the other to the gardens. This allows the gardens to enter the piazza. Each section is two hundred feet long, sixty feet wide and sixty feet high. Each side contains on the ground floor workshops, studios and shops; they will also serve to fit up the court for whatever may be created there on the theme of a happening. On the first floor there are galleries for exhibitions and on the second there are studios for artists.

These buildings should actively be used throughout the year as a free self-supervised academy, as a free community of involvement and exchange. The spirit of the Biennale depending on the experience, discussion and work done in them. These buildings would still be used by the Biennale for exhibition purposes when it takes place every two years.

The square, eighty feet wide, can be closed at each end by two moving doors fifty feet high and forty feet wide. A movable roof framed in glass and metal can enclose the square.

The spaces inspired the project and not the project inspires the spaces.

The entrance building by the lagoon (fifty feet by fifty feet and fifty feet high) is a signature building which will personify the meaning of the Congress Hall. It will act as an information centre, and be used for other services, such as a restaurant, etc.

The gardens should be a site for rest among the trees and should make available more grass areas (without fences) and places to sit. It should be a park more than a formal garden.

Reprinted from domus 1, March 1969

Silence and Light,
Address to the Students at
the School of Architecture, ETH
Zurich, Switzerland
12 February 1969

I'm going to put on the blackboard here what may seem at first to be very esoteric. But I believe that I must do it in order to prime myself.

Don't forget that I'm also listening and I have really no prepared talk except that I put a few notes down just to get the scaredness out of me because, you know, this is like a blank piece of paper on which I've got to make a drawing. And so the drawing is a talk this time, you see. But it is wonderful to consider, you know, that you must see so well that you hear, too. The senses really can be considered one thing. It all comes together. It is the reason why I constantly refer to music in referring to architecture, because to me there is no great difference—when you dig deep enough in the realm of not doing things but simply thinking what you want to do, all the various ways of expression come to fore. To me, when I see a plan I just see the plan as though it were a symphony, the realm of spaces in the construction and light. I sort of care less, you see, for the moment whether it works or not. Just so I know that the principles are respected which somehow are eternal about the plan.

As soon as I see a plan which tries to sell me spaces without light, I simply reject it with such ease because I know that it is wrong. And so, false prophets, like schools that have no natural light, are definitely unarchitectural. Those belong to what I like to call *the marketplace of architecture*, but not to architecture itself.

So I must put on the board something which I thought of only recently which could be a key to my point of view in regard to all works of art, including architecture.

And so, I put this on the board: Silence and Light. Silence is not *very, very quiet*. It is something which you may say is lightless, darkless. These are all invented words: *dark-less*. There is no such word. But why not? Lightless, darkless. Desire to be. To express. Some can say that's the ambient sound—if you go back beyond and think of something in which light and silence were together, and maybe are still together, and separate only for the convenience of argument.

I turn to Light, the giver of all presences. By will. By law. You can say the light, the giver of all presences, is the maker of a material, and the material was made to cast a shadow, and the shadow belongs to the light.

I did not say things yet made—desire, being, that quality, that unmeasurable force; everything here promises the measurable. Is there a threshold where they meet? Can a threshold be thin enough to be called a threshold in the light of these forces? These phenomena? Everything you make is already too thick. I would even think that a thought is also too thick. But one can say light to silence, silence to light has to be a kind of ambient threshold and when this is realized, sensed, there is Inspiration.

Inspiration must already have something of a promise of being able to express that which is only a desire to express, because the evidence of the material making of light gives already a feeling of inspiration. In this inspiration—beside inspiration—there is a place, the Sanctuary of Art. Art being the language of man before French, you know, or German. It says: The language of man is art. It stems from something which grows out of the needing, of the desire to be, to express, and the evidence of the promise of the material to do it. The means, somehow, are there. The sanctuary of art—the ambience of a man's expressiveness—has an outlet, you might say. It is my belief that we live to express. The whole motivation of presence is to express. And what nature gives us is the instrument of expression which we all know is ourselves, which is like giving the instrument upon which the song of the soul can be played. The sanctuary of art—I'm taking this little lesson to say that it is the treasury of the shadows.

I'm sure there is no such separation. I'm sure that everything began at the same time. There wasn't a time when it was good for one thing or another. It was simply something that began at the same time. And I would say the desire to be, to express, exists in the flowers, the tree, in the microbe, in the crocodile, in man. Only we don't know how to fathom the consciousness of a rose. Maybe the consciousness of a tree is its feeling of its bending before the wind. I don't know. But I have definite trust that everything that's living has a consciousness of some kind, be it as primitive. I only wish that the first really worthwhile discovery of science would be that it recognizes that the unmeasurable is what they're really fighting to understand. And the measurable is only a servant of the unmeasurable; everything that man makes must be fundamentally unmeasurable.

Now, of course if you see that, you wonder how you can make a dime—we call it a dime, you say a franc. It certainly doesn't look to me as though you could make a franc out of that, unless you sell it to Zodiac, you know. Well, maybe you can do it, but it is just part of an inner belief that you cannot evaluate a Giotto painting. It defies any analyzation, it defies measurement, because after all, Giotto gave us the prerogatives of painting. He said that, to a painter, a doorway can be smaller than a person. But the architect must use a doorway that is bigger than a person. Is he less in art than the other? No. He just recognizes his realm of expression.

The painter can paint people upside down, as Chagall does, as you know, but he has this perogative because he's a painter. He's representing nothing; he's presenting everything. It's a presentation of the wide realm of expression which exists in man. A sculptor can make square wheels on a cannon to express the futility of war. Unfortunately, the architect must use round wheels if he wants to bring his stones from place to place. From this, you get the sense of that which tends to be the marketplace, and that which never reaches the marketplace.

And this is, you might say, the crossroad, the place of realization—the place where one sort of senses how much from there, how much from here is the content. Giotto vibrates in this area, defies time. No time will ever say he's old-fashioned. Tremendous discoveries of expression lie in such a great man, as it did in other great men. The essential quality which I admire most in Einstein is that he was a fiddler. From this he derived much of his sense of the universal—or rather, you might say universal order was something that came to him from his sense of eternity, not from his mathematical knowledge or the knowledge of science.

Why didn't it reach the others if knowledge was there, because it filters through everybody? Knowledge is available. It just happened to be in him, the knowledge of something else, and so it is in every one of us. Knowledge is very specifically something that belongs to each individual in his own way. The book of knowledge has never been written, nor will it ever be written for man. Certainly nature doesn't need it. It's already written for nature.

So let's talk a little bit about a problem that comes to a man as an architect. Suppose you were assigned to say—and what a wonderful commission it would be—what is a university. And instead of being given a program, saying that a university should be for so many people, the library must have so many books, you have to have so many classrooms, you've got to have a student center, and you have to have schools for the professions—think in terms of *university* as though it never happened, as though it isn't here, so you have nothing to refer to, just the sense of a place of learning, an undeniable need, an undeniable desire on the part of all of us that a place be for learning, something which comes specially to someone who is willing to convey to others what is so special in him, and what becomes special in those who learn, in their own way special as though a singularity taught singularities. Because we're all singularities, and none of us are like the other. So consider a university.

I gave this problem to the University of Pennsylvania, to my students. There was no program. Well, I said, you consider the University of Pennsylvania as probably the seat, because somebody has to have something to put their hat on, so that was the only indication.

Now one student, a German student, in a very halting and most modest way, said he believed the core of the university is the library, but a specific library. He said it was the central library. He said that the library of the university is like the Acropolis. It is the offering of the mind. And he considered that when you go into the library, and you see these books, you judge them as offerings of the mind. A man motivated not by profit of any kind, just by a sense of offering, writes a book, hoping that it will be published. He's motivated by the sense that he has something somewhere in there, whether it is deep, deep in the silence, or whether it is already on the threshold of inspiration. He must be there to write it, and when he draws from here, and when he draws from there, somehow; he motivates his writing a book. And he gets it also from another, beautiful source, and that is through the experience or the Odyssey of a life that goes through the circumstances of living, and what is important are not the dates or what happened, but in what way he discovered man through the circumstance.

The artist feels this when he makes something. He knows that he does it now, but he knows also that it has eternal value. He's not taking circumstances as it happens. He's extracting circumstances from whatever revealed man to him. Tradition is just mounds of these circumstances, you see, the record of which is also a golden dust from which you can extract the nature of man, which is tremendously important if you can anticipate in your work that which will last, that which has the sense of commonness about it, and by commonness I mean really that the essence of silence is commonness. That's the essence of it.

When you see the pyramids now, what you feel is silence. As though the original inspiration of it may have been whatever it is, but the motivation that started it, that which made the pyramids, is nothing but simply remarkable. To have thought of this shape personifying a kind of perfection, the shape of which is not in nature at all, and striving with all this effort, beating people, slaves, to the point of death to make this thing. We see it now with all the circumstances gone, and we see that when the dust is cleared, we see, really, silence again. So it is with a great work. I see a Giotto painting also with a feeling of silence, as though it came from here, you see, as though it didn't come from any sense of the marketplace.

Going back to the university then, this was a center; it was something about the humanities that was really the university. Another part of it was that of the professions. This is the engagement of man in the various avenues of expression, be (he) a doctor, or a lawyer, or an architect, or a bookkeeper, or a nurse, anything. You choose to be a nurse because you want to; you have something that tells you to be a nurse, or something that tells you to be an architect. The university position has nothing to do with the marketplace. The marketplace has to do with the way this profession is practiced by the individual—this is something the university should not be concerned with, except to inspire him in the nature of his profession, and in what way he will, in the end, be the happiest in the exercise of this expression. Problems of the marketplace really do not belong there, because no matter how much you teach it, the tendency will be for the person to find his own way, because a man does not really learn anything that's not part of himself. He might try very hard. He may even pass examinations, but he'll never really be a chemist, even if he studies chemistry, unless he's a chemist from the very, very start. And so, therefore, knowledge per se is to me very doubtful, you see. But knowledge taken to prime your way of expression is not, and to develop a person's talent is not. Very good. Very wonderful. The place, the realm, within which the talents of people can be exercised.

So the university has nothing to do with the marketplace. It doesn't disdain it, because it gets its support from the marketplace. But it still doesn't teach it, because it's useless to teach it. To prepare you for nature's ways, yes. The laws of nature must be known, because there are three aspects in the teaching. There is a teaching of the professional position: responsibility to other people which includes the differentiation between science and technology, which are completely different things. And your specific knowledge that you need in statics or acoustics, those are all very necessary things and belong definitely in the realm of teaching. Thirdly, to prepare you for your responsibilities—conducting your office as a responsibility—and that is to teach the man to be himself, which is delving into the various talents which can be employed in the profession—not all having to do with design, not all with specification writing, but it, somehow, all belongs to it. You're not teaching geniuses, you're just teaching, you know, the nature of the profession, the many facets, you see, among which self-expression can come about. But the most important thing to teach is to know that architecture has no presence. You can't get a hold of architecture. It just has no presence. Only a work of architecture has presence, and a work of architecture is presented as an offering to architecture. Architecture has no favorites, it has no preferences in design, it has no preferences for materials, it has no preferences for technology. It just sits there waiting for a work to indicate again, to revive the spirit of architecture by its nature, from which people can live for many years.

And so the university is a sanction. The library of the sanction place, the places of the professions, the library of these professions are there, hooked up because there is also an offering of the mind, and somehow connected with the unit, with the more objective offerings of the mind, which is the offering of the sanctuary of the Acropolis. You might say objective or subjective—it doesn't really matter. It's just offering.

Now if you consider this, it must be kept in mind the differentiation of a wonderful kind. It begins in mind the differences between the garden, the court, and a piazza. Because your connections are not going to be just colonades and that sort of thing. It's going to be mental, the connection. You're going to feel it in some way. But the consciousness of a planner that there is an association, a kind of inter-respect between the two, is already. It guides the hand, you know, in saying it should be here, it should be there, it should be there, you see. Otherwise it becomes merely land-scraping, I call it, you see. Not landscaping: land-scraping. It is really a conciousness not drawing around trees here or there or stamping them on your plan, you see. I hate that, really I do. So, the connection, then, is the realization of what is a garden, what is a court, what is an avenue, what is a piazza.

A garden is a very private thing. You would say that the landscape architect, or the architect, or the gardener who makes a plan for a garden with his fountains and places to sit, and the trees chosen in relation to porticos and so forth, should make the plan as an instruction for something that will grow into being, and once everything is established that will grow into being, it is full. After that he takes this plan and throws it into the fireplace and doesn't keep it as a record, because the next garden he makes must be completely different, because that garden is very very private and belongs to the individual. It's not a place of invitation, it's a place of... of part of the expression of living.

The court is different. The court is the boy's place. The court is already a place of invitation. I would like to call it the outside-inside space. It is a place which one feels that if he comes to it, he can make a choice as to where he goes from there. And a piazza is man's place: much more impersonal, less defined than a court.

With this so-called architecture of connections, which happens to have no rules, is a consciousness of the involvement of the land and the buildings, of their association with the library. Now there are many things absent. It wasn't sufficient, just the connection. The class was very excited about one aspect which I hinted at. That there must be a place of happening. A place of happening, and, you say, why can't things happen the way they will. They don't have to. The Agora, for instance, was a place of happening—Agora, the Stoa. The Stoa was made most marvelously. It was made like this. No partitions, just columns, just protection. Things grew in it. Shops became. People met, meet, there. It's shaded. You present a quality, architectural, no purpose. Just a recognition of something which you can't define, but must be built.

Today, the general unrest among students should call for this kind of space. You shouldn't try to fight a battle as to who's right and who's wrong, but just create the architectural interpretation of this, which is a place without partitions which will form itself into partitions some day. So it is a recognition of a place where possibly the student, the administration, and the teacher would meet. It's a club of the university, not the student center, so to speak, but everybody's center, and it sits probably in a green area like this without paths whatsoever, because who knows where you're going.

But that's a definite architectural quality. It has the same quality as all religious places, a simple quality of knowing that a stone stands free, that it has something more than just simply singing at random or going through a forest and trying to jump. What is the feeling? It is something in the way of a mysterious decision to make Stonehenge. It's terrific. It's the beginning of architecture. It isn't made out of a handbook, you see. It doesn't start from practical issues. It starts from a kind of feeling that there must be a world within a world. The world where man's mind somehow becomes sharp.

Have you ever said anything significant when you were outside waiting for a bus? Never. You said something significant inside a building, never outside a building. Did you ever say anything significant at a picnic? No. Well, you had a hell of a good time—I realize that—but you didn't say anything that was the mind saying. It was really quiet functioning as humans in the most sparkling, beautiful, amusing way, which is definitely a part of our lives, but it is not necessarily how our buildings start.

Buildings start as a kind of recognition that there must be a place of concentration where the mind, somehow, is given play. And I make a distinction beween mind—and this might be put here, too, because it doesn't belong here, but I'll put it here anyway—mind and brain. Brain is an instrument given by that fellow over there. Mind is this and the instrument. Somewhere in here is mind, mind is the instrument and the soul. Now this is mind. Brain is—I would say the machines we make now, you see, for calculating, for putting into; I don't know what you call them, these computers—these are brains, never the mind. The mind makes this, but it never will really give you anything the brain can do. And the man, the men who really know the instruments, will tell you that themselves. It's the men who don't know it that will tell otherwise. It's like putting a penny in a slot and getting a very wonderful answer worth more than a penny. I'm afraid not.

So they discovered that this was a place of meeting of everyone, a very necessary thing. From this you recognize also that a school of architecture probably starts with a court, surrounded by shops, in which you build and tear down at will. It's a closed court because nobody really likes to show how badly he does things, so it becomes something which amongst your conferees is okay. Outside, not. It's not an exhibition place. There is no admission set for this thing; it's closed. From this grows other things, spaces high and low, but it is a kind of area undetermined, spaces undetermined in their light, in various light, in various heights, and that you move around with a sense of discovering the spaces rather than being named for certain reasons. They're just there and you feel it is a school of architecture because of how much concentration you put into the primitiveness, the fundamentalness with which you made these spaces. These are all, I think, indications of the tremendous opportunities that exist today in architecture. The discovery of the elements of our institutions which need revival, which need to be bolstered up, which need to be redefined.

Palace of Congress
Venice, Italy—1968-79

Now, in the Congress Building in Venice I built—I am thinking of buildings—a place which is the meeting of the mind and a place where expression of the meeting of the mind can take place. It is also a place of happening. I don't believe in inviting shows for the Biennale, saying, *Come with your exhibit, bring your big packages, bring the things you've done.* But rather I say, *Come here, meet other people, and by meeting them something will happen to you.* And it will.

Here in a Palazzo dei Congressi they meet to sense each other's mind. In the Biennale they meet to express something actually, tangibly. It is somehow a place of existence, which I might put here. I'll put it here—existence here, and presence. You see, presence is here, existence is here. It exists. You can feel the thought, but it doesn't have presence. When you describe, when you say, *Oh! It's marvelous! It's beautiful! It's terrific! It's...it's immense,* you are saying words which no university professor understands at all. But when you say, when you see a thing, *Oh, I don't like stone. I think it should be taller. I think it ought to be wider,* you are dealing with the measurable, because it is made. So in the work of art there is the measurable and the unmeasurable.

When you say, *It's terrific,* you're talking about the unmeasurable and nobody understands you, and they shouldn't because it is fundamentally unmeasurable.

Now from this grew other things. It wasn't just the university and the buildings there—which are not yet, have not been made in the university, and there were other buildings; I don't want to mention the whole story. But what grew in it? A realization of the marketplace and the university. And it so turned out that the university here, the marketplace there, there was a place between; it happened to be in Philadelphia, the Schuylkill River. City planning couldn't be here, because it is too politically infested. City planning could also not be here because it is too theoretically oriented. So there has to be a place of happening, a place where the marketplace goes to, where the university goes to, both represented—but they're not particularly here—and this was a place of happening right here, designed by one of the students as a bridge crossing the Schuylkill, and it was a kind of place of auditoria, a place where there were many auditoriums, many that would be the proper ones selected for the kind of discussion which is a generator of the sense of the institutions of man, which a city planner should be most conscious of—not any of these things—but fundamentally first, the sense of the institutions of man which yet have not been made and those which are here, but they're very badly in need of change. From this is the true generator of planning, not from the other things like traffic. To me it's child's play. Traffic—we can really put it into a machine and find the answer. In a certain way you can. At least a help. Not the real answer, but at least a temporary one.

So there must be found in every city really, a place of the marketplace, free of the school, which is, in a sense, the nerve center of worthiness, of that which can make a city really great. Because you measure the city not by the excellence of its traffic system, but by why it has a traffic system—because there is worthiness to serve. And from this architecture of connection between, the whole city takes direction: the university and the other schools take direction by the reason of their courts, their gardens and their avenues, and so forth. The connection is both mental and physical. This institution, I think, is necessary everywhere, because otherwise nothing will progress. The marketplace won't progress, nor will this progress. There must be a ground here, it's a freedom ground at this point. This came out of no program, simply a speculation on the power of architecture to set down that which commands technology, which really writes the program, because after all, if an architect gets a program from a client, he gets an area program. He has to change the areas into spaces because he's not dealing only with areas, they're spaces. It isn't just feelings, they are feeling, ambience. They are places where you feel something... different. As I said, you don't say the same thing in a small space, you see. So a school must have small spaces as well as large spaces, and all classes need not be the same. There's something like a place of learning. Felt so. Taken out of the very essence of your feeling as a person, the various other people to a sense of commonness, which is a tremendous guide to a person's mind.

You say *the institutions of man*. I don't mean institutions like the establishment. I mean, really, institutions being this: that it is an undeniable desire to have the recognition, that man cannot proceed in a society of other men without having certain inspirations that they have—this be given a place for their exercise. Actually, the institutions of learning stem from the way we were made. Because nature, in what it makes, records how it was made. In the rock is the record of the rock, and in man is the record of man. Man through his consciousness senses inside of himself all the laws of nature—except that his instrument, which he gets from nature in the way of a brain, is usually very poor—and when he mixes it up with his sense and desire, he finds that there are plenty of obstructions. He takes years before he senses this himself. But regardless, the quality which he inherited, that part which I say is the golden dust which he does inherit, that which is the nature of man which he inherits, just like his physical being—in this he senses the desire to learn to express. So all learning, you see, stems from the way we're made, only to find out the laws of the universe because it's in you. And so it is with other inspirations which are in us. The sense of physical well-being comes from the desire to live forever; to express. The highest form of expression is art because it's the least definable.

Desire to live, to express.

The institutions, therefore, are established because there is this sense of wanting to learn, and the wanting to learn makes you pay a tax to see that a school is established. Nobody resists this tax because it is in the nature of man that he wants to learn. Sometimes he's beaten out of it because of certain things, like he's scared to be in front of a class. He loses his courage because he's slower in becoming free of this. That's why I believe that no marking should exist at any school, because it's destructive to man. And it's very difficult. Well, I say, I know it is, but really, if you didn't mark anybody, I think you'd find that your class would become brighter. Actually, it is so because people don't grow equally. I had a good experience in this because I was a very poor student, and I somehow managed to get past; but I only learned the things that were taught to me after I got out of school and not during the time, because I was naturally bashful. I didn't want to assert myself, and also I made my lessons three days afterward instead of the day I should. So, all these things are just part of a person.

Now another example of searching for the nature of the problem: a boy's club. I gave it one time as a problem, and the speculation was what would be the first room which one would make, which would present a boy's club? If I were to take the programs issued by the Association of Boy's Clubs, which has a standard program, or whatever it is, I would meet this kind of a situation: I would come to the entrance, and there would be a supervisor who would see to it that you're a boy or a girl. There you would go through, you see, and then you would be hit by a room that is ping pong, noise, absolute stress and strain, because it is good to feel, as they said, that the boy must feel that he's now amongst others, you see. And then there are some guidance rooms, so to speak, where the older boys can be. Well, it just continues. There is, of course, a swimming pool. There is a gymnasium. But I tell you that many people would never join because of that shock of being supervised from the start, never go into a place where you're likely to be pushed around. When a boy is delicate and frail and not a fighting sort of person, he walks into a gang of enemies. Hmm. So, the problem was given, what is the first room? One thought that it should be a room with a fireplace, a generous one, with much seating around it, where one can take a seat so, hopefully, that someone would come and sit by him, or that he had at least a choice not with any strain attached to it. But during the course of the development of the problem, it was found that the best place was a court. You open the door and you're in a court with an arcade around it, and the promise of the kind of room that you'd want to go to all around it. So the man chooses, the boy chooses what room he wants to go into because he's just entering life, so to speak with others, and the sensibleness of this is certainly far greater than knowing exactly how a boy's club works. You don't know. And so you make a plan which you don't know, and it's a far superior plan.

I'll now talk about functionalism. I think you can talk about machines being functional, bicycles being functional, beer plants being functional. But not all buildings are functional. Now, they must function, but they function psychologically. There is a psychological function which is a paramount function, whether it's a factory or otherwise. Just so people are involved; there must be a place for people—even an atom-cracking plant must consider that there are people involved in this thing. There are places for everything, but there is something which has to do with the association of people with it. And that sense, I think, brings about a new era in architecture which doesn't try to make everything be accountable. So, when you are given, as I said, a program by a client in which he gives you how much square-foot area he needs, let's say, for a lobby, which he measures by square-foot area, you usually won't have more than three or four people at a time, or maybe ten or twenty, that's where the elevators are, where the stairways are, from which you go upstairs. Now measure if this were also an entry for a school of architecture. You see how it would fail. But the program reads just the same for a school of architecture as it does for an office building. Pretty much the same. It's measured by so many square feet per person. Three and a half people per acre—that kind of thing. But actually, you translate the lobby into a place of entrance, and it becomes a very different thing. It is a space of entrance, not a lobby. You change it. You change corridors into galleries because you know their value, you know their tremendous association—value when they are a gallery instead of a corridor. And the first thing that must be done of great importance is to make the budget economical, which means worthwhile, which means that you may spend the same amount of money, but the attitude shouldn't be that the money rules what you do. You must find that which is worthy within what is considered for the moment to be a limit, but your duty is also to portray what may increase this limit, in order to bring more to the client, depending on just how you are made, whether you give in to certain things. But the going through this exercise of portraying what seems to be the nature of something is a very essential thing to your eventual powers, which will bring about a new architecture.

Now, I have some other things here. I cannot speak enough about light because light is so important, because actually, structure is the maker of light. When you decide on the structure, you're deciding on light. In the old buildings, the columns were an expression of light. Light, no light, light, no light, light, you see. The module is also light, no light. The vault stems from it. The dome stems from it. And the same realization that you are releasing light. The orders which you think about when you are determining the elements of design—the elements, and how you are considering them in design to be perfected. There is in the design the consideration of the differences between the order of structure and the order of construction. They're two different things. There is an order to construction which brings in the orders of time. They're very much married to each other. The order of structure can make conscious the crane. The crane that can lift twenty-five tons should appear in a specification of present-day architecture but it does not appear now. The architect says, *Oh! They're using a crane on my building. Isn't that nice,* so they can pick it up more easily, never realizing that the crane is a designer; that you can make something of twenty-five tons coming to something of twenty-five tons, and you can make a joint that's so magnificent, because that joint is no little thing. In fact, if you'd put gold into it, you shouldn't be spending so much money, because it's so big. So the realization that joint-making is the beginning of ornament—because I do believe that the joint is the beginning of ornament—comes into being again, you see. What you can lift as one thing should be something that motivates the whole idea of making a single thing which comes together with another single thing. So in the order of structure you make this decision, like when I said that a beam needs a column. A beam needs a column, a column needs a beam. There is no such thing as a beam on a wall. And if you make the decision which I made, that the beam of brick is an arch, therefore, since I did not want to use any concrete beam, and since I was not going to use any columns, it became so natural to use an arch, because it was only part of the wall construction which is characteristic of brick, and I placed everything supported under arches, like big arches which stretch as much as twenty feet, let us say, with a very low thing using restraining members in concrete like this to take the thrust away, bringing the wall very close together, giving a space with that much opening because I made a composite order in which the concrete and the brick will work together. This is a composite order. A sort of sense of structure, a sense of the order of brick, sense of the order of structure, which made this possible. The design goes on and on, speculation of the ways you can do this thing in the most fantastic ways, because you recognize that structure has an order, that the material has an order, that the construction has an order, the space has an order in the way of the servant spaces and the spaces served, that the light has an order because it has an order in the sense that it is given by structure. The consciousness of the orders must be felt.

I just remind you in closing, the story of a very famous Persian poet, who lived in twelve hundred or so, who writes as a poet; I'm not going to recite the poetic language, because I don't read Persian, and also, it's far from me, the words that I read. There was a Priestess who was going through her garden in the Spring, and of course it was a glorious day. As she went through her garden, observing everything, and came to the threshold of her house, and there she stopped in admiration—standing in the threshold, looking within. And her servant inside waiting came over to her saying, *Mistress, Mistress. Look without, and see the wonders that God has created.* And the mistress said, *Yes, yes, but look within and see God.* In other words, what man has made is the very, very manifestation of God. Thank you very much.

Louis I. Kahn-Complete Work 1935-74
ed. by Heinz Rommer, Sharad Jhaveri,
Alessandro Vasella, Institute for the History
and Theory of Architecture
at the Swiss Federal
Institute of Technology, Zurich 1977.

Interview, *VIA* magazine
Philadelphia, Pennsylvania
16 March 1969

I was at the conference on the judgement of urban problems in Cannes in Southern France. There I had a feeling of the person who is concerned, very seriously concerned, with urbanism, or so-called urbanism.

What was submitted as a view of urbanism touched nothing on the uplifting of the aspirations which could lead to finding a way of expression. It was all rather mechanistic, concerned about structure, a great consciousness, rather healthy, about how the services must filter through the building—or rather be the backbone of the finding of the physical shape—that it relied a great deal on it, though it was based on no particular knowledge as to how much you really need of it, because some of those spaces allocated were entirely too big for what's happening—as though you were lifting the bottom of the street somewhere up into space thinking that the whole bottom of the street is being used as an avenue for the circulation of utilities where there are only a few pipes, lonesomely in there, interfering with everything else. You know what I mean? And it could be very much condensed into a much smaller thing, but you see that part of knowledge should not, which some immediately condemn, immediately a need in order to judge these things. I didn't feel that that was so important—the fact that you didn't know anything—because that can easily be found out. But the fact that you recognize that new shapes will come or new realizations of form will come from the consideration of everything—that is very important.

But the conference didn't go much farther than the fascination with the mechanistic, the structural, and several projects looked as though you were building a great big Christmas tree on which you put little balls which are called housing. You could no more pay for all that service, structure being one of them in this case, because it was only serving the little Christmas ball in which you put the house. And the house was so peculiarly made—because it said it had to be independent from the other house—that they were completely unlivable. Even that point, you see, was completely unrealistic.

It never really reached the point where it had integrity. It didn't have that quality of integrity which I think I mentioned here in Thomas Aquinas—where I think it's an excellent definition of beauty, a beauty put in such a way that it isn't beauty to look at but beauty of an emergence of something true to the expressions of man.

And I told you the story about the person who gave his dissertation in an outfit quite unique: The last one that was up for jury consideration was an interesting fellow, wearing sandals, corduroy trousers, a loose blouse in the Russian fashion, dark blue, with a little cord that he wore on his neck to which was attached a little clock. He kept referring to it every time as though he were very punctual about something, which he wasn't at all. It was just a little affectation. And he had a great bush of hair which from the rear as he turned around looked like an Egyptian figure, and he had a beard and a moustache, a rather distinguished looking person, Slavic, spoke very slowly. Next to him, standing on the floor, was a bottle of mineral water—I think it was mineral water, it was marked mineral water—and it was a great big bottle which he took by the neck and took a swig out of it every ten seconds. And the jury just waited—gurgle, gurgle, gurgle, just like this. It was really very amusing. And he had a pack of cigarettes and also some little liquid which he kept putting on his hand and licking every once in a while. Then he had a little blackboard on which he put some figures, symbols, like U for urbanism you see, and D for density, and if it was very dense he just squared it, put a 2 on it. And this was all just something probably scientific, but really it wasn't.

This took a long, long time to introduce you to his mind. The drawings around him were done very meticulously, and they were drawn on some plastic; maybe they were inserted in some way, I don't know how. And he had light behind them so you could very readily see them; when you were in this room you were surrounded by the drawings—in this little cubicle he had made for himself, a little blackboard, a little mat on which·he had all these things that he was using. There was something ritualistic about the whole thing. And the jury was very patient with him because he was so very slow, in delivery—his mind was tremendously slow. But it was clear on the subject matter. His delivery was very, very slow, and what he said didn't seem as though he were the inventor of it in any way: He was not the man that generated this idea, he was really talking like he got these from a book.

There was an American boy and a German girl who collaborated as architects. (I have their names here somewhere, and I should really remember their names.) The young man is going to teach at the university here. He is, I think now, from California. I believe he is, and his project was a town which is being studied by Rudolph and others between Washington and Baltimore—Columbia. And he took that project and used it as a basis for his study. And she was absolutely excellent in her sense of what a place like this should be; she was really the only one who had a feeling of the humans that are going to occupy this. Otherwise, it was all just technology and trustdom in the servant aspect of this—what serves you, but nothing which aspires to what may be the emergence of a new atmosphere of living and new goals of living. This none of them the others has, it was all something else. She was the only one who had that sense, and she talked about places in a way which I thought was...to me, very realistic things, though very far away from the usual mind on the subject. His work was a modification of Lubisnisch's work, you know, who spired his buildings, sweep the ground up with the buildings. The first I'd seen of that was in Tel Aviv when I was a judge in a development right on the sea, and he has this thing just jutting out into the sea, and it was really a very beautiful thing. And I remember Bruno Zevi and a few others were very highly supporting him, including myself, but it was unexplored and I thought in many instances completely impractical. Like this pinnacling of the buildings; you wonder what happens at the very end, because at the end all you have left is an elevator with nothing to serve. There's nothing there for it to serve so therefore the shape of the building is wrong, unless it was a spire of a cathedral with a cathedral down below or something like this. It couldn't ever be used practically but still the shape, I felt, was a kind of dream shape which would level itself out, because plenty of people knock down dreams. But the man who had this feeling was a good man to have such a feeling, and he was a highly emotional man—Lubinisch—and he appeared again in California and was also a judge of a competition there for what they called the Golden something. He appeared there, and he had to leave the room at least four times, he was so emotionally involved in this thing and trying to convey the eventual beauty, the beauty that's implied by this work. So you do feel that they're wonderful people, but you feel as though they haven't been taught, they haven't been encouraged, and it's something to think about.

Oh, and the story of this other man. He didn't win a medal because it was a voting thing. They're 17 judges and out of 17 a few voices was enough, and what he showed as a solution to the problem was really nothing; it was only that he was a man concerned and very much involved, and he said some very good things. Though they weren't his own, he believed in them.

The next day after the announcement of who won medals—there were four of them, one sort of squeezed through the backdoor, just got in—and the next morning as I was going from the hotel to the Congress Hall where all these things were being exhibited, I was met by two very nervous girls who ran across the street against the traffic and just sort of stopped dead. One seemed terribly nervous and ready to cry, the other seemed a little more calm, explaining that this young man had been forcibly lead into the hospital and they didn't know what to do. And they asked me to help. Well, I didn't even know where the police station was, I didn't even know where the hospital was. So I felt that since the hotel was so close, *You come to the hotel and I'll try to get a hold of Lefevre.* Now Henri Lefevre was the man who really instigated all the revolutions—student revolutions—in Paris, a man, a sociologist, who is greatly honored by the students. He was there as one of the judges of the competition, and his wife was there, and I found that they were living in the same hotel just luckily. So I called them, and he was still in bed—it was still early in the morning. I drew him out of bed, and I let all that French flow, you know, those girls were French as is Lefevre. Lefevre is a sort of man I admire very much because he doesn't get flustered. He listens carefully. He says a few words only and gets to work, which is very nice. So he heard a few words—chattering, chattering—but he was saying just a few words here and there. Then finally he got on the phone and sort of brought things together and took this very nervous girl and put her to bed with the help of Mrs. Lefevre in her hotel room, I was sort of free of the problem though it really possessed me, and when I inquired what caused this, I found that this young man had come to the Congress Hall, where all the exhibits were, very, very early and had all the equipment to tear everything down—all over, anybody's exhibit, down the line. That was his intention. He started; when he was caught, he stepped out, of course, and that was the reason he was taken to the hospital.... So there was a lot of drama going on. It was really very interesting and very important to me because as I was in this atmosphere, it sort of was a rejuvenating thing to see the works of men. You sort of sum up things, how things are going and the degree of functional irresponsibility—national, economic. Nothing is considered, and it's all because of lack of experience; there's nothing there that is deliberately foolish or anything like this, though completely impractical....

And the thought that I had, if I were asked, you know, what would be the most important goal to reach in the consideration of what is a city, or what is urbanism, I go back to the thought that a person is the outlet, outlets of expression, and needs to develop his natural talents as quickly as possible. Just think of an architect or, I'd say, a future architect or a man who would go to architecture because of his talents, not knowing anything about architecture. Can you really begin any later than when he's six years old, you see? You just wonder about it. And you wonder about all these degrees you must have first before you study your profession. It seems like one of the worst things is all that academic nonsense that precedes. You see, it's the learning of the tools—the learning of the means by which you can draw, through your natural talents, what is in you. So it seems to me that the places where one finds the peculiar or unique combination is where his talents are brought out, even though it may be in some instances only a person who is available, or an office that's available, where these talents can be developed. Or it can be a school, a place more formally school because of the nature of your talent. Or it can be a shop. It can be a bureau where school is not a formal thing but is a place where you can go as though you were talking about apprenticeship again—but now something less autocratic than that. And if I could think of the first consciousness of what directions, let's say, a city should go, it would be the recognition that there must be many, many more schools of great variety. And you're serving man almost more immediately than you're serving just the question of holding their body and soul together, which is almost disgraceful not to serve.

You might say a country that cannot have a person that is born to live at least in the food and clothing that makes his body go on is just a disgraceful situation. And it's really what's in back of my mind, not giving too much attention to need, because it is really disgraceful not to give need to a person. Need. So to make a plan based on need seems to me no plan at all! You might say need is a kind of service station, you see, almost. That's how little it must be considered as an impetus for an inspiration for that which a city should be. The city should be one of the most exciting places, where you're in the environment of learning yourself, about yourself, learning your talents so that you can be an effective person.

So school, this school, our school, any school, should be serving of the individual, not a band of people, not to serve a political idea. I think that is useless because the political idea is a circumstantial thing. It is a fight for survival, yes, but it's not really developing your talent at the same time. You can't waste, in my opinion, a nickel's worth of time fighting for the right to exist. The situation should be that you fight for the right of developing your talents. Now I know both things must exist, must be there. One of the young architects whom I met cornered me at a point as I was walking out of the building. He said, *Don't you think that the most important duty of the student now is to be political? Is to be part of the political scene?* And I said, *No, I don't think so. But,* I said, *for those who have the talent for their position in the political scene, they definitely should not go away from what their talent is.* And I see also a collaboration between the man of talent in that respect and the one who is preparing himself in a different way. But not to say that politics is important and hence everything must be serving politics.

I was thinking about this when I was saying how true it might be, and I yet felt that there were great areas of not truth about it because, after all, at a certain time you don't think of your talents while a world goes on in this direction. And it seemed wrong to me to think that it was so *set* in its importance. So I don't know what it is—I just don't know. I don't want to say it's politics because politics is like being aware of that which can destroy you and that you have the understanding of man to know how you can avoid your destruction and that of your position and right to live. But it is something which is only serving the right to live—not for the sake of politics itself, but for the right you have to express your talent, you see, which makes a person happy, which makes a person... the littlest thing that he does makes him feel well about the next day and gives him a will to live.

So although I know I'm not very clear about whether a person should now do nothing but political things, I don't think all have talent, and for that reason also, people hang on, people who have no talent for politics that are in politics are simply hanging on to the person who has the talent for politics. They call him a leader, but then in what way are you serving the leader? Wouldn't you be serving the leader much better if you were also one who could express what he's trying to express in a way that's like you in which he's trying to express. If you write well and you are aware of the politics, isn't this better service to the man who is, let's say, able to find his way politically. He needs your support because he needs numbers—but I think quality numbers, not just numbers that you count like so many votes, but they're all quality numbers. One man who can do one thing or another to help what may be the emergence of the right to express.

If I were a writer, I could take this pen and put it down to a piece of paper and write what is right. If I'm an architect, I could also take a pencil. But where do I start? I feel I start with a kind of everyday developed consciousness of the nature of my work. I begin this way. I don't begin with the sense that I now know a great deal about this particular subject. I continue to develop this thing. If I don't have something that stands there unanswered all the time—unanswered, you see—I never really can make an effective line here. It isn't just learning about one thing or another here which is that which makes my pencil move. I know that the next day it will move some other way. But if this stands to one side as unanswered, and I know it is there, then I pick up my pencil and I have a hell of a time starting. I'm in a much better situation when I am basing it on certain bits of knowledge which, after all, in my comprehension of it can be so meagre, because just the egocentricity, or the singularity of the person just blocks him from knowing what this really is. So the development of this seems so important. Now how many of these things are there that you are developing in your consciousness. One senses that places of learning to develop the personal talents is one of the things that could be here, that could start a town. And when you say, well, the guys who know about pipes, they're alright. They should have also these principles in relation to pipes and I have these principles in relation to something else. I have either a sense of making a space that is psychologically conducive to learning or to working. Another man says, *I will serve those spaces very well,* but he also has to know that the other fellow must respect the other man, you see, who is dealing with spaces. You can't absorb all these things and be a combination of all kinds of talent, because there is no such thing.

A man has talent which is an explored thing—it isn't just saying my talent is drawing. Drawings bring about another *consciousness* which is the talent, *not* just drawing the spirit which your talent gives you. You open doors easily with your talent, and you open doors not at all when you are just full of what you've been pumped full of. Either you have knowledge or a practice or anything which is sheer nonsense. You can get out of school and be given a house to design, and you would learn immediately all that has to do with practice, conduct, the air conditioning, all these things because many people tell you about them. You wouldn't need to learn about them. But you have to learn where the doors are that are opened easily and give access to your desire to live, which is really what the talent gives you.

To honor this and to make the atmosphere of learning, be conscious of this. It is the gift which you inherit which can only be in a place which relates itself sufficiently to other places in *one* particular area of places that makes *choice* possible—so you can't find it. You'd never want to ride on a train unless you saw a train.

So if we can speak about urbanism as being not a collection of specialities, but that are just available, that's fine. You develop these specialities which are based on talent, and it drives themselves toward specialities. But what I see at the University, and now you see it, is the *loss* of this value which was rather a prevalent thing, not understood clearly. They were not going to talk down to anybody previously. Everybody did the same thing, but he learned through that same thing, he learned to find himself, very well. This must be heightened, I feel. It must be heightened, because some were respected because they fit into this very well, others were not respected because they could fit into nothing else. Though they found their way, people who even made tremendously good marks or did very commendable problems, you never knew how much help they got from someone else until they were left on their own. Then the help they needed was not there, and the thing dwindled and dwindled and dwindled.

What if their talents were developed particularly and, within the context of this problem, allowed to develop in its way, giving not necessarily that you must make a good design, otherwise you don't graduate, that kind of thing, but simply from a point of view which the talent is recognizable? Then he would have a wonderful variety of attitudes that wouldn't be clear, I assure you, but would be something very exciting to be a part of. And then also the inner respect of one and the other would be something very great and you'd have an immense kind of happy service that exists anywhere—even honoring the person who was of particular genius for one thing or another which could be in one direction or another. So where I previously find I always thought that it was the physical inter-relationships which because you're an architect resulted in spaces which were served—spaces where you lived and spaces that you served—I feel now that what are absent are realizations, like the school. Realization of the variety of schools is a stark necessity where I said it had to do with the institutions of man. It was the same thing, only it wasn't immediate. There wasn't an urgency in it. It had to do with the society coming up to a certain point where the recognition of an institution of man had to come about. But it was too vague, in a way, when you said that the greatest of these institutions is that which serves your powers of expression.

If you had to come to immediate action I wouldn't know where to turn, but I feel you can turn by simply, tomorrow, saying that we must have these schools. And since the schools are not immediately available it is necessary to commandeer certain places where the nucleus of these schools can be. So architects' offices immediately become schools themselves, of a certain kind.

And you say you go to this office and you learn a lot about drawing: you won't know a damned thing about architecture but you'll learn about drawing.

Some people come to this office and they say to me: *I want to work here because I know that when I've worked here I'll be able to open an office.* I'm supposed to pay for this, you see. He wants to open an office and he has just simply the sense that he wants to find enough to do this. And if I were to ever ask him in what way is he serving me, it would really be a very interesting question. I never asked the question; but I wonder about it. But that man, however, is expressing a kind of thing he needs very definitely. It would be very good if it were possible. I know it is very impractical to say this, but it's simply a realization that working for somebody—which is roughly the same thing as what I'm talking about—is not really it (a school) until it becomes a conscious realization. Then it makes the person who is entrusted with the people who are just emerging set up his place with that consciousness. It's a consciousness of this, really.

I'm going to speak in France at the end of this month and the beginning of next because *aujourd'hui* is coming out with an issue of my work and showing some sketches and so forth. When I think of it and when I look through the slides and things that I've done, I really hate all of it. I hate all of it because I know how much is left undone, how much of an encumberance an office itself is. And how much I want to build everything, you know—how one building leads to an understanding of the other. I've always had the feeling that I want to begin all over again, but then where? Where to begin all over again?

And the more I think of what it is—and this is very much like what others have already known from the start which I did not—it starts with the total environment really, where your building fits in with greater anonymity, with greater force, greater reference to buildings in general rather than the peculiarity of one building.

Geoff White: Do you think that—you were talking about this jury at Cannes—the concern with systems, the machines, do you think that's what they're trying to get at?

They may be getting at it, but if you look at the machine as it is, the machine is not there for something that isn't absolutely needed now. In other words, if you think of what you make commanding technology, I believe—I don't think technology's commanding you at all, that all technology that exists now is in business—it's serving something, and look at what it's serving? What's coming out of it? Nothing of great beauty. Nothing of great integrity. It's an instrument made to serve a certain purpose, and the architect, because of his particular view of his role or rather his feeling of expression, his contribution to make living something more beautiful to others as well as to himself, has to command the technology.

The attitude to *use the technology,* which is not really the technology which belongs to the thought that brings about a consciousness of the infinite, the insatiable outlets in the architect. They're thinking *yes* about using technology and that's what looks very nice—trusses, the way trusses look—not even technology because even the potentiality of the crane is not indicated. It's just really complication, it's a new gimmick. It isn't really felt very strongly, and the shapes are very ordinary, and the shapes that are extraordinary are impossible. They're just whims, you see. They come out of dreams right to the drafting board, and it's too quick a path. There's much that has to intervene between the dream, which is unscrambled. It's a marvelous source, because it is the purest psychologically. The desire is very close to dream. In fact, buildings that are just floating, which is your desire—you want to do all these things, they are all there. But they have to be brought to earth, but without losing respect for them. Many of these come out almost directly like a building...like this for instance.

You see a building like this, rising like a building (makes inverted V with hands), you see a bunch of buildings which are like this fellow's I talked about who had this good project. He made buildings like this, the underneath of which is completely useless. You see, he stuffs it with cars. Well, what the devil? The cars couldn't even get around there! The cars are dumb animals that need almost a kind of mechanical room. You don't want to give it a beautiful path to ride in underneath a building. Its only intention is to stop, so it doesn't need this beautiful path, and it's such complication underneath these things. So it's unrealistic, you see, nothing. You come to an elevator up to its point, you see. Really! But dream has this all over the place.

Rolf Sauer: Last time you were talking about the village green—the new village green between the University and the Marketplace. Now when you mention University, do you think of this thought you mentioned last time in the context of many schools besides the University?

Yes, I do. I do think of University, but it means more. It isn't a special place without its tentacles out in all directions.

The university really should touch things that are in town, you see, and find its identity with things in town. So if you had a stock exchange in town, though it is a practical place where things are being transacted every day in circumstantial paths of every day, there is always in the university a sense of its position—not practicality, but its meaning as to whether it serves man altogether. The university, therefore, says *the stock exchange is;* it has this center of belonging. How it's exercised is sometimes pitiful, but it has its knowledge. It is therefore the practical aspects of what happens there. It is not so important to know, for instance, that the Supreme Court is different from the house of legislation because the Supreme Court is a place that relates more to man, that's all. You can call it, if you want to, *where constitutional rights are being held.* In a way it's the same thing because *constitution* is just a concern with man and his rights—in a very general way, not in what happens everyday but in a general way. So you see, what the Supreme Court—what position it upholds is the right position for it. Now, do they actually have to know what occurs there? Yes, this will be of interest to you when you *get* there, but its position in the nature of man is tremendously important. It really has much to do with the dignity of man, much to do, even though you don't think of fairness or unfairness or whatever at the moment court is being held.

So that's why I think the university is not a confined thing, and that its concern, degree, or any kind of distinction which qualifies you, I think, is not qualified by an individual like myself in an office but it's qualified by, let's say, the university. I would say the university—even though you don't go into the university—must be able to qualify you for your right to at sometime convey what is in your mind. So you may have to appear before a board—maybe you appear with certain selected people of a university. At that point you are, one feels that you are, qualified to practice architecture.

I don't believe so much in the State Board being this; if somebody writes an examination that's very useless, no? I think the places of sanction needn't have to be some place where your head is blown off, because it's legal. No, I think it should maybe be at a board of sanctioners—at Harvard, Princeton, you see, other centers or places of environment or rather the encircled influences of learning—and that they review this man, or his works, or ask him some questions, and he's made an architect right away. He doesn't wait until his examinations to prove that he can design a beam which he later turns over to an engineer anyway. If he knows how to design a beam, that is his predilection, so he talks about that.

I know when I was a kid in high school I had no way of learning, I had no way of studying. I mean to say that I was learning all the time, but I had no way of studying. And when it came to an examination I would even read the question wrong—and sometimes when I knew I didn't know the question I would simply write about the Battle of Marathon, which I knew. Now what sense of protection made me do that? So one day my Greek teacher—you see he wasn't asking about the Battle of Marathon, which I knew very well— so he says, *Why did you write about Marathon when I asked you to write about something in the Persian campaign which is a different campaign* (It is probably that which had to do with Cemtem and the campaign which came after)? So I said that I didn't know the other question, so I wrote this one. He excused me, too, you know. He said, *Well.* He was a funny man, we called him *Zeus,* you see, and he was always scratching his moustache, and he was always puzzled by bad boys, and he didn't want to reprimand but he didn't know what to do about it. He was a small man; the other fellows were grown up. So he excused me, and I remember that profoundly as being such a beautiful generosity and right now I don't know either the Battle of Marathon nor the others, because it is really not so important.

Reprinted from *VIA* magazine
Graduate School of Architecture
University of Pennsylvania

Where are the institutions of well-being? Where are the adult clubs, besides the boys clubs or other clubs that a city needs? A city like this could stand easily four Baths of Caracalla, places where you can swim, exercise, be taught about health, not just think that health is what we correct in a hospital. Those institutions are not around. We can afford them; we can signify to the world the magnificence of our present freedom.

We have an incomparable freedom in this country. I believe everybody mismeasures us; nobody can conceive that there is tremendous freedom in this country. It's badly interpreted, but still it's there. The institutions that could come from that are infinitely more than what is shown. If we could hold a congress in Philadelphia in 1976, to which people came—no pavilions, please!

Don't show us what you've done; it's boring.

Tell us what you aspire to do; it's beautiful.

Come to meet as people.

No pavilions, no gadgets.

Just confrontation, confrontation.

Inspired agenda.

Let there be a fight, let there be something from which can come understanding.

Build an oratorium. A realm of oratoria for small discussions, meetings, larger ones, various kinds. That's the offering: come.

Let America pay the entire bill.

Let a place be a place for the meeting of men.

In cities there should be no highways, because the idea of a city is to go to it, not through it.

I think movement of automobiles in a city is fine, parking is not.

Nothing is more ridiculous than a parked car. It's a hunk of tin, that's all. When it moves, it's marvelous.

When you have twenty stories of cars on the street and then you build houses above it, you're destroying the street.

What avenue is more important to the communication of people in a city but the street? Isn't it reasonable to assume that maybe the first three levels in the center of town do not belong to anybody? Anybody builds only as air rights above it and those three levels are devoted entirely to the spreading of the institutions of man—representative places which represent the institutions of man—shops, libraries. All of that is part of this atmosphere of communication, free of destruction, free of preferred location, just simply belonging to, as now, the city.

The city owns one-third of the real estate of its streets. The streets belong to the city. Do you realize it's one-third of all the real estate? They've tremendous powers. They can redesign the streets and make infinitely more meaning to the spaces between buildings. They need but to extend it—in certain places more, in certain places less. Their prerogatives are in capturing place, environment, association, in the center. Above it sit trunks which are called buildings, and maybe they have even heads to express something significant for themselves.

Is that idealism?

I think it's just desperate survival.

Let us call that space the breathing level. At present, we've got the noxious level.

Call it zoning of streets.

Call it zoning of areas.

The first step could be the zoning of streets. Streets don't have to be the same. They're the first place you can attack in the revision of cities.

Mr. Pround, who is director of the new Mellon Museum in New Haven, has this idea to make a gallery which is a place to study the nature of man—particularly the Englishman—which is derived from what he does, in what way he expresses himself in drawing and painting. Mr. Pround believes that out of man's work there is a sense of what that man is.

Jonas Salk was doing the very same thing in knowing what man is through biology. Not so much curing as learning what he is, his potentiality, biologically. What you can expect because of his biology. What you can expect physically from that. What he was trying to express was the combination of both things: what the works of man convey and the potentiality of his physical structure.

I wish that I'd met Pround before, with his simple notion that is really around the corner of your mind. He was electrified by this very simple thing.

Reprinted by permission
University of Cincinnati
College of Design, Architecture, Art and Planning

Architecture has no presence.

Architecture has existence.

It is a kind of ambience in the mind which stirs every man in the profession and raises in his inner feelings a joy and a will to express in the language of architecture that which revives the wonder of even the established, even the smallest thing like a worm.

I know architects who have tremendous commissions, who down deep want nothing more than to be recognized for a small building, in spite of all the great projects, as being a significant contribution to architecture itself. Because most buildings that are built belong merely to the marketplace. That doesn't belong to the realm of architecture at all.

Architecture has no presence except as a work of architecture, which brings it into presence and is offered to the spirit of architecture, in hopes that it will become part of the treasury known as architecture in existence which yet doesn't convey itself in presence.

There is a vast difference in the feelings of existence and presence in all of man's work.

A thought has existence but no presence. It's not material. It's something which crosses the mind, that wonderful instrument which is really the soul and the brain.

It cannot be hoped in any way throughout the entire time of man and nature that a machine outside of man can do any more than be a superior brain. And this is to be welcomed by man very much, because the brain is what man wants so he can express the song of the soul.

The soul is the same in all; otherwise you could measure it.

It's conceit to think it's different.

What is different is the combination of the brain and the soul which gives you a singularity, a limit of the possibility of the unmeasurable qualities of soul, to show itself through the instrument, brain.

Brain is nature's offering, nature's way of approximating what man wants as an instrument.

I believe nature has done beautifully, but as far as man is concerned, not quite enough. We are jealous of the birds. We want to fly like a bird, excel the bird for that matter. So it is with running like a deer or swimming like a fish. There isn't anything that man doesn't want to have as an instrument of his expression, because I think the reason for living is to express. To express that which is fundamentally unexpressible.

Everything that man does must, in its best state, be completely unmeasurable.

The greater the works, the more unmeasurable.

The great works are felt in the commonness, the commonness which the soul, equal in all, gives us. We couldn't really talk to one man in the world if that weren't so.

I had to write an article. I should have said I desired to write an article, but to write is like pulling teeth, very difficult. I'd love to but it isn't my natural talent. But it was a time when a drawing, which is my natural talent, was inappropriate, and I thought, how could I honor so fine an architect as Luis Barragan of Mexico, whom I admire very much though he did very few works. He expressed himself in other ways, in the way he makes his land architecture.

I don't like the word *landscape architecture*. It sounds prissy to me, it sounds frivolous. *Land architecture* sounds great; nobody lives up to it. I don't know one who is a land architect, but I hope they wake up and become land architects instead of land-scraping architects.

I thought of this sense which brings you back, and back farther than back, to a sense of man which we feel within us where there was an overwhelming desire to be, to express. The instrument was not yet evident, but there was this prevalence equal to and as prevailing as the order of nature, as all the laws of nature.

On one side this will to be, to express, the unmeasurable. Coming into contact with the course of this prevalence is another prevalence: the laws of nature, all of order. This desire to express in the ambience of eternity, and that which is in the realm of the universal order, law. Once these were brought together, there was a movement between light and silence.

Silence met light. Light, the giver of all presences.

Material which was derived from light was spent light. Spent light was a material which cast a shadow by the grace of light, and the shadow belonged to light.

This will to be to express moved towards light, light moved towards it, and in its ambience which you may call a threshold ambience, one sensed the inspirations. The inspirations are the same as saying, *I want to express and I know it's possible because I see the mountain. It's a made thing. I must make something to express, I must find the words to express, I must create something which makes expression possible. And I know it can be done because nature has made a mountain or the stream.*

The inspirations are the beginning of all works.

When we speak lightly about inspiration, do we realize what a marvelous word it is, and what a marvelous point in man's realization of man it is?

It is also where the sanctuary of art is because the only language of man is art.

Even a word is a work of art.

Usable languages are only made so that expressions can lead to art. The art of saying things, not just little pebbles which form words.

There also is the treasury of the shadows as though whatever is made belongs to light, material.

Something which is made is tangible and, because it is made, becomes somewhat measurable. When you see a piece of statuary and you say, *It's beautiful, it's marvelous, it's terrific!* Are these the words you would express to the university president who is concerned with other matters? No. Because these are words which are closest to the unmeasurable.

But when you say, *I don't like stone. I think it's too high, I think it's too light,* you're using measurable things which have to do with nature's material existence. It is not impressive to say *It's beautiful,* because it is in the eyes of the beholder. To some you have but to say *It's beautiful,* and the man says, *Yes, it's beautiful.* He doesn't see the same thing as the other man, but still it's beautiful.

Man strives to find his commonness through the commonness of the soul, in expressing more truly what the man sees, hears or feels than any kind of measure that can be employed.

What man makes, nature cannot make.

Nature does not build a house, nature does not make a locomotive, nature does not make a playground. They grow out of a desire to express.

It was beautiful to read a poem by a Persian whose name is Rumy, who lived in the thirteenth century. He writes beautifully. I wish I could say the poem but I can't. He describes a priestess walking through her garden in spring, hurriedly going through it to get to her house. When she comes to the threshold of her house, she marvels at it and is transfixed by what she sees inside. Her maid-in-waiting rushes to her and says, *Priestess, Priestess, look without and see the wonders that God has made!* And the priestess says, *Yes, yes, but look within and see God.*

When I think of the present dissensions, I read into them not disorder, not insult to the status quo. I see in them an advance in the minds of men who can throw to the wind the convenient avenues of getting ahead and show an inner dissatifaction with the way things are.

If you were to offer the leaders of dissension a house free of charge, put them into the most wonderful neighborhood, provide for their food, give them the best of clothing, the leaders would refuse, I'm sure. Because all you are giving them is what they need.

If you were to say, *I will make accessible to you that which has yet not been made*, I think they would agree. They are all looking for what has yet not been made. They would settle for no material goods if only that were brought before them as a possibility.

If I go to a convention of architects and I hear stories about what has been made by the architect, slides showing his works, I have never but fallen asleep. Say the inspiring words of that which is potentially possible, and I am awake.

Down deep, man only trusts desire, not need.

Need is just so many bananas as far as I'm concerned.

Desire is the entire strength of man's striving to live.

Schools should teach the essences of desire, not cram them with people of knowledge because the knowledge, no matter how accurately imparted, rests in one differently from another. Even to the scientist a formula has a different meaning in its relationship to other things he is interested in.

Knowledge feeds the desire to express.

What is so mysterious about this desire to express? Why do we want to learn, a desire which is peculiar to man?

Everything in nature records how it was made. In a rock there is a record of the rock, in man there is a record of man. Look at the fetus, study the fetus. Every step in the development of man is there.

Man's desire to learn is to learn how he was made. If he knew how he was made, he would know all the laws of the universe. If he knew all the laws of the universe, he'd have powerful means of expression. He needs to know to express, not just to know. He only wants to express.

The scientist finds from what already is and gives to the artist—which is every person, not just individuals particularly selected—the instrument of expression.

That brings us to what is school.

School is a place which has this unique ability to serve the talent of the individual. Not just to impart knowledge but to serve the talent of the individual.

No person should be examined where his talents don't lie. I know, I studied physics. I took notes in physics. I took notes so arduously that I didn't hear what was said. Had I listened to the teacher and not taken notes, I would have learned something about physics. I took notes to pass examinations. And even then I had to copy somebody's notes which were more accurate because my mind wasn't in that direction.

Do I love physics? I do. I really do. But to pass an examination in physics is for the man who has a predilection for physics. It's ludicrous to think that I passed physics, which I did, and do not know a damn thing about it.

Had I been asked after the physics to draw physics, I could do it. I could express through drawings what I learned in physics class. This would be my way of expressing physics. I would know physics from that point of view which matures my talent for drawing. I'd get confidence in my power of drawing.

Salk Institute
La Jolla 1959-65

When Salk asked me to do the laboratories in San Diego, he said that he wanted a hundred thousand square feet of space to give to ten scientists who wanted each ten thousand square feet of space. Then he said, *I would like to add one more requirement. I would like to be able to invite Picasso to the laboratories.* That really electrified me. I proposed to him at the next meeting a laboratory of a hundred thousand square feet, but a meeting place which amounted to almost a hundred thousand square feet in addition. These were laid out in a manner which would suit the unmeasurable qualities—and the laboratories were dedicated entirely to measurable qualities. The contrast was between law, which is unchangeable, and rule, the law of the artist, which is changeable. And he bought it. To this day it's on the agenda as something that must be done.

It is the world of the architect to indicate those spaces which have never been and could not have been thought of by the client, but for which the client really wants you. The great client wants the architect to tell him that the fullness of the environment must be presented, from it true choices can be made.

Truth being man's fact. Fact being the realm of the scientist.

I read a ninth edition of the Encyclopaedia Brittanica, and it said Bach couldn't have cared less whether he were original, whether he were contemporary, or whether he used the latest kind of realizations in music. He only was interested in the truth in music.

If the artist finds this, or the architect finds this, it's the one thing that doesn't belong to him.

It's common.

The only thing that belongs to him is the way he expresses truth, not truth itself.

When a dish fell in Mozart's kitchen, it broke, made a terrible noise. The maid screeched because she was surprised, but Mozart said, *Ah, dissonance!* And dissonance belonged immediately to music because in his great genius he was able to prove its beauty through his compositions. But dissonance doesn't belong to Mozart.

Reprinted by permission
University of Cincinnati
College of Design, Architecture, Art and Planning.

In the L.I.K. Studios
University of Pennsylvania
29 September 1969

I want to repeat what I said before, at least what I tried to say before, on the position of element in the work that we do, and this could be done for our benefit as well as McCleary's class. I'll use the blackboard—in the way I see it.

I see *our mind* which, you might say, the brain has many impressions and the mind is really something else. The word that I feel is the most—the most—less heady—I always call it the spirit, but somehow the word *commonness* seems better. It's kind of commonness that there is a feeling that one understands the other, and that it isn't necessarily the words—it can be just a feeling. But there is a contact—one individual and another—through a kind of commonness. It isn't understanding; it's more realization that it is understanding. Or it could be a word we don't know. But it has really nothing to do with really knowing anything—it's feeling the validity of something and that it belongs and that you want to pursue it, but it isn't anything that's really just tangible.

And from this sense of commonness, you might say out of the presence, of the stream and the mountain and the wind and the sun which somehow is there on the other side as being that which is already made—that is the evidences of order.

So it's commonness and order. Now from this commonness, there comes the feeling of realization about something. It may be that the sun gives off heat. It isn't so much knowing about heat; that comes later. It's hardly important to know about it for the moment (except that when you really do know it, it becomes a tremendous aid and simply spreads in the minds of many who have different predilections than you). But for the moment we should consider that there was nothing that gave you tangible knowledge, and it's best to consider your mind as being made of that stuff, than to think that it is made now of a different kind of thing. It's quite the same and one must think that you're really suspicious of things or less satisfied with things but not necessarily imagine now we know so much, therefore we know so much more what to do. We don't. In my opinion we don't. At least, if we do, than maybe it's more modest to think that we don't. It doesn't matter really whether you do or not. This is what I mean.

So realization—that you realize something—that isn't here in the brain at all, it's really here in the mind. This could be called inspiration, if you want; you see, it could be called another thing. It depends on what kind of mind you have, what kind of combinations you have. But realization is a sort of feeling that there is a validity about something. There is a sense that you can reach the other man through something that you're expressing or wanting to make. Right here is all the evidence of this. Because if you hit against a mountain you know how hard it is, you bounce back, you know you got to do something about it. And there is sun that gives you heat—and the stream that always seems to go downhill instead of uphill. And you feel that, when you're making something, you make it in accordance with the laws of nature. And that when you're thinking of commonness, you're thinking of that wonderful surge in a kind of direction true to something else, not necessarily order which made choices of a kind that seem to be, first of all, takeable, or become possible. In a way, commonness, in the light of order, makes you feel about the possible. So there is possible.

Now here the sense of design and elements come in. If you make something, it may be that you have to have two parts, in the making, instead of one part. It's a sense of the form of something, the form of something which has inseparable parts—and these inseparable parts are the elements. That which is different from the other. If you make a stairway and you make a landing, the landing is not the same as the stairway. This is really a part, and that's a part, though to make a unit you need both. We don't construct this stairway the same way as you'd construct that landing. Now sometimes you like to make them become one, and that's all right; that's a question of how, in what way you want to express it. Someone else would express it very independently, others would want to express it as a unit. But in any case, one satisfies. That is a question of design, you see, whether you make this the same as this. You want to make it this way and that way and with nothing underneath, maybe, and so forth—that's a matter of design. But the realization that one is different from the other is a matter of elements. That goes for *many* things. In planning, you know that the aqueduct which carried water just cannot be the same aqueduct that did something of a different nature. First of all, it would carry greater weight and how it's served would be different. So let us just say for the moment that the difference between design is felt here, the elements which have to do with each part. Now you could also consider the entire stair as an element. And knowing this stair as an element, when you consider its entirety, is a matter of coming to the realization of what a stair is as an entity, even before you have found the individual parts. If you think of stairs, you don't think of elements being the stairs around a platform—it's so constructed, really, that you begin to see it as a single element, not as one divided. In designing it you may find that it is different—one is different from the other, but you can also consider that the stairway is in itself an element. Here it is beautifully expressed because it doesn't even try to be of the same construction as other things. It's so independent—it is as though you took it in off the roof and dropped it from some place in heaven—simply dropped it in there, made it independently. You say you ordered the stairway? Well, we better give that to Saint Nicholas because it's such a beautiful thing. Give it to him to do; he comes and brings the stairway with him. It's so independent; that's how it's made, as though it really wasn't part of the fabric of the building, that the skin was one thing, the rounded structure was one thing, the stairway came in as though it has its own belonging. And that is thinking very much elemental.

Now if you think of a design as being a manipulation of needs and *working things out*, you see, you lose that. You lose the sense of it because you don't think of one thing being of significance in itself. When you think of this stairway, it can be actually less wide. Oftentimes you sort of want to have a railing closer to you, you know, from where you walk. And it really hasn't anything to do with how big it is. But a person who is not conscious of it as an element thinking, *You'll find plans like this*. And I've seen them! Plans in which, let's say, this is a big dimension, say it's three hundred feet, and this may be two hundred feet or something like that...no it's one hundred seventy five. Now I've seen, and everybody's seen, a plan with little stairways like this. You're supposed to go up the stairs on this thing? I think of the number of people this accommodates, and think of the stairway that's put in there. Now there's no reason why you can't have an entrance and go for two stairs. I don't think it has to be an entrance to the stair— that's a matter of design, spirit, whatever. But if you don't think of spirit—because immediately when you say spirit, somehow you dismiss the whole thing because everybody seems to know what it is. And it really is the most remote of things. Whereas *commonness* brings it a little closer to earth. You realize that you're really talking to the other guy as well. Here you think that you're quite independent and that it only belongs to you. Here you begin to think that it doesn't *only* belong to you, which is true, that's what spirit is. But commonness is a word which for the moment I'd like to use much more than I use spirit, because it reaches everybody much easier. Spirit is more a private word; you don't talk about it. In the same way one should not talk about God—it's also a private word—because it defiles the meaning of it, by the way. It becomes a private meaning and another meaning that transcends privacy.

So, therefore, you sense that you're going upstairs to another level. It must make you feel that it's an element in the plan, and immediately a stairway may become as big as this (drawing big square). Because it is not just a matter of being wide enough to go *up*, you see, but to be *assertive* enough to realize that to go up is *one of the events of this building*. It's an event of the building, and you know how much of one. It plays on your mind as being important and welcomes you as you rise on the stairway. And it has very little to do with so-called beauty, you see, per se.

And when I talked to the Dean one day outside that building over there, and he was praising that building: *How do you like that building? That's a modern building, now you fellas have what you want*, he said. And I said, *Well, I'm sorry but I think the building across the way is much better*. And he said, *What do you mean, we were going to tear it down*. So I said, *Well, maybe you were, but it contains much better lessons architecturally than this ever would*. And I explained to him: *Did you ever try to walk up the stairway in one of these buildings?* He said no. I said, *I'll take you*. And I took him, and I said, *Well, that's a very, very modest way of expressing it*. I said, *Well now that other stairway, have you ever been in it?* He said, *Well, I haven't*; and I said, *Which building is better?* And immediately he knew this building was better. He didn't need any more than to just walk two steps and he knew it was better. And that modern building was condemned, immediately, in his mind.

I'm sure he thinks of it very differently now, but for the moment he understood why this building was a greater building than that building, because elementally it was completely lost. It doesn't have a single thing in there which is conscious of the elements, and everything is conscious of the elements here: the windows, the stairs. And the elements are a consciousness of the parts. And then, if you think of it this way, what you are doing is *composing* and not designing.

You're composing. Designing is the infighting. When you have realized this, you see, as being the element, then you do all the infighting, design-wise, to make it gloriously itself. And that's where design really sits. It sits in trying to make this work with that, this work with this, this work with the outside. The whole thing is a matter of infighting with itself, and the sense of making each part sympathetic to the other. Design is a matter of making this place work with the outside, and so it is, in a way, what you may call the balance, the symmetry—the same, only one is identical, the other is not, but really it's the same. It's balance, too, only it balances as a hairline balance. This is a balance which you might say is the same as cotton on one side and gold coins on the other, so balanced that it must be thought of in this character. This balance and symmetry is an accounting for all parts to fit each other. If you have a shape like this, and you have a shape like that, or something else like this, somehow or other this shape wants to say something to this, and this wants to say something to that—so they fit together, and they do not bleed out into waste material. You place this one in such a way that you make no space out of that one, and it's lost, and that's a great waste. In our own bodies this doesn't happen. There is a great deal of symmetry, balance, which, even though the shapes are very different from each other, seem to fit each other very well and talk to each other. So a man can really jump over seven feet only because things are in balance—he couldn't possibly do it otherwise. Everything has talked to each other enough, so that whatever movement you make is sympathetic to the other. So design is the infight. You never present a design, you present a composition of elements in which design is present, quite clearly, because they're so sympathetic to each other.

And I wanted to make this introductory remark to what we have said already, but not quite so much in detail. My sense was that in dealing with buildings—in this case, we're going to deal with a very simple building in which the program is not written—we must find somehow in commonness the answer to the program. That is where the program lies; here is where your confidence in being able to make something exists.

Now I have written some little piece—nothing to do with the class. I had to write a foreword to a book which had to do with architecture without architects—they were from Ireland. I don't know how you figure out these things. The book seems rather interesting, the building and such, and I couldn't write much about the book because it sort of talks for itself. You try to analyze it, you know, like Freud would do or something like that; I couldn't see that. So I wrote about things like this: Instead of trying to say that something is singled out as being important, in its time everything is important. And it must be considered that if it is done with sympathy, what seems to be sympathetic today, that it's important still.

If an island is highly dilapidated, and you walk through and you see the sadness of the unattained state, the real estate developer's mind would think, *Well now, this is ripe for redevelopment*, wouldn't he? But to a man who sees this as an evidence of man's work, who wants it to be perpetuated—look at that big gap between that man who wants to perpetuate this thing and that man who wants to tear it down. If you were asked, let's say, to live in that spot, you would at first resist it, because your images of your refrigerators and air conditioning and television would come before you, and you'd say, *Well now, no I can't do that. I've got appointments to make, and certain projects to finish*. You'd give every excuse in the world not to live in this lovely place, because those conflicts do come out for one thing. Live there for a little while and meet a few friends and you're more into it. How precarious, and how much on the brink of changing one way or another, all our minds are in that respect. And I couldn't for the life of me see these structures—encrustations on hills, near the water, and all these lovely places. Anyone who wants to accuse you, it's all right for the other guy to live in it, but not for you—and there's a great deal of truth in that. Nevertheless, what should be the judge of one who has a refrigerator, for instance? I don't have a car, but I have a refrigerator, have a television, have three stories to a house, or whatever you want, as compared to something that when you walk into it, you feel that only another human could make all the walls right for you. And how wonderful that is, actually, and you don't expect the other to happen where you have a refrigerator of your own. Somehow everyone takes their place. Which is better? Big question mark, you see.

So I said it this way: The prevalence of order—I call this a prevalence, because you can say that order, the prevalence of order, is really the universe. And the prevalence of commoness is eternity. Something eternal. Now this is also eternal, but it is eternal in material—material eternalness, I mean universal.

Universal—Material. The commonness, equally as indestructible; it's a prevalence. It's everywhere—and being is of order. To be. Desire to be of order is life. Not living, life. Living is the exercise of life. To live is to express. And we are in a most beautiful profession, or you might say, better still, way of working not of a profession, of knowing, because it touches many aspects of expression.

The spare atmosphere of
Mars tells us of this prevalence to be,
None of attitude, nor of choice
The vectors to the character of forms, living forms, and shapes.

I'm reading it poorly, but the vectors of that lead to the characters of living forms and shape, comes from attitude and choice. And that could be very primitive attitude and very primitive choice.

In outer space, the earth is felt in wonder
as if for the first time.
This marvel, blue, green, and rose
unique in our system
makes us realize that man's work can be like no other.
It cannot be assumed that on Mars, shapes will be like others. So:
The builder seeking a beginning
is primed by the feeling of commonness
and the inspirations of nature
just a fragment of knowing steers wonder to intuition
and to the acts of expression.
In the presence of the mountain, the water, and the wind
the desire to express feels the possible
The site confirms the possible.
When you come to a site, you know it's possible, because the site already tells you it's possible.
The site confirms the possible...
and encourages agreement on the beginning in the making of man's place.
A mere foothold is confident of the settlement.
The first institution of man.
It's the settlement of man, if they agree to come together and live together, that's already an institution, not ordained by anybody particularly on high, just by your own agreement, you see. So institution is really an agreement. It's an agreement, let's say, to study. It's an agreement to have recreation. It's an agreement to have fun, you see, whatever it could be.
The works of man reveal his nature.
First thing you do, you know the nature. Because you are reacting, through commonness, and through the making of things, you make it like nature cannot make it alone, without you, so therefore it does really reveal its nature....
The time of a work holds its own validity
from which the sense of truth can be drawn
to inspire the work of another time.
So another time has its own validity. So you look at it as nothing dead, as though this happened *then*, or this style I don't like. Because it had its validity of the time, and you don't have to prove it within one thing. One thing doesn't have to be considered as being better than the other thing; it is just simply a realization of something which in time had its validity. Otherwise you couldn't have extended it. If the other man that sees it, buys it, rents it, whatever he does with it, it has enough commonness in it to tip the balance, which makes the acceptability possible.
The city, from a simple settlement
becomes the place of the assembled institutions.
What can you say—a city is more than the assembled institutions? Is it the traffic system? What we talk about is certainly not. It is really the sense of the institutions. Where do you study this? I tell you, you don't study it in the universities. It's got to be in your noggin, you know somehow it's so, because it isn't studied.

Now the measure of the greatness of a city must
come from the character of its institutions,
established by those sensitive to commonness
and dedication to man's desire for higher levels of expression.
The place of the island, the hamlet, the mountain
draws us to them for their simple truth.
To leave them for the city must bring revived faith
in new beginning.
A city must ever be greater and greater.
In closing I said:
Commonness is the spirit art, because the language of art comes from commonness, and the spirit is in commonness.
A work of art is an offering of art.
Now, I didn't mention those little houses in Ireland or anything, but simply couldn't because this won't be understood, of course, so maybe this foreword will go into another book . I think it's better with it this way then to try to justify things and modify them in any other way. Now what I've told you somehow is fresh in my mind because I've reviewed this on the weekend that I was away. I wrote it then, and it has in it probably more, more in more detail, you see, of what I was thinking about, and many things I did not write.

When you think of the elements going just a little bit farther—because I think we're gathered here to maybe make this talk out of context of our class for the moment; we'll come to that soon enough, so why not, right?—you're thinking of elements like stairways; you think of walls; you think of a roof being different from a floor. It can't be considered the floor, because it's in the one place, you see, where you can walk on it if you want to but you're not obliged to. Now you can design it that way if you want to, but you wouldn't live on this roof. And so but to separate it is terribly important.

Now you say, *element wall; structure.* If you make structures like this, twenty feet apart, you would have to do this (drawing), and you'd have element column, beam, and wall enclosure. Because a beam needs a column, a column is there for a beam. It is not right to assume that this wall can take this force, but this (column), for this the wall is valid. It's a wall and being a continuous member, it takes these various joists, whatever they are, spreads the load over the wall evenly. One must never think of transferring element wall into a column with all kinds of reinforcing means, to make this load a concentrated load at thirty points, to be able to homogenize itself in the wall sufficiently from here. You go from here to here so that wall is acting on the floor, this beam, and what it must be I don't know. I have no idea what it could be because it's contrary to all the laws of nature to do it, though you can do it engineering-wise. You can actually make it work. But you're going contrary to nature, which means you're going contrary to economy, and that means you're going contrary to poetry. Because economy is poetry. Money isn't and economy is.

Then, if you think in terms of *elements*, also it's well, at the same time, to think in terms of the *orders*. When you're dealing with the mountains and the streams and the wind, you're dealing with *material*. And in that sense, the *order of the material* has to be known. But it's a prevalence of order, which means it involves all materials in all situations. This part makes you have to think in more terms of order; there you must think of prevalence. Here you must think of something which is never really satisfied. And in this case, you've got to go constantly step for step, as knowledge is revealed to you as being closer and closer to the tendency of order. Closer and closer to its *fact*, you might say. And here, closer and closer to the truth. So here you have truth—I mean something which between you has truth. Truth doesn't sit there, but truth sits in here, because truth—this is man and nature. And there is created the realm of truth. Here the truth, here the (?). Here's the realm of truth, and what you make must be true, not right. That's over there. Truth is here. So all that man makes must be subject to, not fact, but truth.

So, it can be, of course that I'm overstepping that which has to deal with the scientist. For the moment, the scientist really had better answer for himself because he knows secretly what his strivings are which contain both these things. The scientist still does, and what he's doing sometimes belongs in one or two facts made available to you. He must become transformed himself from what is constantly pulling at him in this commonness to something that resists purely its realm. He comes back to this, where he wants to express something, because then it somehow must have the quality about it of not only fact, but truth. Something which inspires the other man. This inspires, sure! It inspires, but I think it doesn't *inspire*; it inspires each individual separately. It isn't what you might call inspiration as being probably the same—it isn't. It is only vested in the individual.

So, I'm getting a little bit away from the subject, but I was thinking of the orders of materials. In the making of a brick which answers in every way our desire to make something that we can handle and that's not too heavy for us, we find as a fact that if we make it too big it will warp and we can't organize it very well. So we learn from it what *is* the fact. But also there is a kind of truth in it as well as that. But the brick sits there as out of nature, made by the will of man, out of its limits, out of his limitations as well. And this brick then has a characteristic which you must express, which you must respect for itself. So if you realize that, you can also realize that if you're spanning in a brick wall, here's the brick wall (drawing). There's a brick wall, and in the making of this, this is a brick wall, and this is just brick and it's a brick wall! But suppose you said: I have a wall, but I want to go through this wall at certain places. Then you must make an opening in this wall. Now if you want to, if you're so conscious of the beauty of brick that you can see that brick should give you all the answers—you're so much in love with this material— then you must say to yourself: What is the order of brick? And what is the order, what is the evidence of the order of brick which makes an opening possible? Then you must say that the beam of brick is an arch. You cannot make an opening through a wall, except through an arch. Whether it's a small arch like this, or whether it's an arch like this (drawing), it is within the order of brick (draws flat arch and curved arch) that the beam of brick is an arch.

But this is in a way also elemental in itself: You can make the use of brick itself full of elements, elements which divide the order of brick into various parts, which tells you that if you're dealing with it, you have to deal with arches if you assume it purely. When we talk about balance and symmetry, we are talking about the movement of one thing with another, in its arrangement. Now this can be extended to very many things: for instance, if I were to say that you have a big span of three hundred feet and your span comes to a conclusion somewhere, a terminus of some kind. Since the span is uninterrupted, the spaces are uninterrupted, if one thinks in terms of how the space is served, if you work under the premise that you do not interfere with the drama of the spaces making by any other subsidiary construction, you just hold to the single span as being an event that you want to happen, not a big span, and put little things in it as though it were a box of candies. But you want to see how the thing is made, so therefore a space *does* show evidence of how it was made within the space itself—not just for the enclosure alone, but for the light that you want this space to have, the natural light. And since the structure, you might say, is the maker of light, as well, then you can consider elementally that your source of structure is also the source of light. So you can make your element have many things attached to it, if you decide that light is also revealed by the space, by the structure. And truly it is, this is light and it is gotten from the structure.

So if then you think of it in the terms of large spans, the station points where the structure comes to rest may have to be developed in a greater way than it is ordinarily. It may be that that space becomes a station, not a column. It is also a column, the column must be there as a column. But it's a place where you can develop an event in the structure—it has a right to be an event of the structure. And that could be something attached to it, which if you place there, it's of greater advantage to you to show how it's made than it is if you had it separately. However you can have a difference of opinion about that; there can be something outside the building entirely which serves it. Let's say it is a large span and suppose you wanted to have this place air-conditioned. I think it would be just as valid to consider a building out here, which is an air conditioning building. I don't know what it looks like, maybe it looks like that (drawing), that's an air conditioning building which is outside of it. It has nothing to do with the making of the span and need not be at this point; I've often thought it had to be here, so it is within the space, but it could really be there, as though the building now cannot afford to have anything in it which will supply the source of service to this, because there's nothing there that can give it to you. In shorter spans, you can make them, let's say, exist in areas between the spaces or whatever they are—so there can be areas here embodied so you can serve these spaces. And these are called elements too. They would be elements, they would be the space elements of service that you're composing. They don't have to be like each other. They could be different from each other. But you're conscious of the fact that this space is not the same as this space, so that you don't think of it in this way, in this space. So you're also dealing again with elements: elements that serve, elements that are being served. And it can go out like this—an element out here, but you're conscious of it, being outside. And this may have nostrils, it may have all kinds of things, you see it can have exhausts, it can be a little boat, it can be anything, but it really is terrifically valid—because the demand is there. Because the shape demanded by a different service entirely cannot be the same shape as that which this demands the space to be, out of some aspiration, or other—realization, aspiration, whatever it may be in here, which are the forces of the unmeasurable. Which are here. And these are the forces of the measurable, which are in here.

And so you can see, in the elemental thinking, right from the start, your decisions can be immediate. The inseparable parts. The more you know. And knowing meaning, the more you are made to be active in the attitude towards the wonder of this, you see, that sits there in front of you. The wonder of this is constant and it gives you a headache. The wonder of this can bring you some light; it's almost a source of light. In no way should it be but highly regarded, because this primes your sense of order, which brings to you the sense also of this business of the elements, because you know when you're dealing with chemistry and physics, constantly you're dealing with elements. You know? You don't monkey around with oxygen just as though it were something of a football; you put it next to something and you'd have thought there, and you put in another way, and it just breathes quite comfortably. The elements teach you about elements, and how they must be separated in order to be great, and not be homogenized. That's why it's difficult or dangerous to talk about design, you see, as being anything but the infighting to make the elements more wonderful. So that when you compose them, they marry each other very well, and that for no one do you shortchange the element itself. It can be the column; it can be the beam; it can be the vault; it can be anything that you can see; it can be the mechanical plant, you see, it can be that kind of wires. It can be also that which brings water into a city, you see. So in the sense of the elements, there is also some group design areas that come into your play when you are dealing with the city. In the city, you can consider that water itself has a position which will emerge into its own architecture, as also movement will emerge to be its own architecture.

It's coming more and more the truth that the bridge, for instance, is quite obvious. You see, the bridge is something that you do, that you think as an element of movement. If you respect the river below, you never put a post in it, you see, in order to make beauty out of the element of movement over a river. As soon as you put a post in, you make the river somehow less. If you respect the river, as you respect the tree, as you respect a rock and soft earth and all that, you in some way give reverence to nature, which taught you how to make the first act of expression. And those who, blitheful you know, use it because of convenience of what is called economy which isn't economy at all, it's nothing but irreverence. Then I think you have no question about what to do. What you think of the river and you think: *Gee, what a wonderful opportunity. Think of it! It's one mile long! Isn't that going to be a marvelous bridge!* And the engineer says: *One mile long, how many posts do I need?*

And to strive for this, if it's in your hand, should be what you must do, as an engineer, as an architect. You must do this now. That's why I myself advocate (advocate in my own mind, I mean to say) that the big span makes a tremendous amount of sense. You know, when you think of the ground that's being eaten away, the big span means that you really are respecting the ground again. And though a tree looks miserable against these large constructions, it is still wrong to put a post amongst them.

So, in thinking again elementally, you're thinking always of new things that are coming in which satisfies the sort of sense of commonness which this is. This satisfies commonness because back comes nature, you release nature again—you don't cover it, you work on it. Nothing like this is thought of a great deal, but it must be thought of as being the religion of work. Therein lies the religion of your work, because it's satisfied here. Down deep, this is where religion lodges, right in here. And a religion, you know, in an abstract way, religion.

Then think in terms of this, and think in terms of elements which have to do with wind. Wind is a force. You can really think in terms of an order of wind, and you can think of the architecture of wind. And this is manifest in many villages in India, in many places where the houses were built with wind structures above them. I can't draw them very well but some of them had peculiar looking things on them, which allows for the ventilation to enter in and not allow rain to come in. Now the realization of that—they didn't look to see whether this belonged to the Romanesque period or some other period or whether it looked *Nantucket*, you know. No, it was a matter of necessity, and it was a matter of also sort of looking to this for help. And somehow the sense of this brought about this. And this is really the beginning of architecture, the other is not. And the beginning of architecture as far as Greek work was concerned is *absolute* in the sense of light and dark and light and dark and light and dark, in what is the structure. So that the column, which is here (drawing), and the next column which is next to it and so on along the line, is a matter of no light, light, no light, light, no light, light—is constantly very clear, you see, what this is telling you, in the way of the realizations regarding light. And looking for the light and realizing that light, in the ambience of light, especially when you're capturing it and following it through certain kinds of made places, that you get *here* a very particular place which is called a building. Inside of which you have *that* light which either inspires you or makes you sad, or makes you gay, or you want to greet somebody, or you feel that death is near, or that life is near, or something—you feel it in here.

Outside you don't feel anything. You're constantly in the prevalence of nature, in itself, and the prevalence of order, and there the things become homogenized into a different feeling entirely. Entirely. In a building, it becomes somewhat enveloped in your nature. You know more of your nature inside than you do outside. Because you're with yourself and that's important. It's the most general thing about elements, and it leaves, in my opinion, your mind completely uncluttered with a sense that you can develop on your own. Because it could mean something individually. Tendencies in design, tendencies of approach. So anything you approach, you know, isn't, let's say, categorically from here to there to there to there, no. You can start this trip here, but there's no reason why you don't start this there and do the whole thing according to what I said. I don't think it has anything to do with it. It's simply that when you want to criticize yourself and you want to say, *Where have I gotten?* or, *Must I try something else*, it may be well to think of starting from another angle. And this could lead you to a truer path, probably.

Now we're studying the Mall area, which started with a wonderful motivation, you see, really. And Independence Square—we know for a long time that's existed. But the Independence Building itself is a very little building, not very large, and much love was put into it—I mean so much so that it was almost smothered, you see. The buildings across the way, I remember as a kid, there were all kinds of old shops there. Old established businesses, crowded absolutely from Fifth, Sixth, just dense with all kinds of structures, curiosity shops of all kinds where you bought cotton and wool and ropes and anchors and compasses and, I don't know, odd things made by various odd people, and it was really quite an interesting place. I remember we used to go there in hopes of seeing, to see, odd things and there were plenty of them. People lived there, too, you know; it was just a big glob of involvement. But the shrine was something undeniably important. And though it itself, like any old thing, wants not to be noticed particularly, suddenly it became singled out and had to be given a platform. Now, there is nothing really wrong with this. The destruction was terribly painful, much objection, but the cries of real estate and patriotism matched up in one bundle was so great that you really didn't know which you were talking about at one point. And so it became something which, if you talked about it to a real estate salesperson, they'd say it's valueless; if you talked about patriotism, it's everything; and if you talk about patriotism, it is valueless; and so on down the line. And all the buildings were demolished strongly, one building after the other, except one building somehow just couldn't be demolished—I don't know what it is, maybe a child's stocking that you just don't want to throw away, it's the same kind of thing. Somewhere it stops. Now, when this was done, the buildings around it looked like the people at a funeral—they all sort of looked at each other and said, *Is this what we really are?* across the way, this wasteland in the middle and with the one side looking at the other and saying, *Gee, this is not really worthwhile, is it?* and the other side looking at the other side and saying, *It's not worthwhile!* So great plans were made of the sides of this square, and all these great plans were made alongside of *images*—that is to say, comparing images which were powerful, kind of *evolved* images—one was Park Avenue, New York. And the first projections there that were all drawn out were flanked by tall buildings, all of them the same height, and went right down the line. And it was to frame the square, these buildings. Now, a king could have done that very easily. I mean, he could have said, *That's a building and you want to know what the buildings are? I can tell you, let him sell one building and I'll give you another,* and it would have been done! But then this is America and it has a different kind of rule about it and so you couldn't really do this, no one was at right for it and nothing could really control it. Though they said it should be done this way, nobody could write a democratic order instead of having it. And after a while, though they held onto the possibility of making them all the same, the first customer—you see after all the land is bought as a unit, and then re-sold to various people, the old streets became the boundaries again along here because they couldn't get the transportation coming to agree to go underground in this thing or anything, they just had to go through the street. And they thought, *Well, we can't do it, but it probably may be all right anyway.* You could think.
And so the lots were divided into streets—be it Chestnut, Market, or whatever street, Arch, and so down the line, they had to keep them going through. And the first customer who wanted to put a building contrary to the heights established, he said, *Well, maybe it's all right because after all, it is a democracy, and so we're saying it's fine to make one building taller than the other.* You could think that the cost of the land would have something to do with the economy, which usually is the case. But it doesn't seem to be the case because somebody's going to build a building here that's only three stories. And next to it seems to be the most economical thing to build a twenty-one story building. So there you are—it just fell apart, this whole thing. You can't govern it. It's just impossible to govern it. At least the rules couldn't be found.

Reprinted from *VIA* magazine
Graduate School of Architecture
University of Pennsylvania

If I were to try to define architecture in a word, I would say that architecture is a thoughtful making of spaces. It is not filling prescriptions as clients want them filled. It is not fitting uses into dimensioned areas. It is nothing like that. It is a creating of spaces that evoke a feeling of use; spaces which form themselves into a harmony good for the use to which the building is to be put.

I believe the architect's first act is to take the program that comes to him and change it. Not to satisfy it, but to put it into the realm of architecture, which is to put it into the realm of spaces.

An architectural space must reveal the evidence of its making by the space itself. It cannot be a space when carved out of a greater structure meant for a greater space, because the choice of a structure is synonymous with the light which gives image to that space. Artificial light is only a single, tiny, static moment in light and is the light of night and never can equal the nuances of mood created by the time of day and the wonder of the seasons.

A plan of a building should be read like a harmony of spaces in light. Even a space intended to be dark should have just enough light from some mysterious opening to tell us how dark it really is. Each space must be defined by its structure and the character of its natural light.

When a personal feeling transcends into Religion (not a religion but the essence religion) and Thought into Philosophy, the mind opens to realizations. Realization of what may be the existence will of, let us say, particular architectual spaces. Realization is the merging of Thought and Feeling in the closest rapport of the mind with the Psyche, the source of what a thing wants to be. It is the beginning of Form. Form encompasses a harmony of systems, a sense of Order and that which characterizes one existence from another. Form is what, design is how. Form is impersonal and belongs to nobody. Design is personal and belongs to the designer. Design is a circumstantial act: how much money there is available, the site, the client, the extent of knowledge. Form has nothing to do with circumstantial conditions. In architecture, it characterizes a harmony of spaces good for a certain activity of man.

But architecture has limits—and when we touch the invisible walls of the limits, then we know more about what is contained in them.

A great building, in my opinion, must begin with the unmeasurable, go through measurable means when it is being designed, and in the end must be unmeasurable. The design, the making of things, is a measurable act. At that point, you are like physical nature itself, because in physical nature everything is measurable—even that which is yet unmeasured, like the most distant stars which we can assume will eventually be measured.

But what is unmeasurable is the psychic spirit. The psyche is expressed by feeling and also thought and, I believe, will always be unmeasurable. I sense that the psychic existence will call on nature to make what it wants to be. I think a rose wants to be a rose. Existence will, man, becomes existence through nature's laws and evolution. The results are always less than the spirit of existence.

In the same way, a building has to start in the unmeasurable aura and go through the measurable to be accomplished. It is the only way you can build. The only way you can get it into being is through the measurable. You must follow the laws, but in the end, when the building becomes part of living, it evokes unmeasurable qualities. The design involving quantities of brick, method of construction, engineering, is ended and the spirit of its existence takes over.

Thus Form has not shape or dimension. If I were to take a spoon to represent form, I would say the spoon is a container and an arm, both of which are inseparable to *spoon*. If I were to design *a* spoon, I would make it out of silver or wood, shallow or deep. That's where design comes in. It's measuring it. It's putting it into being. But that which characterizes *spoon* from some other instrument is Form.

Unitarian Church
Rochester, NY—1957-67

I drew a diagram, which I believe served as the Form drawing of the church and, of course, was not meant to be a suggested design. I made a square center in which I placed a question mark. Let us say I meant it to be the sanctuary. This I encircled with an ambulatory for those who did not want to go into the sanctuary. Around the ambulatory I drew a corridor which belonged to an outer circle enclosing a space, the school. It was clear that School, which gives rise to Question, became the wall which surrounds Question. This was the form expression of the church, not the design.

My first design solution was very rigid. It was a completely symmetrical square. The building provided for the schoolrooms around the periphery; the corners were emphasized by larger masses. The space in the center of the square harbored the sanctuary and the ambulatory. This design closely resembled the diagram, and everyone liked it until the particular interests of every committee member began to eat away at the rigid geometry.

At one stage of discussion, some even insisted that the sanctuary be separated entirely from the school. I said fine, let's put it that way, and I then put the sanctuary in one place and connected it up with a very neat little connector to the school. Soon everyone realized that the coffee hour after the ceremony brought several related rooms next to the sanctuary, which, when alone, were too awkwardly self-satisfying and caused the duplication of these rooms in the separated school block. Also, the schoolrooms, when separated, lost their use for religious and intellectual purposes, and, like a stream, they all came back around the sanctuary.

It is the role of design to adjust to the circumstantial. So the final design does not correspond to the first design, but the form held.

Once I saw a building which had grilles outside. It was an art school, and the men were making patterns on their paper. The grilles were also making patterns on their paper. So this was not the solution. I came to the realization that the solution was in a partial solution—to suggest psychologically a solution. I realized there should be a wall in front of every window. I came to the realization that every window should face a wall. This wall should have a bold opening to the sky and an opening for the view. Thus the glare would be modified by the lighted wall and the view not shut off. In this way, the contrasts made by separated patterns, which grilles close to the window make, is avoided.

This wall, receiving the light of day, with its sort of ruin of openings, should be at sufficient distance from the inner wall so that it could never impose its shadows on the interior, because it does not belong to the interior. Another realization came from the effectiveness of the use of breeze for insulation, from realization that there should be two roofs: a loose sun roof independently supported and separated from the rain roof. The designs of the window and its wall, of the rain roof and its sun roof, would tell the man on the street the way of life in Angola.

Dr. Jonas Salk, the Director of the Institute, told me what areas he required. That was the beginning of the program of areas. But there was something else he said which became the key to the entire space environment. He said that medical research does not belong entirely to medicine or the physical sciences. It belongs to Population. He meant that anyone with a mind—in humanities, in science, or in art—could contribute to the mental environment of research leading to discoveries in science.

Without the restriction of a dictatorial program, it became a rewarding experience to participate in the projection of an evolving program of spaces without precedence. This is only possible because the director is a man of unique understanding of environment as an inspiring thing, and he could sense the existence will and its realization in form which the spaces I finally provided had.

So I did not follow the dictates of the scientists, who said that they are so dedicated to what they are doing that when lunchtimes comes all they do is clear away the test tubes from the benches and eat their lunch on these benches. I asked them: *Was it not a strain with all these noises?* And they answered: *The noises of refrigerators are terrible; the noises of centrifuges are terrible; the trickling of the water is terrible.* Everything was terrible, including the noise of the air conditioning system. So I would not listen to them as to what should be done. And I realized that there should be a clean air and stainless steel area, and a rug and oak table area. From this realization Form became. I separated the studies from the laboratory and placed them over gardens. The garden became outdoor spaces where one can talk. Now one need not spend all the time in laboratories. When one knows what to do, there is only little time one needs for doing it. It is only when one does not know what to do that it takes so much time. And to know what to do is the secret of it all.

Architectural students with materials, medical students with their first patients—it is the same experience. From this confrontation many marvelous things can happen. But the initial attitude should be of ignorance and humility.

Experience starts from there; the first certitude to emerge is the discovery of our ignorance and inefficiency to predict the probable behavior of materials and structures. Indeed, things never behave as we assumed they would from the reading of books. What we presumed negligible is not negligible, and the whole theory collapses. Everything is shattered, and we have to start again. Analogies, appearances have deceived us, and, half blind, we proceed along stumbling steps.

This inglorious, painful, and slow process is nothing else than the true process of learning—creating our own knowledge and experience instead of annexing somebody else's work. Research is not concerned with gadgets but with theory, much less with invention than with discovery. And research is immense fun, because what we discover at the end is the great unknown: ourselves.

They will be next to each other but not unified. If I make them completely un-unified, then it will be something pretty ugly, and that is exactly my intention. For to make a thing deliberately beautiful is a dastardly act; it's an act of mesmerism which beclouds the entire issue. I do not believe that beauty can be created overnight. It must start with the archaic first. The archaic begins like Paestum. Paestum is beautiful to me because it is less beautiful than the Parthenon. It is because from it the Parthenon came. Paestum is dumpy—it has unsure, scared proportions. But it is infinitely more beautiful to me because to me it represents the beginning of architecture. It is a time when the walls parted and the columns became and when music entered architecture. It was a beautiful time and we are still living on it.

Take a beautiful tower made of bronze, which was erected in New York. It is a bronze lady, incomparable in beauty. But one knows she has corsets for fifteen stories because the wind bracing is not seen. That which makes it an object against the wind and which can be beautifully expressed. Just as nature expresses the difference between moss and a leaf. How beautiful it would be to express that wind forces are playing. The base of this building should be wider than the top, and the columns which are on top should be dancing like fairies. And the columns below should be growing like mad and not have the same dimensions because they are not the same thing. This story, if told truthfully, would make a beautiful tower, even if it is ugly at first.

1969, *Progressive Architecture*

The Profession and Education Address to the International Congress of Architects
Isfahan, Iran
September 1970

I was reading about the early Greek settlements in Spain—a few people, seafarers, adventurers pulled by the beauty of things around them, the wonder of them, and wanting to extend and find out more.

They were going to school by going on a boat. A tremendous school.

They came somewhere where it was beautiful, it was wonderful, and they agreed to settle. And one who had talent and one who had another agreed to exchange.

Sher-E-Banglanagar
Dacca, Bangladesh 1962-74

I felt that there was in the village a lack of the nation's sense of the institutions of man. The seat of the institutions of man is the measure of a city—not its traffic systems, not its service. Those are implied. The institutions that are there; the availability of these institutions; the exchange of them; the architecture of connection which connects them in which the garden being the private place, the court being the place of entrance, the plaza being the place of meeting, the court being the boy's place, the place of meeting being man's place; city hall is an exchange of the desire for the extension of the talents of the individuals.

It is not the place of the jail and of the other characteristic things around. The City Hall that we have is a sign of misery where you pay taxes and where you constantly feel the disassociation between the people and the seat of government.

The city should have in the new institutions the realm of the auditoria, where the person, when he entrusts representation, should hear him out as to what he feels should be the possibilities of the establishment of newer institutions which stem from the multiple desires of expression.

The place of well-being, the place where you honor the body, is an institution particularly absent. You have hospitals and you have clinics but you don't have the place which honors the body, where you know about the wonder of the body

The university cleaned of specific research could be a place of the mind free of the marketplace. In the universities of the United States there is much research on government necessities. That does not belong in the university, that belongs in the marketplace. Only the purest of thinking and that which leads the individual mind to his specific way of thinking should be the university.

The sanctioning of the professions should also be free of the marketplace. Teaching practice is probably the least important thing you learn about architecture. The difference between the demands of practice, the grooming of the individual, and trying to imbue the spirit of architecture in an architectural student is tremendously important.

A school of architecture may be built today around a very large courtyard surrounded by shops of experimentation in all materials. The courtyard is where you build things and tear them down. It should be a private courtyard not available to anyone else in the university.

The jury room or the place of judgement should be a place of exchange. It is the place of the most honored criticism. It should be the center of criticism but not of judgement.

In a city there should be the forum, a place between the marketplace and the university.

Planning exists in the forum, not in the marketplace.

It should not be mixed with anything political or anything which has to do with the present laws, which make ownership, which often interfere with good planning.

It is a new institution, the forum, which sits between the marketplace, wherein is the profession of architecture, and the university, where the spirit of architecture is felt. The practice is the exercise of the individual.

The village should be a reflection of the town or city, which is the center of the institutions of man. One should feel in the village the contributions of the city.

In the center, the village has its little ambassadors of these institutions: the school, the mosque, the bathhouse. The bathhouse should not be made in so rugged a way as it is made now, because the bathhouse is not the center of cleanliness. The well should not be built by villagers anymore. We know how important the cleanliness of water is, and if the villager does not know how to protect himself by building a well, the government should build a well for him or find a way in which the water distribution would not be harmful to him. That is a responsibility of not just the people who make a place to live.

The village is a wonderful place to live because there you can choose the mountain you want to live near, the land characteristics that pull towards you in a most inspiring way.

It is an apartment house spread on the ground as compared to an apartment house which must in a city be vertical because land is so tight.

It must be a place where everything is; a town should not leave anything out. It should be full of everything.

Tradition is a sense of validity.

It is not so much what you see, but what you feel.

If you feel the reflection of something, it is beautifully stated. It reflects something which you would like to extend the expression of, although you may not know its background. It transcends the knowledge about it. You see it and you feel that you must see it. It is the kind of thing which you would not see in nature without man.

It spells an association of man to man.

It spells civilization.

It spells the tendency towards the meeting of people and finding out about yourself through someone else.

It's like the room; you find out about yourself because the other man is present.

Tradition is a sense of validity. It tells you the nature of man is its worthiest extension.

It is an expression of truth.

It has nothing to do with habit.

It has something to do with expression, which is the core of existence. Whether one does it in the simplest and most unglorified way makes no difference.

Those who do work they do not like are dead people. They are torn away from their natural sense of expression.

People don't want to think that their needs are the responsibility of someone else. It is almost disgraceful to think that you are doing something for anybody if you are just giving them what they need.

What you must give them is a chance to sense their desires, to sense that which is yet not expressed, has yet not been made. Through that you will know your new desires.

We look at the village and see its picturesqueness. The architect doesn't see it so much that way. He sees it as wanting to build itself more beautifully out of what is there. He sees it as a rugged beauty which is yet not fully expressed. He wants to learn the most frugal ways of doing it. He doesn't sense that he wants to use expensive materials. He just wants to guide the hand a little bit. He wants to give a sense of what men together cannot make, what somebody else must make for them.

The city points to the place where you sense what the village should have.

The town comes from a village that has become bigger from cross-advantages.

If you destroyed the village you would be destroying the sense of association between nature and a place to live, because you are far away from nature when you are in a town. You can see the mountains sometimes, but it isn't the same thing as breathing the air and sensing the distance between the mountain and yourself, which a village gives you.

If you hold tenaciously to your village you hold to something which everyone would be envious of as a way to live and a place to be near nature out of free choice.

But you have to be associated with a city.

Every person you saw yesterday would be afraid to enter the city. He would be overwhelmed by what he doesn't understand.

He should come to the city and say, *This is a place where everything can be sensed, where a boy, if he goes through the city, knows what he wants to be.*

What he wants is not necessarily associated with a village, because that part of the unity of a village may not pay out because it buries talents which are left unexplored. There are people in the village who would make better architects than we if only they were touched by what it is to be an architect.

When they enter a city, they go delightedly to their village, because the village is a wonderful place to live and the city is a wonderful place to sense what you can add to the way of life, what institutions you could add to the way of life! You can have the places where you develop your talents so that you can express yourself individually.

In architecture, design must be understood.

Design is a delightful experience because you are making something which will have presence.

But the preparation which comes before this is equally as delightful and enormous.

From wonder is realization.

Realization is realization of form, it is realization of the laws of nature, it is realization of the validity of your relationship with the laws of nature.

The first thing that comes from realization is form.

Form is not shape.

Form is the realization of the inseparable parts of something.

When you consider the form of school you consider a realm of spaces, not spaces spelled out, but a place where you sense it is good to learn.

When you have a two story house you have a stairway. You don't consider the stairway as being one of the things you have to have; you consider it as part of form, an inseparable part. When you consider it as form, the landing can be a room and this room has a window and the window has a window seat.

You are saying, *My grandfather who is infirm will climb half the stairway and, without anyone feeling that he is old and decrepit, he will sit down by the window seat because it is there. He doesn't tell anybody how difficult it was for him to mount the stairway.* That sensitivity is terribly important. You only get that from considering the stair as an element, not a design problem.

When you look it up in *Standards,* and it says that a riser and a tread has to be so big and that a landing has to be so big, you are not talking to architects.

The window is a wonderful thing from which you can get the slice of light which belongs to you and not to the sun.

The window that is also a niche tells you that the living room doesn't only belong to everybody but belongs to you, too, so that if you are disagreeing you can go to the niche.

The room is that sense of space, that sense of completeness. If you had to give only one room to a person, he must have all these possibilities of self expression as well as being able economically to live in one room with his family, no matter how many people are there. It must be made so magnificently in the sense of its elements that, when that family leaves and gets the proper number of rooms for the proper number of children, an older man who has no family can enter this room and not feel that he is living in a degraded place.

Architecture is the making of spaces which belong to the treasury of spaces.

In a great city there is the treasury of spaces. How many different uses are those spaces put to? Can you tell me that a schoolroom wouldn't make a marvelous architectural office? Of course it would. Better than to go into an office building and get that sense of utility, meter-out space, as compared to a space which at one time was full of spirit. How much more wonderful you can make a detail in a school than you can in an office building. Spaces are interchangeable. They are not rigid.

Architecture is the making of meaningful spaces.

It is the composition of elements, which comes from form. Form is the distinction of the inseparable elements. If you take one of them away, you do not have the atmosphere you expect from architecture.

In the development of elements, you get an order, because when you go to make something you must call on the laws of nature. You must know the order of brick—not just brick which is so much per thousand, but the order of brick. If you are using a lintel of concrete, you are composing a composite order in which brick does one job and concrete does another. If you talk to the brick and say, *How happy are you?* you will find he is pretty unhappy. So it is knowing stone. So it is knowing concrete.

In Dacca I knew when I started I would get a miserable job in concrete. I didn't want a miserable building. I realized the trauma comes with the joint when the pour is over. That's when all hell breaks loose. Nothing could be more ugly. We prepared for it by saying our pour should be no more than five feet high and then something must be left at that point, the event of the joint which can make the joint glorious and contrast with the rugged work.

I've waited seven years before the first marble was inserted in that joint. Everyone previously thought they would cover it up with mosaics and tiles. Concrete was poured the best it could be poured and much attention was paid to it, but you know concrete. You take off the forms and then you know what you've got. Now marble has come in and everyone agrees to a man that the concrete doesn't have to be touched because the marble is so contrasting, so fine-giving to that which is rugged. The marble is irridescent like rock candy, it has white but it still has grey in it. You can see through it and it has a gold vein running through it. You must take pot luck from concrete, so the insertion of marble is a complete recognition of the order of the material— allowing the concrete to be what it is, allowing the marble to be what it is. You can expect perfection from marble. You can't expect it from concrete. The combination of the two has brought about a composite order which works, instead of a single order.

In the use of brick, the order of time is important because time is money now.

The order of time, the order of construction, the order of structure, the order of spaces, the order of materials are sensed during the time of design.

Design is the infighting, the time when you struggle to get from the existence in the mind into presence, into something which you expect and visualize. The bigger thing is the composition of the elements and then the perfection of the elements.

In the orders of the city, there is the architecture of water.

I look at the village which is proposed for three hundred thousand people. I know it isn't right. Why? Because I cannot read the order of water. I cannot see how a place in the desert can not have as its most glorious buildings its water towers, its center from where the water is gotten. These towers can be so glorious as to contain the police stations, the fire stations, the center of maintenance. Those centers don't need buildings.

What kind of building is a fire station?

It is almost a garage, and a garage is not a building. It is an extension of the street.

A building should be associated with the institutions of man and not their servants.

A fire station is a dock on a transportation system where, just by pressing a button, you are already on it instead of being in the city struggling to get out of the streets to put out a fire. The order of movement includes all this.

The order of water includes the architecture of water. So does the architecture of the street, which is a kickable architecture compared to the gossamer-fine architecture of the institutions of man. The services must be made of a rugged architecture, not polished—so rugged that you can kick it. It has a sense of its position architecturally.

There is the order of wind, the order of light.

The order of light tells you that the porch belongs to the sun and the place inside the porch belongs to man.

It has nothing to do with *brises soleil* devices to make shade.

It has nothing to do with air conditioning.

It has nothing to do with the architectural elements which talk about shade.

Your argument is that now that you can have air conditioning, you don't need it. What about the protecting of air conditioning? It costs money to fight the sun.

It is that sense of orders which compose the city. It is a sense of the making of institutions of man and being sensitive to new institutions of man. It is the feeling that the city is a place for sensing what you want to have in order to express yourself.

First International Congress
of Architects
Isfahan, Iran

Tradition and traditional, I think, is a very good distinction to make. One has to do with the way of life and the other has to do with the way of living. Tradition really touches on the way of life and it takes in and encompasses the various individual tendencies each person has. Traditional, though it is a fine distinction, can mean that it is a line of tradition only expressed in a certain way which in one period can be expressed differently because of the circumstances involved. I would say traditional is circumstantial and tradition is probably not circumstantial. The value of tradition is that it gives you powers of anticipation, that you are able, with tradition, to find the courage to express that which lasts for a longer period of time than what circumstantially you can judge. It is beyond the circumstances that you express it in. So the golden dust is only an expression of nature-man which distills out of all of this, from which you get the very essence of the meaning of tradition and traditional, and everything that makes that distinguish itself from what nature makes without man.

There is a distinction in my mind between that which sits behind the desire to express and the means of expression. The environmental conditions seek for a means of expression which is appropriate to the environment. And this is the measurable part that you speak about. That which distinguished the choices that were made in expressing it one way or another is something of a motivating thing, not so much the means. That which is the fabric, or you might say, the aura, is part of desire in man which chooses what to make. It chooses what to make, which is grown right out of inspiration, out of desire to know how to make it. How to make it is a tremendous lesson all around us. It has been expressed a certain way and it has much to do with the atmosphere of what you call comfort, knowing it very well in one place as being different from another. So, I believe that is a good way of expressing it. So when the stone is available, it is stone, and when stone is not available you build it in brick. You find a way because there is a great impetuous feeling of wanting by any means to express it. So certainly in this way I agree fully.

I think if you lose sight of the primordial feelings, you really cannot get at the comparison of differences, because what led you to expressing it and finding the means of doing so, a more detectable thing than the former, could lead you away from that which was a kind of face in the expression, which tends to be more singular then the actual expression which can be general.

Anybody will agree that it is good to build it out of brick. But what to make, is something else again. Isn't it wonderful that what to make is really not something that is such an agreement, as is, how to make it? You can find agreement there, but you find invested in one individual a sense of that spirit which tells you what to make. And so it boils down to the individual in what to make and to a society in the making of it.

When you say *monumental,* you have one image of monumental. There is a block in the mind because of the word itself. I have a different one. When you say *vernacular,* I also have a different image than you have. In fact, the word *vernacular* is a new word to me. I never use it. I hear it—today I heard it—and I see no distinction between a vernacular or anything like this, I see no difference at all. I'll tell you why I don't see it.

You see, to me, city planning, for instance, starts with a street. A street is the first community building. It is recognized as a place of agreement. You agree to have a street because everybody lives on it. The same thing—you agree to have a court, and if you say agreement, and you say institution, it is the same thing. Because institution really means you are instituting something which everyone agrees to.

So, therefore, you might say, the courtyard is the first big building which you call monumental, except it does not have a roof. It is a matter of span. It has universality because just to span something, one copies the other, because it was so anxious to have a span. Suddenly when across a big area, which usually starts with a court or a street, one loses the copy from the other. Each one was different. One had a cold climate, and the other a warm climate, the question of span was the thing. The span is simply this. There is no mystery to it. So there is nothing you can favor over another. Certainly the small span which is the base or the route, which is really a collection of rooms and one can define architecture as the making of a room. Just as simple as this, or a sundry of rooms, or a room where you assemble, which really comes from the street. Primarily you must part from the street from which you actually assemble. And from this sense, the borrowing can be felt in one place or another. And the small span somehow, with the availability of the knowledge of making things, could have been the same.

You can learn from a peasant how to build, and from a farmer who plants trees, not to make his land look *pretty* as a landscape architect would, but to preserve his crops by the logic of planting his trees in a certain place so that the wind does not get at them.

It is almost the same kind of thing to say you should forget about architecture, forget that it even exists. Think that it is just a place of enclosure, that it is a way of making, as the peasant makes or the farmer makes.

The architect has got to have a tremendous amount of humility to know that he is beginning all over again to know about it, instead of thinking that it is already so, when it is not. So, if you begin to think that nobody knows what it is, that is a lot better than the statements I hear about the differences, because I see no difference.

Look as you go through those villages. The architects response to it would be that it teaches him something he forgot. That is perfectly legitimate. In fact, if he does not think that way then he is really no architect to begin with. He is remote from this living stream, and he imagines that now it is different, but it isn't. It is really what makes an architect so very dumb, the fact that he tries to make these distinctions between monumentality and nonmonumentality. Of course, there is no such thing.

In a certain economic class, even if they have ten people in the family, they could have only one room. This is said to you. You can give no more than one room. But then, if you take the attitude that even if you must build one room, that it be a room which, when later abandoned in favor of five rooms which this family really has to have, even if you have to build only one room, you build it so that anybody of any economic class that needs no more than one room could go into it. Then this room belongs to the treasure of spaces, whether it be in a village or a town or anyplace else. This could be an architect's view. He would not view building something, maybe tearing something down, as being something he really has control over.

I hold that as soon as you make stations between that which causes shelter and that which made man realize that he has the power to shield himself, from this fundamental stand point, I think you lose the essence of architectural meaning. It cannot be divided. It has got to be considered inclusive. In all humility saying that the farmer does better than you, that is all right. But I don't think you ought to divide it. I think it is dangerous.

Now, if you think that the villager is not using art, then you are greatly mistaken, because it is the true language of man. There is no other language, nothing is truer, because it is that part which contains the most intangible, therefore it is truer to man, because man is essentially born of the intangible and he is only using the tangible to express himself, nothing more. In it lies the great powers of desire which are insatiable, but there is a part which knowledge can only approximate to help him come anywhere close to it. The point is that he has simply that faculty which has more comprehension at the moment, and it is really quite accidental, it has nothing to do with the time. Can you tell me that Beethoven was born because of time? You are wrong. If he were to be born today, he would be a musician, play differently possibly, but the sense of music would be the same. That he played the music a certain way true to the way music was played at that time and he extended his experiences with Mozart is of no consequence whatsoever, whereas the consequence is, what is music about? What is this nature which is music?

So what is in these villages? What is its architecture about? That is what you are looking for. You are not looking for anything else. If you find that, you find the answers to any problem because you find in that the powers of anticipation, that which has lasting, qualities. Any kind of answer to a need to me is very temporary. The only thing that man would accept is desire. It is, today, the reason for dissension all over the world.

In America, particularly today, if you were to give a very poor person something, if you gave him a house for nothing, the true dissenter would refuse it. If you gave him a chicken in every pot, he would refuse it. But if you gave him that which is yet not made, he would listen.

What man is composed of is that which is not yet made, not what is made. What is made has to do with needs, what is yet not made is the very essence of his existence, so therefore nothing but art can bring it up. No statistics can anticipate anything but what has already existed, and that way you can say you would have more of it or less of it, but it has nothing to do with the aspirations of man.

I disagree with any kind of argument which has to do with answers. I only would agree with arguments which have to do with inspirations, how you can recognize it and how you can serve it. It is sort of the trust in the marvel in the making of a room. Somehow as simple as that. The villager makes it beautifully because he is really essentially an artist. Maybe he does not have the language of art, but the trees give him the art, the skies give it to him, the mountains give it to him, he is just the man who is more pure as compared to a man who is cluttered up by all kinds of knowledge. So he made a simple saying and he expresses himself very simply. Maybe we have to go there to find out what architecture is, instead of trying to call one thing monumental and another thing something else.

Monumental to me is nothing. It only has to do with something that can not be added to or taken away from. That is all that monumental really is. It has nothing to do with size. I think the Magna Carta was monumental. A diaper pin is monumental, because it cannot be added to or subtracted from. But the word *monumental* kills you because we think it is only big, or it is ostentatious, or it is made of marble. It isn't. It is just the extent of your willingness to make the effort to make something which can assemble people. Nothing more.

First International Congress of Architects
Isfahan, Iran

You must permit Joy, not one feeling but all feelings.

Your own accomplishment gives you Joy. You must accomplish first the right to be generous.

Consciousness is a prevalence which needs an instrument to play on.

A man obeys a law: that's why he has a body.

Unmeasurable: Knowing it is probably knowing it less.

Knowing things is not the thing that will help you most.

The fault we have in getting knowledge is that we get it in an isolated way.

I am not trying to persuade you. I would consider that as improper use of my time.

You can't be joyful by yourself.

Your consciousness of others is your *intouchness* with what may be called religion.

You must be everybody, not only yourself.

If you close your eyes to the things around you then you close your eyes to yourself as well.

I really don't know that it is so, I only sense that it is true.

A belief doesn't come from knowledge. Knowledge is in man because he is made out of nature. The stuff is it. It is answerable to all universal laws.

Knowledge is that which you draw out of things that already exist.

If you find a commonness between your nature and the nature of another man, you state the nature and find the knowledge behind it. It is the nature you want.

You want things, but that is not a statement, your wanting is not enough. Everybody must want it. You are satisfying what they want.

It must be a part of life in such a way that its destruction would destroy you.

You can't just say you don't know and make it easy for yourself that way...you feel in tensions...you are in touch with what people were not in touch with when there was no architecture.

Oftentimes you imagine you are thinking when you are not, and this often happens when you are not drawing.

Where the energy is, the change will happen.

You are thinking much more deeply into the nature of this building if you are thinking of desire rather than needs.

I like to feel that knowledge is not in man's mind, but stands outside of man's mind, like a book, which he can go to.

There is work to be done and the work will be your teacher. You can be born from the work.

How you make things is the knowledge of experience.

Every work of art is a joyous thing. No work of art comes from sadness. The initial thing is the capability of joy.

It was the place of the art lobby, that is to say, the place of arts and letters. It was a place where one had his meal, because I don't know of any greater seminar than the dining room.

There was a gymnasium. There was a place for the fellows who were not in science. There was a place for the director. There were rooms that had no names, like the entrance hall, which had no name. It was the biggest room, but it was not designated in any way. People could go around it, too; they didn't have to go through it. But the entrance hall was a place where you could have a banquet if you wanted to. You know how you don't want to go into a great baronial hall where you must say hello to someone you don't want to, and this is so with scientists. Scientists are wrapped up in the fear that somebody a little distance away is doing exactly the same thing they are doing. This kills them.

All these provisions and considerations are programming (if you want to call it programming). But programming is too dull a word. This is the realization of the nature of a realm of space where it is good to do a certain thing. Now you say there are some spaces you know should be flexible.

Of course, there are some spaces which should be flexible, but there are also some which should be completely inflexible. They should be just sheer inspiration...just the place to be, the place which does not change, except for the people who go in and out. It is the kind of place that you enter many times, but only after fifty years you say, *Gee, did you notice this...did you notice that?* It is an inspiring total, not just detail, not just a little gadget that keeps shouting at you. It is something that is just a kind of heaven, a kind of environment of spaces, which is terribly important to me. A building is a world within a world. Buildings that personify places of worship, or of home, or of other institutions of man must be true to their nature.

It is this thought which must live; if it does not, architecture is dead.

Many hope architecture is dead, because they want to take over. But they don't have the encompassing ability, I'm afraid. So many people are prone to place too much trust in the machine today. They must never divorce the machine from architecture, which is the greatest power they have.

Next, we may have a city without architecture, which will be no city.

I believe there are unexplored areas of planning. I believe that if you just hand it over to the architects, everything will be fine.

However, there are unexplored architectures in the city... the architecture of order is unexplored. Why must we have very distant reservoirs that carry parts great distances? Why are there no points where great intersections of movement give continuity?

Though for other civic needs we need not be so tight-minded. We must somehow give immediate attention to water, because water is becoming more and more precious. There must be some kind of order to water; the water that is in the fountain and the water that is in the air conditioning plant need not be the same water that we drink.

Gandhinagar
Gujarat, India—1963-64

I am to build a town in India, or at least so I am told, and I think that the most prominent architecture there will be water towers. The water tower will be centered at the points of civic service. There would be water towers, possibly, at the intersection of roads. I could also find there the police station, the fire station. This place will not be a building...it will simply be an extension of the road. The movement just sort of winds itself into an airplane...any intersection could be a place where you catch your plane.

I think Eero Saarinen's solution at Dulles Airport is a beautiful solution of a place of entrance. Maybe the traffic is not the same because the pattern is not the same, but there is the sense that you arrive somewhere, and that you get there all the services, and you go to the place in a car made for that purpose. Dulles Airport is so far superior to these airports in which each company has its own little house. In these airports you're trapped. It's really a conspiracy. They give no grace to man, and he feels so helpless. He is here when he should be somewhere else.

We were talking earlier this afternoon of the three aspects of teaching architecture. Actually, I believe that I do not really teach architecture, but that I teach myself. These, however, are the three aspects:

The first aspect is professional. As a professional, you have the obligation of learning your conduct in all relationships...in institutional relationships, and in your relationships with men who entrust you with work. In this regard, you must know the distinction between science and technology. The rules of aesthetics also constitute professional knowledge. As a professional, you are obligated to translate the program of a client into that of the spaces of the institutions this building is to serve. You might say it is a space-order, or a space-realm of this activity of man which is your professional responsibility. A man should not take the program and simply give it to the client as though he were filling a doctor's prescription.

Another aspect is training a man to express himself. This is his own prerogative. He must be given the meaning of philosophy, the meaning of belief, the meaning of faith. He must know the other arts. I use examples which I maybe have used too many times, but the architect must realize his prerogative. He must know that a painter does not have to answer to the laws of gravity. The painter can make doorways smaller than people. He can make skies black in the daytime. He can make birds that can't fly. He can make dogs that can't run, because he is a painter. He can paint red where he sees blue. The sculptor can place square wheels on a cannon to express the futility of war.

An architect must use round wheels, and he must make his doorway bigger than people. But architects must learn that they have other rights...their own right.

To learn this, to understand this, is giving the man the tools for making the incredible, that which nature cannot make. The tools make a psychological validity, not just a physical validity, because man, unlike nature, has choice.

The third aspect you must learn is that architecture really does not exist. Only a work of architecture exists. Architecture does exist in the mind. A man who does a work of architecture does it as an offering to the spirit of architecture...a spirit which knows no style, knows no techniques, no method. It just waits for that which presents itself. There is architecture, and it is the embodiment of the unmeasurable. Can you measure the Parthenon? No. This is sheer murder. Can you measure the Pantheon, that wonderful building which satisfies the institutions of man?

When Hadrian thought of the Pantheon, he wanted a place where anyone could come to worship. How marvelous is this solution.

It is a non-directional building, not even a square, which would give, somehow, directions and points at the corners. There was no chance to say that there is a shrine here, or there. No. The light from above is such that you can't get near it. You can't just stand under it; it almost cuts you like a knife...and you want to stay away from it.

What a terrific architectural solution. This should be an inspiration for all architects, such a building, so conceived.

What will architecture be like fifty years from now, and what can we anticipate?

You cannot anticipate.

It reminds me of a story.... I was asked by General Electric Company to help them design spacecraft, and I was cleared by the FBI for this. I had all the work I could do on my hands, but I was able to talk about a spacecraft anyway. I met a group of scientists at a very long table. They were a very colorful-looking lot, pipe-smoking and begrizzled with mustaches. They looked odd, like people who were not ordinary in any way.

One person put an illustration on the table, and said, *Mr. Kahn, we want to show you what a spacecraft will look like fifty years from now.* It was an excellent drawing, a beautiful drawing, of people floating in space, and of very handsome, complicated-looking instruments floating in space. You felt the humiliation of this. You feel the other guy knows something of which you know nothing, with this bright guy showing a drawing and saying, *This is what a spacecraft will look like fifty years from now.* I said immediately, *It will not look like that.*

And they moved their chairs closer to the table and they said, *How do you know?* I said it was simple...

If you know what a thing will look like fifty years from now, you can do it now. But if you don't know, because the way a thing will be fifty years from now is what it will be.

There are certain rules which will always be true. What a thing will look like will not be the same, but that which it is answering will be the same. It is a world within a world; that is what it will always be. When you have an enclosure, it will be different from what is outside. And it will be so because its nature is such.

I think that there are men today who are prepared to make things look entirely different from the way they look now, if only they had the opportunity to do so. But there is not the opportunity, because there is not the existent will of this thing floating around. You take the drawings of Ledoux, which are very interesting.

Ledoux has this feeling of what a town is like, of what a city is like, but he projected this, and *town* didn't actually look that way at all, and that was not so many years ago. He imagined this.

When a man sets out to project something for the future, it may turn out to be a very amusing bit of history, because it will be only what can be made now. But, actually, there are men today who can make what is an image. It is what is possible today, not what will be the forerunner of what things will be tomorrow. Tomorrow you cannot predict, because tomorrow is based on circumstance, and circumstance is both unpredictable and continuous.

The very secret of Cartier-Bresson's art is that he looks for the critical moment, as he puts it. This is like saying that in circumstance, which is both continuous and unpredictable, he sets the stage for it. He knows what will happen here, but he waits and waits for it. I know when he was taking photographs of me some years back that I used to enter the drafting room, not knowing he was there. He was in a corner somewhere; perhaps he had waited for hours in a corner, and I didn't know he was waiting for me.

I used to go around the room while he was waiting for me to stop at a certain board. And I did stop, too, because the board was occupied by a beautiful Chinese girl, that's why.

I went over to the board and started to draw, and I hear the camera go clickclickclick. He was ready, you see; he was waiting for the very moment, but he was setting the stage for it. He was a marvelous photographer. He dealt with the subject, you see. In fact, I learned very much about the meaning of one art and another through him, just by making the understanding that his art was different only because he was giving the circumstance.

To what do you relate the fine aspects of your problems?

I really look for the nature of something. When I am doing the school, I would try to solve it by *School*, rather than *a school*. First, there is the aspect of why *School* is different from something else. I never read a program literally. This is a circumstantial thing. How much money you have, and where it is to be, and the number of things you need have nothing to do with the nature of a problem. So you look into the nature, and then you are confronted with the program. Look at the nature of it, and you see in the program that you want...a library, for instance. The first thing that is done is the rewriting of the program. Now this must be accomplished by something which interprets it. Your program alone would not mean anything, because you are dealing with spaces. So you would send back your sketches which encompass your thought about what the nature of it is. Invariably, more spaces are required because every program written by a non-architect is bound to be a copy of some other school or some other building.

It's like writing to Picasso and saying, *I want my portrait painted...I want two eyes in it...and one nose...and only one mouth, please.*

You can't do that, because you're talking about the artist. He is not this way. The nature of painting is such that you can make the skies black in the daytime. You can make a red dress blue. You can make doorways smaller than people. As the painter, you have prerogative. If you want a photograph, you get a photographer.

If you want an architect, you deal with space...spaces which are inspired...and so you need to reconsider the requirement for the nature of the environment which inspired the activity of that institution of man. You see in a school, or an office building, or a church, or a factory, or a hospital, an institution of man.

Do you approach your analysis of the site of a building the same way and try to understand the nature of the surrounding area?

Often the character of it, the nature of it, must be explored because it is there. You just don't plunk a building somewhere without the influence of what is around it. There is always a relationship.

What stimulated your design at Dacca?

This is a very broad question, but since I went through about five or six buildings, I had about five or six different stimuli. It is more or less a recognition of a single element. The stimulation came from the place of assembly. It is a place of transcendence for political people. In a house of legislation, you are dealing with circumstantial conditions.

Sher-E-Banglanagar
Dacca, Bangladesh
1962-74

The assembly establishes or modifies the institutions of man. So I could see the thing right from the start as the citadel of assembly and the citadel of the institutions of man, which were opposite, and I symbolized the institutions of man. (Earlier, I symbolized the institutions of man by making a school of architecture—a school of art and a school of science. Disciplines are different, completely different, although they were both made by man. One is truly objective, whereas the other is truly subjective.) And then the buildings which are called the place of well-being, where one begins more and more to consider the body as the most precious instrument, and to know it, and to honor it.

My design at Dacca is inspired, actually, by the Baths of Caracalla, but much extended. The residual spaces of this building are an amphitheatre. This is residual space, a space that is found, a court. Around it there are gardens, and in the body of the building, which is the amphitheatre, interiors, and in the interiors are levels of gardens, and places which honor the athlete, and places which honor the knowledge of how you were made. All these are places of well-being, and places for rest, and places where one gets advice about how to live forever...and so that is what inspired the design.

I made a mosque entrance. I was setting the nature of it, because I noticed that the people prayed five times a day.

In the program there was a note which said that there should be a prayer room of three thousand square feet, and a closet to hold rugs; that was the program.

I made them a mosque with thirty thousand square feet, and the prayer rugs were always on the floor. And that became the entrance, that is to say, the mosque became the entrance. When I presented this to the authorities, they accepted it right away.

Do you feel that with large urban problems, with five or six architects trying to solve specific areas, it is valid for an architect to seek and express inner nature as the dominant understanding when there is the large scale which requires outer nature?

Actually, the inner space justified the outer space, even though you may give one portion to civic needs. I think the advantage is that one man can do it. I don't think a committee can set the nature; one man does it.

What this one man does is not design the thing. He simply programs it, you might say. He gives it nature.

One man can do this, and not do the building. If you separate this thing without saying its nature, you have nothing which holds it together. It holds together physically, but in the spirit, very little. As time goes on, that which this building really needs to express itself is absent.

You see, when you go into the department of, say, city planning, it should show the promise of the city as you enter. It may be a great hall, in which the city shows its aspiration and conveys it to the public. If you took the program as given, you are saying that a city hall is, after all, only an office building now. Then a great loss would occur. The nature is to inspire, and to give inspiration is probably too strong an expression. I would say that you present your aspiration, something in which you believe, something which you are not afraid to expose. We are trying to say something which is better than an elevator, and a lobby, and a door with a name on it that says, *City Planning Commission,* and then a counter, and a secretary, and a spittoon.

If you think of the city, you think of the realm of spaces, because actually, one must think of the city as having a treasury of spaces. Do you think you can relegate this to any architect who gets a commission?

No—there are some who can think in this manner, and some who cannot. And it cannot be done by committee, or you would be voted down. You would be voted down by every inferior person.... *This is unnecessary....too much money...*this or that. But it blocks the presentation of a potentiality. So if you entrust to a man the nature of each institution of man which wants to express itself, how do you see these buildings?

One man, not a committee, is there to try to make it exist. Therefore, how they make it must be that a man's work appears, and then before you know what is worth, and what is not. It belongs in the fold of social influence, because expression was possible. An emergence comes from that, and then society comes from that. From society, you would get nothing but finality.

Would you comment on the education of an architect, and how to achieve the integration of craft and design? If you were head of an undergraduate school, how would you begin the training of architects?

I think that one method can be quite as good as another. I would say it this way: You have professional obligations in all buildings, since you are dealing with other men and their various interests. You must know the obligations of dealing with the money problems, that clients have the cost of buildings, the paying of bills, specific space requirements, and so on. You must know obligations like this, and understand the supervision, the honesty, that must be there to see that the man is given the full value. We have the profession, but there is a man, and there is a spirit. To teach the man, one is in the realm of philosophy, in the realm of belief, in the realm of the other arts.

The forms of expression are here...this is not expression; this is preparation for what you must know. Your obligations as a professional are those of a man who is entrusted to do a work which is of interest for the people, for, after all, an architect doesn't dish it out of his pocket.

Also, I would say there is the obligation of proper programming. In the professional, I would say that what we were talking about is finding the nature of something in here. The architect finds in his building a certain nature which belongs to a certain activity of man.

If I were a musician, and I were the first person to invent the waltz, the waltz doesn't belong to me at all, because anyone can write a waltz—once I say that there is a nature of musical environment which is based on three-four time.

Does that mean that I own the waltz? I don't own the waltz any more than the man who found oxygen owns oxygen. It was simply that one finds a certain nature. Our profession is shabby only because we do not change the programming. If you change that programming, you release wonderful forces because the individual then never makes the mistake of making something which just pleases himself. You please society in your programming, not in the way you do your lousy building. The architect trains himself in expression which is true. It is the spirit of architecture which says that architecture does not exist at all...that's what the spirit says. It knows no style, no method.

It was designated so that you felt always as though you were walking through a place where people are at work.

Then I present another way of looking at it, say, as a court, and you enter this court. You see buildings in this court, and one is designated as painting, one as sculpture, another as architecture, as history. In one, you rub against the presence of the classes. In the other, you can choose to go in if you want to. Now, without asking you which is better, which is a very fair question, let me tell you what I think is better. I think the latter is the greater by far. In the halls you go through, you will absorb by some osmosis...you will see things. If you can choose to go there, even if you never do, you can get more out of that arrangement than you can of the other. There is something that has to do with the feeling of association which is remote, rather than direct, and the remote association has a longer life and love.

So it is the court. The court is the meeting place of the mind, as well as the physical meeting place. Even if you walk through it in the rain, it is the fact that you are associated with it in spirit greater than your actual association.

So I have asked the question and answered it too, haven't I? That's the best way of giving an examination that I know. You get the best mark and everything.

You make the bridge and invent it; the bridge is not physical. It has to be in spirit, though; its lasting quality depends on it. Now there are other reasons as well. We must not assume that every teacher is really a teacher, because he can be a teacher only in name. You cannot depend on something that is frozen in this architectural arrangement...where actually the connection can be made in far-reaching ways. One does not assume that even a good student can become a successful practitioner, or that a teacher is necessarily a good teacher. One who is just beginning to sense things may emerge to be the best teacher.

Now we take each element in a school of architecture and compose these elements. One of the most important that I know, since art involves the eyes, involves vision and the mind. You see it through association and in other ways. You can close your eyes and see a philosophic realization. You can see it in a way that you can listen to it, something philosophic you can see...with your mind.

You are passing things that dangle before your eyes, and they tempt you in a way to stop your mind. But there are things that happened a long time ago that have been done with great love, and are just a wonder in general.

As for the library, in a school of architecture, the library is not a place in which you are thumbing through the files, you're discovering a book. Architects have hardly any patience with a catalogue. An architect invariably gets disgusted with the first block of the library, which is the catalogue. You know this yourself. Now, if you had a library where you just had broad tables...very broad...not just how big is a table...Maybe the table is a court, not just a table, but sort of a flat court upon which books lie, and these books are open. They are planned very, very cleverly by the librarian to open at pages that humiliate you with the marvelous drawings...things that have been recorded, finished and spread before you, buildings that are magnificent.

If a teacher could make comments on these books, so a seminar is spontaneous, this would be marvelous. And so you have a library which has just long tables, and plenty of room to sit to one side with a pad and pencil, and the books are out in the middle. You can look through them, but you can't take them out.

They are simply to invite you to the lesson of the library. The library is really just a classroom, and you can make it so, and looking at this element, *Library* is different from *a library*. The man who is studying and writing his Ph.D. has his catalogue. It's there, and it is his religion.

In his catalogue, he might see sparks come out, which are books, and the association of the catalogue and the books is very precious to this man. He makes a lot of recordings of the books he is going to swallow up, and he finally writes what the other fellow wrote, only in a different way. But our library is very different in the school of architecture, for you are really treating your minds in a very different way. Every book is really a very, very personal kind of contact, a relationship.

You know what I mean. You've gone through it, and you know what I mean exactly. The location of the library comes from this nature. If you put it on the first floor, second floor, third floor, I think it tests against its nature. You shouldn't be forced to put people through the library. It should be just something in its structure which says, *What a wonderful place to go,* and of course, the location has much to do with it, but essentially, it is its nature which you are after, to convey.

Glare is bad in the library; wall space is important. Little space where you can adjourn with a book are tremendously important. So you might say that the world is put before you through the books. You don't need many...you need just the good ones and there is no such thing as looking for a book in the catalogue. You don't just ask for a catalogue book...it would die in the library.

A student of philosophy who is writing his degree knows how to deal with books that are stacked away. He learns books in a different way. The Avery Library at Columbia is not a true architecture library; you have it on various floors. It is one of the best libraries of architecture that there is. They have the best architecture books, editions that are ancient, but you have to bother to get them, and the impatience of the man who must see something immediately is too great... he doesn't read the thing anyway. If it is in Latin, it is just the same as if it were in English. because he will see the pictures. He will see what he sees, what his mind tells him it is. Then, when you read it, you probably find something totally different from that which it is. What you think it is is absolutely as important as what the man writes it is. It's how you feel it and give service to it, and how you convey it.

You plan a library as though no library ever existed, and you say the same thing with the classroom. You know how dirty classrooms get, and how full of passion the whole room is, quiet passion, violent passion, whatever it may be, but the room is full of it, and you have no patience to clean up anything. In fact, when the classroom is orderly, you lose everything... that is to say, you really don't find anything. So the classroom is not a pretty room, but it is a room which is dedicated, with light, and plenty of space to work in.

You can't mete out the square-foot area for a man's work, because some people require a great deal of room, and others require little room. You've got a series of desks, and you've got to hang your drawings on the back of your shirts, if there is not room for anything. You just have to see a place which is very broad and full of light. And there must be high spaces, because the whole lesson of measurement and association with dimension must be part of the room. I think you just feel that you are in a room that is sixty by sixty, and from this you can tell what a room eighty by eighty would be, because you know what sixty by sixty is. You don't have to have that big a room; your mind can take care of many things.

Man can work in seclusion, but, you know, when you have an idea, if you're a really good person, you just can't help telling that idea to somebody else. You want to share it immediately, and you don't want to hide it. In a sense, that's our nature. If you had stolen that idea, you would be hated for the rest of your life, but to convey it is just an urge which everyone has. You can't help it. Any one of us, in a sense, is a teacher, because we want to share that idea, and because sharing the idea has another meaning. The other meaning is that you know its validity through sharing the idea.

The confirmation by one man with a sensitive feeling of its validity is like getting the approval of a million people. This would not be true if you were dealing with a mathematical problem, but it is true when the problem has to do with aesthetics, with art. If that man is honest and will tell you what he feels, then you have a tremendous approval, that of feelings which strike the soul. The location of the classroom, of course, is important, but it will not influence anybody. I think that the power lies in working on your own. If it is an inspiring place to work, don't worry about the campus benefiting by it. If it is an inspiring place to work, you see, the greatest service is given to the campus by its just being there.

There is a point about meeting, and there should really be classes, like seminar classes, and they are mandatory things. You just don't go out and have a seminar because the mood strikes. I do not think that there should be rooms designated for seminars in a row on a certain floor, because a seminar is really an inspired thing, and you should hold a seminar like this one, and you should sit around and hold it. As soon as you make it on the second floor, with all the seminars lined up, it is no longer a seminar. There isn't the spontaneity in back of it, and in this sense I think you might ask, *Shouldn't the school for sociology and the school of architecture have a meeting?*

Yes, there should be a meeting—if either one is prepared for the other. If you groom yourselves in the motives and the objectives of the sociologist, and you know this before you enter a seminar, and if the sociologist is willing, also, to understand the essence and the spirit of architecture, then the seminar would be tremendously beneficial.

Otherwise, you will have a cockfight. One would just not understand the other. Each one would go away thinking, *Well, be doesn't understand me.* And the other fellow would say, *He doesn't understand me.* I find it so.

Now there is this to consider: I think the teacher is essentially a man who does not only know things, but feels things. He is the kind of man who can reconstruct the universe by just knowing a blade of grass. That man can bring anybody together. He can bring a sociologist together with the archaeologist or the metallurgist. Somehow in him, he has a sense of the laws of the universe. Because of the way this man was made, he senses it, and through this sense, he doesn't say, *The hell with sociology.* No...he respects all parts. With such a teacher, the meeting would be wonderful. It would be a great benefit to the architects, and also to the sociologist.

Reaction to your work means approval of millions, even though only a few are present. It's the kind of thing in which you learn that what you present you can believe in, and that is a tremendous thing. So you can call it a jury room, if you like, but it is a room where you meet, where classes all meet, for a kind of review of an experience in doing a building...starting with a piece of white paper.

It could be the most valuable lesson to call on people and get some reactions—maybe violent reactions from persons of certain beliefs. You don't have to take their marks, you see. Marks are the teacher's concern. I think to have this person who comes in give you a mark would be asking too much. He is reacting, and his reactions shouldn't be marked.

I am against marks in juries. I really think it shouldn't be considered just a grading session. If a teacher says a man could enter the jury, that's the end. I think a student shouldn't stand there shaking like a leaf, before people he doesn't know, and say his piece, after he has worked all night, and maybe two nights ahead. He is nervous as a cat, and he gives it his best, so I think a jury should never have a mark. The jury should just be a place where you know you are not going to be called down. You're just going to get a spirit, and the atmosphere should be cheerful.

Around this, I think, you can build a school. You have so many rooms. The rooms can have rough walls; it doesn't matter. You can pin things up any place you want to. You can throw paint on the floor. The classroom can be like a Jackson Pollock, but when you come to the jury room—no. There should be something wonderful about it, and it should always be a friendly room. It's always a sanctuary, you see. It is not a room where you sit around as if you are on trial. It is just a great room. It is the sacred space in the school of architecture.

In The Hall of the Mountain King: A Block Party,
From *Thursday's Drummer*
Philadelphia, Pennsylvania
25 February 1971

Who are they [the people directing Philadelphia's Bicentennial celebration]? If this is a relevant committee charged with the responsibility of seeking worthy ideas, then why don't they call in people who have some ideas?

What the 1976 celebration needs most of all is an editorial, but unfortunately if you're not asked to give your ideas it means you're not wanted. So far, anyone who speaks outside of this closed committee is only talking to be self-eliminated.

Fresh ground and new buildings aren't necessary to feel the spirit of the creators of our independence—Jefferson, Franklin and the rest. You don't need new buildings to properly convey their spirit. Let's take Philadelphia as it is and add something viable to what's there already. This doesn't mean buying new furniture and new drapes.

This also doesn't mean that we have to buy a new house, because it's already there. Let's measure the distance from 1776 and take the city as it is and make what we have available to the other cities of the world. Let's do this by making the area from 6th Street to the Delaware River in Center City more hospitable. We can use the old Quaker meeting houses and other churches, close some of the streets and place a dome over a few and use them as meeting places.

Maybe we can add a few new, small satellite buildings for our grand 200th birthday block party that I envision, but we don't need the usual clap-trappery of the bigger nations showing off to the rest of the nations and the smaller nations trying to compete; that is all wrong.

Isn't this a good idea—to bring back the spirit of the young men who translated the spirit of independence into an inspiring document with plenty of sparks? The Declaration of Independence can be brought into focus again, since the main purpose of the Bicentennial, it seems to me, is to sense new inspirational beginnings. This can bring the beauty of our independence and freedom back to the world and away from political maneuvering and commercial circumstances, which give us a false sense of our idea of liberty and freedom to the world.

Freedom is being misinterpreted now. Our problem is to find ways of bringing it back to the world in a modest manner and not a selfish, pretentious way. This will give Philadelphia an opportunity to repair its fences. The city can do it by itself without the Federal Bicentennial money.

I'm for the meeting of people, not for showing off our productive genius. Discussions and a continuing talkathon with representatives from all of the nations of the world at the Bicentennial should be centered around the new availabilities of everyone to reach new agreements. *Institutions* to me mean agreements, not *buildings* in the old sense of the word. Isn't it an *agreement* when we provide schools for everyone? Isn't it also an *agreement* when we give recreation facilities to all?

Let's call the Bicentennial celebration an *agreement*; that we conduct an almost *inspirational dissent of a bloodless revolution* to translate the deeper meaning of 1776 to 1976. Why isn't the spirit of that event open for discussion?

The coming new *agreements* needed by all of us are those that can help mankind. This can be done by inviting people from all over the world who have distinguished themselves in science, the arts and political life to participate. The discussions can be centered on an *inspired agenda*, not the reading of papers. The agenda about our concerns for the rest of this century can be plastered around the city on giant billboards. The meetings can be held in Independence Hall, the meeting houses, the streets, including the cobblestone alley—open to pedestrians only—that runs next to the First National Bank in Independence Hall park. We can have a great block party.

The city's only major contribution to this project would be to clean up the streets, plant some trees and clean house for the celebration. This grand party and meeting of the minds could provide a joy of good promise and generate new ideas to solve our problems.

Reprinted by permission
©1971 *Thursday's Drummer*

Contributed by Harry Jay Katz

On the roof of the Ducal Palace
Venice, Italy
26 February 1971

The roofs of Venice are nothing short of fantastic. When you climb them as I did and take a tour of the roofs [of the Ducal Palace], it is a sea of lead which you see in front of you, and lead is an undeniable material for roofs. This lead is thick and has turned the right color; the roofs look like snow in this spring weather. How much of a lesson this is to us: the importance of finishing our buildings and giving the ground on which the building is built back to the roof, which is really the reflection of the ground which is occupied below. We are prone to forget the roofs, because they are not seen and teach the importance of them.

I have to climb the roof again. This moment I would love to feel how it must have been to construct all this. What gives me courage in my lack of historical knowledge is that the man who built it did not think of history either, but simply did the job and built it as a roof. The size, the construction rhythm of the lead plates and the making of joints manifest the truth of the statement that the joint is the beginning of an ornament.

From below, the upper part of the roof looks extremely handsome; you can see how the joints are made to accommodate the size of the sheets and the passage of water.

Contributed by Renzo Salvadori

Van Eyck to me is a significant architect. He's more than significant, he's a great architectural mind who has had little opportunity.

He does things experimentally. He made a room in a school in which he decided that it was best to make the doorways very low for the children. I disagree with it absolutely because the child aspires to be able to go through a room that his father goes through.

It's a miscalculation. If you do that, you would have to make a stairway for infants in your house, and a stairway for young people, and a stairway for a very young person who's going to become a young man. You'd have to make a stairway for a middle-aged person, and you would have to make a stairway for old people, and you don't make that kind of a stairway.

It's general, the stairway that does for all of them.

For the very young man the stairway must be so precise for when he is jumping up to the fourth floor in no time flat.

To an old man the landing is a blessing.

If you put on the landing also a window and a bench where a person can sit around a window, like a window seat, and put a couple of books there, too, while this young man is driving up the stairway the old man can stop at the landing and say, *You know, I never looked at this book. This book is fascinating.* He sits down, he reads the book, and the young fellow says, *Grandpop, aren't you coming up?* and he says, *No, I'm interested in this book.* Actually he can't climb the other stairs.

It's part of the making of the stair which sets in this quality, through which is the well-being of everything you do.

The isolated statements out of context could mislead you. What Van Eyck was doing in his way I would not question. He's one of those people who are trying to find the truth in things constantly.

I heard him speak one time when Le Corbusier disbanded the *CIAM*, and a new team called *Team 10* grew and had their first meeting. Aldo Van Eyck made a speech about the meaning of a threshold just before you enter a room. It was magnificent, because through this he could build a whole architecture. It must be so true that in it lies all the other truths of other things that support it. He first spoke of it in Dutch, and he translated it into English himself, then into German and French. His gestures were not the same, somehow. He was very good, too; you couldn't leave. If you couldn't understand one language it was a fascinating idea to listen to the same thing in other languages. It was a magnificent event. Since that time, I respected him as being tremendously significant.

In the same way there are buildings of invitation, in which you say to the people of foreign countries, *Look, it's my party. Don't bring your houses here, everything has been provided for. We'll build your building and you come and we'll let you put exhibits in. We'll give you all kinds of availabilities: power, light, partition material. Just come!*

The theme of the exhibit is this: Whatever you want to tell your nation you can tell here, so other nations can also see. Bring your children, bring the men of significance to this country.

Let the meeting be born out of inspired agenda, not agenda that's only prepared papers. By the meeting of people, you say different things. You're not the same person.

It's a place of meeting people who are concerned about the world.

We have printing presses in many places where announcements can be day-by-day on what's happening by the consensus that is being brought about by these people.

It should be where the Declaration was signed.

The people who made this country were motivated by something which the world has never known, a country which has wide frontiers yet undiscovered. England could never have held these people in check, tea party or no tea party.

In the Bicentennial are places of invitation, a series of modified Crystal Palaces within which exhibits will be divided and made available according to the dictates of the show that you're putting on.

It's the living place for ecological exhibits, where nations bring their problems which have to do with the order of air, the order of light, the order of sound, the order of movement, the order of spaces to the world.

The availabilities are being destroyed by man. Man ought to guard this carefully, otherwise he really will eliminate himself.

I believe in bringing young people to these exhibits, children, so that they learn how one senses the nature of nature in relation to how it is defiled.

The wars of the future should be putting a pack on your back and making the Sahara a wheatfield. It's much more exciting because you can command the sun.

The sun is an availability. You can use it as a resource.

These lessons of fairy tale quality can be brought into the minds of young people and old people.

To feel where their position is in relation to the gradual destruction of the world is the theme of the exhibit.

The first fight should be to keep the streams pure. I believe in making aeration fountains all through the Delaware, all through the Schuylkill, to get the aeration into the water so you can put the fish back. Not fountains for beauty, no! Fountains to make the stream right again.

Dissension is based to a great extent on distrust of the motives of another person.

I believe in this country.

The representatives are lousy.

There is much more benevolence in the leadership than what's shown.

American exhibits should be ruled out.

There should be no boasting, no beating of the chest as to how well you can make glass. The important thing is something to do with living.

Silence and light, that which you desire and that which is the availability.

Need is something which is only disgraceful not to give.

Need is not regarded as anything today. If somebody gives you something, you take it away in a hurry and don't even say *thank you*. It's not right. Your birthright should not have to grovel for that which you need.

The only thing that should be honored is the seeking of desire in people, which has the promise of new needs. That makes sense to me.

A person needs housing, and somebody needs a pencil. It should be organized differently. It should be always available. It used to be a great thing if you could buy one corn for each person. Now you buy four corns and throw two away, or one is left uneaten on the plate. It's awful to have that kind of society.

Spareness and just enough have tremendous power.

The desire for equal ostentation is like saying you want equal poison.

The meeting here should be the meeting of new agreements of institutions, of which they have none in Pakistan. No one in Pakistan can say *I can go to school because I want to learn*. No, you just live and die. A tremendous lack of availabilities.

The nations getting together to give those availabilities would be a great thing in understanding and joy.

I'm saying it like a Pollyanna, but I think it's practical.

I don't believe in judging anybody.

I do believe in criticism.

Criticism should only be constructive, not destructive. I don't believe in what is called the critic today, who purposely picks the weak things just to make mincemeat out of it. He doesn't pick those things which are difficult to explain. A critic should know his subject in an impersonal way.

I saw Mrs. [J.F.] Kennedy many times when she was trying to pick an architect for the library to commemorate her husband's life.

We were having lunch, and she said, *You know, I don't think of my children the same way as when John was alive. I think of them differently. They're not there in the same way.*

A journalist would pick this up and say, *Jacqueline Kennedy doesn't like her children.*

What makes her say this? The death affected her entire existence. And I also detected in that a quality of wanting to be herself.

When I met her the first time, I said, *There's a woman who would not have anyone but a king or a pirate.* She now has a pirate. Previously she had a king. But in the end she will only want to be with a poet. She has those qualities.

History is that which reveals the nature of man.

What is has always been.

What was has always been.

What will be has always been.

Nothing could come about unless it's within the nature of man, so it makes no difference when it occurs as far as the nature of man goes.

The circumstances cannot be the same, but the value is the distillation of the nature of man out of the circumstances.

You cannot anticipate the future.

You don't know what I'm going to say the next moment.

Therefore what you build is the level of your comprehension today only. You cannot tell what you'll do tomorrow, so you can only build what is true to you today.

But it must have the power of lasting quality because tomorrow is the next today.

Today is always tomorrow and always yesterday, too.

The past is only a manifestation of what could have happened today, only the circumstances were not in its favor.

There are new availabilities as one discovers that nature has secrets and secrets and secrets, and they are still forthcoming, which releases out of the knowledge of them new availabilities of expression.

How do you integrate sites in Italy such as Siena or Carcassonne into your architecture?

I have not integrated.

That's the point that is missed in the statements that I've made. People don't understand what I've said.

I respect Carcassonne—not because it's the only example. I haven't scurried around the world and picked on one thing and said: *Carcassonne!* I come upon things all the time which are new to me, which were there all the time.

I happened to be in Carcassonne, therefore I like Carcassonne, that's all. People imagine I took that and put it in my notebook, and the next job that came around was Carcassonne.

Carcassonne impresses me not because it's Carcassonne, not because it's a military thing, just because it's a clear picture of a purpose well expressed.

Richards Research
Buildings
Philadelphia, PA 1957-64

I would admire a safety pin for the same reason. If I happened to be impressed by that, I would have said the towers at the University of Pennsylvania were inspired by a safety pin. Then you would really be surprised! But it has nothing to do with Carcassonne or San Giminiano and those places. They record themselves as being marvelousness that they are phenomena of man's nature, and if they are well-said they become the example for all things you do.

Mellon Center for
British Art and Studies
New Haven, CT
1969-74

The Mellon Center is as much inspired by Carcassonne as is the Medical Towers.

Carcassonne comes to my mind as a well-done thing in the same way that a wonderful person comes to mind. They are symbolic. I always thought that if I'd marry anybody it would be somebody who would make a swell grandmother. I certainly wasn't going to marry a grandmother with wrinkles all the way down her body. The point was that a good grandmother was a good person, that she lives a good life—especially if she makes good apple pie.

[Vincent] Scully wrote about *The Old Testament* as if I had said, *They got me*, having read *The Old Testament*. I never said that.

He had been criticized by another critic of architecture because he mentioned that Frank Lloyd Wright's building in Florida was influenced by Hadrian's Villa. He remarked to me that the building I did—I think it was the Salk Institute—was also influenced by Hadrian's Villa.

Actually, somebody else in my office showed me a picture of Hadrian's Villa, and I was impressed with the ins and outs of these two buildings. He showed me how close it was to my own building, something I'd never seen before because I'm unhistorical by nature.

Scully, who is an historian, sensed the desire, saw these pictures, and then put things down like that, but it's completely the opposite.

Fitch, who is a good critic, said, *You may say something about Frank Lloyd Wright, and you can't prove it. But Lou Kahn's alive and kicking. Why don't you ask him if he felt that way about Hadrian's Villa?* So he called me up and asked me, and I said I did not. I said, *If it was in the book all this time, why didn't you correct it?* And he said, *What can I do to correct it? It's printed.*

One of the most dastardly things that happens to a man is being quoted incorrectly.

Richards Research Buildings
Philadelphia, PA
1957-64

When people went around the Medical Towers to inquire how the scientists liked the spaces, most of them thought they were great but didn't have enough space. I think it's a wonderful design. We have certain availabilities we never had before. But one doctor was criticizing everything, the sun coming in through his window, a speck here. The journalists picked that up immediately, and Vincent did, too, because whatever journalist is in him he included.

Since that time, every man reading the book wants to know what's wrong with that guy, and not what could be behind something which they may have to peer into to see what it is.

If a guy is willing to die for something he's doing, he's right. In some way, he's right. It's the best sort of evaluation you can give a man.

People often feel my buildings are expensive. They're not. They're actually very close to the budget, but the word gets around that they're expensive.

They cost more because I reveal the truth in those buildings. They need things they never knew they needed before.

In the Medical Towers, I worked right to the very cost. There wasn't a penny more given to me and the building suffers because of that. If I had had more experience, I would have advised them that the rooms they intended to have were too small.

I gave them clear rooms, rooms that had no partitions, because a laboratory is a place of constant change.

I only made corner windows because I knew the running window would be defiled. The windows were in the places where you needed light. Everything else was in darkness.

I think I worked it out extremely well. From it, the whole line of architects began to think in terms of the serving areas and the areas served. The idea doesn't belong to me at all, because to discover differences between areas served and the areas that do the serving is just a sense of what modern architecture should be like.

Of present architects, who would you say are the most promising?

You can't predict the future.

The most sincere are the ones with the best future.

It may not be measured by what is called success, but those who search for the truth, no matter how ugly it is, are bound to find the more lasting expression.

It has nothing to do with professional practice, because practice is purely marketplace.

One who is the least sincere can be successful in the marketplace.

One who derives the most joy from what he is doing may not be in the marketplace, because people in the marketplace are not joyous people.

If he has availabilities for his expression, considering his individuality, his singularity, he is bound to be a very happy man. He gets it through the meaningfulness of his existence.

I met an architect who was working on a tremendous commission. I had just come from Baltimore and there was the possibility of my getting a small building to do, and he was working on something that was two or three million (dollars). He was complaining, *Of all the things I've done, I haven't found yet the thing that would be the source of my expressiveness.* I pitied him so much, and I said, *You'll never find it if you can't find it. There are such tremendous availabilities. I can't write but a little ballad, or maybe a minuet. You have the chance to compose a symphony, and you're complaining.*

Just because he didn't have it in him, he would still say, *If only I had a house to do where I could really express the things I want to!*

It doesn't make any difference whether it's a house or an outhouse. They are things man does with equal delight.

Why are the Richards Building windows blue?

It's sun-inhibiting glass, but it didn't prove to do what the glass people said it would do. That's what accounted for the silver paper that some used to cover their windows. Now all they have to do is get the right glass in there. They're not so poor that they can't put in a more modern kind of sun-inhibiting glass. That's one of the big complaints that they have that is easily corrected. I felt very angry with these people.

When you say a thing is poetic, you're giving it the highest compliment.

Poetry expresses that which is trying to eliminate the word, to express something to the mind. It tries to say nothing and convey its power.

When a thing has poetic quality, it has a transcending quality.

Poetry is an aura of religion bathing over the words of man.

I am reminded of Le Ricolais' definition of the intuitive sense. One question the class asked me was *What is the intuitive sense?* I knew better than to answer the question so I turned it over to Mr. Le Ricolais. He said, *The way to look at it is: What made man decide to do the first thing, to express himself for the first time?*

We dismissed knowledge because it wasn't there.

He said, *Maybe you could express it by saying that everything begins with poetry.*

It's a sense of validity without the word.

It's a servitude to thought.

It is that which conveys a nature to you indelibly through the language of the spirit.

It is not defining or overdefining something which ruins it.

When I first thought of order, I made a long list of things I thought order was. I exhausted myself, and finally I said, *But every time I write what it is, it becomes less.* So I eliminated all the things it was and just left the *is* there: *Order is,* and somehow it became something clearly in my mind.

I didn't know what this meant, so I took it to a person whom I regarded very much, somebody who knew the language beautifully.

I said, *Order is—do you feel any power in that?* And she said, *It's so tremendous in power that you must keep it this way.*

Saying that to me was a confirmation. We saw right away the glow. It didn't glow before. Then everything else I wrote had this image that order is. From this I really began to write, because I felt that I had something in what I said that didn't have to conform to how things are said.

It's impossible to express anything by group.

It's crystallized in an individual's mind. All the orders come to him with a completeness that no one can have by coordination.

The realization of a form is the realization of inseparable parts of something.

It has nothing to do with shape.

It is the realization of something that doesn't belong to anybody, not even the man who realizes it. But the man who realizes it is in a sense a leader, and he could through this realization assign any number of projects to prove his realization. This is design.

Design is the act of making glorious, making true, making operational those parts which are inseparable in form.

This is shape-making.

Each person chooses a different shape to make that which is answerable to form, so there can be many collaborators in confirming the sense of form realized by an individual. In that sense collaboration is fine. That's why you call in an engineer, that's why you call in an acoustical man, that's why you call in an expert in one thing or another.

You are working out a design, which means you're putting reality into an element in form. When you're thinking of something with inseparable parts, you've got to find the right material, you've got to find the right physical character of it. That's why a committee can't do it.

You call the man who realizes a sense of these things *a radar* about the nature of man. He can use a little bit of salt, a little bit of pepper, and a lot of cinnamon, because he knows that is what serves it, not something that had to do with a vote, a consensus.

My first feeling with regard to a client is that I'm going to reveal things to him of which he doesn't have any inkling.

If I get a program from a client, it's an approximation of need.

What I try to insert is that quality which touches the desires of people beyond needs and that which would motivate similar desires on the part of those who may use the building after the client who orders it.

It must have qualities beyond the dictates of the moment.

A house of greatness has the quality of being a personification of house.

My sister came from California because I'd been given the Book Award. She was reviewing things that happened when we were kids.

One time I was not well, and she substituted for me, playing the piano at the movie house where I worked. I had had about four lessons on the piano, and she had had only one, so we were not too expert at what we were doing. Nevertheless we were determined to make a living, which had to be done. I coached her on what she should play at certain moments, because I knew the film, and I had it all worked out when you played *Hearts and Flowers,* and where you played the *Indian Dance.* She could play, she just went to a piano and played. It happened to be that the film was changed, but she went through the routine anyway. It was really funny. She explained it to me. I'd forgotten about it completely.

I played in two movie houses. When I finished the one I had to run in no time flat to the other, which was about eight blocks away.

One day the proprietor called me. He said, *Louis, I'm afraid your job is over because we're installing an organ.* At the time, organs came in as an advance over the piano. He said, *I guess you can't play the organ.* I said, *Yes, I can,* not having ever seen one, and he said, *That's great, that's wonderful. I was worried about it because I couldn't find a relief organist. They're pretty rare. Nobody knows how to play the thing.*

That Sunday—the only day the movies were not open, we had the blue laws that were most strict in Philadelphia then—when he was installing the organ, I talked to the fellow who was a pianist and an organist as well; he played in churches. I said, *I'm in trouble, I have to learn to play the organ this Sunday, because I have to play Monday.* He said, *Lou, that's all right, you'll be able to play the organ. I'll teach you.* They were installing it, and he was testing it, and instead of worrying about testing it which was not too important to him, he sat down and taught me to play as soon as that organ was installed at four o'clock in the afternoon. We stayed on until nine or ten o'clock.

I really could play. I only had to learn to use the legato system instead of being free to play any staccato whatsoever. What I had trouble with was the bass. The feet never operated for me, and the foot pedals gave the quality to the sounds. I learned to play a few, but I couldn't learn it altogether since I had no formal education. But I said I was prepared enough. He said, *If you can't use your feet, it'll be all right. It'll stand for the two hours you're playing, we can forget about the feet.* But I wasn't going to forget about it. I wanted to learn, and I managed to use my feet to some extent.

Come Monday I was scared stiff, of course. I got at the organ, and I was surprised—the thing was very responsive. It was electrical and no pain at all.

During intermission, while they were changing the films, I made drawings which had to do with amusing ideas, funny people, drawn on slides. *One minute, please,* that sort of thing. They were projected while they changed the film. While that was going on, the proprietor said, *Lou, I didn't know you played so well, but you play too loudly.* That was the footwork; I didn't know how to control it. So I said, *Suppose I lay off the feet,* and he said, *That's a good idea.* And so we were in agreement. I played right on through until I graduated from college.

Then I got a job working in an architect's office, and that was very different. But I was able to go through school. Every year for four years I borrowed the same amount of money. I paid it off and then I'd borrow again. My credit was very good.

That reminds me of school. Penn was a nice school then. It was highly religious, not as if it were a certain religion, but religious in the sense that transcendent qualities were considered worthy.

We learned to respect the works of the masters, not so much for what they did for themselves, but for what they did for others through their works, which were a high use of the language of architecture.

When I saw the pyramids, they seemed to talk to me and tell me how they were made and tell me the wonder of their beginning and the audacity of thinking that the desires of man can be so extended that they will also extend the will to finish it over a period of time. To force people into slavery in order to make it tells me something of tremendous cruelty and arbitrariness, but it also tells me that there is a guarantee that you may not be living your life the same now as you will some other time.

The transmigration of souls is only a method. It doesn't mean anything to me.

But the question *Why anything?* does mean something.

In the question *Why anything?* there is the unanswered.

Death unanswers everything.

And this cannot be left without an answer: *Nothing is destroyed.*

Whatever we make comes out of life, therefore it's a living thing. It may not jump, it may not talk, but it's living.

The work of art is the making of a life. It's constantly revealing, as though it has in its age developed a sympathy of things that, through the circumstance of living, confirms more and more a great work of art.

It doesn't die, it isn't stylish—it's more than these.

I draw a building from the bottom up because that's the way it's constructed. It depends on gravity. You begin with the way all the weights can be distributed on the land, and then you build up. If you do that, then you draw like an architect.

I've started at the top and drawn that which gives to the sky, then gone down. Because you have the freedom, because you are doing a drawing and not a building, you have the same right as Chagall has. He can stop the building right in the middle of the sky and indicate ground, and say, *The hell with it. I'm not going to go any farther.* You are conveying something which shows the prerogatives of a painter, one who knows he can defy gravity.

Often when I speak to many people, I speak to only one person who is smiling, because there is an approval there that gives me the courage to continue. When I see a grim face, one that seems to want to object to what I'm saying or doesn't absorb it, it kills me. I must move away from his face immediately because I cannot find a rapport.

A person smiling is like one million people who are smiling at me, because the one person is plenty confirmation of approval.

At one time I tried to please everybody, and it destroyed everything I wanted to say.

Contributed by Robert Wemischner

At Independence Hall
19 May 1971

We're up here on the roof of Independence Hall.

This is my city.

When I was a boy I went sketching in Independence Square. I recall how much I loved American history, of which this place is the center. How I suffered when I read about an American soldier falling in the line of battle. To think that two hundred British soldiers were lost compared to one American!

This is the city of availabilities.

When I was a kid, one could avail oneself of places where one could learn without having the money to do so—it was all free. I went to several art schools in this city and I felt that it was a wonderful thing to have these availabilities.

Now I think about the city in the same terms of availabilities. A city is measured by its institutions—not by its traffic systems, not by certain mechanical services, but by the way a man can find the places where he can develop his expression. A person who has a natural ability to dance will learn on his own Latin or any subject, if he has a feeling for it. The city should make it possible for an individual to develop his talent. This city is famous among American cities for its availabilities in the arts: painting, sculpture, writing.

I have no theories about the city except that we be very sensitive to the constant awareness of the need for new institutions.

In back of me is Independence Mall. Before it was built it was a point of great controversy, because this building huddled amongst the buildings of development around it and took on a scale which related to the street. Now it has been given a more glorious position, as though the mall is a celebration of Independence Hall. Now that it has grown up to be a little older than what it looked like when it began to be constructed, it begins to take on its own rights; whereas previously everyone thought, including myself, that no building around it should be touched, but that it should fit amongst other buildings as though it were an incident in the growth of the city.

This mall proves that there are many people in the city, not only myself. They all have their aspirations.

Things are done not the way you thought they would work out, but they seem to be sympathetically part of things anyway.

People have a great commonality about them which makes you realize that one person and another are equally sincere.

When I was a boy we used to throw the football out of a window. That was a time when the horse was a pedestrian and the cars weren't around. We could race against the horse if he was no more than a good runner.

The playground was the street.

I still think that the playground should be the street.

The street is really a room, but it's a room peculiar to itself.

It is a room by agreement, as though the buildings that flank this room agreed to build this room.

It is the first community place.

From this outside room with the sky as the roof must have come the notion of having the first meeting place. Weather conditions suggested a roof, which made a simple enclosure which you also called a meeting house, within which you could put some benches.

This notion didn't come from me a long time ago. It came through the contact I have with young students who don't have much of an axe to grind. They are looking for their position in the way of how their predilections can be exercised and channeled. I am inspired by their sincerity, by their not being in the marketplace, by not taking that position in the battle of wits. Many things are drawn out of you which couldn't be drawn out otherwise. Although they never could predict what ideas I would come to, it was through their presence that I realized the street was a room by agreement.

With this simple idea I could design any city in the world and it would be instantly human. Consider that all these devices to serve this notion can be employed through an inspired technology which can transform the city. And it comes from the simplest poetic image.

The streets have lost their sense of agreement, because now everybody goes to the streets whether they belong there or not.

The streets have to be given over to this sense of agreement.

You can define streets as rivers, as canals, from which you derive the sense of a dock.

Garages should be part of the design of the streets, not the design of buildings. The whole street idea should be one of which the garage is a part. Garages are the harbors of the waterways which you call streets.

The analogy is a way in which you teach yourself to teach.

Images and lessons can come not out of knowing, but out of having knowledge come to you in a way which conveys the commonality which knowledge itself cannot convey. All my work comes not from knowing anything, but from taking knowledge and transmitting it through myself into the sense of commonality.

What is projected, everyone can receive.

Not for the Faint Hearted
from the *AIA Journal*
June 1971

On drawing

One day, as a small boy, I was copying the portrait of Napoleon. His left eye was giving me trouble. Already I had erased the drawing of it several times. My father lovingly corrected my work. I threw paper and pencil across the room, saying, *Now it's your drawing, not mine.*

Two cannot make a single drawing. I am sure the most skillful imitation can be detected by the originator. The sheer delight of drawing has its way in the drawing. That also is a quality the imitator can't imitate. The personal abstraction, the rapport between subject and thought are unimitable.

To an architect the whole world exists in his realm of architecture—when he passes a tree, he does not see it as a botanist but relates it to his realm. He would draw his trees as he imagined they grew because he thinks of constructing. All the activities of man are in his realm, relating themselves to his own activity.

A few years ago I visited Carcassonne. From the moment I entered the gates, I began to write with drawing, the images which I learned about now presenting themselves to me like realized dreams. I began studiously to memorize in line the proportions and the living details of these great buildings. I spent the whole day in the courts, on the ramparts and in the towers, diminishing my care about the proper proportions and exact details. At the close of the day, I was inventing shapes and placing buildings in different relationships than they were.

The sketchbook of painter, sculptor and architect should differ. The painter sketches to paint, the sculptor draws to carve, and the architect draws to build.

On Stopping Our Pencil

In Gothic times, architects built in solid stones. Now we can build with hollow stones. The spaces defined by the members of the structure are as important as the members. These spaces range in scale from the voids of an insulation panel—voids for air, lighting and heat to circulate— to spaces big enough to walk through or live in. The desire to express voids positively in the design of structure is evidenced by the growing interest and work in the development of space frames. The forms being experimented with come from a closer knowledge of nature and the outgrowth of the constant search for order.

Design habits leading to the concealment of structure have no place in this implied order. Such habits retard the development of an art. I believe that in architecture, as in all art, the artist instinctively keeps the marks which reveal how a thing was done. The feeling that our present-day architecture needs embellishment stems in part from our tendency to fair joints out of sight, to conceal how parts are put together. Structures should be devised which can harbor the mechanical needs of rooms and spaces. Ceilings with structure furred in tend to erase scale.

If we were to train ourselves to draw as to build, from the bottom up, when we do, stopping our pencil to make a mark at the joints of pouring or erecting, ornament would grow out of our love for ducts, conduits and pipe lines by pasting acoustical material over structure. The sense of structure of the building and how the spaces are served would be lost. The desire to express how it is done would filter through the entire society of building, to architect, engineer, builder and craftsmen.

On Winking at Chapels

As a problem in architecture, consider a chapel of a university. Is it a space divided for denominations of set ritual or is it a single space for inspired ritual? In search of form for such a chapel, its concept may come from how you think about its undefined nature.

To invent a circumstance, let us imagine the feelings of a student of architecture after an inspiring criticism. Full of dedication to his art, he passes the chapel and winks at it; he doesn't go in, he winks at it. This is inspired ritual.

The chapel has a central space which for the moment we won't describe; around it is an ambulatory for those who don't want to enter. Outside the ambulatory is an arcade for those not in the ambulatory; the arcade overlooks a garden for those not in the arcade. The garden has a wall for those who don't enter and merely wink at the chapel.

On Winking at Wonder

Form comes from wonder. Wonder stems from our *in touchness* with how we were made. One senses that nature records the process of what it makes, so that in what it makes there is also the record of how it was made. In touch with this record we are in wonder. This wonder gives rise to knowledge. But knowledge is related to other knowledge and this relation gives a sense of order, a sense of how they interrelate in a harmony that makes all things exist. From knowledge to sense of order we then wink at wonder and say, *How am I doing, wonder?*

On Interplay in Architecture

Richards Research Buildings
Philadelphia, PA 1957-64

My medical research building at the University of Pennsylvania incorporates this realization that science laboratories are essentially studios and that the air to be breathed must be separated from stale, waste air. The normal plan for laboratories places the work areas along one side of a central corridor, the other side of which houses the stairs, elevators, animal quarters, ducts and other facilities. In such a corridor there is mixed together with the air you breathe the outflow of contaminated, dangerous air.

The only distinction between one man's work space and that of another is the difference in numbers on their doors. For the university, I designed three studio towers in which each man may work in his own bailiwick. Each studio in these towers has its own escape subtower and exhaust subtower for the release of isotope air, germ-infected air and noxious gases. A central building around which the three major towers cluster serves as the area for facilities, usually to be found on the opposite side of the corridor in the normal plan. This central building has nostrils for the intake of fresh air located far from the exhaust subtowers for vitiated air. This design, the result of consideration of the unique uses to be made of its spaces and their service requirements, expresses the character of the research laboratory. From what I have said I do not mean to imply a system of thought and work leading to realization from form to design. Design could just as well lead to realization in form. This interplay is the constant excitement of architecture.

On *House* and *A House* and *Home*

Form is what. Design is how. Form is impersonal, but design belongs to the designer. Design is prescribed by circumstances: How much money there is available, the site, the client, the extent of skill and knowledge. Form has nothing to do with such conditions. In architecture, it is a harmony of spaces good enough for a certain activity of man.

On Law and Rules

Man makes rules which are of the laws of nature and of the spirit. Physical nature is of law. The laws of nature work in harmony with each other. Order is this harmony. Without a knowledge of the law, without a feeling for the law, nothing can be made. Nature is the maker of all things, the psyche desires things and challenges nature to make that which expresses the inexpressible, that which cannot be defined, that which has no measure, that which has no substance: love, hate, nobility. Still the psyche wants to express just that and cannot without an instrument. Law is the maker of instruments. The violin—beautiful out of the law, how the upper and lower diaphragm of the violin lends itself to the strikes of a bow, and the vertical strip dividing the two members are in a sense a continuous column. Even the sound holes in the upper diaphragm are cut so that little of the continuity of the beam is lost. Law leads to rules. A rule is subject to change, being man-made.

On Things Disliked

I do not like ducts; I do not like pipes. I hate them really thoroughly, but because I hate them so thoroughly, I feel they have to be given their place. If I just hated them and took no care, I think they would invade the building and completely destroy it. I want to correct any notion you may have that I am in love with that kind of thing.

Congress Hall, Venice, Italy

I can see the Congress Hall as if it were a theatre in the round—where people look at people. The curve of the meeting hall is slight in order to retain the sense that it is really a street-like piazza gently sloping. The whole structure, reinforced concrete with marble details, is conceived like a hanging bridge supported on the two ends by two columns...where also the stairs and elevators reach the various levels.

Because this is delta country, buildings are placed on mounds to protect them from flood. The lake was meant to encompass the hostels and the assembly and to act as a dimensional control. The assembly, hostels and supreme court belong to the Citadel of Assembly...suggesting a completeness causing other buildings to take their distance.

Salk Institute for Biological Studies, La Jolla, California

The original concept of the three parts which expresses the form of the Salk Institute—the laboratories, the meeting place, the living place—has remained. The acceptance of the separation has made Dr. Salk my most trusted critic.... When his belief in what constitutes the nature of a laboratory space was fully realized, he could not turn back.

Institute of Management, Ahmedabad, India

The plan comes from my feelings of monastery. The unity of the teaching building, dormitories and teachers' houses—each its own nature yet each near the other—was the problem I gave myself.... You notice I made all these buildings answerable to each other, even though the scale of the house and the dormitory and the school is so different.... The fullness of light, protected, the fullness of air, so welcome, are always present as the basis for architectural shapes.

Reprinted with permission of *AIA Journal,* June 1971
©1971 The American Institute of Architects

From a Conversation with Peter Blake
20 July 1971

What the man does is a chunk of man.

It's natural for me to give consciousness to a room, as though the dimensions of the room and you in it have a rapport. No speaking is involved, just a rapport.

I like to think that the room is a living thing. The work of art is the making of a life.

Nature makes nonconsciously what man makes consciously.

I want to give to the wall a consciousness.

All living things have consciousness. A leaf wants to be a leaf. I do not say that a wall wants to be a wall in the same sense that a leaf wants to be a leaf. You must instill this prerogative into the wall, because the wall is not a living thing.

It's a way of revering that which comes out of man, which must be considered miraculous or incredible. The incredible parts are those which nature makes nonconsciously, like a rock, or a mountain, or the streams, or the air. But that which man makes, inspired by nature's ways and finding availabilities through nature's constructions, is a miracle of man and the availability. That which is made in that sense is given, in my mind, a consciousness.

It wants to be a wall.

It's proud to be a wall.

Wallace Stevens said, *What slice of sun does your building have?* and I added *What slice of sun enters your room?* as if to say that the sun never knew how great it was until it struck the side of a building.

The sun goes along.

Man makes something; the sun is inspired.

A work of art has in it already an inspired technology; the way of making it is something which is invented.

I associate the street with the desire to be a street. It comes from the natural agreement that man has in him, which comes out of his sense of commonality.

The street is really a room by agreement.

The meeting house stems from the sense of agreement that a street has.

I live on a favorite street in that it has a dimensional ending. It's only two blocks long and, you begin to see it as a room.

A long street that goes on and on can only be distinguished as rooms and rooms and rooms by their intersection characteristics, because they are different from the actual stretch of the street, and they tend to make that part of the street characteristically a room of its own.

A long street may be considered a succession of rooms.

You can build all of city planning around this notion.

It is a kind of agreement.

The sense of the extension of the agreements is the inspirational source of city structure.

Architecturally we borrowed and stole from the European and did many works which would inspire the European. The more intimate beginning sense of city comes from there. I would trust more that which came out of the original inspiration than I would that which comes out of circumstantial convictions which modify those conditions. The inspiration is European, because it is more where the beginning of a city is.

The circumstances here should give you different shapes and different forms, but a street must be answerable to the original inspiration street.

If streets leave you and you don't have any street any more, then there's a new generative force equal to the original sources in Europe which should give you a completely different aspect of places around which buildings are built.

The streets in India and Pakistan are free for the animals and the motorcycles and the people.

It's one grand vehicle!

It's the only available means of communication and so it isn't categorized for this kind of a street or that kind of a street.

A street as soon as it opens is already available for all kinds of things. There's something about it which makes things naturally gravitate towards it. Here, we are more likely to divide because we don't want anything to interfere with the intentions of a street. There, the people and the animals and the motors take over. You feel even more the sense of a street there than you do here.

There are streets in all our cities. The original sense of their making, though it stems from a European source, has now been defiled. The sense of its original agreement, as though it were agreeable to two sides, as those who occupy the street, is lost by the inroads of indiscriminate traffic.

Those streets should not be called streets anymore.

The traffic must go away so that they can become streets again.

I don't mean traffic altogether. I mean traffic which destroys the street as an exchange, people to people and buildings to buildings.

In the American city there must be new definitions of new characteristics which should not be called streets at all—just vias where no communication other than this traffic is expressed.

You don't walk on the water in Venice. It's a street, even though it's purely a water transport.

The service of the building is gradually reaching such a high cost as to equal half the cost of the building. And everything is done to conceal that half of the building.

The catastrophe of good materials changing to cinder block is happening only because the equipment that must go into the services of the building is increasingly more important and more costly.

We must give it a rightful expression.

If we were able in our structures of the future to isolate the equipment of the mechanical as though it had its own aesthetic existence, just at the spaces have their own, then we would free the building of all the subterfuges we use to conceal the services of the building.

Mellon Center for
British Art and Studies
New Haven, CT 1969-74

In the Mellon Center for British Art and Studies, I tried to express more dramatically this very point. In the original studies I made for Mellon, there were instruments outside which looked or will look like something independent. Instruments of different natures are for the supply of air, the exhaust of air, the machinery that goes into making the air the way you want it on the interior of the building.

I have to abandon these because of the excessive costs, although I think I am abandoning something which has a meaning in the expressive possibilities of building. Now, on the interior of the building, I am making points that have equal expressive power, which will be the source of distribution of air. These will be made, hopefully, of material independent of the material of building.

They will not be clothed in the material which supports a building because they're not supporting anything. They're simply there as a kind of Franklin stove that sits in the middle of the area. It's going to look like an air maker or air controller.

Buildings will emerge with greater honesty.

When I was in Venice discussing future projects there, I thought an area could be set aside for industrial estate, which would be punctuated by the instruments for the control of the ecological condition. You would see fantastic instruments which may be called smoke eaters or chemical destroyers, which stand there quite markedly as an indication of man's genius to invent a technology.

You can hang the buildings if you have foundation conditions which warrant the care with which foundations must be made. In Venice you have water problems, and also you want to be able to let the water flow easily from the Adriatic into the lagoon. The arching of structures below for easy movement of water would be excellent.

Just think what opportunities there are for expressing man's regard for nature, and still man's living and working can go on the way he likes it to.

Salk Institute
La Jolla, CA 1959-65

The separation of served and servant spaces is beautifully expressed in Salk, in that you have a laboratory for experiments and a laboratory of pipes which you can see downwards or upwards. This space is just as tall as the space where experiments are made. These rooms have large pipes that feed downwards and upwards. You walk in to service these areas. They are just as important as the biological laboratories, since controls have to be made on very small areas in a laboratory. The temperature may be very high in one place, and very low right next to it.

It all comes from what Dr. Salk called the *mesenchyme space*. One serves the body, and one is the body itself.

Olivetti-Underwood Factory
Harrisburg, PA 1966-70

In the Olivetti plant, the ceiling is a ceiling of light. Light looks right through it. It isn't as though it were covered. The light must be close to the work, and then everything which serves it in the way of conveyors and other piping is above the level of the light. It is all open to view. Also the window in the Olivetti plant is above you.

Jewish Community Center
Trenton, NJ 1954-59

The first building in which I was unable to demonstrate the separation of servant spaces and the spaces that were served was the Trenton Bathhouse, a little building which required places for girls and boys to be separated while they were dressing, and entrance to a large pool.

The problems of separation without mazes, and finding the areas where enclosure must be and where openness can be has set up a sense of difference between the servant areas and the areas served.

The hollow columns which I invented for it, which were containers, became the servant areas and all other spaces became open, served by these hollow columns. From this came a generative force which is recognizable in every building which I've done since. Those constructions which serve were differently conceived than the structures of the rooms themselves, as though they were servants serving the spaces.

It is the emergence of clean spaces again.

The structural systems can be integrated into this idea. It is the recognition of the difference which makes you conscious of the serving structure, rather than having structure because you like it.

Structure should be characteristic of one activity of man against some other activity of man. That relates back to the Salk building in which the servant areas are the rooms between the actual laboratory rooms.

An architect is a composer.

Truly his greatest act is that of composing and not designing.

Design is the infighting to make the composition concept hold.

He does all these wonderful nuances within the design to strengthen the elements which are inseparable from each other.

If I can conceive of the elements which cannot be taken away from each other—if you take one away, the entire thing is broken apart—then I have constant hold of the process of design, design being that of the intimate details to make the elements live and work well with each other.

What takes all the time is design.

The composition is almost immediate.

Composition is the characteristic of one building as compared to the characteristic of another. I think I am composing music when I sit down and play because I have no notes in front of me. And at times, if I have some element which has resourcefulness, I can by just keeping that element in mind extend it endlessly, provided I keep that element in mind. But I can't as soon as I just ramble and play freely without the sense of something that holds it together. Notes are the prerogative of the music composer.

There aren't notes, but there certainly is structure and the separations between the characteristics.

In structure you might see the notes in a sense. If you think of the Parthenon being made of columns and spaces in columns, you can say the columns are no light and the spaces between columns are light.

The columns are notes, and the spaces between are intervals between the notes.

They are the light intervals.

Structure is the maker of light in that sense.

Salk Institute
La Jolla, CA 1959-65

When you ask who has been my favorite client, one name comes sharply to my mind, and that's Dr. Jonas Salk.

Dr. Salk listened closely to my speculations and was serious about how I would approach the building. He listened more carefully to me than I did to myself, and then he recorded these things in his mind.

During the time for our study, he constantly reminded me of premises which were not being carried out. These premises, which he thought were important, were also the basis of his questioning in his own way of thinking. In that way he was just as much the designer of the project as myself.

The man who orders what is to be done must be fully prepared with the essence of what he wants to do.

This transmitted to the architect can be equally inspiring, as though shapes that never occurred to a person would occur to the architect. If the sense of the building characteristic as compared to another building is purely in the mind of the person who orders it, in that sense I consider him my favorite client.

There are other clients that inspired me in other ways. But in as complex a building as a laboratory, he did as much as I did in formulating the servant and served areas.

My proposal to separate the studies from the work areas came from the principle that the study doesn't need all the equipment and services that the laboratory needs. I felt it a tremendous waste to have a study within all his availability. To get away from the laboratory was also important. But I never forgot the fact that although one can choose to go away, the other may not.

The studies were separated and became sun shields for the laboratories, so they worked together—an integration of the means which has one part of the building and another part of the building sympathize with each other, helping each other become themselves.

Mellon Center for
British Art and Studies
New Haven, CT 1969-74

In building the Mellon Center, the buildings which flanked the other side of Chapel Street were removed. The project is conceived as going from High to York and beyond the church. The Mellon Center will tie in with what will eventually become the art library.

Let me point out two features of this building.

These end structures are mechanical towers. They contain all the mechanical equipment which is hooked up with the building on every floor. They were made to be outside to develop their own shape, instead of being buried in some undistinguished area in the basement, as is usually done. They are brought out into the open.

Another characteristic is the expansion joint between the two buildings. I emphasized and dramatized the expansion joint, causing it to have two entrances at this point instead of the usual one. I felt that this was in itself an aesthetic emergence, rather than what was just necessary.

The shops along the sidewalk were inspired by the general feeling of the students of Yale. I felt that they had a wonderful point in not forgetting the continuity of the shopping characteristics of the street. I therefore dedicated the lower floors to commercial activities, and the building is above.

The street has a tendency to enter the building.

The street, with only its sidewalks being the pedestrian way, is not sufficient today with the greater number of people and the demand for freer movement, not just simple linear movement along the street.

The shops go into the building.

You enter a large open space which has protection above, and there the shops continue on the first level. Though there is no Mellon entrance at this point, you do see the building of the Mellon Studies as you enter the building for shopping purposes. There is on this level a protected area, places to eat and enjoy yourself.

The enclosed street connects up with the entrance on Chapel Street. And these two openings connect to the interior street. This is a shopping street and it has protection above.

This building is made of a framework of concrete with spans of great variety made possible by a *virandel* construction of floors and walls. When we needed large spans, the *virandel* went through the entire point from floor to floor and released free spans. The area below where the shops are has spans up to eighty feet, so that there is no sense of direct structure relation between the building above and the one below. The idea was to free the area as much as possible for pedestrian movement, and to free the shops so that their arrangement was not inhibited by columns.

I have reduced one level to make a better relationship between the area of the books and the area of the pictures. There is a collection of paintings, rare books, prints and original drawings. By making the books on one floor and the gallery above, I was more able to express the connection between books and drawings.

The drawing is also a book, and who pays for a book?

Nobody does. You only pay for the printing, because the book is a dedication of the mind.

Contributed by Peter Blake

Architecture and Human Agreement,
Lecture at University of Virginia
Charlottesville, Virginia
April 1972

Human agreement is agreement without example, a human response to something that has natural accord in the same way you say, *It's a nice day.*

It is better than reason.

I think it was Leonardo who said, *If the heart is right, the mind is right in vain.* I believe that thoroughly. When things go wrong and someone tries to soothe your feelings by explaining that it could happen to anyone, it never reaches you deeply because you know in a total way that you have failed, or it isn't the way it's stated.

Knowing is one thing and knowledge is another.

Knowledge is in a book that is incomplete. It will always be incomplete. Knowledge will always look for that marvelous point when everything else relates to everything else.

What we get from knowledge in the way of knowing does not warrant any acclaim except in what way it alters you.

Knowing is of value where it passes through your singularity. You relate it to those qualities of human agreement, those qualities of human response which only you can give, which make you unique. It is tremendously valuable that knowing can prime your singularity.

In dealing with the problems of the Bicentennial in Philadelphia, I was handed recently a list of particulars that the Bicentennial would take care of. It was a very long list. They handed it to me to fill in those aspects of my profession that may have been left out. They were very proud of this long list because it seemed all-comprising.

I said, *It think this list is too short because it's so long.*

I purposely said it so they'd ask another question.

It was really a question of how you can comprise any list at any time in history, because you always know there is the man around the corner, who has just discovered something or felt something to be true, that would not be answered by this list.

When I read the *Encyclopaedia Britannica* on architecture, I feel that it's most inadequate, and when I read it on physics, I say, *Isn't this great, isn't it wonderful that so much is included.*

We should talk about and try to find our inspirational sources.

If one could only touch the inspirational sources, the list could be extremely small and everyone would be satisfied.

The inspirational sources are the inspiration to learn, the inspiration to meet, and the inspiration to express.

The inspiration to learn stems from how you were made because, in what is made there is a record of how it is made. The important step of the making must be recorded psychically as well as physically.

The sense to be made encompasses all the laws of the universe and all the psychic directions.

To learn is only to find out how you were made.

If I were to teach city planning I would teach it from the inspiration to meet.

City planning is quite useless to teach, because if an architect knows how to beautifully create a house, he can also create the plan of the city.

If I go into a store to buy something, the first thing the seller should offer me is a cup of coffee. Meeting produces a different plan entirely from the mere hurried exchange of one activity and another.

Inspiration to express is our inclination.

The professions hardly describe it.

If you are in the profession of architecture, it is likely that you are not an architect. If you are an architect without thinking of the profession, you might be one.

The profession kills your incentive. You are thoroughly protected. If you were to ask the professional institute of architects to give you a list of those whom they would recommend as men who would inspire them in their work, they would give you a list of the entire membership. Their interest is purely operational. There was never a meeting that I went to in which I felt the pulse of a man who, out of the very desire to live, desire to express, says it in a way his singularity tells him.

In trying to find three sources of inspiration, I have expressed the third in different ways. I thought at first it was the inspiration to well-being. That I ruled out as being an overall sense, a motivating sense. It is just the inspiration to express, because we live to express.

The reason for living is to express.

It is the instrument on which the song of the soul is played.

It deals with the mind instead of the brain.

The brain and the soul is the mind.

The brain is what we try to make in machine form, and I think a machine would be tremendously successful in being able to calculate, in being able to deal with information much more readily than the brain, because the mind interferes with it.

The mind is always looking for something which is yet unexpressed, yet not said, yet not made.

You fight against that because the mind is a desire thing. The brain is a need thing; it's just so many bananas.

Desire is insatiable, and it is the root of dissension. It is opening up the avenues where desire can be felt.

The yet not made, the yet not said is what motivates man. What has been made already is just an indication of the wonder of the mind.

Desire is the motivator of the new need, and as soon as it is a need, it becomes a measurable thing and therefore less respected by the human.

When you speak about inspiration, you've got to think, because you want to know what inspiration is. I try to think of it because I made a statement and I have to defend it. I answered the question in no time at all, and spent four or five months trying to think of how I could substantiate it.

A man goes to the mountain, saying, *I need you because I feel you can express what I want to express.* The mountain says, *I'm busy, I'm basking in the sun, I'm having a hell of a good time. What do you want from me?* And he says, *I tell you, it's quite marvelous.* And out of his pocket comes a little something, with some columns and pediments.

The mountain says, *What's that?*

It's you.

Me? You mean to tell me those blocks are me? feeling the raggedness of his side, seen so much in the glancing light. *If so, I suggest that you go around the other end where it will be so much more advantageous to you.* The mountain becomes a collaborator as soon as you show him how beautiful he is in the form that man makes him.

Isn't it marvelous that, out of what's around, you get the feeling that you make with the aid of nature what nature itself cannot make? Nature does not make a house, it does not make a motorcycle, it makes no airplane. Only through man are they made.

We must admire deeply the original examples. Those which came out of sheer inspiration and what may have been the source of inspiration, those which lead you to choose one or the other to express are a mystery.

The first feeling must have been a sense of beauty.

Since we come from nature, we had the advantage before we were made of rejecting that which was attractive in the way we could be—a bird or, God forbid, a crocodile, or a microbe, that being worse, although I know a microbe wants to be a microbe.

As we made those choices out of the seed of us, something must have felt this germ so thoroughly that, in the course of inviting suggestions by nature, we rejected them, and nature agreed along the course recognizing the tendencies, the vectors of the seed.

Beauty must have been the first feeling of man. In the presence of nature, total harmony has to be answered to because all laws of the universe are involved in everything nature makes.

Beauty is not good-looking although that's not a bad idea.

It's like truth.

Anything that happens is the truth, whether you like it or not. You cannot strive for truth—it just happens.

Fact is different from truth. Fact is measurable, truth is not.

Beauty is the sense of rapport. It is the same kind of sense as human agreement.

The motivating power it has is to instill in you a sense of wonder. When the astronauts went into space, I followed them and saw this marvel, rose and blue in the distance, and the beauties of Paris and the wonder of Rome left me.

Just wonder came back.

Facts, knowledge, nothing. Knowledge left me entirely.

The one thing that couldn't leave me was Beethoven's Fifth or Toccata and Fugue. The most unmeasurable somehow stayed. They held on. They weren't lost because they still retained the marvel and wonder in them.

From wonder comes realization.

It must be so...feeling. No facts, just the sense of beauty, wonder, realization.

Realization leads to form which is distinguished from shape, form being the sense of the inseparable parts of something. If you take one part away, the whole goes. When you think of an axe, you think of a sharp edge, a butt end and a handle. If you take any of it away, the axe disappears.

From form you recognize the elements of form, and the elements are the first recognition of where design enters your work.

Design is putting something into being.

Before—in your sense of beauty—wonder, realization of form, the inseparable parts were all in the mind. There was nothing about it you can see.

Design is that which puts into being by making the elements more pronounced for their duty in creating a form. Every element is perfected so the sense of wonder can be re-reflected.

When man makes something it must be unmeasurable in the end.

When you do a work of architecture, you soon forget how many bricks you have to account for and what you have to devise in calling upon the orders of nature to make what you have to make. In the end all those things are not known to anybody but yourself as a struggle of bringing things into being.

A man says, *Ah, that's wonderful!* and that's the sum total of it.

When I think of how sensitive a person must be in regard to human agreement, I think of Gertrude Jeckyll. She was a great landscape architect who worked with Lutyens.

Lutyens, an architect with wonderful feelings, had also his limit, like all people have their limit. His houses were superb. But when the buildings got too big, he called upon uncompleted things in him to make them. I saw that in my many trips to India. As much as I admired his buildings in Delhi, I felt his houses were greater. He responded so beautifully to the landscape architect Gertrude Jeckyll that his porches that looked into her gardens had the feeling of satisfying a greater order sympathizing with the garden itself.

Gertrude Jeckyll was also responsive to what would sympathize with his architecture. She was going down the steps of one of her imaginative landscape works, and a little boy was running down those steps gingerly. She said to him, *Johnny, I see you're up so early.* And he said, *Aw, Miss Jeckyll, I'm supposed to be invisible!* She admonished herself deeply for not having sensed that he was invisible.

When I graduated, an architect from Chicago came to the school, a mountain of a man with a splendid vest and imposing figure, who twiddled his chain as he went along. He said, *I can give the class three important points of advice in being an architect. One is to get the job, two is to get the job, and three is to get the job.* That is what is being practiced.

The fight for the job is enormous.

And once you get it, all study leaves you, every interest leaves you.

I know it because I have the same sense of jealousy as everyone else, at this fellow getting something which has expressive content, that I'd just love to be part of. And of course it's always the inferior person who is getting the work, while we have it in us.

But if something, whether it is a strong rein or a little one, draws you back—it could be someone telling you that the building you built is good—you forget about that commission.

I'm sure Mozart died thinking he did nothing, because what he had yet not expressed is what motivated his will to live.

So it is with all of us. We want to express.

What we have expressed we fight for to the last ditch. When it's finished, it's finished.

Kokoschka, in a BBC interview in London, had to explain to the interrogator how he proceeded with his portrait painting. He said, *It's simple. I follow my subject everywhere, sometimes in embarassing places, and I study to the very last moment. In fact,* he says, *I fall thoroughly in love with my subjects. And when I am finished with what I have done, I fall thoroughly out of love with my subjects. Because in the painting, in the expression, lies the next painting.*

In the same way, in the building lies the other building.

It remains unexpressed.

This is the truth, the way man is. He must go through the circumstantial flow wherever he meets.

You can't anticipate circumstance.

You don't know what I'm going to say next.

You follow the dictates of circumstance or the advantages of it, whatever you grab onto.

The value of your work is the value of being, the degree of the unmeasurable that you're able to bring forward, that which you couldn't do without in the exercise of making something as an offering.

This is a residue that falls, the golden dust that falls. If you put your fingers through the golden dust you will be able to reach the powers of anticipation. You can predict that which can last a long while, in the same way as the first one who put a capital on a column and constructed the beams that gave you an enclosure.

If you imagine yourself as that person who did the first building of that nature, you would feel you had left that mark which gives you the feeling of well-being as an expressive person.

One can never forget the lessons of the beginning.

The beginning is a breakthrough.

There is no precedent.

It is from feelings of beginning that one measures man.

The only overriding inspiration is to express.

When one finds that, he finds the love for living.

Today, with factory operations and a man making half a shoe, all he does is find a moment when his labor union can charge more for his services.

He's wasting his life. Nobody can pay enough for that.

He just makes half a shoe and cannot show off to his son or his wife that he made this shoe.

So it is with every contribution that a man gives as to his singularity, that which makes him different from another man.

Every man is decidedly different from another.

In contrasting the sense of art of the West and that of the East, rhythm is the difference.

The Oriental does not make portraits of nature. He makes the rhythms of the rocks, the rhythms of the atmosphere, the rhythms of the clouds, the rhythms of the streams.

The tip of his brush is his soul.

When he makes his calligraphy, one recognized immediately that fluidity in being able to use his rhythms, done quickly and fleetingly. He invents the mountains when he actually sees them. He doesn't paint portraits of the mountains. The streams are not recognizable streams, they are the essence or spirit of streams.

Our Western abstractions are not inferior to the other; no, it's just a different attitude.

But the marriage of both can be because the human agreement is there, only it's expressed differently.

There's a beautiful touch of philosophy given to us by a Japanese poetess, who believed paradise was not a place, but something within us, individually. She said, *Because we are in paradise*—she meant herself—*everything around us does us wrong. And when paradise leaves us, there is no pain because there is no concern.*

Published by permission,
University of Virginia
Charlottesville, Virginia
April 1972

From an Interview, *VIA* magazine
Philadelphia, Pennsylvania

I was relating my experience with the Art Commission, where architects present plans of schools on land available in neighborhoods, often too small to have a playground big enough for the pupils to come and at least meet each other at that moment as the whole school in play. School therefore has to assume several yard periods. And that you related to your own time in school, when the assembly was really in a sense the classroom. And the yard certainly was one. And now you get the order to have a classroom which will assemble a half or even a quarter of the school, and the yard is cut down to just what is barely necessary to have only a period, a small period, of meeting outside; you get some fresh air, that's what you do, natural air. And all these seem like the beginning of a paring down of even that, you see, smaller rooms and smaller playfields— once the idea of the total assembly doesn't become an important part of school.

So I wondered whether you couldn't just eliminate the playground altogether, and really consider that it has no more power. I don't want to say it quite categorically. My mind switched to thinking in terms of a large piece of land, which would take the place of what? Of the small, inadequate playgrounds which are distributed around neighborhoods.

This, I know, would meet with a great deal of disfavor, but when you look at the plans submitted, of meted-out places for swings and for sandboxes and for any other hard-surface play, and everything is measured to Graphic Standards proportions, of just minimums, you realize that the architect is bound hand and foot. His imagination can't span—cannot suggest even the elimination of some relatively unimportant, let's say, elements of play, and make even a superior playground by not offering the usual standards but simply a clearing itself, and let the imagination do everything else, the imagination of the child, I mean to say. And from this I thought of the idea that after all, if you did nothing else but had as a premise to assemble land in reservation, even if you do not build on it right away, that the act of the clearing itself, knowing that the open land is an asset without even knowing its purpose.

That's what I meant about the power of a location being a beginning, already a beginning when the land is an asserted piece of land, waiting for the most agreed upon use. The recognition that the size of the land gives a sense of orientation to a neighborhood—a section of the city, if they were larger patches of land. Immediately you are in keeping with a sense of associated uses, similar to the anticipated associations that William Penn thought of when he allocated even in the forests surrounding the initial development of Philadelphia five locations upon which one should not build. It's the sense of having or, let's say, employing the natural feelings of such a force, of simply a clearing, and is greater than all *standard* planning, or all the good that's expected from what has been directed through planning.

A large location, one large location of land you see—I feel it is very true and the other is not true. The small piece of land associated with the school, where everything is measured out, is wrong because that measurement is a kind of established standard, and possibly repeated and repeated. You say that a swing requires four feet on one side and eight feet on another, but the spirit of a swing isn't there. And also you might say do you need a swing? Maybe a clear piece of land in which you have no swings would make the device for swings, or the device for other play to come out, merely because it is a large piece of land. And the other, which had everything accounted for, is a deadly thing.

The spirit of play cannot be found with these little piddling postage stamps. Why give any play, you see, if you cannot give it in full? Because the spirit of play is not just meting out so many square feet so you can just sort of stretch your legs. You either give it or you don't. Therefore abandon the idea of a playground entirely from a school and just simply make a clearing somewhere worthy to play in, and that is then a recognition of part of man's desires. There it's expressed. It's not expressed in the others, that mete it out like spoon-fed...a token idea of what play is. Play is wild! Play goes in all directions.

A large piece of land. Now if you can't afford to build anything, the act of making the recognition that there must be a large piece of land is a better act than fitting it out. The fitting it out will come. Not only that, but you will be able to sense what you cannot sense as an appropriate space today. Maybe the first act on that piece of land is to build a kind of shelter, not unlike that of a stoa, which is unpartitioned, and it's there as a kind of shelter which is secure in shelter because the trees won't shelter you during the rain; so this is built as a kind of first thing. You wait, you go under this thing when it's raining, you wait for the rain to be over, and you go back to play again, or you go home, or wait for a bus. But this gives you a sense of the validity, you see, of the establishment of play, and this is what you're supporting. When you're establishing that, your act can be very, very primitive and be truer than giving free notebooks and that kind of thing. That doesn't mean anything!

You don't give any notebooks, but you simply are there in class without anything at all. Believe me, you'll learn a tremendous amount if you don't have that classbook. If you can't give it in the spirit, you see, which means beginning over again sometimes rather than thinking that it is just a continuation in better and better and more and more...rather not that, but strip yourself of the accumulation of established means and begin again in those primitive ways to catch the spirit of learning—where you don't have so many availabilities.

But you still can feel the raw desire that's in back of the agreement to have such a place. The word *agreement* is a wonderful word, because it's a simple, down-to-earth, bread-and-butter word, and we need it very desperately. And the word *institutions* has bad repute, because it sounds like it's shackled, and confined, and running in one direction only. And that's what I mean really. Look how much spirit there is—you can see the open space. Would you have any hesitation to say that you have made a good act? Not a bit. If you can establish that as being truer in spirit to play. Or even if not play, just a clearing in the light of many houses—that a clearing is part of many houses. Just that. On that a school can be, and also may be; a meetinghouse—could be just simply that. Or a place of shelter. And the freedom of this area; where things can be for play!

The garden. It has to do with, not nature in the broadest sense, but nature as it applies to a place which has been chosen by man and is developed for man's use in a certain way. And the architect is called in as the advocate of nature, and makes everything in the deepest respect for nature by not imitating it at all, and not allowing himself to think that he's a designer if he imitates how, let's say, the bird plants the tree. But he must plant the tree as a man, a choosing individual. And then there is how he thinks, in the garden, as the interpreter of a personal thing— the gardens belongs to a person. It is not a place of invitation; if it is an invitation, it's a very intimate one.

He must make a drawing for the garden with the idea that things will grow and that his drawing is really only an instruction for something that starts. And that even every balustrade or every fountain or the choice of stone is something that belongs so much to this garden that the next garden must begin over again. So therefore he must destroy his drawings of the garden once it is instructed to be built, put it into the fireplace. All details, all ideas of the garden must go into the fireplace, because it really belongs to no other garden. Therefore he keeps no record of it; he must begin again as though it were the most intimate act.

You might say that nature is the workshop of God, that it is the saws and the hammers and all the means of instrumentation. But the desire to be something, if it strikes this instrumentation, if, let's say, nature makes a nod and says, *I can make it*, the desire is somehow in back of it and is a tremendous thing. It is really the incredible. It is the part which is completely unmeasurable. It says to nature something which is not invalid, and nature makes that which it could never make had it not been for the spirit that wants it to be made. Because if nature would go on making what it makes, there would only be the matter of the sun shining and the rain falling and everything just really being right in its place because that's the way gravity wants it, that's the way the winds want it, and that's the way everything that is measurable wants it.

Reprinted from *VIA* magazine
Graduate School of Architecture
University of Pennsylvania

With all the forces we felt in regard to what we originally wanted to build, the determination to bring it within the budget has actually made it a greater building. I believe that thoroughly. I see all the ideas I had before and they do not in any way surpass what, in simple terms, in modest terms, in terms appropriate to our religion, has been brought about. So I am deeply pleased.

I feel it. I wouldn't say it unless I could say in all modesty that it is good.

That's about the best you can say of anything, that it is good.

Because when you say it is *very* good, that is actually less.

Good is good.

I feel the great continuum here. This place never looked on paper to me as it looks now. With the people assembled, the place is made, I see it at the time of the Holy Days with everyone present, and it works.

It's part of the whole, and the fact that we have been so reasonable and so sensible in making the school such a part of the sanctuary that it blends into it makes the place even more significant than if we had all the space that separates them and waited for just the day, the two days, and for the extended time on our High Holy Days.

I'm pleased that we have been frugal because it's the very basis of learning.

In feeling the great continuum, which one must feel, you must always say when you have been in the synagogue, *Is it worthy of the Temple?* Though it's only a branch of the Temple, one must feel the synagogue is part of the Temple.

What was has always been.

What will be has always been.

And what is has always been.

It's the sense that reflects the beginning, and the beginning is the confirmation of all things that follow.

We have captured in modest ways such a place. We had one stream that went through everything we did. It's what Leonardo said, that when the heart is right, the head is rightfully bent.

The vectors of two people are reconciled.

The third vector can lead you right off.

When I am alone with a person, I become generative. What I say, I never said before. Or if I did say it before, it becomes a confirmation of what I said before.

A third person changes this event into a performance in which you say exactly what you said before. It is that sensitive.

I know the close and undisturbed associations we had on this building, in which you questioned me because you understood the importance of the principle—whatever principle, yours or mine—and that it couldn't fly away, it couldn't be destroyed by reason. It had to justify the aura of that principle—that was the point that was understood, not so much upholding the reason in back of it or trying to find out what it was.

Our reasoning never met because the background of reasoning is different from one person to another.

Commonality, which lies in the principle, is the only meeting point of that principle.

It is something which prevails in everyone.

It is like saying: *Isn't it a beautiful day?* Or: *It's great.* Although it is understood by each individual very differently because of his background, the sense of its belonging in the affirmative or in the refusal is complete. That must be considered phenomenal evidence, one worthy of being preserved.

I believe in a kind of psychic inheritance and that is what commonality is made of. It is not just physical, but it is part of the same family, mind you, because I don't believe there is a difference between the physical and the spiritual.

There are two joyous paths. One is the desire to be to express; the other, to be to be, just for the sake of being. That is the source of the material because it had to be an equal, non-differentiated battle to emerge, by the physical, by the desire to express.

One had to retain its unmeasurable quality, and the other the instrument to make expression possible.

The one felt that there must be an instrument on which the music of the soul must be played, and that in the light of the completely ephemeral, the beginning which couldn't have been anything that one can describe.

The source is a touch.

It is unbelievably sourceful and all-powerful.

All these words fail you because they are wrong words. When you say *powerful,* you think of forces.

There must be a word like *God* which simply comes to you and that settles it.

I express this in architecture by saying that architecture begins with the making of a room.

144

This room has its measure, it being small or large.

The world outside is wide and complete and stretches out into the universe. There is this world within a world which is a case to the violin, the violin being the soul of the person. And so it is the violin and the violin case.

If it is a large case, the violin doesn't fit very well. When I speak to an audience of people, I always center around a person, especially one who is smiling because I feel there is a human response. I feel as though I am in a room by myself with just that person. Then I can speak. I want to say something which I have never said before, although I hate myself because there is plenty of source for this, only it is in the wrong place, amongst many people.

It is from the event to the performance. As soon as a third person enters, you begin to try to prove to this person that you are also worthwhile. It spoils your generative sources.

J.S.: Three kinds of states, really: one when you are alone; one when you are with another person who makes something like this possible; and if there is another, that is the third condition.

Just a different condition. A lot of things happen with many people in a room, remarkable things. But for the priming, you need the presence of another facet of the commonality.

J.S.: When you are with another person of this nature who makes you feel this way or allows you to feel this way, then you are turned on. Whatever is the mechanism in you is activated. It needs to be touched and when that happens, a great deal that is in it is suddenly revealed. It is important enough to know that it does happen.

That is the main thing, not to try to ferret it out, because you will find that it is an endless thing to actually know what it is, even to define it. It is the sense that it has common approval, the nod of approval.

J.S.: For the average person it is enough to know that this kind of mechanism exists, that that kind of a process goes on, can be experienced, and has value. For a few others who are interested in probing the nature of this process, that is another matter.

You can't deny the man who wants to know the nature of it. You must say, *That is his dish of tea. I will stay back in my poetry, and his dish of tea is to do the other.* The point is that he gets some joy doing it. Joy is the kind of thing which responds to the will to be to express.

His will to be to express takes on the particular avenue through whatever avenues are open to him.

The pot luck you get from nature is your brain, the instrument which makes all these things possible, allows for certain avenues to open and others not to open. The predilections of a person, the natural talents of a person are remarkable and must therefore be brought out as your real human resources.

They are not the resources which deal with needs. They are those which make a man desire to live altogether. It is a beautiful thing.

I will speak about this when I get to London. It is important that the room is the beginning of architecture, and that a plan is a society of rooms, and that rooms talk to each other.

J.S.: Yes, the most important thing is for people to have the sense and understanding of the nature of things and of relationships, to express themselves in whatever metaphor is natural for them.

The time may come when it will be possible to put all these different things side by side and discover what they have in common. I am interested in discovering the convergence in what has diverged and in that way arrive at the source, meaning the nature of the beginning and relationship of it all. The plan of the cosmos and to the laws of nature.

Which are one law, and that is order.

J.S.: That's right. When you come down to it, order is the word that I use constantly, meaning plan, meaning relationship.

Meaning inherent. If you exclude the word *plan* for a minute and relegate it to rule rather than order.

J.S.: You mean use the word *plan* for the word *rule* rather than *order*? That is agreeable. They are two different things.

The plan is something that one must define somehow. It needs to be defined.

J.S.: It defines itself, Lou.

It defines itself, that is the point.

J.S.: It defines itself in the way in which it is expressed. By looking at the different ways in which it is expressed I would like to understand it. The understanding arises from what is implicit in what is explicit. Only by understanding the explicit do you comprehend the implicit.

That is absolutely so. But the understanding is also singular because you are involving a person. The person is speaking, the person is living. It must be assumed that the other person knows something and sees the implicit in his own way. That is why it is dangerous to define.

What a beautiful search that is.

Leave it in a sense of question. There is a profundity in that.

Putting your fingers down on it is actually the end of the world. You know you can do it, but that is the end of all things.

J.S.: The moment you express what you feel, you have brought something to an end, and you have to go back into the beginning of becoming again.

Absolutely. That is not satisfactory to you because it gives you another starting point from which to go farther and to go deeper into it.

You live to express.

It gives you a sense of the will to live at that point because there is so much still to peer into.

If you have come to a point, at that point you start the voyage all over again.

But your instruments are less and less and less. The availabilities are less and less and less. One must at that point experience more, allow a kind of youthful abandon, go over all this with less concern and simply rest, with almost deliberate intention to either prove or disprove it—either one is allowable.

Allow that which presents itself to you to be a new starting point.

That is when history is of no value, except circumstances are essential to draw out the nature of man.

You can't do without living, and in living there are circumstances which impress themselves upon you as being realizations.

Realizations come to you.

At that point, to live in the Himalayas, to live somewhere else, is what you need. You need contact with a tremendous sweep of singularities to realize that in commonality lies the seeds of understanding, of comprehension. That is the time to talk to a common farmer, who has attachments like you have except that he has not found the same things that you have, and doesn't understand these things because his work is different and his course of life was different.

You speak about your interest in gerontology.

Aging is the thing that you fight, only because you know what a tremendous adventure is always before you.

It is the finding out of self, or the nature of human, I would say, rather than man—like man is the species and human is something else.

J.S.: This morning, many of the things that I said in my dictation parallel so closely what you have just said that I am tremendously impressed by the parallel way in which certain minds that are in existence at any one point in time operate. It is almost as if they have the same or similar capacity to perceive. They perceive the same things, but they express their perceptions in different ways.

A person must have architecture inasmuch as he has existence. Therefore, he is an expression of some kind of order. What is the order of which this person is an expression?

You want to have some understanding of the mechanisms in the sense of what is right and what is wrong, and how these judgements can be made so that it might then be possible to build a better, healthier, more useful instrument; one that is free of disease, free of disorder, free of malfunctioning—one that functions to the fullness and maximum capacity of the self.

That is true, when you think of nature as giving the instruments to what may be favorable to man as well as unfavorable.

I would like to take the view that the microbe wants to be a microbe, and that you are selling him short.

J.S.: There are two kinds of microbes, just as there are two kinds of men.

Sure, there are two kinds of men, there are two kinds of microbes, but they all want to be what they want to be.

J.S.: Ah! That is intrinsic and that is given.

That's it. Nature accommodated anything that wanted to be. It is impartial.

What are the levels of inspiration which can touch nature? What is this that can want to be, which nature somehow wants it to not succeed to be? Nature rejected what it couldn't do.

Or does nature reject nothing, and make anything that wants to be?

Our atmosphere is favorable because our natural phenomena are there to make it favorable. Nature couldn't care less if all the atmosphere became sulphur, because it would still be as natural as it is with oxygen.

Nature is the most unjudging thing there is.

It is there, it happens, and therefore it is still in order.

There is no such thing as chaos. If it happens it is already in accordance with order.

We made the atomic bomb and it is in the nature to make it with nature's approval, but the course of things doesn't make the bomb because the atmosphere in which we live, the balances in which we live do not uncover constant phenomena of atomic explosion. But somewhere else it could be.

If one were to study nature for the phenomenon of order, and the earth's composition or some other composition, it is either favorable or not favorable for whatever may be action in the course of life.

The scientist must be driven to not just study the phenomena that are available to him, but also to study the possibilities.

The atomic studies were valid, but their use was invalid. That must be talked about, because men like Oppenheimer cannot be constantly placed in the wrong position. They must be put in a good position.

J.S.: But this is all part of the nature of things also. If you think of nature as being an experimentalist, allowing things to happen and letting them be judged in the course of time....

Nature is highly experimental. It is a phenomenom of becoming merely because things are fated to become.

J.S.: But that is what an experimentalist does.

The experiments a human does must be completely distinguished from this, in my opinion.

J.S.: I think we are talking about two different kinds of experimentalists. The words *experimental* and *experimentalist* often put off people who think the way you do. That word is inflammatory. Now that you have put it this way, I must have you see that the experimentalist of which I speak does exactly the same thing that you do.
I am not talking about a manipulator. I am talking about an experimentalist.

There is the distinction between the measurable and the unmeasurable.

J.S.: If that is a different sense of the experimentalist, then let us use the word for the moment, and see if we cannot dissolve the negative attributes of that term because of its association.

All right, let me try it.

Nature is there; it is to be.

To be is manifest in nature, and I see it in whatever is the succession of equilibria, so close to each other that there is no time between each state of equilibrium. There are just the circumstances.

If you can call circumstances experiment then I would agree to use the word *experiment*. One thing impinges on the other so that something else happens, and it is a constant succession of happenings.

Nature works nonconsciously.

It is also subject to eventual measurement. Maybe measurement will never be achieved, but the point is that it lends itself to measurement and the explorations of the scientist to find even those minute episodes in the one-melting-into-the-other kind of condition, which nature so gracefully does without any effort whatsoever because the order is so absolute that it can take anything in its stride.

The artist begins with a sense of beauty, which means total harmony in the same way that nature is a total harmony.

Nature is total harmony of the means that are available to itself and to man.

In man there is also this seeking of total harmony which he sensed at the moment of the first sense of consciousness. That is the human order sense, the response sense. It was the moment of the presence of the realizations of total harmony which he sensed nature has.

His presence, which is different from his existence, is manifest. Existence could have been before manifest. The theory of existence before sensing presence. This must have been even before something visible was present. When it becomes visible, becomes touchable, it has presence— against existence which has every promise of presence.

You have all the laws of nature to help you make presence because it was already there and working, it is just a question of how long it takes. But nature could care less.

The experiment is something which has to do with the will to live to express, and it is the greatest reverence for nature itself, for having had a nonconscious genius for making whatever has the right wind of demand for presence. I see it as only a matter of offering a reverence and the expansion of this feeling on the part of man producing that which may hopefully become a work of art. All things that are expressed don't quite reach that which deserve that accolade though they are involved in art because man's language is art.

He has no other language but art, and so he simply offers.

He doesn't experiment so much as he offers, and he would not allow it to be brought as an offering unless what he has done somehow expresses a reverence for beauty, a total harmony.

J.S.: But he experiments with ways of expressing what it is that he offers.

He does this, but if one could only eliminate the word *process* as it applies to nature and humans both. If one says one is process and the other is not, that is rather an arrogant statement.

For making beer you've got to use a process. Making an experiment is a process.

J.S.: No, let us use another word and that is *procedure*.

Procedure is a better word than *process*.

J.S.: Procedure is involved in a process.

You can't call making a painting a process. The word *experiment* is better than *process* in that sense.

You proceed. The word *process* means procedure, doesn't it?

J.S.: The word *experiment* should be used as the artist experiments with various ways of expressing, communicating, conveying.

Yes, and he doesn't start to express, because he doesn't know.

J.S.: No. That is saying that he is deliberately proceeding to express something that he has preconceived.

Rather, the conception seizes him, and he becomes an instrument of that process of expression, and in order to give fullness to the expression, his capacity to reflect the meaning of what is sensed is expressed in his capacity to experiment with various ways of representing or reflecting in its true form what he has sensed.

This should be stated and restated in so many ways.

It is like a poet who writes a line which he believes to be the ultimate line, which when written becomes the un-ultimate line. He begins to tear down his whole objective which is to write poetry without words, but he is forced to because the limit of the medium is such that words are his medium.

Why does he come to a stopping point when he knows that he has not come to a stopping point? It is because the next poem is already half generated in his mind. He can't stop writing this one unless he realizes that the next poem is already there.

It's something tremendously important in a man. It's the reason why Bach must have died thinking he did nothing, because what he was interested in was yet not said and yet not made.

As we speak about this, I know that many times we must speak about it, because these words stand in the way—the word *process* and all that.

When I review doing your building, I do not see it as a process.

I see also a recent thing that I did in which somebody whispered in my ear, *Let's start from the bottom and go out.* To him it meant something absolutely different.

Just like Barragan who came to the site and said there should be no trees. Then he proceeded to design it, and it was impossible. He made steps, he'd go down and up, have a garden here and a court there. I saw a single sweep going from building to building. And he is the one who inspired me to do what I did. And you, too.

J.S.: I had to come back and suggest that we make a court rather than a piazza, a plaza out of it, with benches so as to put the human scale into it.

But then somebody came in and wanted to put little flowers into it.

These are all the things that had to be held. What power was it that held it? What fighting? What willingness to block a move that you knew was not exactly right?

When this fellow came in with the ball of tricks, saying there must be the smell, and there must be the sound, and all this tomfoolery, he came in with the kind of stuff that one puts before clients and mesmerizes them into a swooning act.

Courtesy Jonas Salk
Founding Director
Salk Institute for Biological Studies

I love beginnings.

I marvel at beginnings.

Beginnings are that which confirm its continuation.

I revere learning because it is a fundamental inspiration. It isn't just something which has to do with duty. It is born into us.

The will to learn, the desire to learn, is the greatest of inspirations.

I am not revering of education. Learning, yes.

Education is something which is always on trial, because no system can capture the meaning of learning.

In search for beginnings, I have come across the thought that material is spent light. I liken the emergence of light to a manifestation of two brothers—knowing quite well that there are not two brothers. Nor that there is one.

One is the embodiment of the desire to be to express. And the (other) one—is to be to be.

One is light nonluminous, and the one is light of a prevailing luminous (sic). And this prevailing luminous can be visualized as becoming a wild dance of flame which settles and spreads itself into material.

Material is spent light. The mountains, the earth, the streams, the air and we are all spent light.

The will to be expressed, which I mentioned as the first brother, is the center of our desire. The desire to be to express is a motivation for living.

There is no other motivation for living than to express.

I began by drawing a diagram, calling the desire to be to express, *silence;* the other, *light.*

The movement of silence to light, light to silence, has many, many thresholds. Each threshold is a singularity. Each one of us has a threshold in which the meeting of light and silence lodges. This threshold is the position or the aura of the inspirations.

Inspiration is where the desire to express meets the possible.

This is the possible, the possible of anything. It is the maker of presences.

Here also is the sanctuary of art.

It is also the center of the expressive urges, and the means they have found to express.

I made this diagram to be read from left to right, and here in mirror writing going to it. All to mystify, to make you look for even a greater source than this. To put nothing in front of you that is thoroughly readable, so that you can strive to find what goes beyond this realization, always looking for a source, a beginning.

It's in my character to want to discover beginnings.

I like English history. I have volumes of it, but I never read anything but the first volume. Even at that, I only read the first three or four chapters. My purpose is to read Volume Zero, which has yet not been written. That's a kind of strange mind which causes one to look for this kind of thing.

From such a realization, one thinks of the emergence of a mind. The first feeling is that of beauty. Not the beautiful, just beauty. It is the aura of the perfect harmony.

From this aura of beauty, on its heels, is wonder.

The sense of wonder is important because it precedes knowing, it precedes knowledge.

When the astronauts went into space, the earth appeared as a marble, blue and rose. I felt nothing less important than knowing. Paris, Rome, the wonderful works of man—all of which came from circumstantial conditions—left the mind as being of little importance compared to the sense of wonder that prevailed.

The toccata in fugue remained because it was the most distant from the measure. The unmeasurable was the one thing that captured the mind, and the measurable made little difference.

When you see a gentle stream polluted, your sense of wonder about the stream leaves you. If the stream is still clear, you feel something ominous about being near this stream which soon will fall from its position of wonder.

Never must wonder leave our mind.

If you stop to think of other inspirations, it's pretty hard to find them.

City planning must be part of the inspiration to meet. A school is also part of the inspiration to meet.

Another inspiration which is on trial is the inspiration of well-being. Well-being includes ecology.

The original inspiration which came to us when architecture became apparent was an inspired movement. Its beginning didn't have a title; it had an undeniable urge to be.

There is no such thing as architecture.

There is the spirit architecture, but it has no presence.

What does have presence is a work of architecture. At best it must be considered as an offering to architecture itself, merely because of the wonder of its beginning.

When people talk about architecture being in one niche, and urban planning being in another, and city planning being in a third, and environmental design being in a fourth, these are purely marketplace divisions. It is destructive when a man says on his stationery that he is all these things.

The man who feels architecture as a spirit cannot title himself this way, because he would consider it pure dissipation of his original inspirations.

An architect can build a house and build a city in the same breath, if he thinks about it as being a marvelous, inspired, expressive realm.

From the first sense of beauty and from the sense of wonder which follows it comes realization.

Realization stems from the way we were made. We have to employ all the laws of the universe to be. We hold within us the record of the decisions which made us particularly human. There is the psychic record, there is the physical record, and there are those choices that we made to satisfy the desire to be which directed itself to what we now are. This nucleus lies in the leaf, it lies in the microbe, it lies in everything living.

There is a consciousness in all living things.

We would understand ourselves, if only we could capture the consciousness of a rose which must perforce have such simplicity that we would be able to solve our problems with a glow of presentation and offering that we cannot now do.

From this sense of realization comes form.

Form is not shape.

Shape is a design affair. Form is the realization of the inseparable parts of what is in realization. Design is to put into being what realization tells us. Form is the nature of something. Design strives to employ the laws of nature in putting it into being.

At that moment you put the measurable into what you are doing. Previous to that, everything is unmeasurable. Whatever you make has both in it.

Design demands an understanding of the order.

When you are designing in brick, you must ask brick what it wants or what it can do. Brick will say, *I like an arch.* You say, *But arches are difficult to make, they cost more money. I think you could use concrete across your opening equally well.* But the brick says, *I know you're right, but if you ask me what I like, I like an arch.* And you say, *Why be so stubborn?* and the brick says, *May I just make a little remark? Do you realize you are talking about a beam, and the beam of brick is an arch.* That's knowing the order, it's knowing its nature, it's knowing what it can do and respecting that. If you are dealing with brick, don't use it as another kind of secondary availability. You've got to put it into glory because that's the only position it deserves.

If you are dealing with concrete, you must know the order of concrete. You must know its nature, what concrete strives to be. Concrete wants to be granite, but can't quite make it. The reinforcing rods in it are a play of secret workers that make this so-called molten stone appear marvelously capable.

Steel wants to tell you that it can be an insect in strength.

The stone bridge is built like an elephant. You know its beauty, its harmony, by the extension of the material to its fullest capabilities. When you are just covering a wall with stone you must feel that you are doing an inferior act though that can be said of the very best of us.

To get all these things together and act in the purest manner might isolate you very much.

However, the religion in back of it is important to have in order to make the move. If it must be one step downward, it's made cautiously and in full knowledge that you are doing it.

A group of architects were chosen to collaborate on the development of the Bicentennial plans for Philadelphia. It was a difficult thing to get all these so-called prima donnas to work in unison. It was how I think in terms of silence and light which made it possible for me to propose the scheme which finally was selected as representative of what everyone was trying to do.

The original concept was that of making a street. I praise the idea of the simple notion of the street, because the street is really a community room.

This has tremendous binding character and was an immediate starting point, instead of thinking of the various items that should be in an exposition. We drew a building—it looks pretty angry, but this is a building. This had three different buildings. Here was a series of buildings together. It doesn't matter what the shapes are.

This building was the courts of the expressions. This was to be programmed by the great expressors: those who are interested in moviemaking, printing, painting, sculpture, architecture—all of the expressive urges.

This building was to be programmed by the great scientists, who could convey the manifestation of light, of air, of water, of land. We'll call this the court of the natural resources.

Here was the forum of the availabilities. The meeting of these was connected by a great street which had a canal and other transportation studies in the center.

Flanking the street were alcoves, within which there were many availabilities shown: auditoriums and various places, and results of a meeting of silence and light. This all took a minor role because the participation was the offering of these availabilities which were made on the street.

The theory was to invite all people who are learning. This didn't stop with your college work. It was for everyone, and it was particularly directed to those who have no notion as to what availability is: the Indians, the Pakistani, the Chinese, and the people of many African countries. The greater part of the world has not an immediacy of availabilities.

The availabilities are there to make possible the urges of expressive instincts.

This brings you to city planning.

A city is measured by the character of its availabilities.

School is an availability.

I believe in schools of natural talent.

A boy, no matter how young he is, who shows aptitude for dance, should be sent to a dancing school above all things. I assure you he should also avidly look for other schooling, but the center of his interest should be what he does naturally.

You never learn anything that is not part of yourself.

Everything you learn is attached, glued on, but it has no real substance in you. If one is led to his natural predilections, he will eventually learn the most difficult subjects merely because he has the freedom. But give it to him immediately.

School should be the center of freedom.

There should be no judgement, there should be no comparing one person with another.

If you have a classroom of thirty students in which freedom reigns, you would have thirty teachers.

It would bring about a program for schools which is not given to you by the School Department.

Think of a corridorless school. Instead of a passage, which a corridor is, you have a hall oriented toward the gardens. A hall which you may call the classroom of the students that vies with the library for equal importance. Two fireplaces mark the ends of the hall. There are window niches that allow for places one can go to in the meeting place which is the school room, the students' school room, free of obligations.

You would not find that in a program. You shouldn't find it in a program.

The architect realizes the opportunity to express the realm of spaces where it is good to learn. He must begin all over again. He disregards the program and discovers the nature of a room where it is good to learn. He would never present a series of rooms called *Seminar Room One, Two, Three, Four, Five,* and *Six* and so on, but would consider a seminar room as a discovery room. There would be rooms not named for anything, that would have various orientations from which one can choose the environment where it is good to talk with the number that are going to talk in this room. So with classrooms, so with the library which has this disdainful title today of *Information Center.* Just how far that is from the original inspirations is unbelievable.

A book is tremendously important. Nobody ever paid for the price of a book. They paid for the printing.

In a theater one must distinguish the auditorium and the stage as a violin, a sensitive instrument in which one is to hear, in which a whisper could be heard without amplification.

The lobbies and all other adjunct spaces are merely that which compose the violin case. That is the distinction. The violin and the violin case look completely different from each other.

Going backstage in many of the theaters, I saw the inside of a wastebasket. As the actor emerged from this wastebasket he seemed calm as though nothing happened, but behind the stage the mop is right next to the person. I decided to think of backstage as the actor's house, and I designed his house half a mile away from the theater. I regarded the green rooms as his living room with its fireplace. The rehearsal rooms, the dressing rooms were a function of that house. I even installed a chapel where a man could think of his lines alone without being prodded. I built a porch outside his house, which faced the street on which it was built, then wheeled it to backstage and presented the porch of the house as that which you see when the curtains are opened.

I was trying to discover the nature around which design was possible.

In building a house you consider the bedroom as being in a field with no roof so you can see the stars. Then you discover that the room isn't just a sleeping room, but it also can become a sickroom. And then you need a cup of tea, and then you long for the kitchen; and slowly, stealthily, the bedroom creeps to the kitchen—maybe even begs for forgiveness.

The living room is the same with all its freedoms.

So also the kitchen.

It combines in a loving way, an understanding way. Its strength is gathered not by looking into how things are made now, but by how they could be made.

The city also must be considered in terms of what way it can be made, not in terms of how we correct what is already made.

The most inspirational point from which architecture can be understood is to regard the room as the beginning of architecture.

You know when you enter your room how you like it, the way no one else knows. The windows of the room are the most marvelous. Wallace Stevens, the American poet, said something to architects. He aspired to be an architect. He said, *What slice of the sun enters your room?* as if to say that the sun never knew how great it was until it struck the side of a building. Can you put that in a UNIVAC machine?

The plan is a society of rooms.

The plan is one in which the rooms have talked to each other.

The plan is the structure of the spaces in their light.

Structure is the maker of light because the structure releases the spaces between and that is life-giving. The spaces could be an entrance or a window or even a little building which has windows in it because the distance between the columns is so resourceful. Concrete has such tremendous power and could have very little material. The play of what may be within the column disciplines is an endless study.

The form of a school has to do with the conversation of the various rooms and their nature and in what way they supplement each other to make the environment rich with the feeling that it's a good place to learn.

Consider elements in a house, where the living room contains a bay window where a boy admonished can sit and feel that he's away or he's in his own little room. Consider a stairway that goes from one level to another as being measured by the agility of a boy with all his coordinating faculties who has in him this desire to run up the four flights in no time flat.

This sensitivity is exemplified by Gertrude Jeckyll who was a famous architect who did many gardens for Lutyens. She was explaining sensitivity in the making of her gardens. One morning she was ascending a stairway in one of her gardens and a little boy whom she knew was running down the stairway at the same time. And she said, *Oh, Johnny, you're up so early.* And he said, *Oh, Miss Jeckyll, I'm supposed to be invisible.*

The order of movement, the order of light, the order of wind, the order of water may be reconsidered.

Gandhinagar Master Plan
Gujarat, India 1963-64

I had an assignment which could not be carried out: the building of a city of eventually five hundred thousand people, the capitol of Gujarat State of India known as Gandhinagar. The Summamati River is dry except when the monsoon comes and mountains of water go down that basin. It all goes to the sea. I thought of bridges that straddle the river bed, which could be reservoirs at the same time capturing and storing the water that goes down at the times of the monsoons. From such points there would be viaducts that run to stations in the future city. These stations would be the center of the fire stations, the police stations, the center of maintenance, the center of air conditioning, the center of water supply. The mango trees which are sacred stayed just where they were. They became the point of departure for the area, the sectors of the living quarters. The streets were oriented in accordance with the wind. There the employment of the utilities—which also follow the water lines, the natural features, the stations of water which mean a tremendous amount in a town in India—was the basis of the plan. It had no other theory in back of it but that of these orders.

Did the world need the Fifth Symphony before it was written?

Did Beethoven need it?

He designed it, he wrote it, and the world needed it.

Desire is the creation of a new need.

A city should consider all its spaces as belonging to the treasury of spaces.

It is an environment of broad availabilities constantly growing to new availabilities. The architecture of connection could be felt throughout the plan. The localities served by the orders of service should be distinctly a different architecture than that of the institutions.

I know that *institutions* is not a word to use, but it's an excellent word. It tells you that there is an agreement in back of the making. Institutions are there because of the inspirational quality which made them at the moment when silence and light meet in a realization, but they have lost the inspirational impact of their beginning and have become operational. They aren't felt in the same way they should be felt. Nothing in a town which is fundamentally a meeting place should be made unless it is made in a way which is deserving of its position.

A town can be bypassed today because we have transportation. The automobile can take us away and it can thumb its nose at town.

A town must become more and more resourceful, more full of availabilities.

Everything must be in a town, and must not be dispersed.

If a town is considered, it must not just be a chunk of townspeople who have moved to this new locality. It should be the great opportunity to make new expressions of everything that is in the town you just left.

Today it is a community room without a roof.

The walls that flank the room are the buildings that are on it. It is established by human agreement.

Human agreement is as simple as *Isn't it a nice day today?*

Agreement is not equal in each, but there is a sense of unanimity without example. It is what made the school a school, or what inspired the first room. It was an undeniable agreement that this man who seems to sense things which others don't should be near the children so they can benefit from such a man. This simple beginning when the teacher didn't call himself the teacher and the student was not called a student was the beginning of the sense of school. So it is with other buildings that present themselves as belonging to the original inspirations.

Today there are many institutions that must be established for availabilities.

The city place is nowhere in any town in the United States. It used to be the village green. Now it may be the place of the auditorium. It may be the place of invitation where the Mayor can invite a guest to the town without sending him to the Hilton Hotel. Places where people can come and have their studios—places of invitation. Institutions are quasi-meeting groups that want to uphold some aspect of our democracy.

In the city of Philadelphia there are about two hundred of these groups that protect citizens from what the institutions are unable to cope with. They are not set up for it, their laws are not for it, but they protect the rights of people. Housing associations that are not officially ordained report miserable financial conditions: They have sixty-four dollars and ninety-four cents in the treasury, and they are not sure whether they are going to have a place to meet next time because Mrs. Jones is going out of town. Why shouldn't they be honored with a meeting place? This place is not anywhere. Why couldn't the mayor have his offices there?

Every time I talk about it I seem to be unable to add anything to the few remarks I've made now. But I know if I were honored with such an assignment my mind would open to it.

I want to tell you something more about a room.

A room is a place. A small room is a place where, if you are with only one other person, you can be generative. You can say what you never said before. The walls seem to talk to you and give you a sense of what you want to say. The vectors of two meet.

Let there be a third person, and it becomes entirely too complicated. You resort to lines you've said before.

In a large room it becomes purely a performance, unless you find a smiling face which keeps telling you that what you are saying is worthwhile. Then maybe you can generate something. But I assure you that everything that I tell you now, I've said before.

The room is a marvelously sensitive thing.

If you were to speak in the Baptistry of Florence, though it is a large room, its proportions, its shape, its octagon can make you generative.

The shape is like a personality.

Such is the power of spaces.

When you hear of pre-fabricated systems you feel the tremendous loss it would be if one had to resort to them for all buildings that are built.

I want to make my last remark in reverence for the work that has been done by architects of the past.

What was has always been.

What is has always been.

What will be has always been.

Such is the nature of beginning. The power of accepting the qualities of commonality, of human agreement. It is to be trusted beyond any kind of operational system, to be trusted far beyond the discoveries or the statistical analysis of things as they are.

Because things as they are have nothing to do with desire.

Desire is the real motivating force for living and expression.

Thank you very much.

Courtesy International Design
Conference, Aspen, Colorado

I started to say I don't know a damn thing about what *The Invisible City* is. I feel I do know what it is, except it's hard to explain.

What it is is a man. It is possible if the man is there. The more the human is like others, the more he really is the artist. And the artist is the only animal that should be tolerated in this world. A scientist is just like an artist, but he is turning off the unmeasurable. When he writes a paper, he had better be an artist when it comes to expressing himself.

Why do you discover things in nature?

If you discover oxygen, it doesn't belong to you.

It's really to serve expressiveness, because your course in living is expression. You go out in the fields and find gold, or you find oxygen because man is tremendously adventurous, but you're serving expression in the end.

How do you like museums the way they are now?

I would say the first museum—not the way they are. I would not look at anything the way it is. I just forget about the way it is.

What is its meaning?

What is its inspirational source?

A museum is part of learning, if you make it a part of learning. It's with many, many apologies that you must take the elegant marbles from Greece and put them in the British Museum under an air-conditioned system. I think you ought to walk on your hands and knees to Greece to see them. Take it out of the museum!

I don't know how to answer the museum problem, but I know what has to happen. Attitudes must be created. It's a great thing when you consider it an availability. But if you see it in a sad sense, if you see that you have it and the other fellow doesn't, then it's not right, because there's only one of its kind.

Why can't that one of its kind sit in its original inspirational position?

It's a sad affair. Too much money is spent. If only you had just museums of your own place, things that you regard so very much that you don't want to let them disappear.

Attitudes would change if you had to go in all humility to places where things originally were placed.

How has the concept of *The Invisible City* affected architectural design?

I was more conscious of the idea of *The Invisible City* than I knew. The sense of doing things has to do with the feelings of the nature of it and what it wants to be. I speak from that. I spoke from it from the first time I recognized that I had powers of my own.

It stems from the realization of what made the first act altogether.

It certainly wasn't knowledge.

It was the sum of ability that you inherited, and it is your intuitive sense which has a record of all the stages you went through. There's a residue there—both psychic and physical. The choice is made to satisfy a seed urge to be human.

An American city is different in concept, and it has enviable things.

The measure of a city is an unmeasurable measure.

What is the quality of its availability? I know all the troubles which come from impetuous decisions which our cities have had. There were decisions which came over a great period of time because one project follows the other in rapid succession. But still the measure of it is the availability. I know of no country that is as rich in availability as America—and not as elegant, and not as beautifully made.

A museum seems like a secondary thing, unless it is a great treasury. A treasury, a guarded love for your source. Oh, what a place that would be! Not just an accumulation crowded together. You go through halls and halls and halls. The Museum of Cairo is a confined building that looks more like a storage house than it does a museum.

A museum should spread out.

The first thing you want in most museums is a cup of coffee. You feel so tired immediately.

A museum needs a garden.

You walk in a garden and you can either come in or not. This large garden tells you you may walk in to see the things or you may walk out. Completely free. You're not forced to go in. You go to see one thing or you are taken there to see it, and it's part of the visual history, the sense of the unmeasurable.

If you were starting over again, sir, what would you do?

One thing I'm going to tell you—I'd be much younger than I am now. Otherwise I wouldn't take the proposition at all.

It's all very right because I'm the guy who starts every day all over again.

It is just to what level of realization; the level of realization is always in what way you are conveying yourself.

If you take anything from anybody else, it must be that which doesn't belong to that man from whom you've taken it. There is that aspect of a man who is that generative as to offer first of all what doesn't belong to him. And this you can steal, rob, take—anything you want, because it doesn't belong to him.

The servant space and the spaces served—that doesn't belong to me. It is something which guides me in everything I've done. I express it my way and the guy who takes the expression is a sheer dope or a thief or a moron.

He shouldn't take what is expressed; he should only take the source which causes the expression.

If I had known that from the very beginning, I would have felt happy though the other man made beautiful things. Most people can only feel happy if they rip out an advertisement for a job in a newspaper so the other guy won't get the job.

People share by offering.

Circumstance is a running timer of the nature of humans.

If a battle is fought, the circumstances cannot be anticipated except through a sense of commonality with which the plan is made. The battle must happen and its course can never be anticipated or understood, but a new sense of anticipation is born as the result of it. Anticipation which belongs to man entirely, that of discovering his nature.

Your question is a good one, because you might say a good question defies any answer. I don't know why I'm pointing out your question over somebody else's; it's just that I was glad I could answer you.

This morning an educator told us his definition of change. He called it *novelty and continuance simultaneously.* Could you go beyond this and expound on your idea of change?

First of all there is physical change. Physical change is just a course over which you have little control because it's nonconscious. Every pebble on the beach is the right color, the right position, the right weight, the right material because it is nonconsciously made. The succession of equilibria is the interplay of the laws of nature, which is really only one law: order itself. It is never chaotic. It is simply changing. Every change is equally in equilibrium as the one that proceded it.

Nature doesn't speak about ecology, only we do.

Nature couldn't care less if all the air were sulphur. We'd suffer, but nature wouldn't suffer. Nature would go along with no problems whatsoever.

Change, nature's concern, is nonconscious.

Change in man is conscious. It has to do with rule and not law.

Rule is made to be changed; the essence of rule is to find a greater rule which can hold people's sensitivities together and relate to it together. The longer it lasts, the stronger is the rule, but the welcome of the new rule is tremendous.

I don't see novelty in change at all. It's too weak, too ephemeral. Change is a movement in which commonality is involved, and approval without question is involved. I'm sure the intended meaning is the same, but I have to put it in other terms to make it understandable to myself.

In America, we are talking about the city. The sense of liberty is so great, but we don't realize it because we are now questioning things. The sense of liberty causes the kind of dissension we have here which would never have been dissension in any other place. When a law is made in America, you just get yourself a lawyer.

How would you deal with improvisations?

Improvisations. The rule is so great that improvisations can enter it and still sense themselves as belonging to the rule. There is a time when the rule is not holding up and there is a wild scramble for other expressions. But they will never be of any value until a new rule is found.

There is a sense of commonality in a rule. It's made because it touches many. Its confirmation must always be by many.

If you can see Los Angeles!

You know what they say about Los Angeles—it's a series of places looking for a city. That about sums it up.

It's really a road with some things stuck on the road. And some trees which disguise it with difficulty.

There seems to be a race between poles and those long palms.

It's on wheels.

It's the greatest place to deserve a martini in my life! I really deserve it.

I felt Los Angeles is the closest to truth. It's a startling truth if you define truth as I define it, as being anything that happens whether you like it or not. It's a manifestation of what's possible. Therefore it's the truth. First you must begin. It's a revealing truth.

I don't know how to judge it. I'm not sure we know what a city should be.

There has to be a movement which conveys a sympathetic empathy, a quality of approval of whatever is happening. Los Angeles, you might say, is a great big happening. It does not epitomize the American city. It's just a succession of things that happened.

What would epitomize the American City?

I don't know that anything does epitomize the American city. The core of it is a tremendous core of availability because it is naturally given. The nucleus of the American city is the sense of freedom and the sense of offering because of the freedom.

It isn't that the city is good-looking, but it could become the city beautiful.

Beautiful, the first instinct of man, has nothing to do with good-looking or more beautiful. It isn't even beautiful—it's beauty. Beauty means total harmony. Its beauty would rise from a total harmony that one feels about offering something which came from a very short past in which what was available gave vent to many expressions.

People who came over from foreign countries realized that right away. They came from countries where nothing was available, to a place where things were available. They found there cause for expression—sometimes beautiful, sometimes ugly, but it was available, and they expressed themselves.

But there were gaps in the expression because things were done impetuously. Many people who went right into making money when they came to this country were led away from what they really wanted—to be in a school and to learn something. There are people who at all costs would like their son to go to the university, even if he doesn't want to go. This would not happen in other countries. He would take his position because there are class positions.

The core of availabilities lies in the tremendous resources the country had when it began. The frontiers were full of desire, and they brought out the desire aspects in us.

Because of recent changes in technology and world economics, the city functionally is changing or has changed from an organism to an organ. Do you care to comment on that in regard to architecture?

At present the city is not expressed at all. Even the street is the same on which the horse or pedestrian used to be. The place where the car stops and where the horse got a drink is the same place. It is part of the design of the street and not part of the design of the building. The water trough should have changed from a water trough to a new design of the street.

A building must be an expression of a realm of spaces where it is good to be for the purposes it is meant to be. Not crudded up by having five and six—or even twenty—stories of cars before you come to the actual places sitting on the cars.

The street is destroyed and the community of the street is destroyed.

The car must be found a position, not in buildings but in how a street is made. That may cause us to have new contours, and the level which you call the street may be above the present level.

The design of the street should not be a proud design such as *We did our police station with prefabricated elements*. So what? What have you accomplished if it isn't part of the order?

The city should be a collection of organs. It is an organism in a physical way which frames the organism in a psychological, non-resistant way.

I've spoken about the order of water, but there's the order of wind, the order of sun, the order of streets.

The architect builds with an order of structure.

The order of construction is a builder's order.

The order of times is very important now. Do you realize that buildings cost one percent more if you wait one month? The order of a building is economy, which means it's the right thing to do rather than that it costs less.

Do you feel competition complements or acts against inspiration?

Competition doesn't act against it. It's part of the urge to express. You take to competition because you want to express. It's a necessity. Because it stimulates, it activates, and you can so easily fall into conveniences. You would not know it were lunch time if you were working on what you love. Lunch becomes a terribly important thing to many people because they're not on any path whatsoever.

If you are conscious of some place or need that satisfies you, would you talk about it a little?

No such place exists. I feel that it is the next thing that satisfies me most.

How do you know what a city or a street might want to be?

A street has to prove itself in being. You have to feel the validity of street as an undeniable creation. That means you've got to go to the very source of it. You've got to see it before it was ever made and senses its validity, and from that you'll know. It's something you can do in whatever way your faculty gives you this insight into its nature.

It never would have been unless it had a source which was so strong that everything that followed it belonged to that seed.

It's just as sure as when you plant an oak seed, you're going to get an oak tree. The shape you don't know, but it's going to be an oak. If you put it in a crowded place, it's going to be one cramped-looking oak; if you put it in a free place, it's going to spread evenly because all the air around is equal.

I am a little uneasy about order. I think the American society in general is a disordered society. How do you deal with that issue?

You're sort of pushing order on top of disordered situations.

I'm not pushing anything—just remember that. I'm not pushing it—I've just presented it.

Ordered city is not the same as order. It has to do with orderly.

Nothing is on trial in nature—nothing.

It has its own rights, so deeply that nothing can destroy it. It changes, but it's still nature.

When you think of physical sense, you think in terms of that which has a natural kind of opposition, because it approves its own position.

What is there about Los Angeles that has a lesson of another city? I don't know of anything in Los Angeles which another city should have—nothing. Who wants a dirty street? But there are dirty streets.

Is Las Vegas an example to the next city because Las Vegas is the truth? Is it an example of a city?

Courtesy International Design
Conference at Aspen, Colorado

From a Conversation with Richard Saul Wurman
Aspen, Colorado
June 1972

What do you tell a man, and how much can you know? All I do is to dwell in my own sense of what a thing wants to be. If it's a school, it has rooms where it's good to learn. And that goes for everyone, even though they use inner systems to learn.

When I first came to India, about twenty-five years ago, I was invited to beautiful parties. The Minister of Education was there, and he spoke of the dilemma in Calcutta where there were a hundred applicants in the school to study chemistry. That never happened before. They had only ten benches for chemistry in their laboratory. He told an elaborate story of how he modified the English system of examination to make it so that the right ten people would get this position. He went through a very grueling kind of systematic elimination, and all this seemed silly to me. Here were a hundred people wanting to study chemisty. When he got through explaining his system, everybody was full of praise.

I said, *Mr. Minister, wouldn't it be a good idea if these ten, who by your system won the right to study chemistry, would have to teach nine others what they learn? And as a reward for teaching these nine others, they wouldn't be examined.*

It hadn't occurred to him, and he thought about it and said, *Maybe that would work. But that does not occur to the Indian. It occurs to somebody out West because he has a sense of the availabilities, and the Indian simply doesn't.*

I said, *Do you realize you could use the same system in the villages? If you were to have the first students who got out of school be obliged to go back to the villages and teach all the villagers to write their names, then everybody would be able to read the newspaper.* The sense of education must be whatever path is available, no matter how modest, to make sense of an availability. The school has this invisible quality which is made with the realization that it must be a good place to learn.

A city is where a boy, just by being in the city, will know what he wants to become.

He has a sense of what is available, and he doesn't feel that it's inaccessible to him.

That doesn't mean a good place to be educated—that would rule it out immediately. There isn't an ounce of inspiration of desire in that, not at all.

If a man has a natural ability to dance when he is only six years old, he should be sent to a dancing school. I assure you he would learn Latin on his own when he got bigger, only because he had the privilege of expressing himself as early as possible.

The school needs great revision. Present movements have definitely shown the inner courage that lies in everyone.

When I went to school, to think that you would flunk an examination was nothing short of catastrophic. There are people today who say, *It doesn't bother me if I don't go to school for a couple of years.* This is something which is blossoming and is of tremendous importance to everybody.

Reprinted courtesy of the International
Design Conference at Aspen, Colorado

I remember a time when Peter Smithson came to Philadelphia. This was every bit of twelve or thirteen years ago. He preceded all those who are wearing the most individual clothes. He came in with an outlandish outfit: pink shirt, Irish green tie—and with his drawl. He speaks very slowly. He speaks always with the idea of twisting everything to some bit of humor. He was very modest to me. No matter where he goes, he immediately sticks his feet up on the table. He's completely relaxed.

He was speaking at the University of Pennsylvania about his entrance to New York for the first time. He mentioned that he was going through Hoboken. We were all shocked, because it was such an unsightly way of coming into the United States. We were trying to cover up for it. We said, *Oh, that's a pity. You might have come in this way or that.* He was listening, sort of smiling. Then Ian McHarg—he's a master of invention, you never heard anyone who can begin and end without a change of breath, an accumulative thing which grows and grows into a great cloud—and in the end he said, *You came to the anal end of America.*

We all said, *I wish I'd said that.* Then Smithson said, *No, I disagree with you all. I think that's a reality.*

I was completely fascinated by his comment. The architects complain about the way things are, but they are always too late. They complain after the fact but don't have any voice in anticipating what could happen.

It has to do with correcting the path of circumstance and not having powers of anticipation.

Man knows another man's nature, not in a specific way of what he will do, or what the result or actual circumstantial act will be, but he has a feeling of his nature. He has a sense of order which is all-absorbing of the aura of conditions that come together and talk to each other.

From this comes my suggestion of zoning a street rather than zoning the houses. A street is a path of unanimity, whereas the individual interest that may be in every store is something which you can't predict. The street is more all-comprising in its nature than each individual fighting for himself.

If man would take the broad issues, he would find a better answer. You can legislate broad issues much more easily. If you try to please everybody, you've only got to give concessions beyond what is economically valid.

One mistake the architect made was not to distinguish economy and financing. All the time he was talking about economy, he was meaning financing.

Economy is poetic. It's a beautiful balance. It's the kind of thing in which you'd say you'd rather build the right thing in cinder blocks than in marble.

Financing is circumstantial. It doesn't have the many facets that economy can offer.

I couldn't agree less with the conditions of the writing on the wall. The best thing is to neglect it.

Criticism must always be constructive. Don't bother criticizing something that is worthless. You could treat it much better by neglect than by writing about it. You can do better by taking that which is truly offered.

How do you react to the charge that the role of the architect is
diminished in today's society?

In his eyes it isn't diminished.

Architecture is a quality which comes out of man. You respect the fact that it can emerge. You criticize those who don't honor it sufficiently by what they do. But you can't condemn architecture itself because it just waits for another time when it is again honored. I don't worry about that because it is circumstantial.

Architecture is not honored enough. It is not used enough. But the fact that eighty-five percent do buildings not using the architect is no indication that architecture is dead.

There is a difference between an architect and architecture.

Architecture is there, waiting for the architect to appear. Not everyone who is building a building is necessarily an architect. He is in the profession, but is he an architect?

Are you saying unequivocally that architecture and the architect
should not be in bed with the developer?

Not in any way. Just the way he shouldn't be in bed with the builder. The builder can't specify something and then also say that it's right, because he's tempted to say it's right when it's really wrong.

I see architecture as belonging to that undeniable emergence of man's expressive nature.

It must be considered nothing but marvelous that it ever emerged.

That is the point from which one must work.

Nobody ever reached architecture; they only reached an offering to architecture.

If this is not in the architect's mind, he can contribute nothing.

Something operational, something mechanical, something which is an enclosure will work, but it will not have the power of making what is called a visible city.

A visible city takes into account the places of invitation, the sense that you are in an area of expression which architecture can offer.

What do people have to contribute to architecture?

They have everything to do with architecture in the approval of sensing what an architect can do, as being something he likes to feel he's part of. They're not in the game, they're simply reacting to it. It's the human response. In this way they contribute. They cannot sit in committee and decide what is done. An architect should be the one who senses the nature of what he is doing, and offers this nature.

The first thing that one should feel is that it's the only thing that he ever wants to be to satisfy his will to express, which is fundamental to the will to live. When a man is in his work that way, he can give his best.

It has nothing to do with aesthetics. Aesthetics is something that follows you, not precedes you.

Let the other fellow explain how wonderful it is aesthetically. Your approach had nothing to do with aesthetics whatsoever. It is a nature of spaces where it is good to learn, good to do what you have to do, that you are trying to make. This induces the will to live.

I can only explain by explaining the marvel of a room. And the marvel of the plan as being a society of rooms.

Nothing is farther from the spirit of architecture than to make the architect a servant to the manipulator, because a manipulator lives in another town than the one he builds in.

There's a story told about you, that they had to break into your
office to steal the plans for the Salk Institute to get started.

It must have been an Irishman, because they have wonderful imaginations! I don't think he had it very clearly, because the place is not locked. That's why we lost everything. It must have been the first set of plans, right? Because I built with the second one.

I don't know of any set of plans that has been done on time.

If the man is clever, he makes a contract which says that any delay caused by the client must be justified by the client. An architect doesn't feel this way about it, because he's so anxious to express. It's his very life. He would never put conditions in that may scare the client off. So he promises the moon. At that point, it's just a new moon. He doesn't tell them, but the moon is promised.

Who is to tell the moment when, if you eat pencils and spit ideas, your plan will be ready?

The more thoughtful, the more time. But now, with escalation conditions, every month you wait, you increase the project by one percent. That's serious, because often that month's increase far exceeds the architect's commission.

Some years ago, you pointed out that one of the first things an
architect does is to take his client's program and change it.

That's almost mandatory.

Sher-E-Bangladesh
Dacca, Bangladesh—1962-74

It's the same when you are designing a city. I didn't design a full city, but in the capital of Pakistan there's a reservation in the town which contains all the buildings that serve as a legislative capital. They gave merely a rough indication of the kind of rooms they needed, because they anticipate so many people. They had a very small number of galleries for the people to participate in the Assembly. I felt that, in time, they would include many more people and select people. They would be prone to do that rather than allowing the public to come in. I increased that, and they agreed with me. All through the planning, it was a modification of the first plan.

I heard someone say that architects are the true dictators of
our time.

I wish it were true. They are not dictators at all.

Alvar Aalto said that? He would say it, because he's not a dictator. He describes himself as the kind of dictator that does not include men like Mussolini. By dictator, he means teacher. It's like changing the program. You can't be a dictator, because somebody else pays for it. It must be approved. He couldn't get a dime from what the other fellow wouldn't take out of his pocket. I think it's just a way of putting it. It sounds rather European.

You talked about the school of architecture as first being a
courtyard available to everyone, and of a library throughout the
school. Could you expound on that?

It has to do with any school, rather than the school of architecture specifically.

The small space and the large space. Without even knowing *why* the large space and *why* the small space, you know the same thing doesn't happen in the small space and the large space.

Some can work very well alone, and some can work only with others. It wouldn't be true of medicine, where the classrooms are most important. In architecture, the classrooms are less important because you are exploring in your drawings, in your model-making.

It is a large room. If you call it a studio, already its name implies a system.

The system must change from day to day.

Therefore, it is a place where the system is never designed. It has to do with spaces where you need a lot of room and a lot of natural light. In a school of architecture built by Nescti, there is no light. I think that's fundamentally wrong.

I always wanted to have an office in an abandoned school, because the walls were free, the windows were large, and the ceiling was high. Somebody else may want a smaller room. If I were doing ceramics or making ornaments, maybe the high ceiling would bother me. But it might not. A small scale would be very good for a person who wants to be in such a place. He relates to the things he has around him. It could also tell him that the little thing is beautiful as a little thing, and equally as important. One does not know what is specifically good. Only in a general way is it good.

The institution is not the building.

The institution is the agreement to have that which is supported.

It is an agreement that this kind of activity is natural to man.

It is an undeniable part of the way of life.

Isn't that what man has become? I don't have a sense of my beginnings in our culture. I don't have a deep respect for what I am.

Your beginning is in yourself. It's there, but you haven't found the sympathetic ray that makes you feel you really have it. You only discover it yourself. Nobody will give it to you, but it's through the other person that one senses himself.

In a classroom, when the kids are free, every student becomes a teacher. Freedom implies freedom of expression, that you are doing what you like to do. There you gather your will to live.

When you gather this will to live, you feel there's offering coming from it.

A man who is happy offers everything. He loses nothing by it. It doesn't cost him a penny.

The offering is not wide enough. It is not given sufficiently freely, because man is struggling to hold on to the little bit that he is able to express. He is held back from expression because the power structure makes it difficult.

The man who graduates from architectural school should not be left to the winds by having to work for an architect who can teach him nothing except enough to get his credentials. He should be given work to do. There's plenty of work to do. If he is given work, there will be a great deal of fighting—because why did you give him this, and why did you give him that? It will be a terrible mess. And if you work judgement into it as to who should get what, you'll find that judgement is worthless, because he does not develop his fullness when he really needs it. His fullness is something he works into and feels the power of. So my suggestion, though idealistically you'd want it, would be more difficult than the way it is now. You tumble around until you fall into something. You get good and dirty, and then you say, *I don't want to get dirty again,* and then you go in again and find a modified edition of the same thing, until you feel yourself into it.

There is no one who can make a common ideal. The ideal is a purely singular thing. It has nothing to do with anybody giving you your ideal. It will be made by yourself. This tumbling process is a rather good way of evolving the person. That's what man is doing when he's hitting against circumstance, because circumstance is unpredictable. He takes pot luck. That's why the great continuum means a great deal to me. Nothing is ever destroyed. Whatever may be the conditions which make you feel it isn't true, it appeals to the sense of living more that nothing is destroyed.

If you ask the question, *Why anything?* it gives you the answer immediately.

You spoke before of the manipulator....

The manipulator; oh, yes. I don't know anything about him, really. I just like to accuse him, that's all.

If you work for a manipulator, you are your own manipulator in your own way. The money-maker's life principle is very short. Maybe the architect's justification is that it will soon go down, so he can't be accused of what he did.

Architecture will never be given its rightful beauty of existence without the work being distinguished from others who can build a building.

Not so long ago, if you were building a building, you could have gotten any industrial organization that does heating, another one that makes windows, another one that moves partitions. They'd give you the service to make the plans for the installation. The architect became a kind of assembler, and was more discerning as to where [these parts] may go. But essentially, it was a maze of sundry parts, and the only permission that the client would give to the architect would be to have the architect tell him what kind of marble to put in the lobby.

What is the entity of a high building? In what way do you express the elevator? How do you make the space where the elevators are plentiful more than the space above? Only the architect can do all that which shapes a building. Wright did it intuitively in his Mile-High Building.

Financially, that box equal below and above works out. You are borrowing money off so much square feet, and it appeals to the bank because they have little measuring ways of knowing whether it is economical. They don't even look at the plans. They'll say, *What kind of windows do you have? We have aluminum windows. That's great.* That's all they do. It's just, *By golly and geez, those buildings do come out somehow as being something that will last long enough for the financing to work out.*

Much of the new housing is built on individual lots. Do you consider this kind of housing architecture?

Architecture doesn't cross a line and say, *Because it's only a little thing, I don't consider it architecture.*

Architecture crosses all lines.

It doesn't stop at the building, it doesn't stop at the location, it doesn't stop even at the confines of a town. You can't set out to make it architecture. It is really an offering, and it becomes architecture because of this quality.

The nature of a house is downbeat.

It's a place that's shared with no one.

It's a place where it is good to raise a family.

It's a place that must also be good for another, if he moves in after this family is gone.

It must have the quality of house, rather than just *be* a house. It must have the quality of a good place to live. Anyone going into this place should feel that he could belong. That would be the requirement of what would make this place belong to architecture.

The problem with the apartment is that it's the closest thing to a house. The floor is a contour; the elevator is just a place to stand.

The yard is just as much on the eighth story as it is on the fifth story. A true apartment must have its yard on the level where the apartment is. The yard above may not be as big as the yard below, but the yard is essential to the house. Within that area, can you do it financially or not is the question of the apartment.

A dormitory is also a kind of apartment, but the dormitory is one place where you are temporarily away from home. It's a lonely place. Therefore, it must be a place where you feel that you are making house in relation to your room.

Erdman Hall Dormitories
Bryn Mawr, PA—1960-65

When I built the dormitories at Bryn Mawr, I made each sector relate itself to an important arm of the dormitory: the dining room, the entrance, or the living room. It's a girls' dormitory and it was a matter of making house. I put fireplaces in all these areas as being the feeling that a man is present, because somehow you associate the fireplace with a man. A dormitory is different from a motel; it's different from any other kind of living quarters.

Most apartment houses look just like office buildings. Putting token balconies on them doesn't save the situation at all. Going onto a balcony is precarious. If you are on the eighth or tenth story, you don't use it because you feel as though you're going to drop off. Therefore, the yard would have a trellis that encloses you almost entirely, and that's where you'll plant your foliage, like vines.

The apartment house should look like the Hanging Gardens of Babylon.

Can you do it? Let that be up to the strength of one who says he can find a way.

Your first example, or two or three, would immediately make the budget of apartment houses a different thing entirely, just because somebody had the sense that he would do nothing but this. He believes it is in his nature so much that he is able, through his talent, to make the client realize that he has something there that's wonderful for him to invest money in. Recognizing the nature of the apartment house for the first time is the role of the architect. He will never find it if he succumbs to the arms of the developer.

If the architect senses the nature of the apartment house, that doesn't belong to him. It only belongs to him as far as he expresses. The offering is not so much his design as it is the sense of its nature.

The commonality is in stating the nature of what he is doing. Not the way he did it. He can be a lousy designer, but a marvelous architect.

When you are trying to relate your architecture to the people and place where you are working, what qualities were you after in your second capital of Bangladesh or East Pakistan?

First of all, may I rephrase the question to suit myself? I never use the expression, *my architecture*. I'd say, *my expression*. Architecture is a prevailing thing and has nothing to do with ownership.

Sher-E-Banglanagar
Dacca, Bangladesh
1962-74

In the capital I recognized the fact that a deep porch was the answer to the serious sun problem. One deals with the coolness of a shadow before you get to a window.

I offered the Pakistani a way of building a house. I did it much beyond the objections of everyone there. They gave me particulars, like the plinth, the platform of a building, can have fifty percent useable and fifty percent unuseable. They would add corridors and porches on the plinth. In my buildings, there is a hundred and twenty-five percent unuseable space, not fifty percent, because the only way I could express it was with deep porches. Their idea of a deep porch is that it is as wide as it is deep, because I studied it from its value, not from the lip service you give a porch. If the building is smaller, it is even more important, because people sleep outside.

The idea was very attractive to them because they don't have to answer to the people politically. I think those who have representation and control over budgetary conditions would have objected to it very strongly, and I probably would have failed to have full expression made. But where opportunity is, let's just be done. I argued against *brises soleil* for that reason. *Brises soleil* was a way of cutting out the sun, but it also brought in heat, because all those surfaces gathered heat. It wasn't equal to the coolness of a shadow.

What did you have in mind in your fantastic use of circles and half-circles and triangles?

Those are porch openings.

It was done because they have earthquake conditions in which the force this way and that way is equal to the force this way. The arch is this way, and the other takes care of the forces the other way.

I couldn't carry it out to full consistency because I couldn't get my wits together enough. I went as far as I could go.

In the Legislative Chamber, they wanted a room of prayer that was three thousand feet square, with a closet for rugs. They didn't have a sense of a room for prayer. They judged that not all members of the Assembly would go there, only some who feel like it, like people who cross themselves before they go to bat.

I presented the idea that this closet space for rugs and the space of three thousand square feet should be infinitely bigger. I had an outlandish figure of thirty thousand square feet, which I immediately changed. The point I wanted to convey was that it should be a full-flown mosque and that it should be over an entrance, so that the mosque would talk to the Assembly, and the Assembly would talk to the mosque. I knew the orientation of the chamber was characteristic of such a place, which had to face exactly towards Mecca. And I knew from what I'd seen how deliberately the town turns not to Mecca, that I felt the Assembly should also turn from this. To place this properly as an adjustment to an interior space didn't please me. I though this should be more nobly expressed. I was working with them out of the very ways in which they could evaluate things.

That very same day, it was approved. The head engineer, Kapilideen Ahdmed, called the President, Iaphan, and explained things to him. Iaphan agreed. And Ahdmed spoke to me and said, *You have something there.* It fitted beautifully. It fitted politically. The people would love it. At the same time it pleased him, because he was a very religious man. You'd walk into his office at the time of prayer, and in the middle of a sentence he would say, *I'm listening,* and he'd go to the closet, pick out a rug, sit himself down and pray. I waited until he was through then resumed the conversation.

I said to Kapilideen, *I'd like to put the Supreme Court here.* He said, *No, you wouldn't get that through the Chief Justice. He doesn't want to be anywhere near the Assembly. He wants to be far away.* But he said, *I'll arrange a meeting with him and see whether he'll agree.* We had a meeting that very morning—with tea and biscuits and people serving. I explained I wanted to put the Supreme Court near the Assembly, and he said, *Oh, no, don't, I can't bear to be near those rogues.* I made a sketch of the whole complex. He looked at the mosque entrance, he looked at the Assembly, the gardens and everything else.

Well, he said, taking the pencil out of my hand, *I'd agree to put the Supreme Court here,* and he put it exactly where I wanted him to put it. He said, *The mosque is sufficient insulation for me.* Look how the mosque worked to bring together a plan which was symbolic as far as they were concerned.

This is an architectural attitude. The architect should work to bring about a relationship, the architecture of connection, of the realm of spaces, where a rapport of buildings and spaces can be felt.

This was not the solution to a problem. This was before the solution.

The architect's work is not in the solution.

It is in setting the nature of something and putting it into practice.

See the marriage between the operator and the architect. He's a servant. He's a draftsman, that's all.

Do you design spaces specifically for children?

That would be a great mistake. A child wants to be an adult, and there is always a teacher within the child.

A child is in a room where he grows up to be big. Does he abandon that room because he's become bigger?

There are playgrounds, certainly, and children use them intermittently, but I even question that, especially the gadgetry that's made. They are so very heartfelt, but so contrived. You put a child in a field where there are some trees here and there, and he'll invent castles, he'll invent anything you could imagine, just because it's a field. Nothing is disturbed by all these little bitsy things like running through pipes. It is so forced. After a while this guy says, *It's a pipe, and I don't want to go through it.* But if a teacher says, *Imagine you're crawling through a pipe,* he would do it. He'd crawl so cautiously you'd have no idea there's no pipe there.

The mind of a child is completely uncluttered and full of wonderful mysteries. He's evolving. He came out incomplete except for one thing: he knows what to do and does not know how to do it. Many professions can be clobbered into non-existence, especially those who try to invent itsy-bitsy things.

There is an incomparable teacher, Aldo Van Eyck. When he speaks about architecture, it is lovely. He has little things and shows you how big they are. But he also built a room for children which he regrets to this day because every teacher has to duck through that doorway.

On the other end of the scale, would you like to see gigantic things built?

It's so rare we get them built, that we welcome getting them built.

To get them built means that there is sufficient area of commonality of agreement. This is the achievement. Like this man (Christo) who builds draperies—he drapes Miami Beach. One should not interfere with a man's way of expression. It's his private business how he expresses. Art is not something that is or isn't, because all men deal only with art. If he is expressing anything, he is dealing with some form of art.

Technology is one of the possibilities that can be commanded into service. It shouldn't be considered a substitute for anything. It is something that can be commanded once it grows up to be associated with the thing you're trying to make.

If you try to pre-fabricate houses, you'll find them twice as expensive. Still, you can rest your hopes on it because the technology has not been perfected.

On the question of houses, you must declare war.

You must not question the cost of making the housing situation better. You're not going to ask the general, *How much is the battle going to cost? Are we going into it or not?*

You fight it because it must be fought.

Housing is the one thing that nobody will give you, because it makes no money. It doesn't even take taxes. The taxes that support a city are all commercial. Houses lose money. The attitude towards supplying them has more words to it than action. People talk about it and don't do anything.

The Russians are doing something about it. They're pre-fabricating everything, because they can print the dollar to any value they want. They have a stockpile of pre-fabricated units, enough for architects that are not yet born. It's not an inspired technology. The architect can solve his problem by considering that the way to do it is already settled. I was invited to one of them. There was a hole in the living room big enough to put your fist in, which was never corrected because they had to do things in a hurry. The toilet had no door inside, and the piping was all exposed. The piping was used to hang clothes on. Everything was rickety. Nothing fit.

Pre-fabrication was never treated in a sensible way. The plumbing and all the things that serve the spaces could be manufactured, but the spaces must not be pre-fabricated. They must always be free to be done many ways, because there are many kinds of reactions to kinds of space, depending on what you aspire to.

Reprinted courtesy of the International Design Conference of Aspen, Colorado

When I spoke at Kikotaki's house in Japan, there was a room like this. It was a different world—a whole row of faces in very pleasant forms in the corner of the rectangle.

I was the only one sitting. In this row were all wives and ladies that were invited, and they were in the corner. They were serving tea, and they had all the equipment for serving tea and biscuits. They had to come back and forth. Over here were practicing architects—young, old. I was sitting cross-legged on a pillow, and they were all standing in various poses. There were some of them looking like Samurai—wild, you know? These Japanese have beautifully chiseled features, thin and wiry people. I could see the sword just like this. Some looked like Buddhas—just blocks for faces. And over here was a solid block of students with one student here, two students there, four students here. It was very gay. The formality of it was good. Just faces and lights.

The first day there would be a certain number of speakers, the second day the speakers that were there before might be there again. The stage of the speakers accumulated as though they were all equally responsible. It is the same thing as the inspired agenda because you are never losing sight of the person who spoke before.

From *House & Garden*
October 1972
On the Colonial House

The Colonial house is a marvelous house. It has an eternal plan in my opinion. No matter how much variation you put into it, it's still an eternal plan. It has a hall and a stairway that goes up to the bedrooms. A landing that is a room for the old man to stop and rest on the way up. You can get in the front and you can also get in the back. The dining room is separate and when you really have this separation, it means independence, independence even for the mother who is setting the table. Today, we put the dining room in the living room and when guests come they see the table. The hostess is constantly rushing in and out. She may go gracefully from place to place, be charming and all that, but the charisma of the house is disturbed. I say today you can still use the Colonial house, the room separations make responsive places. One can become the place where you go away while somebody else is doing something else. If you blend spaces in the Colonial way, you have a society of rooms in which each one has its character, allowing delicate differences to express themselves. In a way, people meeting in them are different people from those who live in divisionless spaces.

On Craftsmanship

A craftsman never wants to cover his work. In a good drawer the dovetailing is not hidden, the joint is the beginning of ornament. The joint is where ornament begins. The less the craftsman enters into something, the more there is a modification of the craft.

I have reached a time where I realize I have my own way of expressing myself, an approach, an attitude toward building that is so tied up with the integrity of the building that I could not disguise a joint, nor could I disguise the material itself. So I couldn't apply anything to it. I could use decoration in a sense that things that are put there are themselves something—a sculpture or a painting. But, you know, I go into houses where what I do is not—and I love the houses. There's a unity that I don't try for because it isn't in my nature. I insist the way the walls are made be completely evident. And it's exactly what a craftsman looks for.

I have no color applied on the walls in my home. I wouldn't want to disturb the wonder of natural light. The light really does make the room. The changing light according to the time of day and the seasons of the year gives color. Then there are reflections from the floors, the furniture, the materials, all contributing to make my space made by the light, mine. Light is mood. The color of light is very pronounced. We know that a red light will cast a green shadow and a green light will cast a red shadow. A blue light will cast a yellow shadow and a yellow light will cast a blue. It's surprising when a sunset is truly a prevailing red, not confused, you will see an inky green shadow. Ever since I knew that to be true, I grew away from painting and depended on the light. The color you get that way is not applied, but simply a surprise.

Design is personal. There is in general no perfect design. The striving for perfection is never realized though the desiring of perfection is the constant motivation of the artist. In the work completed is the seed of the work that follows. A man really only does one work.

The quality really that an impressive work of art must have is commonality, not the peculiar, not necessarily the original.

A Word About Beauty.

Beauty is an all prevailing sense of harmony, giving rise to wonder, and from it, revelations.

Poetry. Is it in beauty? Is it in wonder? Is it in the revelation?

It is in the beginning. In first thought, in the first sense of the means of expression.

A poet is in thought of beauty and existence. Yet a poem is only an offering which to the poet is less.

A work of architecture is but an offering to the spirit Architecture and its poetic beginning.

Excerpts from an Interview with Patricia McLaughlin,
The Pennsylvania Gazette
Philadelphia, Pennsylvania
December 1972

The greatest offering, the greatest work, the greatest *part,* the most wonderful part of an artist's work does not really belong to him. He is a catalyst of this eternal quality, and he can only claim the way he himself interprets it.

Picasso opened new avenues. His paintings belong to him, but the new avenues do not. *Things* belong to him, but the new avenues do not. In that way you explain the catalyst—he was just there, he senses it. It is these qualities which the next painter—or the painter next to him, put it this way—recognizes as an opening to his own talent. That's why Picasso has many followers. But if they imitate him, they're no one, you see? To write like Mozart is meaningless, right? To be influenced by Mozart's eternal quality—*eternal quality*—is the seed which stimulates the true artist.

I know what it is: it is my desire to sense Volume Zero. Volume Minus One. A search for the *sense* of beginning, because I know that the beginning is an eternal confirmation. I say eternal because I distinguish it from *universal. Universal* deals with the laws of nature and *eternal* deals with the nature of man. If man's nature would not approve, a beginning would be impossible. So beginning is a revelation which reveals what is natural to man—it never would have happened. What the human approves—human as a larger term for man, instead of man simply as the species—is natural to all humans. I would say the beginning then, is natural to all humans. The beginning reveals the nature of the human, right?

You can say that the first school was an approval of something within us, in our desires, revealed by circumstance. The circumstance *primes* the giving of man's approval. I put it this way: a man was under a tree, who did not know he was a teacher, talking to a few little ones, who did not know they were pupils. They approved of each other, and the first classroom was built. It was the beginning of *school*.

You're not a philosopher by having read philosophy, not at all. I think you are a philosopher because you are just *naturally* one. And if you call yourself a philosophy major, you are calling yourself almost nothing—just about as much value as a multitude of doctors of philosophy these, which I believe is really a false title. It's a false title to be given a doctor of philosophy in a subject—because he went through the mill, you see. I think a person who seeks this title as a stamp of approval in the eyes of those who mete out jobs in the marketplace is really in the marketplace. So if you get your Ph.D. so you can get a better job or you can teach, I think it's a marketplace idea, which should not be fostered by the University.

Everybody lies, by the way, in one form or another. It's not a good word. Lies many times protect us. It's rather a mystical thing—it could be the way you want it, and not the way it happened. You know, there's something wonderful about that aspect. I don't think *lie* is a good word to apply.

In that sense, I lie many times—it's only because I have so damned much fairy tale in me. I never lose sight of the thing. I believe the wish, the fairy tale is the beginning of science. I think if I were to trade my work for something equally as strong in me—as impelling in me, rather than strong (strong is a self-evaluation, and that isn't good, isn't a good idea at all, not good to write about—I hate that, by the way, anything that you may write about which seems as though I have put myself on a pedestal, this is something that I really hate to read—but *impelling* is something else, is something that drives you) is to write, is to be the writer of the new fairy tales. And maybe to use whatever talent I have in drawing to illustrate them.

We knew that the museum would always be full of surprises. The blues would be one thing one day, the blues would be another thing another day, depending on the character of the light. Nothing static as an electric bulb, which can only give you one iota of the character of light. The museum has as many moods as there are moments in time. Never, as long as the museum remains as a building, will there be a single day like the other.

My mind is full of Roman greatness. The vault has so etched itself in my mind that although I cannot employ it, it's there always ready. The vault seems to be the best. The light must come from a high point where it is best at its zenith. The vault, rising not high, not in an august manner, but somehow appropriate to the size of the individual. Its feeling of home and safety come to mind.

Rick [Kelly] wanted to have the flexibility, not by devices, but by how the spaces evoked flexibility. We met well on this subject.

This side of the building shows the decision of materials. Concrete does the work of construction, of holding things up. The columns are apart from each other. The space between must be filled without using the material which does the heavy work. The travertine is a fill-in material, a wall material, an enclosing material.

In olden days the columns were close to each other. Today they can span a hundred feet and the dome-like vault has the properties of a beam. How marvelous that is.

I put the glass between the structural members and the members that do not construct because the joint is the beginning of ornament. That must be distinguished from decoration, which is applied.

I look at my work with a sense of what is forthcoming. The yet not said, the yet not made is what puts sparks of life into you.

This building feels—and it's a good feeling—as though I had nothing to do with it, that some other hand did it. Because it is a premise constructed.

From KIMBELL—YEAR ONE, Produced by Patsy Swank,
October 1973, KERA/Channel 13 Public Communications
Foundation for North Texas, Reprinted by permission.

I would like to see the Exeter Library as seen by other eyes.

I want to be surprised by it.

I have never thought in terms of ordaining a wall for a painting to be painted by a painter, but I was always hoping that a painter would see the building and suddenly come to the realization that he never realized what painting was until he saw the building, and this would make the building greater.

I do my work as far as I can go, always hoping that someone could make it greater.

The space induces the project.

If you have a space, something happens, the programs then starts. It doesn't start before you make the space.

The windows are larger at the top and smaller at the bottom, and in the depths of the arches you see changes. They form a gradation of forces that come down from little force, where the forces are dancing like angels, to the bottom, where they are grunting. When you look at the building, you don't feel it's doing that until you inspect it, and then suddenly the whole thing looks that way to you, unostentatious instead of being blared out unnecessarily and with too much force.

The jack arch can only take so much pressure. I widened the jack arch as much as I could, adding the cant below, a little rise to make it somewhat like an arch. The larger the span, the less arch you have because it doesn't require that much arch.

The ornament is a recognition that a joint is ceremonious. A joint implies ornament.

From all sides there is an entrance. If you are scurrying in a rain to get to a building, you can come in at any point and find your entrance. It's a continuous campus-type entrance.

The white colonial-looking wood building, the red and white atmosphere of Exeter, tells a story of how the building was conceived, because I thought immediately of satisfying the sense of reception, the feeling of human agreement one feels when entering the campus.

You feel it's right. You hold it as a test against what you do.

To build something which tries to mimic these buildings, or to make a building which looks completely apart from all the other buildings, never entered my mind once I came there.

I see the building as a brick building, a brick facade in depth as though it were a brick building.

The brick structure was made in an old-fashioned way, and the interior structure was done in today's techniques.

I couldn't see myself building a concrete building inside and facing it with brick so it looks like all the other buildings. I wanted to make a brick building. Though it is only seventeen feet wide, it's still fully a brick building, and there is fully a concrete building inside of it, following it.

The reading place had the connotations of being age-old and built according to old techniques, demanding that it not be helped by anything, but be on its own.

There was a brickyard in the area which had been making bricks since colonial days. It supplied much of the red brick that was used at Harvard. It had to go out of business. In the course of my design I decided I wanted to use brick, and they called my attention to this brick place. I deliberated because I had never used bricks that were quite so irregular. But then I thought the bricks were marvelous, and it was brick which had been used on the campus. So Exeter bought two million bricks; they bought them out.

I like travertine. It does marvelous things. I knew I could get large pieces and I knew it could be shaped easily. Some of the large stones could be used as cut out of the quarry, in contrast to the brickwork, which had many joints.

The name *carrel* implies something which is in the construction itself, which you find as a good place to read. It's a natural outcome of structure which says, *Why don't we set a bench there? It's a good place to be.* Then you give them the name, rather than saying, *We'll have carrels.* If you see in a program a direction to the architect, *We want so many carrels,* what is lost is the discovery of the carrel.

You go back to the wonder of having discovered it, and from there you get the sense that you have no right to have a carrel until, by your construction, you rediscover the carrel.

The carrel is the place to be. It is a place of no glare, because you are so close to the light that glare is impossible.

The major light is above the eye line. You do not feel any distraction or glare because the opposite wall is so close that the light entering the narrow reading room reflects on the walls opposite the room, sends it right across the room. If the room were deep, the glare would be very strong.

I made the carrel associated with the light. It has its own little window so that you can regulate privacy and the amount of light you want. If you like the sun, you have it; if you don't like the sun, you don't have it.

Over that is a general window which brings light back into the room, and gives light to the carrels on the upper level of the reading place.

Originally I had shutters on the larger windows. I feel still that shutters would be good on certain elevations. They didn't have to be on the north, and possibly would have been most advantageous on the west. This was not done because they can be easily installed at any time, and money was running out. The blinds were an equally good solution. Shutters were more trouble, but though they could have caused more housekeeping.... Housekeeping is a good thing for the regard of the building, it's mothering the building. People only care for a building if they have been through it.

The carrel is the room within a room.

It is also the room which gives you a sense of the books present in both the upper level and lower level.

If I made the reading room the same dimension in height as the books, I'd feel as though I am in a piece of furniture, a highboy, and I'm on the second drawer.

It is a sense of the presence of the books. In the reading room you've got as many books as are allowed in this particular way of expressing it.

I'm not sure the large reading room means very much any more because it is only a place where boy meets girl and nobody reads.

I developed my thought independently. There was no requirement for a large reading room. But they did want carrels, they said so exactly, so I took that as being categorical and worked on that attitude.

It was a guiding thing to feel that the position of the reading room would not be on the interior, because I don't like any reading room that has light from above. It's difficult to read in light from above.

The interior chamber was to be used for entering, and being in a place from which all essential services can be felt: the catalogues, the reference rooms, and the service desk.

It's a connecting architecture.

In the central room I chose the kind of structure which shields the light so it is not pouring down. Any structure giving light only from above is subject to damage, because rain and snow will eventually make it a maintenance problem, whereas a clerestory light gives you light from the sides of a beam.

The thought of having a little dark in your corners could be considered classical architecture.

It was important for the central space to go all the way up because it wants to be the place of books.

If you could have seen all the books, that would have been good.

The fact that the books are different is the reason for making the large circular opening. I was careful not to convey the will of having a circular opening in a wall by not making the circular opening an attraction in itself. I touched the upper arch of the circle and the lower arch of the circle to the very end of the column, so you get the feeling that it is really a beam touching the column. I actually wanted nothing there, but the columns needed to be braced. I used the circular opening as a brace for the columns, though it is more than you need for a brace.

You don't feel a wall there at all; you feel that it belongs to the whole system of bracing.

The rooms on the upper floors are the rare book rooms, the lounge and the seminar rooms.

It is a quiet place.

It is a place one knows he can adjourn to.

It is a place where there can be the participation of student, teacher and management.

It's a free, unobligating room.

It proves to be good because it is now regarded as a community function place; people do gather there.

The internal life of the structure is one in which the strains are held in check.

In a great tall office building the columns on the street are growing and the columns above are dancing like fairies. The column takes the whole load, and there is a great beauty in giving this quality to the column.

You see many office buildings in which the columns are the same above as they are below, and the whole sense of engineering becomes only professional. It becomes as you want to see it before you know its nature.

Imagine buildings overhead which do not have their feet, so that the land can be again freed from the burden of the legs of support.

Gravity says, *Support you gotta give me.*

Concrete frees all gravity demands, defying gravity by satisfying it.

What is so marvelous about concrete is that you don't necessarily have to make references to the ground for everything that may be above. You can consolidate the entire construction above you and truss it in a way that concrete reinforcement is made, and then decide at the entrance that you can conserve the amount of support. You dramatize the support at that point, which no construction can do except steel and concrete.

The arcade is a landscape thing. It belongs to the building, certainly, but it also belongs to the entrance and belongs to the grounds.

The brick building comes right down and is the reading room and arcade.

You enter at any point, and when you open the door and walk through into the building itself you are in the concrete part.

All the struggle of structure above is given to certain walls to take and gives the freedom to the open space, as though there were large spans below and smaller spans above.

It can be called a transfer structure, which is an open truss beam that takes the entire weight of the concrete bookcase.

It is a transparent beam which does not obstruct the view of entrance and the sense of the area below.

A truss can be a concrete arch.

At no time could I have done this building if I hadn't had the absolute order dictation of the face around the periphery looking for a light, the interior space where the books were away from the light, and again the emergence of light in the center—placing books however in the section where there was no light so that they could be seen in borrowed light from the windows of the periphery.

The order was always being tested.

As long as I only had the struggle of arrangement so that I could get as much as possible out of it, I had no fears.

There is one illustration of the library in which there are no tables. It is a great imperialistic room, and many tiers of books are stacked along the walls, and there are people handing down books from on high to people who are lower. There are no chairs to sit on, no tables to read on, just a feeling of what a library should be—you come into a chamber and there are all the books.

This also belongs to trying to find the nature of a *library*.

If you were given the first commission before libraries were ever built to build a place where these books can be, what would you do? That is the thought you have about its nature when you are given the privilege of designing a building.

There could be indecision as to what a library is. It depends on how much you love the book, how much you think it should not be taken out and its being so precious that nobody ever disturbs its location.

The book is an offering.

Think of the writer of poetry. His book is on the shelf and nobody looks at it. He's in the library watching, and nobody notices it. He knows the hours, the days, the years he spent in the writing. Finally he gets to the terrible succession of things that he has to do—promises, concessions—and then it becomes a book.

Nobody ever paid for the price of a book.

How precious a book is in light of the offering, in the light of the one who has the privilege of this offering. The library tells you of this offering.

Very good is less than good.

A good question is a *Why anything?* kind of question.

A good question defies the greatest answer.

What is modern or not modern, what is traditional or not traditional, is put in the form of a question, but never in the form of a solution.

The period in architecture is never over, it's simply the method of change, the interest in change. What is desired has been given a new outlet.

A work should raise a question. I do not do anything conclusive, but something which raises a question.

Potentiality is infinitely more important than what is done.

What is done goes through a path of nothing but obstructions. What keeps you up is something that you never give in to. As long as the thread still holds, whatever that thread is, you make compromises.

I never make compromises, but I make substitutions for the time which are no bother to me, but I make a great issue of them so it appears as if I'm giving up a lot. But the harm is done just the same in giving up something.

What could have been in your path which could have given you something that could have carried it on to a better conclusion than the design you have?

How beautiful the mind is. The aspirations built in man, his motivation to be, is the core of all ritual and all design.

In every man's life there is the sense that somehow, within the sphere of his singularity, there is a completeness that's tremendously valuable, though it may not be marketable.

There is a difference between criticism and judgment. Judgment is *verboten*.

The Supreme Court is ridiculous, and so is the court in general. You want to feel that you are protected from arbitrary acts, but the sense of laws and rules made to punish is inadequate.

If I were attacked in the most arbitrary way, I would feel tremendous injustice, and that is a waste because I want to finish my work—which, of course, is never finished. I know a white-haired man is an easy mark, but when I walk down the street I feel as though I am absolved because everyone knows I have work to do.

I was always looking for Gessett's *History of England*. No book of history ever meant more to me. I had only one volume of it. The second volume was to start with the American Revolution, but the gallantry and the knightly acts of the period before that time fascinated me.

I went through Wanamaker's one day and saw Gessett's *History of England*, and I said, *Boy, this is something I'd pay anything for!* I didn't want to look at the book for fear I'd be disappointed, but I did. There were color drawings, there were photographs. In the older book there were all drawings, no photographs, and I realized how degenerate the damn thing was.

I was interested in the old Gesset's *History of England*, with only those illustrations made by Genvoviel, who knew a horse very well; he knew a rider; he knew the actions of a knight with an axe, a shield and a sword; and he knew the gamble of living in the scenes he portrayed.

I can never forget a drawing he made of Carroll who was killed in the Battle of Hastings before William the Conqueror, and how arbitrarily he was treated. When his friends wanted to bury him in the chapel that meant so much to him, the French refused his burial because the French king, who was the victor, resented a breach of promise which Carroll had made to him years before in a collaboration between England and France. I wanted the book for no other reason than this illustration.

I picked up this book which is crowded with illustrations, and the history of England went by the board—it didn't mean a damn thing.

When I looked through these old illustrations they reminded me of fairy tales. I thought they were the most wonderful things.

I always wanted to be an illustrator of fairy tales.

And possibly, if I could ever muster the talent, to be the illustrator of history.

Reprinted with permission, The Library
Phillips Exeter Academy
Exeter, New Hampshire

John C. Cook: You have just returned from Dacca, where you are buildng the Second Capital of Pakistan [now Bangladesh], begun in 1962. Are you satisfied with those buildings now being built?

Sher-E-Bangladesh
Dacca, Bangladesh
1962-74

I saw the buildings recently. I think they are wonderful, and now I recognize that my idea of landscaping is completely different from what I first thought. I want nothing but grass as a setting, a great carpet in front of a strong geometry.

JC: You've just decided that?

Yes, now. Before, I thought I needed everything. But I don't need the picturesque.

JC: But the people who will live there might want some trees.

If they want trees, then that's their concern. I must make it so strong that they don't want them.

Heinrich Klotz: Your famous Yale Art Gallery comes to mind at this point. Specifically, the enormous bare brick wall on Chapel Street which comes down straight next to the sidewalk—no trees, just a narrow strip of grass. The architecture students have fiercely objected to this wall because it is so alien to the pedestrian standing there waiting for a bus. No bench, no shade, no space, just a wall. It may be a wonderful wall, but it's hostile and too monumental. How would you answer this criticism?

Yale Art Gallery
New Haven, CT
1951-53

Personally, I must answer, *Nonsense.* Yet I must give another answer, because I always respect the other man's opinion. If it's the collective opinion of more than one person, I have no regard for it whatsoever. If it's the opinion of one person, I have a great regard for it.

I don't think it's monumental; I don't think it's anywhere near monumental. A wall is a wall. I consider rain as important to the wall, so I introduced those ledges to wash the wall at intervals. I could have left the wall bare—just for monumentality.

HK: This is a picture of your design for a high-rise building for the Universal Atlas Cement Company. Would you explain it to us?

Office Building
Kansas City, KS
1966-73

It's a building which personifies, in a way, how a structural order must have the power to make itself, not as a willful design but as a characteristic. And it's a kind of belief in the potentiality of man willing an order, a psychological order asking for a physical order. At the same time, it recognizes that the characteristics of a physical order are the measure of it. It is desire calling on nature, the maker of all presences. In this case, it was allowing a physical phenomenon to evolve without interference; but knowing that the spaces which evolve are useful for man.

HK: It is not a Utopian design?

It is not, in any sense, Utopian. Before design, there is existence as form with its undeniable elements; there is, as yet, no presence. Design is to give presence. It calls on the physical orders for approval so that the nature of the spaces and their making are one. The height of a ceiling in a room was chosen basically as eleven feet, which became the module of the tetrahedron.

HK: So you didn't need a central core?

I had no need for an ordained central core. The vertical spaces needed for elevators were inherent in the course of the spiraling of the structure upward. Nothing was broken in order to accommodate. The acceptance of the tetrahedron also reveals spatial opportunities. The structure teaches. This is the natural shape which a tetrahedral system will make without interference.

HK: So it does not need to be held up by a backbone?

No. The building makes itself strong by reason of its triangulation. The spiral form is natural to the tetrahedron, so the shape is not mine at all.

JC: You are well-known for having a very personal way of explaining what you do. You said earlier. *The designer gives presence by calling on nature to satisfy the requirements of man.* Would you expand on your conception of the role of the architect?

To sense the spaces that the desires of man present...to find the inseparable parts, or the form of the *society* of spaces, good for the activities of man. When he designs, he has always the inseparable parts in mind. He calls on nature to find a means to make.

JC: Is this nature, for you, something constant or is it a set of historical circumstances?

What is has always been. A validity true to man presents itself to a man in circumstances. A man can be a catalyst to a validity. Yet it has to await its realization. It has to be given presence.

JC: *To be given?* Somebody has to give presence.

Presence against existence! Yes. Somebody has to. But validity is always there as though it were in the air. But, circumstantially, it could only grow to the realization when one says, *I realize it is so.* The artist is only a vehicle for what always has been. Nothing can really be given presence unless it already exists potentially.

JC: Does the artist provide the realization in any individual way or is he simply the agent who taps what is there?

The artist senses human validity. Validity transcends time. What is has always been. What was has always been. What will be has always been.

JC: In this sense the artist is a philosopher. Where is he as a maker?

I agree. The artist works by motivation, which is the drive to his work, but the artist by his work does not satisfy motivation. He is always greater than his work, therefore he seeks more opportunity for his expression.

JC: Can science lead the artist to more decisive answers and expressions?

The wish in the fairy tale is the beginning of science. Man knows quite well that he's not going to fly just by wishing it, but he must still satisfy that wish. Man's first sense must have been Beauty, a sense of total harmony. Next to it Wonder, then the realization of the opening of the doors of the treasure of form which inspires Design, the process of shaping into Presence. Presence emerges from a wish and Rule. Rule guides the maker to seek Order. Order is nature, nonconscious. Rule is man's order.

Man lives to express. What motivates expression serves Art. A work of art is an offering to Art. Everything turns into itself, you know. There is no sort of ending.

HK: I have the impression that you no longer distinguish between subject and object, you do not acknowledge the difference between human subject and the objective world. I am reminded of Heidegger's ontology.

Yes.

HK: In another sense, it reminds me of Mies van der Rohe's credo. He might say, *What I did was actually nothing individualistically important. I only did what time and my presence have given me. And I just expressed what had to be expressed.* The artist, when you interpret him that way, is humble, and presents his work as an offering.

Yes, yes. He is tremendously grateful. Grateful is not the word, but he feels serving. What you're saying is exactly right, and your analogy with Mies makes me feel terribly good, because I know that the kind of humility and sense of joy that he is expressing is the very essence of my thought. You cannot make a work of art except in joy. Mies is expressing a joy of being. He was in a certain position where a certain realization came about. That source of realization is a truth which is man's fact. Anything that happens is a truth.

HK: Did you want to do anything else, before you became an architect?

I would say that it happened quite circumstantially. There is no denying that I would have been either a painter, sculptor, musician, or architect, because of my love for that which yet is not. If I had to describe the very core of the decision, it would have to do most basically with that which is in question, that which is yet not. You see, it refutes need. It only deals with desires.

HK: By *needs,* do you mean everyday desires for money, shelter, bread, and all these other...

Need stands for what is already present, and it becomes a kind of measurement of the already present. Desire becomes a sense of the yet not made. That is the main difference between need and desire.

HK: Doesn't the architect ever build just for needs?

No. Never build for needs! As an art a space is made a touch of eternity. I think a space evoked its use. It transcends need. If it doesn't do that, then it has failed. One might say that architecture is directed by function more than painting is. A painting is made to be sensed for its motivation beyond seeing, just as space is made to inspire use. It's psychological. There is something about a building which is different from a painting. When a building is being built, there is an impatience to bring it into being. Not a blade of grass can grow near this activity. Look at the building after it is built. Each part that was built with so much anxiety and joy and willingness to proceed tries to say when you're using the building, *Let me tell you how I was made.* Nobody is listening because the building is now satisfying need. The desire in its making is not evident. As time passes, when it is a ruin, the spirit of its making comes back. It welcomes the foliage that entwines and conceals. Everyone who passes can hear the story it wants to tell about its making. It is no longer in servitude; the spirit is back.

HK: What do you do with a client who wants to have a building that's nothing but utilitarian, a pure instrument of everyday needs?

You build what he thinks he's getting. There's no problem there. I also get what I want.

HK: In other words, you are not talking about art when you are dealing with a client.

No, no.

HK: You're talking about his needs.

The art, then, is the art of trying to find the words in common, the words which get you away from your code, in order to reach him. That's very important, to you and to him.

JC: We have been talking about individual buildings. How would you build a city? Or let me put it in your own words: What is the nature of a city?

The city is the assembly of the institutions of man. In other words, the city is the place where the institution occurs to man. The gathering of men and legislation establishes the institution of what is wanted commonly. I believe *availability* is a more meaningful term today than institution. The measure of a city is the character of its availabilities, how sensitive it is to man's pursuit of well being. The traffic system and other needs are only the servants of availability.

JC: Where is the sociologist in this scheme?

He is an observer and advisor but not the planner. A social plan is an arrogant plan. One has to make a distinction between a way of life and a way of living. One is general, the other is personal.

HK: By making such a distinction, do you mean that you achieve a variety of architectural foms inspired by the urges of what you call availability? If so, one would not have to invent..

Yes! You don't invent. You don't force invention without motivation coming from a sense of commonality. You don't invent circumstances, but when they happen, they reveal human nature.

JC: Let's take your Philadelphia City Plan of 1952-53 as a specific example.

Plan for Midtown Center
Philadelphia, PA
1952-53

First, I love my city and I want it to be good. This means to me that its acts in the process of development are true to its particular character, sensitive to its scale in relation to its people. For example, it is a place where one can serve the validity of an open field without limiting it in size because land is expensive, regardless of how much you know about the cost of real estate, or whether it's sensible or not to put a playing field in a city. If you know that a child who lives in the city loves to play as much as one in the country, you cannot make that playground big enough. It's a powerful right.

I have no questions about the existence of the city, not only because it is there, but also because the city is inevitable. It answers a prime inspiration: to meet.

HK: Would you tear down Philadelphia in order to build a new one, if you had the power to do it?

No, because you wouldn't know where to begin. The city itself becomes a point of departure. There is so much left in the city already which determines its paths of happenings. The results cannot be anticipated. The circumstantial things which happen cannot be anticipated. This is the difference between a plan and what happens because you cannot plan circumstances.

HK: These considerations which you mention now are not evident in the plan as it has been published. When I look at this plan I have the impression that the city means the traffic in it and how the traffic flows.

I have one remark to make, right from the start, which has to do with a broader view of the 1952 plan. I believe that a city is measured by its availabilities. The plan does not touch on this question. It doesn't give anything but a sense of land disposition in the order of movement. So, therefore, I try to find a physical validity to movement. I distinguish certain streets from others by the sense of their movement value. Now, in this plan, the importance of stopping was emphasized. It's getting somewhere, then stopping. And the design of stopping is what I was really concerned about.

HK: That's the new aspect about it. When you drive around Manhattan, for instance, you are forced to go on moving because everybody else moves.

Yes. You have a hard time stopping. When you want to stop, you've got to keep moving. You see, the whole thing is not very smart.

When you think about the meaning of moving, in relation to stopping, you get a much bolder solution. Any building, even an important one, would be torn down if it obstructed the order of movement, which includes stopping.

HK: What does stopping mean in your sense?

Stopping means that there is a strategic station where the car can be parked in relation to a sector of the city.

HK: Then, that could mean a parking garage?

It could mean that in the system of movement, the intersection of a street could be a station for stopping. If you say it is a *garage,* you would hate it. But if it is a building for stopping, in a city of movement, then it's something else. It could be just as important as the most important place in the city.

I would say that, in 1951, I sorted out the idea that the streets are rivers, in a sense, and these rivers need docks and wharfs, need station points. Out of this grew the sense that there were strategic areas where the docks were larger than at other places. At that point, I conceived that the station point could also be in the form of a stadium surrounded by parking; the center, with little capacity for parking, was the stadium. In a sense the shape of the stopping place provides the space for the stadium for nothing.

HK: There were those enormous round towers.

Yes. They weren't just parking garages. There was obviously no sense in wasting natural light on a parked car, so I planned to use the outside edge of the round towers for hotels, motels, or even offices. In the inner core were to be the services for the car, and on the outside were to be the living and working spaces.

JC: Returning to the traffic pattern for a moment, don't you think that an uninterrupted flow through the city is important?

No, I think the uninterrupted flow should be outside the city. Inside a city, there should be very organized flow to places of stopping.

HK: As vehicular traffic increases, won't our cities finally be stuffed with cars? We may eventually have to ban all cars from the inner city. This is certainly the case in Europe.

The closer you get to the heart of the city, the more the contours of the land must change. This part of the city could have its spaces which personify the country—maybe on the third, fourth, or fifth level. The contours below, which are now the first, second, or third levels, must surrender a broad area in order to make the services to it possible, no matter what the transportation system may be.

HK: Does this eliminate the pedestrians?

No. It's a city for pedestrians. But on new levels.

HK: This means that you would have to change the city to quite an extent. It could mean that the houses we see out of this window would have to be destroyed for such a new traffic system.

In the impetuous acts of building in cities, you would hurt buildings very little if you modified the first levels and established new entrances on the levels above, leaving the vehicular traffic below. The top level would have no cars at all and would be truly a street, not a road; it would be purely pedestrian. I think it important to consider streets as something which can be used to bring about great changes. The intersection is a piece of city-owned real estate. By acquiring the four corners, the city can add property to the making of a new street-building for the needs of movement.

HK: Then the new levels you speak of also become a building.

Yes. The street will become a building, certainly. I see that the city doesn't realize how wealthy it is. It should consider the land above the streets as its property. What is the real estate value of one-third of the city?

HK: But if the street becomes a building, where is the open sky, the fresh air?

Wait a minute. The mere fact that the real estate is there as real estate and that it can be built over is not realized. It's only considered as a street, sky over it, very beautiful, and please don't change it, you see. The streets themselves have not been used, even though they are worth billions of dollars. Fresh air and sky would be above the vehicular level.

JC: One approach to city planning is to determine what has been called *the anatomy of ambience.*

It doesn't ring true to me, *anatomy of ambience.* Ambience is something that must be felt, and it is not a physical characteristic that can have an anatomy. If you would say *spirit of ambience,* I would like it better. I don't believe in sociology as judge. No sympathy for this whatsoever. I wouldn't like somebody to say there should be a certain social pattern or even to anticipate a social pattern. I don't think you can do it.

JC: You can't plan a city sociologically?

Only if you're fascist. It's the only way you can do it. You have no idea about one individual meeting another individual. This is completely unpredictable.

JC: One denies spontaneity when the sociologist plans the city?

Absolutely, you deny every part of it. And nobody can ever make a pattern, except a completely rigid and inhuman pattern. As long as the city planners try to make a science out of it, and not make science work for that which is human, I have no use for it. City planners who make a walk in the sky, say, a linear walk, are not really thinking humanly. People do not walk in straight lines, except when they meet a train, but they're not enjoying at that moment. City planners imagine that there's a great enjoyment in being up in the air. It's the same thing when New Haven builds towers for old people. Planners think of this from the sociological viewpoint, distinguishing old people from young people, and so forth.

HK: Let's say New York asked you to build the five-mile renewal strip on the East Side. How would you proceed?

I would first proceed by being elated.

JC: Do you really think that an architect can be a *homo universale*? Is he able to know everything he has to know in order to build such a city? Is an architect able to know it without asking sociologists, psychologists, city planners, traffic engineers, and statisticians?

When you build a house, you are able to talk to the family. When you build a church, you are able to talk to a committee. But, when you build a city, you are probably unable to talk to the inhabitants—let's say 50,000 people. That means you have to abstract the whole problem. Suddenly, you're all by yourself. But in a way, a house is not different from a city. I know that I will not have many people here, and there's a certain limit which you say is *house*. In the form *house*, I also think of commonness. I think of every person who can live in this house, not just a particular person. In the same way, every person should be able to live in the city.

HK: When you build a city for 50,000 people, you have to think about what kind of facilities these people will need: shops, services, streets, etc. Simple, straightforward things. Some architects now start to employ sociologists for basic information. A huge block like Le Corbusier's Unite at Marseilles includes a lot of shops which are not used. He thought that all those people would need those shops on the center floor, but they are hardly used. That means he probably reached a statistical solution only. So many people, so many shops. He didn't consider that people want to leave the building in order to shop—the desire to go outside. The statistics forgot the psychology. Maybe Le Corbusier should have consulted a psychologist, as some architects do today.

It's a pity, though. I don't think you should. I would never have that problem, because I know the difference between shopping and buying. Maybe Le Corbusier misunderstood. Shopping isn't necessarily where you buy. It's the very nature of commercialism, that it cannot be isolated. You don't go to the baker next door just because he's there—you go to the best baker. It doesn't work mathematically. It works until you sense the realization: What is its nature!

If it's unsuccessful, it's not in the nature. The crocodile must want to be a crocodile for reasons of the crocodile. It has nothing to do with man's reasons for the crocodile. It's most remarkable that order can be the same for everyone and design can be so different. What the crocodile wanted to be meant that his predilections, his urges for wanting to be, were somehow different from yours. There must be nothing but a state of wonder in you. You must be so full of wonder that you wouldn't want to touch a crocodile. You wouldn't destroy one. You can almost say it's a condemnation of humanity when it destroys animals which are really so innocent.

HK: You're not a hunter?

I'm not a hunter, but I understand the cul-de-sac. I would be the one to defend the hunter because I know that man can be this way. He is not inhuman; he is very human, only his predilections run in this way, and he cannot avoid being himself.

HK: It's a kind of fate?

It's not fate. It's a kind of nature which expresses itself. I believe in education because it implies method. You cannot force a man to know what is not part of his predilection. People say you have to try to develop your mind. That does not ring true. A man cannot be changed, as far as his predilections are concerned. He can exercise what he has natural talent for. He develops by being able to express it. He will pick up a book and read it. But you can make him hate this for the rest of his life if he has to read something not a part of his predilections. It's not a matter of training, but if a man is jealous of those around him, of their singularities, he will pick the book up; otherwise, he won't bother with it.

I would never enjoy being a lawyer, for example. Some people would die for the law. I never felt the least jealousy of the doctor. But I felt terribly jealous of one who could write. This kind of beauty got me to the point where I couldn't see straight. Why was it so difficult to know where to put me? I had to be put with my own little private war going on with myself, with others, and that made me strong. So, if you show me a few tricks, like picking up a pencil right, I'm operating. That means I'm happy.

I must overcome my shyness near a tape recorder; it bothers me. Therefore, I wrote something for you. Let me read it. *Man's spirit created architecture. Its wonder crystallized in the great styles. The styles of architecture in the future are unpredictable. The inspirations which will give presence to the yet not thought of, yet not made, will depend on the visions of our leaders. An inspiring leader will be the natural collaborator for an inspired architect who by his work will reveal the spirit of architecture in a new way.*

JC: Sorry to interrupt you, but what do you mean by a *leader?*

By *leader* I mean a person with vision. The great leaders all had vision. Even the most despotic.

HK: Of course, we might think immediately of Hitler and of his architecture, a complete failure.

Yes, but he felt he did not need an inspired architect. That was his trouble. If he were really a great leader, he would have realized the greatness of another leader.

JC: In the twentieth century, we have had many great leaders who didn't inspire good architecture. Roosevelt didn't, Pius XII certainly didn't. Mussolini and Franco didn't, and Stalin may have been the worst.

Maybe it's not as direct as I put it there. By a leader I don't necessarily mean a national leader. I mean a leader like Jonas Salk. He's a leader in a true sense of the word because he was really not a person who thought of himself first. A leader isn't just a man who wants something; it's usually a man who wants to give something. Don't think of Hitler and Stalin, think of Oppenheimer and Salk, Beethoven and Newton. Then you have what truly are leaders.

JC: Well, you are talking about great men.

We're always talking of the great man. Hitler was bound to be a failure. What he wanted to attain would not answer the immediate comprehensions of commonality. He proposed *a giant race,* for instance. People are not giants. It's an assumption which you cannot apply to man.

HK: Let us be specific about the distinction you make between needs and desires. Your Unitarian Church at Rochester, New York, consists of one great inner assembly room surrounded by an outer shell of small rooms used for church school, kindergarten, and social functions. The outer wall of these rooms is broken up with alcoves projecting the window line. By doing this, you achieved a very special interior space and, at the same time, that famous cubistic exterior.

At first, these alcoves seemed superfluous to the people. In talking with them, I learned that they didn't know what to do with them. They were totally consumed with the attitude that every room and every part of a room has to have a function. They were somehow frustrated, wondering how to use them, until they learned that they had no specific purpose. But the children in the kindergarten like to hide and play in them. They were drawn to spaces which were apparently superfluous. The the adults began to appreciate them by experiencing these spaces. The whole room would have been without character, as rooms can be, if these *superfluous* alcoves had not added spatial interest, evoking the unexpected in their light.

Unitarian Church
Rochester, NY
1959-67

I worked on the Unitarian Church in two stages. The first stage was just the entrance and the main building. Then I added another piece in it, which was done later. In both cases, the amount of money budgeted was very small. But in both cases, the people who administrated the spending of the funds and the planning of each little portion were very exacting about their needs. In my first designs, I had much bigger spaces, more wonderfully conceived, I think, richer in environment, and capable of delighting so many more people, but I had to give them up because of the frugal means. If I have to get more frugal, I look to the Shakers to help me out. Previously it would have been richer, with many more facets to which one could respond.

But I knew I couldn't give up those alcoves. What you say about them is true, I think. Their use—and their appreciation—can come from desire and not just merely from need. If you didn't have these alcoves, the rooms themselves wouldn't have been able to transcend need at all, in any way. They were essential in my plan all along.

I wasn't dealing with a personal place for somebody, but with a place for many. Even when serving the dictates of individuals, you still have no client, in my sense of the word. The client is human nature. It makes no difference if you are serving one person or many. This church building is a little world within a world, just as a house is its little world within a world. But, nevertheless, they are very different. The one makes a home. The other makes a place away from home, where home is also. So you never lose sight of the home, because a person coming from his home to a place away from his home must feel he is in a place where home is not away from him.

JC: The one who gives you the commission...?

Instead of saying *the one who*, let's say *the way of life that gives you the commission*. Forget about who it is, whether it's a king or a simple man. You don't take a commission from a person. You take it from the way of life. That means that when you are designing a house you are designing it for the person, but you are designing it also for the person who will take it after this person. Otherwise, you don't serve architecture at all.

You can't make terrific castles which no one can afford, because the way of life won't let you; it tells you that you can't do it. There are no kings any more. Today, an ordinary person—a schoolteacher, for instance—can tell the architect what he wants. Now this is the way of life telling the architect this. So it really isn't a schoolteacher, nor the shopkeeper, nor the baker, but the way of life which commissions you. The expression of an era can come only from architecture, which has the way of life as its commissioner.

JC: There are clients who behave like kings, and might not even reflect the era in their wants, who have extravagant and fanciful ideas. How would you talk them out of their fanciful ideas which would ruin the building.

To order *extravagance* is unmotivating. It is not the issue. The issue is truth, is it true to the era?

JC: Or let's say you have a client who wants separate facilities for blacks and whites in a bus station or a doctor's office.

I would tell him absolutely, *That is not true. I couldn't do it for the world.*

JC: Or you have a client who wants to build a Miami Beach Hotel with a French Provincial lobby.

If he thinks it's the way of life, he's wrong, because somebody is telling you, *Print this;* and you say, *I can't print it.* To me, that is something which is not going to distinguish our era from another era. No sir. It won't do anything of the sort. The same thing is true in the theater. When you copulate on the stage as an expression of the freedom of expression, theater is no more, symbols are defiled. The act becomes incidental and circumstantial, a whorehouse in the wrong place. Theater does not depend on the literal. In fact, the very essence of theater is analogous to my understanding of the essence of light: It is infinitely more brilliant than it would be if I had to illustrate it.

JC: We would like to know more about the process you go through from the primary stage on intuituion to the final result, or, in your own words, from desire to realization. How do you go from the wish to the building.

Let's take the specific examples of your two skyscrapers, the one with the tetrahedral design which was never built, and the Kansas City tower. The first is a fantasy, the realization of a wish. The second has gone through all the stages of the demand for practical needs. It will be built. These two buildings turn out to be very different. The Kansas City tower is more familiar to a city block. Why are they so different?

That's a wonderful question. Why are they so different? This is wonderful. You might say that the tetrahedral skyscraper was something which had truly to do with the fairy tale: You wanted a skyscraper to come about and not have to learn anything about skyscrapers. Just wave your wand and have it. It is the employment of freeing nature, the way nature makes things—with a very inaccessible answer to what dictates its making. Its dictates are tremendously irrefutable. It's very far away from history. I knew that one had to take care of the wind when a skyscraper is built, but I didn't know anything about the formulas for wind. I didn't want to graft on a wind idea but to find an order which takes care of the wind. I knew a triangle was nondeformable, and I trusted that this would do it. It was really waving a wand. I never deviated from the natural spiral growth of the tetrahedrons.

HK: Could it actually have been built?

Yes. But, you see, it's out of range with the society of leadership—which is really what I mean when I say *leader*. The society of leadership is not there. You see, I am always dependent on someone else for the carrying out of a project; that someone is a man with his own predilections.

What I wanted in my tetrahedron design was freedom to discover. There are drawings which one makes having no client. They are marvelous drawings, manifestations of sheer heart. Think of Boullee or Ledoux, who did drawings which haven't the demand for serving anything other than the spirit of architecture. What is very big in the mind simply must come out.

HK: There are weaknesses in Utopian architecture which one has to recognize. There are architects who want to force their Utopian ideas, and architecture which wants to resemble the greatness of architecture rather than the realness of life. Even Boullee's gigantic exaggerations tend to create an unreal world of pure fantasy.

He's still a man, that means the wonder of a singularity revealed can touch another. It's the judgement which is bad. Just now, you were judging—too ready to classify. That is very much the habit of historians. They make up their minds about what they want to kill and what they want to save.

JC: But there is one kind of Utopian architecture which grows out of reality, and another kind which is imposed upon it.

If you eliminate the fairy tale from reality, I'm against you. It's the most sparkling reality there is. Utopia somehow is a reality, it's in reality. That's the point: Utopia is real.

JC: Is there any Utopian architecture today?

No. I would say that Utopia inspires. But Utopia itself? No, there's no Utopia. But if something were really Utopian, I would excuse everything about it. It would be, in a sense, an expression of youth. It would be like Boullee and Ledoux.

HK: Today there is a misunderstanding of Utopia, taking its clues from a hypothesized vision of life in the future, a vision determined purely by expected needs. It is conceived as a mechanical megastructure of functions—like Warren Chalk's Plug-in Living Unit. It is more futuristic than Utopian.

That's another thing which you cannot say. Because you can only build for the present. It isn't a question of the present conceived as though it were a formula, and, in the other case, the future comprehended in a formula. There is futurism in Beethoven, but he's not a futurist in any sense. He knows the sense of something; he knows his realm so beautifully that he can transcend the present. That's all. Whoever builds never builds for the future.

JC: Let's say you are given a commission, a specific project. Do you begin as if you had no client—with dream drawings fresh out of desire?

It must begin there.

JC: Must every project begin with that kind of....

Absolutely. It must begin without a client, because the client must not order. If the client orders something, it will just add up to an assembly of given elements, and he hires you only because you can choose materials and make it look handsome. You've accomplished nothing, absolutely nothing. You're not in any sense an architect. You're an exterior decorator, maybe.

JC: Did you conceive the Kansas City tower in terms of its environment? How does it relate to the street and to the other buildings? Did you worry about that?

No, not really. I didn't worry about it because there has to be a society of interrespect which the buildings themselves give you. If around you there are buildings which you do not honor, then it's a natural tendency to establish yourself clear and simple as being the one which you hope is honored. But when you work in the presence of something else you honor, then be very deferring, as though buildings themselves were people, as though they were living things.

JC: Was there nothing around you to which you could refer positively?

No, there wasn't.

JC: In looking through one of your sketchbooks, I noticed some drawings of Roman work—especially of Hadrian's Villa at Tivoli. I wondered if these Roman ruins exert a special influence on your work, particularly on the buildings at Dacca and Ahmedabad.

No. I would say *influence* is another one of those words which can be misinterpreted by everyone. It could mean that you sat down and copied it. I'm not constructed in this way. I'm not one who takes things verbatim from some place. I think things out for myself. Even if I read a scientific statement, I would draw out of it what's me about the scientific statement. I wouldn't take it merely as a matter of fact or use it as a source from which to work.

JC: I have seen a comparison of Dacca and Hadrian's Villa; they were printed side by side as a kind of explanation....

Ridiculous!

JC: You think that's ridiculous?

Absolutely!

JC: That's an easy way out. Why?

Maybe some external features, or some fragment, maybe. The circle, for instance. I would never think of using a circle I saw somewhere else unless it conformed to a sense of order in which I am looking for something that answers it. The difference is very great. If you look at it very carefully, some of the circles are really not a circle. They're even broken in the center, and I chose them for earthquake reasons. In Hadrian's Villa, you see the use of some circular forms, which I know very well. But who owns the circle? It's ridiculous.

JC: But you can't deny that your brick arches remind one immediately of Roman masonry work.

It's the nature of masonry work. When you use brick, you come to certain solutions which sometimes look like Roman brickwork, because brick is brickwork. I don't hesitate to do it, even if it does look Roman, because it's the order of brick. Where in Roman brickwork would you see the segmental arch used like this without having much buttressing of masonry? That restraining member made a composite order, brick and concrete. The use of concrete stems from knowing brick for what it is. I would never be able to do this, nor come to this realization, unless I respected brickwork in general, Roman or otherwise. Nobody possesses it. This is not a shape of any kind. It's not a motif. It's in the order of brick.

HK: The large openings in the screen wall at Ahmedabad and Dacca seem to have a predecessor in an ornamental motif at Bryn Mawr College in Pennsylvania. In your dormitories, there are door handles made out of flat plates into which circles and semicircles are cut.

Erdman Hall Dormitories
Bryn Mawr, PA 1960-65

I know. That's true. I have a tendency, even in my drawings, to make a round opening, to make an opening somehow, or an arch....

HK: This is a combination of shapes, appearing for the first time in the door handles at Bryn Mawr. Isn't that door handle somehow a screen, a miniature of your great walls in India and Dacca?

No, that's going too far. It isn't that way.

HK: But regardless of size and function, can't one have a certain liking for a particular form?

Oh, certainly, but I have an entirely different interpretation of that. Even if the shape may be the same, it has more to do with structure and the sense of forces within the plane. If I had a door with a rectangular panel system in it, where the panels are already square or rectangular, I would readily make an opening conforming to the given shape. But if I have a flat surface and have to punch a hole through it, I want to ease the opening, I want to arch it as though it needs no frame. It's the sense of forces that I see in the door—these forces are playing and resisting my making an opening, as if I were making an incision in the door. The door is apprehensive about how much it will be destroyed. I make it the most benevolent opening I can, and that means this shape.

It isn't a liking it so much as a belief in it. It comes from belief in it. I would never play around with new shapes just to avoid being stereotyped. As a means of forced variety, I could never do it.

JC: In the wall of the house of Ahmedabad, there is the suspended horizontal concrete member.

Institute of Management
Ahmedabad, India 1962-74

The restraining member which keeps the arch from pushing out. It brings it back into the wall. I call it a composite order. I recognize in which way concrete is helping brick to be used again. Brick has within its own death, because it is not resourceful enough. If I had not found the composite order, the whole project would have been concrete.

JC: Why was it necessary to have that long segmental arch at the roof line?

On top of each house is a terrace. They sleep on the roofs and, therefore, I needed a balustrade, and I needed that opening created by the segmental arch so that the air doesn't get blocked. If it were a railing, there would be no privacy. If I put a curtain on the railing, there would be no air. Somebody might use rails, but I didn't want another material. I wanted to extend the order of brick and not have many, many materials enter the scene—like a man who is very rich and has too many dishes to eat from. No. I wanted to eat frugally, so I extended the order as far as I could. That, to me, is symphonic. It's the same thing as writing a waltz, and you don't try to write a symphony into it. You are dealing with a single kind of composition of materials: brick and concrete.
The concrete helped me avoid great heavy walls and achieve as much air as possible. The concrete was like the strappings on a trunk. You make it out of wood, but you use metal to reinforce the wood. That's also a composite order.

JC: In the tripartite composition of the facade, if I may call it that, the concrete restraining member of the central section seems to be unnecessary; the flanking concrete members are enough to hold it up.

Yes, I could have done it that way, because the two restraining members, one on each side, are all you need; it has enough muscle. But it really does need it for another reason. I need the opening for the air in the center section as well.

HK: Do you sometimes think back to your early training, the time when you were drawing Corinthian capitals and Beaux Arts plans?

Just in the sense of appreciation of the meaning of order. That training made me understand order—that is, an aesthetic order.

HK: Decorative order?

No, no, because it wasn't really decoration, it was ornament. It was ornamentation of the joint, of the event; that's what it really was. I recognized that a capital had to hold its volutes out to invite the span. It had to reach out, receive it, and the receiving of it had to be bigger than what the column was. This was a tremendous realization, and it's no different now in concrete from what it was a long time ago in columns.

HK: You wouldn't use a column any more?

You can't. If you use a column today, it's never really a stone column or a brick column, because it doesn't have enough force, enough power. If you were to make a big building today using brick columns, your spans would be short and your construction would be very heavy.

HK: Could we say that the clarity of the joint, your celebration of the joint in your architecture, today refers to the meaning of a capital?

Yes. To make it more understandable, it is really the celebration of the meeting of material.

HK: What is the function of those huge walls with circular openings?

In those hot countries, you need a porch which protects the building and the people from the sun. At Ahmedabad, I did not plan for air conditioning because no money was available for it. Here, the worth of air conditioning is almost nil because the orientation of the buildings is right. The fact that you're always thinking in terms of never allowing the sun to come in makes the maintenance of air conditioning much less. These walls are sun screens, and they give you a wall of reflected light, which cuts the glare that comes from the openings.

HK: That defines the function. Yet, they became incredibly impressive images.

I know. But if I had been looking only from the functional standpoint I would have made a brise-soleil. But, since I was thinking in terms of architecture, it has to become a porch. And the porch is a room. Out of it came something which was more than just taking care of the function. You can take care of it with screens or some adjunct means, which is not in any sense a kind of architectural identity. But I created buildings within buildings. The sun screen became the exterior wall of the porch which protects the interior building from the sun. In a sense, the porch is an offering to the sun.

Of course, there are other ways of shielding a building; Ed Stone's American Embassy building at New Delhi is a good example. He built a beautiful interior court. I mean it's beautiful if you don't stay too long. It's beautiful because there's constant water play for quite a large area. There's a very large pool and from it comes a very diffuse spray, and above the pool is a brise-soleil through which the sun shines. You do not see the sun, you see only the spray, and there's a glow of light in there that's really quite mysterious. But when you get close and you see the brise-soleil, you hate it because the sky is broken up into little diamonds and looks very, very ugly. He could have gotten something extremely beautiful by letting the water make the porch.

I made porches out of brick. Concrete was very expensive. I used it only for floors. I used no concrete columns anywhere. Brick was used for the walls and supports. And since there is no beam because there is no column, the arch became the opener, the making of opening.

HK: From the beginning, you had to deal with a rather conservative construction method.

Yes. It's an ancient construction method.

HK: Therefore, you have arches which remind one of the Roman arch.

Right. The word *conservative* is not the word to use. What might be called a conservative or traditional construction answers the demand of today for a larger opening; this might have been demanded in ancient days as well, but they didn't know how to answer it. Now, concrete becomes the reviver of the potentiality of brick. The concrete member holds the thrust of the arch in and allows it to extend almost to the end walls without sending a thrust against them.

HK: So you were able to keep the walls thin and save material.

Well, I was able to make large openings. That means you could open your mouth bigger because that brought in more air. I found a partner in concrete for the brick.

JC: Could you tell us something about the concept of Ahmedabad?

Institute of Management Ahmedaba, India 1962-74

It is a national institute of business management established to bring together men of various castes who have talent in the field of management. It is patterned after the school at Harvard. They had professors from Harvard help initiate and demonstrate methods of teaching.

I had the whole campus to design myself. It was somewhere in the neighborhood of sixty-five acres of land, on which there were to be a school, dormitories, houses for teachers and servants....

JC: All around a natural lake?

No, it's a lake I made. I make a lake. The dormitories are right next to the school, as if they and the school were one. In the total plan, the dormitories and classrooms are held together as a unit distinguishable from the rest of the campus, which is composed of faculty, administrative, and servants' housing.

JC: And you respected the caste system when you made this plan?

I simply took the country as it is. I want to create an atmosphere in which the students will not feel that living and learning are separate. That is what the dormitory-classroom complex achieves. Even the porches serve as classrooms. The porch of each dormitory house becomes a transitional space where living and learning meet. The porch not only protects you from the sun, but also can be a community room. Next to the porch there is a tea room; tea is the national drink, you might say. It is served very often. Each student's room opens directly onto the porch, thereby avoiding the need for corridors.

But let me describe the whole dormitory plan. The dormitories are made up of a series of complete houses. They are an assembly of houses turning toward the breeze. Everything is closely knit, because the closer the buildings, the better they protect from the sun.

JC: The plan of each house consists of rectangular rooms opening onto a triangular porch facing a square.

Yes, and in that square are the toilets and other facilities. The entrance stairway is in the triangular porch. You enter the porch and you are indoors.

JC: Is the unusual juxtaposition of these two shapes, square and triangle, demanded by the sun and the wind?

Yes, they serve as vents to draw the air, and also as shade.

HK: Could you just describe the classroom building plan?

Yes. The building combines classrooms, library, administration, dining hall, kitchen and center court. The major entrance is a ramp which leads from the parking lot into the center court.

I didn't want a bare court because they can be devastatingly hot. I put an amphitheater in the court itself, and this amphitheater is nothing more than an awning-protected place where everything can happen. It's really a place within the court which is protected from the sun. I did not want an amphitheater staring at you, not being used.

HK: Also, within the court in front of the library there is a surprising arrangement of arches which turn away from the axial pattern of the ground plan.

Again, it is a porch which protects from the sun and turns toward the breeze. The arches refer to the oblique axis of the dormitory plan.

JC: There is another suprising shape in the ground plan, the round kitchen attached to the square dining hall.

The kitchen is made like a big ventilator because they make so many foods which are highly spiced and so smelly that the kitchen is made as though it were a big fan. It's really a kitchen inside a vent.

JC: It's a great exhaust.

The client said that the kitchen should be a mile away! I told him that I could make it close and still have it a mile away! I then invented this idea, which he accepted. The kitchen is still sited away from the center of the campus, and the breeze carries the odor away. At the end of the plan, where the kitchen is, I have placed a cooling tower for the air conditioning of the dormitories and the administration areas. It is also made like a giant vent in which the air comes in at a certain point and aerates the warm water of the air conditioning plant. The water is pumped up to the top of the vent, then it flows down across multiple glass surfaces upon which the air can play and cool the water. Then I pipe the water to the air handling units, which regulate the temperature and give cool air to the interior.

HK: You put all the service buildings at the same end of the campus.

Yes, you want to keep the exhaust air away from the buildings. The cooling tower is also the water tower, by the way. It's a tank for the water supply; they have their own wells. So I integrated all those things.

Gandhinagar
Gujarat, India 1962-64

I used a similiar idea for a city in India, where those towers punctuated the entire area. It is a beautiful idea. It was to be a town on a large river, which is dry in the summertime. This city is known as Gandhinagar, which means *the City of Gandhi*. This river becomes flooded in the time of rain. The water comes from the Himalayas. It's a beautiful sight to see, because it comes, as they say, like *galloping horses*. Suddenly, you see this big gallop of horses coming down the dry river bed.

My idea was to capture this water at intersections, with structures over the water—kinds of bridges—and bring the water to the city, and hold it in tower reservoirs. This way, the city would never be dry in the summertime. I began the city with these important stations, the water towers, which would also be utility stations. Water is a gift to a city in India. Water does not always come in pies. Here, it is a river source, and it can be dramatized here, whereas in other cities it cannot be dramatized.

Another primary consideration was the mango trees. There is a law in India which prevents taking down a mango tree. Consequently, I made the sections of living depend on where these trees were. The sectors were also determined by the connections between these towers and the mango trees. The government buldings were to be built along the river. The monsoon rains, as they fell from the land to the high banks of the river, form very picturesque and sculptural erosions. My thought was to make a park out of these washaways, firming up the ground with brick construction, following the contours as they are, just making them firm so they wouldn't continue to wash away. They could have become the most magnificent nature-inspired playground you can possibly imagine. Those shapes! Of course, this didn't pan out. Now the army engineers are doing something there. They are starting to ruin this area. Really ruin it. It's horrible. I had even planned for the industry which would make the bricks to build the town, and the reject would have been used to firm up the river banks. It was to be a city of 500,000 people.

HK: What are they doing instead?

They are building a boring gridplan town.

HK: In a recent lecture, you discussed your project for the Congress Hall in Venice. Your first point was that you had to assemble a large crowd of people, and you went to the blackboard and drew a circle. The circle was somehow a symbol for you of the assembled crowd.

Yes.

HK: Then you went on to say that the building had to be on a long, narrow lot. So you cut off the upper and lower parts of the circle.

The remaining center part you kept as the basic concept of the ground plan. This seems to be an illustration of your way of thinking. Your conceiving, your thoughts about the needs of a building, somehow materialize and merge as primary forms.

That's very well put. I don't know how one identifies the first idea, but for me it is usually the sense of the building in its core, its full meaning, its nature, not its shape. Its nature was that of involvement, of participation. A simple shape which only emphasizes a direction doesn't have the nature of participation in it. It is, on the contrary, analogous to watching or hearing, not participation. The fact that I could adjust to a site which was narrow had to require that one side looked to the other. But the shape should not be adjusted to that narrow site in such a way that it becomes purely directional, because there would be no participation.

HK: Isn't it rather arbitrary to see an assembled crowd as a circle?

Participation may not mean that every person speaks up. If you are in a theater, you have no participation, you are observing. It may be true that you are involved because you feel the person next to you, but it's really pretty much centered around yourself, there's actually no participation. It is just a performance.

Palace of Congress
Venice, Italy
1968-74

The Congress Hall, which was started with a sense of form, which was a pit or a bull ring, had to adjust itself to a narrow area. In the center of this is the organizational position, and this center was the dimension I had to include to make sure that people saw people. It was a confrontation of people with people.

HK: It is an arena, a bull ring, as you say. Isn't a circle a bit too simple as an image for a crowd? Isn't it too rigid, this forcing people into a bull ring? Couldn't it be as it is in Hans Scharoun's Philharmonic Hall in Berlin? Although a large crowd of people assembles around a center, the crowd is broken up into smaller units. The primary emphasis is not on the simplicity of the whole, but on the complexity of many parts achieving assembly and participation.

I wouldn't do what Scharoun did, but I appreciate immensely what he tried to do. I could show you early sketches of what I myself had in mind for Venice. It was the same kind of thing, in which you did not hold rigidly to the geometric shape, but felt as though there were separate areas of people rather than a geometric disc plan.

But, you see, my sense is different. I don't see in a painterly way. I don't see it even as a sculptural thing. If I were to place one group here, one group there, one group here, I would be forcing them more into an area than I am in placing them in a very general frame, where their minds can make their groups, not the architecture.

HK: You don't like a casual arrangement?

No. I don't like it nailed down. If you could move it and change it every day without making a *nature* out of it, fine.

HK: On the other hand, it could be that an architecture of casual shapes would reflect on the the minds of the people, and make them casual. Maybe the audience in Berlin needs to be loosened up?

I think maybe what you say could have a big influence on me. I'm just telling you this. It could have a big influence on me, and I can with easy readiness employ a value which gives more casual arrangements than I do. But there's another thing, which constantly pushes me in other directions: I see a building in an anthropomorphic way, as a body. I don't want to be conscious of how my body functions. I always just expect it to be tremendously resourceful. I have need for things which my body can always handle: to run, to jump, to move quickly, to move slowly. I want to take *any* position, not just certain selective positions. Therefore, my tendency is to make a room without any willfulness, except that which the inspiration of the room itself can offer.

In an assembly, people choose to get either close to or far away from the speaker. If the people grouped themselves into groups in the midst of multiple choices, which the arrangement at Venice gives you in an orderly way, then I would say that what they are doing is truer to the nature of men gathering than a structured arrangement of seats. I don't like to freeze them, because not as much happens as when it is laid out as a field in which anything can happen.

It is best not to be conscious of limits, no matter how glorious these limits are.

HK: When Mies van der Rohe and Hugo Haring were together in Berlin during the early days of modern architecture, a constant question was, *Should architecture create specific spaces which tell people how they are to be used, or very general spaces which allow people to decide for themselves.* Haring made very complicated, irregular, but highly interesting ground plans. Mies, of course, created the *Vielzweckraum.*

Yes, the all-purpose room.

HK: Mies ended up with huge spaces defined only by the outer wall; the inhabitant defines its use. Your Venice proposal relates to this idea, yet you and Mies are quite different.

Very different. I am much more conscious that the space must have the evidence of how it was made. If a Mies space is undivided, and has this relationship, I would agree with him. If he subdivides his general space, I would not. I make a space as an offering, and do not designate what it is to be used for. The use should be inspired. That is to say, I would like to make a house in which the living room is discovered as the living room. I will not say that it is a living room and you must use it as such. Also, the bedroom, which, in a sense, must also be a living room, never has the specific characteristics of a bedroom.

HK: I've noticed in the way you describe your buildings that the functions everybody else focuses on are secondary to you. For example, when you build a library, you have to have spaces for bookshelves, catalogues, desks, and so forth, but the sum total of all these spaces doesn't make it a library for you. Incidental things that are in it, such as a little space where you can drink a cup of tea, make the life real.

Yes.

JC: When we were discussing the proposed Mellon Center at Yale, you said, *As long as I have considered only the functions of the building, I still cannot build the building.* A building which simply functions wouldn't be a building in your sense.

Mellon Center for
British Art and Studies
New Haven, CT
1969-74

No. Nor would it have a lasting quality. It would not have the quality of being in a life, of being in a living thing. When you make a building, you make a life. It comes out of life, and you really make a life. It talks to you. When you have *only* the comprehension of the function of a building, it would not become an environment of a life.

JC: In the Mellon Center, you said it is essential to emerge beyond the solution. The building begins *after* you have solved the problem.

Oh, yes. That's certainly what one means about the character of the spaces. One thing is the need of the space, and another is the character of the space.

JC: And the need of the space is not always identical with the character of the space?

No. The need of the space is definable. The character of the space is not definable. The building can be high in character, or low in character, and still function.

JC: When you have met all of the problems that you are supposed to solve at the Mellon Center, how far along is the architecture?

After you've solved the problem, you can begin to be concerned about the architecture. That's where it starts. It is that assembly of spaces where it is good to be, where the function is almost not discernible.

HK: You would not agree that form follows function.

No. You could say that form follows function if you think of form being a nature, that the answerable part to the nature is that which is intended to function a certain way. If you can consider how the building will affect the individual, that is not a question of function.

I just believe that the word *function* applies to mechanics. But you cannot say that it should also satisfy *psychological function* because psychology is not a function. The function aspect is that which gives you the instrumentation upon which psychological reaction can take place. You might say it's the difference between the mind and the brain. So the function aspect is the brain aspect; but the mind is not something that you can regulate with any kind of requirement. The beginning of architecture is after the function is thoroughly comprehended. At that point, the mind opens to the nature of the spaces themselves, which are released only in the mind after the functions are understood, and the spaces emerge in their psychological satisfaction.

JC: That means, in your words, *the building has a mind.*

The building has no mind, but it has the quality to respond to the mind.

JC: Could we have an example? Let's take the Bryn Mawr dormitories. What was the process by which the result became more than function?

This is a very good and pointed question, and I need more than one try at answering it. But let me attempt it. First of all, for the function of this building, the rooms were for one person only, so that any strife that might come about between one person and another is eliminated. With this situation, a person may seek out whomever he or she wishes for companions.

JC: Was that the primary fact for the program?

This is not purely a physical but already a psychological consideration. I don't exclude it. These are humans, not machines. There should be a dining room, a living room, and a place to come in.

JC: Again, as in Venice, these elemental requirements of the program find immediate expression in the ground plan: the dormitory has a tripartite layout based on three squares.

Yes. The functions are simple in this building. Now, for the requirement of an entrance, I have made not simply an entrance, but a meeting place. I considered it not a dimensional problem, but an environmental one. What I did was to make an entrance room equally as important as a room dining room, a room living room; that central entity in the ground plan became the entrance meeting place.

I insisted on the presence of fireplaces, because I said that a fireplace was a man in the room. That's what is required in terms of function....

JC: For a girls' dormitory?

I insisted on the fireplaces, so that the sense of invitation is felt. I counted on the receptivity of the girls to these rooms, because there are fireplaces which are sort of man-things—a man usually makes the fire. My clients needled me about keeping these fireplaces. They succumbed to the psychological importance of the fireplaces. They were costly and the building was very strictly budgeted. They felt that I was right, that they were a part of the *life* of the building, the character of it.

I mean to say that a dormitory is not, after all, an apartment building. There is a sense of communal living in not placing the dining room away from things. Therefore, I surrounded the dining room with students' rooms, as if each area of combined living has its own environment of responsibility. So those who live around the dining room or the living room felt as though they could identify themselves, as though they belonged somewhere. If you belong in a block where all the girls are away from the facilities, you would not have the sense of belonging which a house should give you.

The entrance hall was always common. Therefore, it was the place where you entered, and it was answerable to nothing except entrance. One is led to divide the house into two parts, one around which there is an environment of pure neighborhood, the neighborhood of the living room, the neighborhood of the dining room, and the other, which centers around the entrance, around which there is a sense of the street. The geometry is good, because there is a sense of division in the places.

JC: You actually joined three houses, three separate units.

Yes. Now, the central rooms have nothing to do with function. I could equally make it function if I had designed a block of dormitories with corridors; you could walk from your room to the corridor to the dining room. But I rejected that for very basic reasons. Here, there is more a sense of pulse. It is, in a sense, a house, because around you are always the things you associate with; they aren't made into separate elements you have to go to. They are in the center of living.

The reaction which came back to me from the students implied this very sense of feeling at home, not really in their *own* home, but they felt the sense of home, the dormitory sense of home. Nobody was fooling anybody that it was home, but the fact that you're associated with a common facility, that you have a sense of invitation, that you have your section to live in, and you can go to another section to enjoy common spaces—all these add up to something much better than living in a block of rooms separated from all other facilities. It *does* function, of course, but the distinction of the Bryn Mawr building is that it has this sense of invitation. I am around the courtyard; I am around the dining room. There is something communal about this, which is missing in others.

Another important aspect of the design is that I did not try to make connections with unknown places. Somehow, you're not going from place to place, really. It sort of blends together. It becomes one house, instead of three divisions. The linking space between the units is a delicate point. I go through it not feeling that I'm going through an odd space. The transition has value in itself.

JC: It's possible to have three main community areas with rooms around them and not have the sense of *mind* or sense of joy which you have achieved there. There must be other things that go into making the character.

Yes. What it really is is the *mood* in these places, and it is gotten by the character of the natural light reflecting in through the concrete shell. You'll see it especially at the close of the day, when the lights come on inside and the light outside is still in fullness. Then you feel like *living* there. And that is what really makes the *mind*.

JC: You seem very far away from your former student Robert Venturi, who is seeking *ordinariness*, a refreshing alternative to the *heroic idiom*.

If he could only use the word *commonness* and express it in the simplest of terms, I would agree.

But *ordinary* for the sake of being ordinary is not in the nature of man at all. He doesn't *know* it's ordinary. Unconscious ordinariness can be the most beautiful; but it's never given because it's ordinary as a virtue. No. I don't agree with that. There is such a thing as a need to begin all over again, which I think is great, rather than simply accepting what is already given. Certainly, that quality of beginning over again, making something which is not special, but something which is a new beginning, which can also have the starkest simplicity without the slightest sense of conscious exaltation, can be very, very great. What, after all, is ordinariness derived from? It is the sum total of all the solved and unsolved practical problems. It is an interpretation of man which says, *We have problems, economic problems, site problems, technical problems, etc., and we have to work so hard just to make a building stand up.* And then it is known to be ordinary because of this. And, because there is a repetition of similar problems everywhere, almost everything is ordinary.

I still believe that all buildings belong to architecture. Ordinariness could inspire beauty, but not if it's meant to be ordinary for ordinary's sake. I can see how a building could become beautifully ordinary. Then it has a tremendous validity in the ordinariness.

HK: That's actually what Venturi tries to do.

Now, if he's looking for the beauty of this ordinariness, then I'm definitely for it.

HK: He is reacting strongly against the present-day trend of creating dominating heroic architecture.

How could anybody not agree to this? But I'm afraid the word *ordinary* is what I'm not sure I want to include, except passing through the hands of a poet.

HK: Ordinariness that passes through the hands of a poet isn't ordinary any more.

No, wait a minute. There must be a beautiful way of saying this, because it has to do greatly with what is called simplicity, in the sense of the word. I have made statements about the Richards Laboratories towers. I have said, *These shafts are independent exhaust.* Now they are being taken as showpieces. I wouldn't think of that. They are not worthy. These ducts are generalized units for certain services, without knowing what they are. I wasn't making jewelry out of exhaust ducts. They are simple, but they are not ordinary. I sense the differences in instruments in the broadest way, but I don't know every mechanical detail. First of all, I don't know the instruments that well. I cannot distinguish one thing from another. So I put them all in one great big wastebasket, and that's the exhaust duct. But to pull it out and make a submarine out of it, that's ridiculous!

Let me put it a different way. The space you live in can be beautiful, especially if it is unfettered by all these other things. I don't believe in pipes in living rooms. I hate them. I believe they should be in their place like children. I want to remain ignorant of how the mechanics really work. I'm impatient with the restrictions of mechanical and construction engineers and with details about how every little thing works. But its *place* I think I know. I want to express that which is worth expressing, that which has grown to be a distinct characteristic. When one is characteristically different from another, I don't want to make a homogeneous mixture of the two. I want to bring out the difference. But I care very little if one pipe goes east and the other goes west. I don't want to make a special characteristic out of pipes, because I know that mechanical things are the first things that are going to be changed or altered; but the space you live in must be alive for a very long time. The space is a new landscape, which is to last as long as the material lasts. But the spaces which are serving it are made to change. Their position must be very general and they must be big enough for change and addition to take place. That is truly the nature of architecture. It is not giving service an individual shape.

A room has a nature, just as a certain part of the world has a nature. When you go into this harbor, you know you're there. You go into this room, and you know you're there.

HK: When you separate service shafts from the spaces, you actually create shapes that have an impressive image. They are not ordinary wastebaskets.

I think this is very important. I think this is the beginning of the modern plan, as far as the distinction between service and space goes.

HK: The first time this separation was done in an explicit way was in the Richards Laboratories. But the idea seems to be at work already in the Yale Art Gallery in the ceilings.

Richards Research
Buildings
Philadelphia, PA 1957-64

Yale Art Gallery
New Haven, CT 1951-53

Yes, the ceiling was the beginning of such a realization. There's no question about that. I simply made a service space out of the ceiling, and it can be read as such. In my first sketches, the ceiling was a series of vaults; the space for the pipes was above the vaults. This scheme was unsatisfactory because the vault intervals determined where the room divisions had to be. So I had to discover a multidirectional construction, which was open and had the characteristic of having space already in it. That was what the tetrahedral ceiling gave me, what I'd like to call a *space slab*. It was as though it were a single slab, only it was an exposed articulation of this slab. A ceiling of forty feet in one span would require a thickness of twelve inches of concrete. This was my guide. I thought of this idea, which would give space for air and light at frequent intervals, as well as provide for multidirectional partitioning. The partitioning could not be fixed because of its being a gallery, so I made multipurpose spaces, which are rather like Miesian spaces. At that point, the consciousness of releasing the serving spaces from the spaces served had not yet come, but the essentials for doing it were certainly there. The ceiling is really a place where the many needs are accessible. The solution derives from the feeling that the way a place is made must be visible and not concealed. It was the revolt against the hung ceiling which caused all this to be made. It was the first ceiling of that type.

HK: Were you inspired by Buckminster Fuller?

No. Because Buckminster Fuller's work was structurally much more advanced. It does not apply to a flat ceiling. I understood very well what he was trying to do, but I never had a desire to make what Fuller was making, nor would I want to make a building such as Le Corbusier makes, even though he was my teacher, but didn't know it.

JC: The Yale Art Gallery had, as you said, rather Miesian spaces, but your concept of space is entirely different from his.

I always think that the client presents you with the need of certain areas, rather than with certain spaces or certain rooms. He presents you with area requirements, and the architect has to translate these into spaces. Spaces have to be entities.

No. Space is not a space unless you can see the evidence of how it was made. Then I like to call that a room. What I would call an area, Mies would call a space, because he thought nothing of dividing a space. That's where I say *no*.

No matter how many partitions are in it, Mies would always call the whole area a space. I would call any one of the four divisions a space, but, after you divide it, the whole thing is not a space any more. I would call this a space, provided it is never divided. What you see in the third diagram are four spaces. I consider these four rooms. Mies would consider this a space within which divisions could be made. In the Miesian spaces he allows division, but for me there's no entity when it is divided.

HK: Why do you insist so much on showing the supports in your rooms?

Because I think that the room likes it. That's why. The room feels its entity, its completeness, it has a right to have a name. It can be called the *east room,* for instance.

JC: But in the Miesian plan there can be *no east room.*

It cannot be given a name.

HK: Can't it be given a name without showing the supports?

No, because it's not yet worthy of its name. Ask that kind of room how it is made, and it will have to say, *If you go next door, you can see the columns of me in that room.* And this is what stops me from naming it. But going back to the third diagram, each of these four rooms has its own character because of the light. One has north and west light, one has south and east light, and so on. Each room has its own character. And, if I were being delicate about this, the window of one would not be designed the same as the window of another. Now, each room has its own light, and if I go to the east room at a certain time of day, my memory tells me to *expect* something there. The structure is the maker of the light. The structure can make an opening, just as a column and a beam can. This is an opportunity for light. And that means if I hide the structure I've lost the opportunity. I go through an immense amount of trouble. If I didn't assume that I needed to do this, my plans would be vastly different. I regard natural light as that which makes a room have its nature, its characteristic, its mood.

HK: You would always deny artificial light?

I do not believe that any room is worthy to be called a room itself in artificial light. That means that any interior room would have to break through the ceiling to get the natural light, as is the case in the dormitories at Bryn Mawr.

HK: In other words, there are two major elements which individualize a room: structure and light.

Structure, which *gives* the light.

HK: Then, actually, this square you drew with divisions is alien at the outset to your concept. You should take it apart, as you actually did in the main building design for the Trenton Jewish Community Center. There, every single entity of space is separated but related to the others. You start out with a given area, define the spatial entities, and then combine them again as an entity.

Trenton Jewish
Community Center
Trenton, NJ 1954-59

Yes, combining again. But, you see, I did all that in order to teach myself. It was a matter of teaching myself its meaning. The Community Center has this feeling of defining space so that each facet is clear in itself, and also gave room for those areas which would serve the larger areas. It had to be reasonable that the passages and the areas that serve, which are between the actual rooms, could be useful, and make the spaces themselves be more useful.

Bathhouse, Trenton
Jewish Community Center
Trenton, NJ
1955-56

JC: So you could use the space in between the units as a service area, as a corridor, for instance, or it could be incorporated into a room.

Exactly. That was a very exciting period. The Trenton Bath House gave me the first opportunity to work out the separation between the serving and the served spaces. It was a very clean and simple problem. It was solved with absolute purity. Every space is accounted for; there is no redundancy. I used hollow columns as entrances to the rooms. I used them as a maze, a baffle, and I used the hollow column itself as a storage area. I used it for toilets, which must be enclosed. And I found, during the expression of this very simple building, the concept of the serving and the served spaces. The desire to employ this with greater extension came with the order for the community building, which I never built because it proved in *their* eyes too expensive. It was really a very inexpensive building. But there were some spaces which they felt were not necessary; strictly speaking, according to their own program, I would say that maybe seven percent were not. I invented certain uses for these extra spaces. Where they wanted four rooms, I may have had five, all of which did not prove to be necessary.

JC: Just as you define the service shafts of the Richards Laboratories as separate units, you define service units in the supports of the Trenton Bath House.

Yes. I thought of a support as being a hollow column which can be used. That's the only place where I could put the services. So the source of support, the column, became the place which harbored the services of the building. The columns of yesterday, which were solid, could be made hollow and contain something. But even the old columns (pillars) sometimes contained something, too. They knew that the mass wasn't altogether necessary because it was only the edges of the mass that supported the building, not the mass itself.

HK: Like the pillars of the nave of Saint Peter's in Rome.

Yes, like those niches and passageways which open the pillar. Actually, this idea comes for me from the real reverence I have for *pochet*. You know what *pochet* is? Each one of the supports of the Trenton Bath House is made out of four walls enclosing space, and this stems from buildings of old, which have tremendous areas of *pochet*, which are the spaces within the structural supports. My hollow columns, which contain rooms, are similar to those piers in Saint Peter's which contain a space which is a passageway. The sense of the hollow column is really what inspired me.

The opportunity to introduce the hollow support idea came as a lucky circumstance, which made each element in the bathhouse accountable: the maze, the toilets, the kiosk, the chlorinating plant, the storage spaces. They were all useful in the hollow columns somewhere.

HK: Let's assume that we have come to you as clients. We want to build a house for a family of families, not an apartment building, but a house where families would share certain facilities in common, and yet maintain some privacy. Let's say that we want a common playroom for the children, a common kitchen, and some sort of central meeting place for all the families. The rest of the rooms would emphasize privacy. The goal would be to provide community and the sharing of responsibilities, as well as the possibility for retreat. The present one-family unit today, with all its problems, may be too isolated.

What you say is tremendously attractive. My thinking regarding the meaning of the street comes to mind immediately. The street, which is a room, is the unspecified position of common space. But you are looking for something which becomes consciously more specified than the street, which is a very general room. But, when I think of something that is a generator of conception, the street becomes the starting point. No matter what is built, it must be good for another reason as well. So the street still stands there, without being specific, as the first answer to your problems. In a sense, the community room of early American architecture, where people met on the village green, was this kind of home, except you met not for family interengagement, but for general meetings.

A family of families has similar connotations. You surrender certain rooms commonly, but what you keep as strictly yours, as I see it, must have in it the living room and the kitchen. I am talking about a way of *life*, and you are talking about a way of living. I feel there'a a difference between the two. The way of life asks for a common acceptance, no matter how humble. The way of living asks for the right of privacy. A conception of the way of life surrenders freedom to a way of living.

What you want, in this house, can only be successful if the scheme has within it the connotations of the way of life itself, so that the house, when it changes hands, automatically adjusts to the way of someone else's living. I can't help but say that within your idea lies a great beauty, ultimate beauty. But is it a way of life? I say *no*. Is it a way of living? I say *yes*.

HK: Would you build a house just for the way of living?

No, I wouldn't. I should reject it. However, if this is sincerely thought about, it might be a new realization of what is really valuable and what is not valuable. If this is designed in a way which respects the way of life, I think it would be a great advance in the building of places to live. Really good.

HK: We are living in a time when *the way of life* is changed by the way of living. What appears to be merely arbitrary and momentary may eventually become part of the essence of a new way of life. The distinction between ontology and history is not so apparent as you indicate.

I sense that what you say is a thing of great beauty. It could lead to a new sense of planning and a kind of truer economy.

HK: Not only economy. I think it gives a new sense of family, too. In a three-family house, children will grow up in a very different way. They will not focus upon their mothers and fathers alone, but on other families as well. The distinction between *us* and *the others* would not be so rigid.

I agree. But, you see, people, according to their various ages, change their attitudes toward life, and then living is altered.

HK: You mean that a certain time will come when we shall realize that we have outgrown this house?

That's right.

HK: And then we have to tear it down.

Yes. But, more important, the rooms which are common must not take something away from that part which you consider your own, the place where you are not answerable to any rules or regulations which are implied in the common rooms. There must be a place where you can make your own cup of tea. Such a plan is almost a revelation of how little you fear other people. It's almost as if you learned not to respect as much fear as you did before. But, I'm afraid that man has established a completeness for himself too firmly to live in such a house. You cannot break out of that very quickly.

HK: It might be enough to have one big common room and a common kitchen.

No. You cannot take away that which is the memory of a house, of *your* home. You can forget maybe your bedroom, you could even forget sometimes your living room, but you can't forget your kitchen. The memory aspect is tremendously important. Also, there is the aspect of invitation, which is lost if your kitchen is lost.

HK: Do you think it would be better to build three separate houses on this lot?

No, but I would like you to think about the religious place of each family. I think one of the most religious of rooms is the kitchen. If you build around the kitchen, it would be a tremendous lesson in interresponsibility. But I really think the kitchen must be your own kitchen. Otherwise, you would always feel as though you couldn't invite anybody. The way you make a cake is very important, because you want very much for the other fellow to like the way you make a cake. And don't forget that the kitchen is the woman's domain and can cause any amount of jealousy.

The young people don't have such a violent sense of ownership. However, I could readily live in a social area such as this. The thought of immediately having this kind of family is very wonderful. I feel much better when I know the other person is there, but I don't have to see him. If I had a room next to another person, I would feel even better. Then, even the closed door is communication, yes? The *next* thing that would make me feel better would be having a garden between his room and mine. It tells me that more can be done with the architecture of connection. It tells me we must meet again.

Office Building
Kansas City, KS 1966-73

Let's talk in terms of systems.

You're erecting this thing and you have spans. It's a delaying thing in my mind in the sense of coming up with the construction and forming a truss, and then coming down. It's a race against time in building the building up with a truss, then it's a matter of technology that comes down from there, using the forces of nature the way the form expends itself and also expands.

This is the delicate part of the building.

The structure is proving to be economical compared to other construction, but the mechanical system is way off. The load cannot rob the economy of the structure by having a mechanical system that takes it away. This is a competitive building. If the ingenuity of the structure is there, the ingenuity of the mechanical must also be there.

You can't beat the cost of throwing it into the pot as usual.

The truss is the point from which everything hangs. You want no interruptions in the hanging area except office space. Any intermediate floors are used for the sake of the load.

Everything that hangs is office. Everything that's in the truss area is used for special purposes which enhance the civic character of this building.

This building will be a point of civic importance.

One looks up and says, *Up there they have the restaurant*; not; *There they have the ducts and machines.*

If anything is built on top of the truss itself it should only be the heliport. I even resent the floor which is designated for the cooling tower purposes up there, because it is already an intrusion on the simplicity of the statement of the tower having an area of truss with special things on it. I would like to see everything underground rather than up there.

I like the idea of the cooling tower being in this area, though I think it's too husky, too big, too clumsy as it is now.

We're very hard pressed to express the club, the restaurant, the heliport, and all those things up there which deserve the right location.

That crummy old machinery belongs somewhere else.

You look to downtown like mad because there's no other friend you have. Downtown must be a friend.

The essence of it is meeting.

If the stores could contain the courtesy of meeting and the feeling that meeting is important, they would catch on.

The heliport is like an address. It has a lot of meaning because you know you can get there.

Let's talk about cooling towers later. The part that holds this building up wants to be expressed not in any kind of commercial or mechanical way. It is an essential part of the service and should not be obstructed. We'll find a place for the cooling tower. I wouldn't worry about that. We'll put it somewhere else. This building is clean as a whistle in other ways, but the mechanical wants to stay out of this area.

The question of aesthetics I'm going to leave out entirely because it's a private affair.

Whatever we do we have to know what the cost is to install an alternative system. What would give us a competitive advantage in having this building on the market instead of something else?

This building is still on trial, if it must be taxed so heavily that the building is just waiting for the dough with costs you can't stand.

An intermediate floor is necessary, or one above, but the logical place for it is in the truss area. Kick the club out of the building. You can't put it on the roof, and the reason is quite simple. If you are expressing a building that's hanging, what you don't want is a heavy head. You want the grace of the truss that's hanging the building to be the culmination of the building. If you start adding to the top of the building you are producing something which erases the picture of its grace.

Suppose you had a system where the core came up and at certain intervals the core gets wide. A peripheral area around here. And the core was like this, bulging out at certain intervals around the periphery but still useable area around it. The idea is not inconceivable if you're talking about saving a great deal of money. At certain floors you don't have quite as much rentable area, but you have services in the core—not somewhere over there or somewhere over there.

The core is made so it serves the rooms like a tree does all the branches.

Of course the client would hate your guts for making such a small floor at these points, but it's the only positive way to keep the integrity of the building.

We're talking about speculation to keep the integrity of the building.

We're not talking about how much it hurts to do it, just can it be done?

Reprinted by permission, Arnold Garfinkel

Architecture and Human Agreement,
A Tiffany Lecture
Philadelphia, Pennsylvania
10 October 1973

Essentially, every man deals with art even in the way he walks, the way he uses his legs, or the way he turns a page. Even his conduct in a restaurant has to do with some form of art. It is choice, it is noticing the grace of your actions.

Art is really the only language of man; all other languages serve to bring art into the fore.

Man lives to express; the reason for living is to express.

What comes to my mind is the first feeling of man when his eyes were opened and he saw things around him. I don't mean a certain time when man was born. I cannot conceive of man before human. *Human* is what we really are talking about.

The first sense must have been of beauty. Beauty has total harmony. Not just beautiful, not the very beautiful, because anything less than total beauty itself lacks this perfect harmony, in the same way as *very good* is less than good. There is something about the immeasurable word which, when made measurable, becomes less.

Art strives to communicate in a way which reveals the human. It is the unexpected that one experiences before a work of art or when dealing in the realm of art. It is what has yet to become or has not been that you are dealing with. An artist is not dealing with something that is recognizable before it is made. Even as it is described, one does not know what it is until it is interpreted.

Then beauty is the first feeling, the first experience of being human, the feeling of some overall harmony that is accepted without any doubt whatsoever. The knowledge that comes later helps to modify or measure the beauty of feeling, of not knowing tremendous harmony in what is evident and what has not yet been expressed.

Possibly the first counter-feeling or sympathetic feeling is that of wonder. Just a sense of being in the presence of beauty motivates an overwhelming feeling of wonder—wonder and the sea of knowledge, sea of knowing. From it comes the realization that you define the universe, more than just knowledge about laws, which only touch the content of that which you may call *order*.

Order takes in all laws, those which are made, those that are invented, and those that are still not invented.

From realization comes an all-important working force which we know as *form*.

Form is a realization of that which can exist or which can be made present. Form is the reciprocal part of something. When you take one part away, the form disappears. It cannot hold together. Form is a realization of that which can be.

You sense the inseparable parts so there is no question of its nature. It is completely different from *shape*.

Shape is something that a man chooses to interpret form.

Mere existence is not presence. To give presence to something, to translate the realizations which come from the sense of form, to preserve that sense with everything that you have at your disposal and to give presence to that which has existence in the mind—that is what design is all about.

When an executive feels the need for the true expression of his product he must know that product is genuine, that it has given presence. That message, and the expression of his product, the executive can convey to the artist or to the designer. It is really a question of singularity to singularity. If you get a direction from a committee, I am positive the product will be less, the expression will be less. The individual has the ability to see it all as a unit and from the sketchy first realizations there can be a fruitful exchange between the designer and the man who wants the design made. This exchange can make the executive a better executive and designer a better designer. It is human to human.

The artist is an expressor and the executive is a wanter or a desirer. Together, both are powerful.

The designer, who is not a specialist in certain kinds of designs, is not a designer at all. A designer is only important when he reaches a subject absolutely freshly, as though he never knew anything like that before. His whole desire is really his own desire and that is to make that present which is yet not present. The essence of that desire is to bring into being that which is not yet said, yet not made. It has nothing to do with need. If you need a designer, then you actually want him less than if you desire one.

Singularity to singularity, executive to designer, is the very act of teacher and student. That is what teaching is all about; instruction is something else. The executive must be the teacher because in him lies some kind of secret as to what he wants to obtain which the designer can give him. I can assure you that one man doing the locomotive, with the same chemistry in back of it, would design it differently than the other. That is how delicate the choice of a designer is.

Every individual is completely different from the other. The desire to express as being is an aura which lives within us, in all of us, in some form or another. The farmer has it, the architect has it, the businessman has it, the painter has it. And the other powerful force is nature itself, which is the maker of all presences. What is desired can only be made present by knowing the laws of nature or, better still, the order itself. There is really only one law: order. In order, there is no chaos; it cannot be chaotic.

To travel from *the desire to express* to *the means to express,* there is within each individual a scientist who would hold back his sense of desire and allow nature to come to it. By holding it back, he holds back the movement of what may be any poetic thought to avoid that which may make what he is searching for have too much singularity. Better still, too much of the undefineable or unmeasurable limits because he is looking for the measurable. If he means to get the measurable pure of what may be his other senses, it is desire itself.

The poet marches towards the means and marches for a long, long time, hoping the means is never necessary. But he finds the means is necessary because he has to print things and he has to say some things. He can't just leave out all the words, which is really his intention, and so nature is held back. The means, the word, is the maker and once found the poet is able to send forth that which has the greatest power of transcendence in his poetry.

Everyone has this talent of the measurable and the unmeasurable in him, but a man like Einstein would be one like the poet who resists knowledge because he knows that if he were to talk about what he knows, he knows it is only a miniscule part of what is yet to be known. Therefore, he does not trust knowledge but looks for that which can be order itself. Like a poet, he travels a great distance resisting knowledge and then when he does get a particle of knowledge, he reconstructs the universe.

The director, if he truly has in him the aura or the brilliance of what is a kind of totality of purpose, becomes equally as intangible as the artist. He deals first with the intangible before he makes it tangible. The executive, or the director, must know what he wants and must turn to someone who knows how to express it. Both are gamblers in this sense, great gamblers because that sense, the desire to see something which is worthy to come forward, is an overwhelming feeling and nothing operational is respected.

It is much like the daring act of the first people in the United States who, by their sense of freedom, did things that other people wouldn't dare to do.

The purpose of design is to take what is visualized as the inseparable part or parts and apply them to what nature can make. The designer will not make a design for appearance alone. Instead it is something that answers the laws of nature and has or takes a shape that is true to the element. Many times in early industrial design, it was nothing to make a stream-lined comb just to give it a nice shape, which looked like something that is to be hurled into space as though it were made for the purpose of movement. Now that is true of egg-beaters, and toasters, and many other things.

An airplane, on the other hand, is made without these considerations of selling. They are made to conform to the very strict laws of nature. The shape is true to itself. The expression of it is still not yet finished. The reason is that the desire in man for creation will never be satisfied. If planes took only two hours to get to California, nobody would raise an eyebrow. But if you were to touch the desires of man, you would find that what man really wants is a flying carpet which would take him anywhere for no cost at all. He would need no pilot, nor gas, and he would be able to keep it under his bed to do with it what he wants. I am sure this desire will never be realized, at least not in my time. But the nature of desire is insatiable. This motivation will always exist where there is any possibility of creating a sense of the completeness in something before it actually has presence. This will to express is an intuitive sense which is in part an answer to the sense of how we were made. All of learning is answerable only to the desire to know how we were made, which is also the reason for living.

How does one make a good choice of a good designer? There are no formulas. The right choice stems from the man who has faith, who has a sense of a certain completeness which he may not be able to describe but knows through his intuitive sense. He is a man who may have only a small parcel of knowledge but who knows he can make it because of the undeniable force in what he is doing. If the desire of the director or executive is there, the artist can pick it out and move with it and do more with that man than if he had been given the most minute instructions of how it should be.

Now when I was speaking about silence and light or the desire to express and the means, I tried to say that all material is spent light. It is light that has become exhausted. Creation makes me think of two brothers who were really not two brothers. One had the desire to be, to express; the other had the desire to be something that becomes tangible which makes the instruments upon which the spirit of man can express itself. If the will to be is to become something of the predominance or the prevalence of the luminous, then the luminous turned into a wild dance of flame, spending itself to become material and this material, this little lump, this crumpled lump made the mountains, the streams, the atmosphere and we ourselves came from spent light.

This drawing of Leonardo da Vinci's, of a section around Siena, looks like a crumpled kind of thing, like spent light. He is such a marvelous artist, I am sure he didn't think of this particular evolution. I am positive that to make such a drawing he had a sense of wonder. It is an inaccurate map, but it tells you somehow that this world is the product of light.

This drawing shows that light is an important part of architecture.

Greek architecture taught me that the column is where the light is not and the space between is where the light is. It is a matter of no-light, light, no-light, light. A column and a column brings light between them. To make a column which grows out of the wall and which makes its own rhythm of no-light, light, no-light, light—that is the marvel of the artist.

An architecture must have the religion of Light. A sense of light as the giver of all presences. Every building, every room must be in natural light because natural light gives the mood of the day. The season of the year is brought into a room. It can even be said that a sun never knew how great it was until it struck the side of the building. When a light enters a room, it is your light and nobody else's. It belongs to that room. The Kimbell Art Museum uses all natural light. After some initial designs that I made, Richard Kelly put the blueprints to the computer and came out with a shape that sent the light along the vaults. The vaults can span a hundred feet without any column. I didn't allow anything to enclose the building.

Kimbell Art Museum
Fort Worth, TX 1966-72

At the Salk Institute of Biological Studies, two of the buildings are not yet built but one is. Salk told me that he wanted to have a laboratory to which he could invite Picasso. He stayed overnight in Philadelphia to talk. I came up with the idea that what he wanted was a place of the *measurable*, which is a laboratory, and a place of the *unmeasurable*, which would be the meeting place. Biology is not just scientific or a simple task of finding that which is measurable. There is an *unmeasurable* quality, even in matters scientific. I, as the interpreter of his ideas, gave him a plan that was terribly expensive, which is why that is not built. Part of the design concept, however, did motivate the making of this building. We are still reserving space for what should really be there—the art library, the gymnasium, the dining hall. We still work in collaboration because Mr. Salk is as much a party to the design as I am. Although collaboration in the Arts is not possible, collaboration in that which *motivates* the Arts is possible.

Salk Institute
La Jolla, CA 1959-65

The studies behind the Salk laboratories provide shade for the laboratories. It was necessary to have light but not sunlight. Part of my design is this meeting house which contains a place which overlooks the canyons beyond the sea, a place which one might call an individual chapel, an unnamed place which could be many things. It is the entrance from which everything else comes—the seminar rooms, the rooms for research fellows, the library, the bar, many things.

The first architectural plan I made for Bangladesh, the second capital city of Pakistan, started with the slightest hint of what the total design was to be. I was inspired by the devotion of the Moslems to their prayers five times a day and was struck by the anonymity of the mosque. There was no preaching, one simply said prayers. Yet it was a community building, used by all, without any direction. Bangladesh is a religious state which made me think that the assembly should look to the mosque, just as the mosque should look to the assembly. The mosque was a citadel of the assembly around which the members would gather. The judges and other dignitaries of the assembly were to live on a lake and across from it were the symbolic institutions. I made this distinction because legislation is that which brings about the institutions of man and makes things available to the people. It is an expression of life.

Sher-E-Banglanagar
Dacca, Bangladesh
1962-74

I felt it was important to make a distinction between the place of legislation and the supreme court. Legislation is circumstantial law, and the supreme court is concerned with law in relation to humans. When I presented this idea to the judges of the supreme court, the Chief Justice said he did not want to be near the assembly. When I sketched the mosque which was next to the supreme court, he took back his words because the mosque provided insulation. The mosque was the pivotal center of the plan, the center of life. Always the artist or the *expressor* must work closely with that which had to be expressed, which in this case were the functions of the government.

In the plan of the assembly, the mosque is at the entrance. It turns slightly more to the West because of its relationship with Mecca. I purposely did this to emphasize the uniqueness of the mosque in relation to all other human needs.

On one of the buildings now being constructed, there are no windows because the heat is very great and the sun very strong. All windows must recede to where the cool air can open to the rooms. The outside of the building belongs to the sun, the interior belongs to the shadows. It is a place where people live. The porches are round places behind the windows. These openings, which are merely porch openings, can be seen only on the inside.

Hurva Synanagogue
Jerusalem, Israel 1968-74

This expresses the same idea in the Hurva Synagogue in Jerusalem. I am using the stone of the Western Wall and inside of it is a concrete structure. These are cool stones compared to other structures. Concrete is warm because of the reinforcing rods which heat up.

An administration building is not simply a building that sits here and the factory sits there. Instead, the administration building is here as well as the factory. The loftiness of the factory structure is required because of overhead structures. It is also suitable for putting a floor between which made it possible to create a base for administration purposes. This building is only half the size that it will eventually be. The windows of the place have natural light which floods the factory with light. The idea of dividing the factory from administration seemed snobbish so I brought them together in the same area.

Government Hill Development
Jerusalem, Israel 1972-74

There is a part of old Jerusalem called Government Hill. On this hill the English have some houses which were part of their administration idea. Here I built a community center which was for all the people of Jerusalem, whatever religion or sect. Now, of course, all these things are greatly in question.

Fine Arts Center
Fort Wayne, IN 1961-65

When I had a theater to do in Fort Wayne, Indiana, I thought that for the theater to be effective for the whisper of the actor, the auditorium and the stage must be like the violin and the violin case. The auditorium and the stage were constructed so that nothing touches them on the outside. They must be completely insulated and independent with not even a pipe near the structure. My original idea was to build an actor's house half a mile away from the site. I even thought of building a chapel so that an actor could practice a soliloquy. I also thought of building a porch to the actor's house to make it a hospitable place instead of a small room behind the stage. After I planned this imaginary house a half mile away, I wheeled it, theoretically of course, back stage. I would not have thought of the porch, which is actually an ancient idea, if I hadn't designed the house away from the conditions of the theatre.

In designing these buildings, there is a completely different construction. The demands were met by taking each element and by giving it shape which is the nature of design.

L.I.K. Symposium
Kansas City, MO

Palace of Congress
Venice, Italy 1968-74

The Palazzo del Congressi in Venice: this was a congess where the people sat looking at the center, and from there to another center which was a ballroom overlooking Venice. The shape was very close to the sense of a congress which is to bring people together—the meeting of Asiatic-Africans and Europeans, and all others.

From a Conversation with Jamine Mehta
22 October 1973

A work of art is an offering to art itself.

The hope of the offering is that art can convey itself as belonging to the multi-facets which touch the feeling of art.

Are you taking art? That has no meaning.

Do you know art? No meaning.

Do you feel art? Yes.

Knowing isn't that important. What is more important is your sense of beauty. Beauty does not need to know, but it induces knowing because from a sense of beauty comes wonder. They are so close to each other.

Wonder is the forerunner of all knowing.

Wonder is the primer. It primes knowing.

It begins with the revelations of knowledge, which enters the singularity as knowing. The will to be cannot be that sophisticated when beginning, and this is the whole motive behind becoming and being. What lodges inwardly is the song.

The song of the spirit is the motivator of to be.

In the spirit the song is untellable, unrealizable because it does not rely on any means which nature can give it, which instrumentally makes it profitable.

Think of the prevalence of the spirit which has in it a will to be, to have, to possess.

Some aspect of spirit is nature, is means. It starts as a prevalence of the luminous. It is as though the spirit were aware, but too corporal to say *aware.*

Luminous comes from itself. It's the beginning of all material.

As soon as you can say *beginning,* already there is something which makes beginning possible.

With it is a spontaneous thing which never had any beginning. The spirit, so blazingly magnificent, which is using descriptive terms which belong to the already material, even though it is seemingly nonmaterial, it is a promise, a self-revelation. You've got to feel it.

Stay away from making the error of beginning.

If you get too close to beginning, it goes farther and farther away from you.

Stop in midstream and allow that which will be forever unattainable.

In the deepest part of the human mind is a clue to beginning which will never be found. There are words which stand in the way. One is symbolism. But it doesn't stand in the way if a symbol is a brink between life and death. If it's there between existence and presence, the meaning could be there.

The word *symbol* needs to be put further back into consciousness, because a symbol can be something which one tribe can understand and another tribe can't understand. There are aspects of human response which don't have to depend on a symbol. They can be felt without a symbol.

Symbols are gentle reminders.

They are stones left to find your path back to where you want to go back to.

The more you get to the source of something, using the word *symbol* as something you don't accept until there is no way you cannot accept it, the more it would be better put as a question.

Around the question is the nonacceptance of anything categoric. It is kept away from understanding. It arouses interest rather than giving you an answer.

To know all the laws of the universe and use them, man would have to live forever. If he knew that he could live forever, he would first exact from nature that ability to live forever. And then when he has it he would not bother about knowing anything because he wouldn't have to know.

A poet can write the most beautiful and meaningful poetry, being ignorant of its nature. Or he's so mixed up, he makes it the way he wants it. Still, everything we make, everything we do, must go to the maker of all presences. If you want to make something, you want to give it presence.

Order is the only thing that can give you presence.

Order is the sum total of all the laws of nature. All the laws are no more the individual laws, but order itself is that which encompasses all the laws. It would be unnecessary to spell them out if order were understood as order.

It is not two things: order and spirit. It is actually one. There are no fights between spirit and order. It is the center of eternal harmony where the spirit realizes that there is that which can make the spirit feel.

It is an eternal agreement of spirit that can feel.

All of nature is a glow of the luminous. The luminous which has no material in it has, because of the eternal agreement, that which can make material. This luminous turns into a wild dance of flame. The flame spreads itself into material, and there is the promise of instruments of being. And there is, in a limited way, the desire *to be to express*.

You can't say it's creation, but then you've got to say what was before creation.

What is that which precedes aura? It's only silence.

But it is the silence from whence comes the wind, from which the stars evolved as the senders of the luminous.

The dimensions must be put this way. You can not measure them in miles, you can not say in how many years has man emerged.

Art lies in the replay of the odyssey of our making.

In there is the instinct of the man who wants to tell a story. The telling of a story, the putting down the incredible, is the evidence of art, man's language. It's incredible because that which was not dependent on the workings of nature still lodges in us.

The wish in the fairy tale is the beginning of science.

Science is trying desperately to put it down as it is, and the artist puts it down as it really is.

The fairy tale is that which lies in the desire *to be to express*. It stems from the tale of the artist in which, with the presence we sense, there is the desire for superior independence from the material. You shouldn't regret that the material is there. You wouldn't be here without it. But being here is the point and the transcendent thing is not being there. What man responds to has transcendency. It can transcend the limits of nature's offering to the desires of presence.

I see symbol as being multifaceted. It's like looking into a mirror in which everybody looks alike because the distinction between one and the other is miniscule.

Symbol is the rallying point around human agreement, human response.

A great work can become symbolic, not because one person has anything to say, but because there's a human sympathy that brought us to it. In using symbol one must see it as having that quality. In writing about it, that quality must also be evident to the person you are writing to, so he doesn't gloss over the words. If he goes to the dictionary to find it, everybody has the same dictionary, but it won't help him because the dictionary only deals with the word.

What can make the word glow is in the area of thought.

It cannot glow just as a word. Let the thought bring out the quality.

The Mona Lisa should affect everybody. This has the quality of being symbolic. You see what it is, but it has this quality of being symbolic. Some people would disagree with this. They would put it on the basis of happenings. This could also mean a great deal. You must account for happenings, but you must also consider the Mona Lisa. It is something that was brought forward. It didn't just come there. Through a person, something has manifested itself as having the qualities symbolic.

The means look like a great benevolent benefactor who simply is there and says, *Look, tell me what you want, and if the laws can do it, I'll make it*. Nature wants this because it keeps the whole course of interplay of equilibria. It could conjure up new explosions which are a kind of physical joy, instead of psychic joy.

What makes something and what desires something come from the same source. There cannot be a division between a nonconscious nondistinction and a conscious nondistinction. Therefore it is a worthwhile beginning.

I feel it delightful to venture into what from a higher intelligence would seem completely stupid.

I am all for that, because nothing drives you on more than being insulted so you can prove yourself.

Let's think about work.

Think about work in which you're not even lifting a pencil. It is this work that one talks about, because when you lift your pencil you are putting down something which is motivated by that concern.

What is the area of concern? How do you give an instrument, which is really not a pencil, to a person which makes him hope to pick up this pencil and put something down on paper?

He has not come into the realm where hard work, constant attention, should be. It is as if you are fighting a war with unpredictable enemies around you. Your plan must be terribly good. You know you are going to win the battle eventually. You have calculated that it's going to rain at a certain time because that's going to help. The enemy doesn't know it because he comes from a foreign country.

The work is here. It all takes time to do. It's the part that's measured by time. Then there is the calling in of others who are just as concerned about a certain aspect of their study as you are about the whole of which they are a part.

But at one point nobody is there but the teacher and your fellow human next to you—human to human coming with an element of motivation, with instruments.

If you say, *Distinguish structure from the space that makes the space,* that's what we talk about in this class. It is making separations. The served area, the area served. That is not hard work. It is realization. It is guiding the mind. You can put the pencil and paper away.

I had a very interesting experience yesterday in class.

One student had a building, undistinguished, but he had a good sense of taking what is there and giving it to himself. He had a little court that he found in the wake of taller buildings. He borrowed the open space, and he gave off some of the office space, too. He put a roof over this area to enclose it, and underneath was a fountain.

I saw red when I saw this style. With the space frame over it, glazed. This felt so negative to me. I couldn't see it. I had the hardest time explaining why it shouldn't be there. I failed to convince this man, and so did I fail to convince others in the class. I noticed clearly that the response wasn't there at all. They didn't see any reason why you can't put a fountain under a space frame, glazed in very neatly.

A greenhouse is part of a farmer's understanding. It is how he prepares plants for his use many times. It can be thought of as a cradle. This man wasn't using it as a cradle. He wasn't going to release the fountain to the outside when it got good and ready. No. He wasn't thinking of growing a tree so he could actually plant it outside. That dream was in a zoo. And the fountain was also in a zoo.

I always wanted to make drawings in which I took everything out and just showed the important parts of the structure. Such fill-ins as where toilets and furniture are on a plan did not show as much concern as setting down the framework. The framework is the final decision of how everything will work out even though not specifically furnished or indicated for this use.

I cannot say the bathhouse in Trenton was the first time I knew about architecture, but you can sense that as evidence if you believe it is evidence, since you are making a commentary on it.

Bathhouse, Jewish
Community Center
Trenton, NJ 1955-56

Yale Art Gallery
New Haven, CT 1951-53

When I had the building to do for Yale, I had a different idea about what the ceiling should be. It wasn't a tetrahedral ceiling. I tried to make it a place for lighting or air. I was thinking of it in this way, but it wasn't deeply thought about in my mind at all. I didn't think of it as being servant areas and areas served.

I don't know whether I did the bathhouse at the same time that I did the other, or whether it was after that. I can't remember anymore. But I know that the definiteness of the hollowed columns was the beginning of the realization of served and servant areas. Earlier drawings I made of the bathhouse showed walls and mazes. I made all kinds of maze drawings, a maze of getting in and out and trying to get corridors. I even painted the outside walls so it would look well.

When I found these posts which are hollow, in which I could insert the services, I didn't care what it looked like.

That was a big thing.

I did it because I knew it had the qualities which carry beyond itself. I didn't intervene by still trying to make it look well. I didn't care. But on the other hand, the fact that I've painted one wall so that you know where to walk in was an indication that I still wanted to make it significant, understandable. I said to myself, *These walls are bare. Do I know where to walk in? Do I want to say 'entrance'?* It was in areas where the full trust of its taking care of itself still didn't come.

I think the bathhouse came after Yale. I don't know chronologically what happened. But I had a sense that the bathhouse was a harbinger. In it was a clue to what would happen later, but it wasn't caught. I made some attempts to make columns. Before, I didn't think of columns like this. Nor was it good to think about it because it's too complicated. I did it because I was trying to develop something emerging out of it. In the bathhouse it was clear.

The way to trust realization is to find the means.

The means is a lump of space altogether that is released by structure.

They dance in front of you—it could be the Baths of Caracalla, it could be the Crystal Palace, it could be anything which structure is releasing.

Structure is the maker of the room.

It is also the giver of life to this space.

You imagine people in it, and you test people in it to see whether they'd live there. It doesn't come so much from the operation of the school, but from whether you can hold a school in this room. It doesn't have to be a special place. It stems from the realization of spaces.

Suppose I were to say that columns were the enemy of a factory. Why do I say this and use columns? It is for the same reason that somebody would write a composition with the idea of writing another one. I wouldn't go into why I did it. I'd make the statement that it is this way. Then there is a factory which has columns. The statement is what one should aspire to. It is the teacher in me that says this, hoping someone would be able to make this possible and to have a much more logical approach to things.

Olivetti-Underwood Factory
Harrisburg, PA 1966-70

In the Olivetti job, I came to sixty-foot spans which led me to a construction I never would have found had I followed their instruction, which had been twenty-foot spans. This makes it understandable why I would say that a factory use no columns. It doesn't mean I adhere to this principle as though it were something over which I had full control. I don't. When I am painting a canvas I have absolute control over it. When I am making a piece of sculpture, I have another command. But in buildings where so many factors are involved—money, other people—a precedent is always set in regard to these things.

Magazines say, *This is the way it was solved.* You aren't talking about the painting and how many ways it was solved. It is a different prerogative. The solution to the problem, as a reference, is an undeniable part of our work, but it is not the teacher.

Silence, beauty, not of knowledge.

Experience is a record of the honesty of our making, from which beauty is sensed.

It comes from joy.

I've made the path sudden; it could be a path of many steps between. It shouldn't come as a shock, from which comes beauty. It may even come when you take a breath because, after all, there's much more before then, when a thing is visualized without being made to order.

You can understand a city in terms of time and circumstances playing on it. You can't make a series of idealistic things which are failures.

There must be a value put to that which is not built. The sense of it has its position as though its value were finished.

I'd much rather write cryptic things, and then do something.

The order, the form, the design, and the inseparable parts—without this you are left with just one of those parts which is separable to nothing. It becomes a single building. How much more wonderful it would be if these values were not lost. I didn't fail. It's just that the circumstances were such that the whole thing could not be brought about.

Fine Arts Center
Fort Wayne, IN 1961-65

The Fort Wayne Arts Center has a value in itself. All of these steps trying to express it clearer and clearer had to be given up. Only one thing is built so far. It's built in such a way that we may have to find other things to build next to it, which is always a possibility.

The value of uncompleted things is very strong. They have emphasized whatever is circumstantially possible. They bring out understanding of things as they are going.

If the spirit is there and it can be recorded, what is lost?

The drawing is important, the incomplete scheme is important, if it has a central gravitational force which makes that arrangement not just an arrangement but something which gives a richness to the associations which are lost. Recording of that which has not been done must be made much of.

Realization is unclearly defined, but it impresses you as being in the nature. You look for inseparable parts. It doesn't come right away. You don't know what they are. Think in terms of space, images which are undivided. It's like a series of images where you gather the sense of architecture from what you've seen through a book or in a room with a person.

Events are what happen to you and what you react to, but you react your own way because you are a singularity.

I have always in my mind the gratitude of being: first of all, of having something responsive in me aroused by what is available, and also the irony that if I weren't in a certain place I would be somebody else.

If I were somebody else, I would never have been an architect. My associations at home would never have led me to those circumstances where people dealt with great sums of money, which is what architects deal with.

Even though my father worked in stained glass, his associations were not so much with architects. He was more associated with those places where stained glass was made. He was not in a position where he discussed stained glass, so he never brought back any architectural qualities. He was also more interested in flowers and birds than writing love letters for people who had trouble writing. When he was in Russia he did write for all those people who were illiterate, such as officers in the army. He was popular because of it, and he was entrusted with many things.

I wouldn't have been an architect if I hadn't gone to Central High School, which was a good school. They had a course in architecture given by the head of the department of art. It was a mandatory course. It was a matter of listening to lectures and then making five plates of the various important styles: Renaissance, Roman, Greek, Egyptian and Gothic. I helped half the class make those drawings and tried to disguise them in such a way that one wouldn't know that I did them. But there was some evidence always that I did those drawings. When the teacher pointed it out to me and said, *Did you have a hand in this?* I said, *Yes, I did.* He said, *Well...I think that's all right.* He was a very nice guy. People who went to school with me remember this very well because nothing worried them more.

I had dreams that I wouldn't pass swimming. It was a school of fine arts, but you couldn't graduate unless you passed swimming. I didn't do it until the last days, and I had to have a stick pointed to me so I would make the last lap. It was impossible for me somehow. I don't know if my breathing was bad, but I was helped, so I consider it all the same thing.

I was always trying to test my physical prowess. I was sent to get some groceries. There was a little street I had to pass, and I always tried to make it in one jump. The distance was quite a distance, but it wasn't so that one couldn't make it. When I was just a kid I always had my toe touching on the street side, not on the pavement. One time I almost made it, but I fell backwards and hit my head on the pavement. Somebody helped me to pick up the groceries. I lost my sight. I couldn't see anything around me. I knew where I was and I walked home thinking of what I would be if I lost my eyesight. I was ready to adjust to the whole thing right there and then. I walked up the three flights to where we lived, and I let on that everything was all right. I sat down in the corner, and my eyes cleared up.

But I remember to this day what I decided I would be. I thought the best thing was to be a musician, because it wasn't necessary to see everything. My mother always wanted me to be a musician, but my father thought I should be an artist because I used to draw all the time. That was my delight. In school days I never really studied, I just made drawings.

I remember having come over with my mother and sister and brother on the boat from Estonia. I was five years old. Because I could draw, I made drawings of whatever happened. It was a long voyage because we went steerage, and you do have a good chance to see what's going on. We were on a certain part of the deck—that was our recreation—and I made drawings of things. It was pointed out to me that the smoke from one boat was going the other way. It was a very slow boat and the smoke was faster than the movement of the boat, or the boat was arrested at that time. The captain called my attention to it. And because he liked the drawing so much, my mother thought we would give it to him. As a result we had oranges every day. And that was really something—oranges were a rare thing, and I was very proud.

When I first saw New York, I was put on a carrier—it could have been a trolley—and I saw the buildings go by. I didn't think I was riding at all; I thought the buildings were passing by. I thought that was very funny. I looked at my father who had met us in this country, and I told him about that. I don't know what his reaction was, but I said, *In this place, the buildings are moving.*

I remember the other stories in which there were projects, or the imagination was working.

I was playing with a little boy in the neighborhood before I went to school. Already I was about seven years old, and we didn't know children started school at six years old. We lived in a section of a poor neighborhood where most people spoke very little English, and they didn't know their way around. Many kids were hanging around. This was in North Philadelphia, somewhere very far east—Third Street or Second Street. It's where many people came when they arrived, and where rents were little.

My father came to Philadelphia first. He escaped from the Russian Army and came from the east because the Russo-Japanese War was to be fought. Nobody liked doing anything for Russia because it was not a comfortable country. He came to this country, and we followed soon after. My father's brother was already here in Philadelphia, so he came to work with my uncle.

I remember that I was born on an island off the coast of Estonia. I remember mud streets and that my aunt was a schoolteacher. And I do remember coming to the class one time and sitting around the desk.

I went to visit my grandmother in 1928. She had a one-room house near the place where they kept fish. There was a sterno stove in one corner and two sacks of dried fish, a chair, a table and a bed. I slept on the floor, she slept on the bed. I lived there for months, and I used to see the fishermen bring in their catch. A frugal existence. She had nothing except what her children gave her. It was a time when the Russians had taken everything away.

There was a time before that, before 1917, when we were at home here in Philadelphia and my father got the message that my grandfather had died, and that he had left his hotel to my sister and myself. Almost in the wake of that, the Russians took over, and they confiscated the right to hold the property. My father tried to get an exemption from that, because it was the only hope he had of having a decent existence, but that fell apart. They lost everything, so my grandmother was in poverty. But her daughters and sons, my mother's brothers and sisters, went to Riga where they were very well off and could send a few pennies to my grandmother.

When I went to Riga to visit my uncle's relatives, I recalled the places my father and mother used to speak of. I visited the areas of Riga and saw my people. I was very much moved by it.

In the place where we lived, we had a common stove which several families used in an open courtyard. I remember I took the coals out of the fire and put them in my apron, and they flared up. It was a heavy rug-like apron. I was three years old. It flared up, and I tried to protect my eyes, which I did. My hands were burned, and my face. It was a traumatic experience.

In the early times in school, I probably was promoted or thought of as any kind of a student only because I could draw. My arithmetic was pretty bad. I could not for the longest time find out why, if $1 \times 1 = 1$, 2×2 wasn't 2. I couldn't get it through my head. Studying was always tremendously difficult for me. My first teacher's name was Miss Apple, and she put stars printed in ink on my arm to tell my mother that I was a distinguished student, not in the academics, but in drawing, or in anything that had to do with making up a story.

I was tremendously bashful and self-conscious because my face was badly scarred, and sort of lumpy because it hadn't yet healed properly. But, being prodded a bit, I could talk about a tree or an apple or something like that. I used to get stars for that. Anything that had to do with not studying. Studying was something that never got through to me, but in oratory fashion I could learn most things.

It bears out the fact that people only learn what is part of them. What I went through has taught me many things about teaching. The position I hold now as a teacher is within the limits of the person, where everything can become.

I never looked up a document as a teacher.

I never referred to a book that one must read, as a teacher, except something I may have found out of the blue and read one chapter of. Never was there a reading list.

Teaching is conjuring up the nature of things. When we talk about a school, everything stops in the mind. Suddenly school becomes like an ember; it's bright and has a nature. This experience comes from your intuitive, a record or odyssey of your making which experienced many rejections and many receptions. Even though the experience is little, it is no different from the experience through which a great scientist gets his sense of order. From the most minute smidgen of knowledge, he reconstructs the universe. It isn't important that the circumstances be right. It can be as little as a safety pin which can reconstruct the locomotive.

You're lucky to be alive. And from that and your singularity, the world is before you.

You don't have to be a special presence.

The experience opens up avenues which are different from the avenues that are opened up to another singularity.

It is important to know the base from which you trust yourself as a teacher. This is what I think a teacher is because that's what I think I am. There could be other people with other views. It is singularities to singularities.

There cannot be a definition such as *What is a teacher?*

It is *In what way am I a teacher?*

I teach best when I never refer to how I did it.

The instructor is out of it.

Teaching is when the person has gotten from me a sense of commonality through singularity. The common thing—every singularity lives in it. You can, just with the raise of an eyebrow, make yourself understood. Just through expressing yourself without words.

The example of what has been done is a source of inspiration.

The inspiration is when the desire to express meets the possible.

When you see a beautiful painting, the desire to express is there. The way it is expressed shows that it is possible. And the way it is expressed belongs to the one who expressed it. You can't use it.

At the point you receive this as belonging to you, not to the man who sent it, the words are changed. You receive it differently, just the way knowledge is received by each one in his knowing differently.

When I'm about to leave for school, something passes over me which makes me feel terribly wealthy. It makes me feel as though I am about to go on a pirate ship and have another venture with humans.

The way I conduct my office, too, is built on the finding of a nature, and even going so far that the program becomes secondary. The program becomes roughly a consideration.

An auditorium is not considered for the number of people inside, but simply for the nature of the auditorium. I could only work when I defined an auditorium as a violin and the lobby as the violin case. I knew how much separation had to be between the two. The ideal violin case would be one in which the violin was suspended and never touched any part of the case. This gave respect for the whisper on the stage.

The case was supplying the instrument with secondary things like the lobby, toilets, stairways. The stage was not the stage but part of the audience. The stage and the auditorium were one.

Backstage was the actor's house. Backstage was no more backstage. It was something which I would build half a mile away, develop it as a club from which the actors come out. A place where the fireplace is, where the living room is, where they made up and rehearsed. I even thought in terms of a chapel where the soliloquy could be said without the director present. And maybe a few little places up there where someone can take a sneaking view of what's happening when nobody's looking, because that's part of the mystery.

I couldn't accomplish these things because the four clients could not see it. Oh, they were fascinated; they listened like gentlemen. Then the listening was compared with money, and the thing became somehow a different thing.

But I never lost sight of what I was thinking. A poet wouldn't lose sight of it. What he couldn't express in one poem, he would express in another.

The same thing could be true of the composition finished, if you found that in the finishing there were vast incompletions. Or there could be the birth of another thing which could be magnified from the most frugal needs into something that has magnificence.

Why don't I refuse commissions, instead of taking them all on?

This would be an unheard-of thing for me to do. I could no more do it than the man in the moon. If somebody came to me and hit me over the head, I'd say, *Look, I don't want to see you,* but not for any other reason. It's because I can sense right away that it is an expressive possibility to be done. In this way I am like other architects—except those who are remotely attached to what they are doing by being businessmen; they are concerned with keeping the payroll going, which of course one must do, too.

But the violin and the violin case. The sense that a school must be made of rooms that are not like other rooms. Still, I build schools with rooms like other rooms, but I never forget what I really want to do. I believe it.

The wish in the fairy tale is the beginning of science.

You'd wish you were somewhere else if somebody were about to hit you over the head. Imagine that you were able to move your finger and disappear. People won't be satisfied unless that's impossible.

You don't absorb any more than what is possible.

But circumstantially you can be led to many realizations which would not be so if your circumstances were different.

I expressed it when somebody asked me what tradition was.

I was in Luis Barragan's house, and we were talking about tradition. He showed me many books of Spanish historical happenings, and he showed me a book full of mythical things, beautiful drawings and diagrams of skeletons that were talking and making love, crazy things the mind can make up, which he had in his collection of books that fascinated him.

We were sitting around talking, and there were people draped on the floor in beautiful dress, drinking champagne. It was a beautiful house, a tremendously personal thing, and very convincing.

We were talking about tradition because he was showing me books that were thoroughly Spanish in mentality—the proud faces that would take any punishment and to whom death was an experience, that part of the Spanish nature. Even in the Spanish castle you can't find the door; it won't let you. Unlike a Scottish castle, where obviously there is a door and a moat, and the entrance is there somewhere—just try to get in, that's all. They also sneak bedrooms and stairways into the walls of the castle. They don't know how alive the walls are because they are full of things that are worming in there, making the hall itself a livable place. The Spanish castle has none of this. It's a wall, nothing else. You rot, or sleep, or do anything you want in this great big chamber. There's no chance for an opening, except what is essential.

We were talking about tradition. Barragan said, *What is tradition?* My mind went to the Globe Theatre; I looked through a chink in the wall to see what was happening. I noticed they were putting on *Much Ado About Nothing.* The audience was standing in the first level, and there were some people in the balcony. At the first movement of the actor, he turned to dust. And the second actor, trying to utter a word, also turned to dust. It was a funny analogy. I was trying to say *Could I see what happened back then?*

You cannot recapture what has happened. What was valuable was the golden dust that fell from this, which was man's nature. If you can, from what happened, derive man's nature, and if you could put your finger through the golden dust, you would have the powers of anticipation.

That power is what the artist has.

He knows he's writing what has yet not been said, yet not been made, and yet he does it with a feeling that it comes from the truth.

The truth is something you can't seek.

The truth is something that happens and then you know it. It is an undefinable quality, and it must happen.

The truth is anything that happens whether you like it or not. It is the manifestation of the truth that you are seeing. But you must filter out of it, or crystallize out of it the happening itself, because that is only a vehicle for conveying the nature.

In explaining the teacher, if I may call myself that, the meaning of truth is constantly on my mind.

It is why I listen so tentatively to the person who is as boring as hell. I am listening to just how meagre is his intuition.

The mind, which is the brain and the soul, is what gives the singularity to a person. He is not the same only because the degree of the unmeasurable is unable to come out. Just how much of the unmeasurable he has is what distinguishes him.

You listen because the story of those who are unable is important to those who are able.

The teacher makes no choices and he has no favorites. He would be shortchanging himself if he were that way.

When I see Indians on the street, I never see them smiling. I see children smiling, but grownups, no. I would like to know what it is. It brings me close to India. There is something I could learn if I could know what there is that is only bound in dire necessities. What I'd like to see is the moment when the Indian is not frowning.

The Indian is concerned with the unmeasurable. When I speak to B.V. Doshi's father-in-law and I mention things which are ordinarily interesting to people, he says it is so and he gives me references to confirm it. He is a man of knowledge, and on that basis we can talk very well.

I couldn't talk about world affairs, because always the next day it's some other thing.

I feel an affinity not only with Indians. I was in Germany not long ago. I went over with the State Department to three countries: Belgium, Germany and France. In Germany I felt that I was completely understood by half the people I saw, and the other half, who knows? This was a matter of speaking to husband and wife, and one did not understand, and the other did. In Germany there are two wonderful traditions. There are the great classical musicians, and there is also a strong operational sense. They are good craftsmen, and they are ruining the cities. The architects are not very good.

I met father and son in Frankfurt. It was a delight to meet these two people. One was talking to the other as though there was teaching going on. They spoke enough English and I knew enough German to understand what they were saying when they were trying to explain themselves to me. It was delightful to see the loving details they applied. Still, there was no power in their architecture. There was nothing strong to hold it together.

I learned four chapters of Chuang-tze with great difficulty. I look at the book once a week, and I don't know what I'm reading unless I go through a struggle. I did read a few chapters, and I like very much the association of architecture and the orders which were a part of it. Defining the inseparable parts, not making an accounting, a listing, a categorizing of what happened—that's what I read in Chuang-tze. There was a categorical respect for his talent. We never questioned him. We never thought he was anything but great.

Le Corbusier was a revelation to me. He made me realize that there was a man alive who could be an inspiring teacher. Through his work he could teach you. This was not true of works of old, because they belonged to their era and you could not sense the human decisions, the time that brought it about. That would be a wonderful thing to know, but in no history do you find it. Having a man living and producing that which others are not producing, that which you sense has the quality of giving rise to inspiration—that had greater power than works of old.

I felt I could throw away the books, which was what was in the air at the time Gropius advocated throwing away the books.

Somebody asked me, *Hasn't the image of Le Corbusier faded in your mind?* I said, *No, it hasn't faded, but I don't turn the pages of his work any more.* I don't turn the pages, though I know that they will be turned again.

At one time I thought the ideas of towers with big open spaces around them was a wonderful thing, until I realized, *Where is the bakery shop?* And the park was not good enough.

If you consider that what is has always been, then what is must be looked at as what has gone awry.

Corbusier is; therefore, architecture is. It mustn't be judged as being poor. It must be judged as architecture which the mind can conjure up.

I was despondent because I had ideas about great garages, with shopping underneath, which could become models, in the same vein as Le Corbusier's towers. I couldn't exercise it. I thought they'd be magnificent-looking structures seen in the distance, so that every little boy would know what the city was about. Smithson quieted me by saying, *Lou, you must consider that what you have said has its place in architecture, though you didn't build it. It's in the thought.* Now I don't think my idea is quite as valid as I thought. There are other ways of managing it, and this way is not the best. It belongs to architecture. It's still there in its right to be seen again, and somebody else looking at it would see a different thing.

Savalia, an Italian architect, made conceptions of various levels which were never built. At the same time they were too much to ask because things were running pretty well without all that stuff, and one would never spoil a city with such suggestions. But today they are valid. That's what I mean by turning the pages again.

If circumstances are different, new validities come about. The fact that a man is inventive is the main thing. The man has done what nature cannot do.

Boulet's factory had the feeling of being a very important operation. It belonged to the dictates of a Napoleon. And people thought: *The world is great, that this thing can be.*

This is no different than what I'm talking about: the station which would be the new utilities of the city. You don't vest buildings which are here with all the burdens of air conditioning equipment. This takes care of it. The spaces are released again, and they dance like fairies. The city could charge for the upkeep of these facilities. The thought of Boulet was an immediate inspiration that something central would take care of work which has the experience of being central. This has a different nature than where you work. You are separating natures. That thing will remain there whether you are building a factory or building a city, because there is a sense of separation, that it has an inseparable part. You've discovered a part, an organ that can make things live.

Le Corbusier's idea was an organ, too, to release land so there would be open spaces for kids to play in. There was an exaggerated statement of all the ground. You are living in the country. These houses are just big houses instead of little ones, and the ground is all free.

But he forgot the bakery shop, and the intimacy of going down the street, and finding the house of a person who lives in a certain way because he is a singularity. How singular can you get when you live in an apartment?

Most people would say, *Oh, unlivable!* They should be talking about how sad that this cannot be.

From a conversations with Richard Saul Wurman
Flight to San Francisco, California
October 1973

Theological Library
Berkeley, CA 1973-74

I am building a library which is an all-religious library for various sects. I can't speak about religious sects. I just know the Catholics, the Jews and the Moslems—I have a vague idea of the various sects. But I don't have a vague idea about religion itself. I feel conversed with religion as a very sacred part of the intimate. But as far as people practicing their philosophies of religion, I can frankly say I don't know anything about them. None of them seem to be of the quality of religion itself.

Richard Saul Wurman: Don't you feel that the intensity with which you work—and the straight-line manner in which you work—is a kind of religion?

Yes, I do. I am so trusting of the intuitive. No knowledge can spark equally the delight of the feeling of self-resourcefulness which the intuitive gives you.

I only want to be recognized for my potentiality, not the facts that occur by the play of circumstance.

If I said, *That isn't the truth,* it is the truth. Whatever is said will be the truth. Even if it is said without thought, even if it is said without feeling, it's true because it was said.

Anything that happens is the truth. You can't seek the truth.

I decided to make things hard for myself.

I can be so bankrupt, time-wise, and a person comes to see me. Everybody in my office wants to say, *Why don't you just defer seeing him?* and I have no graceful way of doing it. It's almost my style of conducting my everyday court. Somewhere down the line it's rewarding in that the business is finished and never deferred. Even the air of resentment at the little time makes the time I have left over more poignant.

I get more daring if I'm making a drawing which I have to wait a long time for than I would if I were to sit down with all the comfort in the world and draw line for line without being pressed. This happened to me just this morning. I was waiting for the lines of a perspective to be made. I had a plan that I would go to bed at three a.m. It wasn't until three a.m. that I got the drawing to do. Even then, it wasn't outlined to the point where I could dash through it. I had to start with a feeling that nothing is ready. I put clumsy lines on the paper and decided I would rub nothing out— not a thing—and I didn't. It was like talking to myself. I just put line over line, and it's a lovely perspective. The people in it are joyous. They're playing. The kids are distorted, and they dash in one direction, intending to go the other. It had all the things I want to do myself: the agility which I always admired, the prowess which I always admired. I never draw a person who is fat. I always draw one who is lean, because I don't like my belly.

I said, *What am I doing? Nobody will like this.* I want people to like it.

I look for the response from an agreement without example. Just the feeling of agreeing. It will eventually be a feeling of a work that's worthy, even if it doesn't get response right away.

It's that feeling of commonality. A person says, *Oh, it's lovely.* I have my idea of what's lovely about it, but the fact that they have that response is what eventually comes in recognition of a work that has in it some degree of eternity. The facts are just temporary things and can't really know lasting value.

United States
Consulate Buildings
Luanda, Angola 1959-61

In the Luanda project, I wanted to make the shield out of paper, though concrete was the more logical material. I was not looking for concrete to do a great deal of work. It was ribbed, it was economized, it cost a lot more money than using it brutally. The point was that I wanted to express the fact that the concrete was not asked to do any work, that it was able to stand up like a piece of paper when you bend it.

Sher-E-Banglanagar
Dacca, Bangladesh
1962-74

In Dacca, I placed the wall in front of the windows. The windows are very light. I'm sure you say, *The craftsmanship was not what Lou wanted.* But still, my choice of the marble in unison with cement is inspired technology. I wanted to recognize the fact that the concrete would not turn out well.

The concrete is made like rotten stone. The marble inset mixes the fine with the rough, and the fine takes over.

If a man imitates what I do, that man is stupid, because I already don't like what I did and to copy it only hurts much more.

I say to him, *Why don't you copy something I haven't yet done?* This would be worthwhile. In the way a thing is imitated you feel the precariousness of the *yet not complete*—what you feel you can do, but never do.

The intuitive is the potential, that which is true to everyone, but which not everyone is able to bring out because of the difference in the instrumentation that man has.

RSW: Was there somebody in your life that allowed you to set out at a certain time with the confidence that you could survive doing what you wanted to do?

233

George Howe. I read a letter one time that he wrote, recommending that I be a Fellow of the AIA. It was the most laudatory letter, and it really did pinpoint the potentiality as though he were reading my mind all the time. This gave me tremendous confidence—more so because he never showed me the letter.

I wouldn't have seen it if it weren't for my secretary, Louise, who said, *Lou, you must read this letter.* I said, *I don't want to hear it, I don't want to read it, unless George would show it to me.* But she wouldn't let me go. She said, *You simply have to read this letter.* I said, *No, it wasn't shown to me, and I'm not going to read it.* So she said, *All right. Are you coming for dinner?*

She took the letter with her, and then she said, *I want to read you something.* I was rather dull about this thing. She read, and it was written so well that my name did not appear until the very end. It was simply a description that I couldn't recognize myself in. It was something that had to do with some kind of gift, and it was beautiful. In the end, it turned out that he was talking about me all the time.

George did have an influence on me. His gaiety in the light of adversity—I thought there was something very wonderful about this man.

My mother held true to the absolute confidence in me. When I was three, my face was burnt. My father said, *I think it's best that he dies.* And my mother said, *No, he'll live and be a great man.* She would say it, she was that kind of person. My father didn't have much influence on me, though he had lots of talent. My mother was so unselfish. She was someone good to go to.

And then there was a lady whose daughter I liked very much—(she wasn't my first sweetheart, but she was certainly my second sweetheart)—who couldn't read or write. She would listen to me hours on end explaining to her physics and poetry, and she would say, *Isn't that wonderful, isn't that wonderful!* I was very much in love with Ada. I was in love with her because she was so terrible in school. I thought maybe I could teach her something. They were just simple notions that I had. She was extremely honest and forthright, like her mother. She was plain and good. I always wanted to talk to her and tell her things.

An interesting thing happened the other day. The Swiss, Heinz Ronner, came to burglarize the office. I mean burglarize in a very loving way. It was a thing that had to be done. They discovered drawings lying around, things bundled up. They opened everything. If they saw a bundle marked, *Prints,* they didn't assume they were prints. They looked in it and found drawings I've been looking for for a long time, just piled together.

Office Building
Kansas City 1966-73

There was a drawing I made of the first idea I had for the Kansas City Tower, and it looks no more like a tower or anything like what is hopefully now going to be done. I wanted a truss where you could live and be special in its spaces, from which would hang a building, it being so complex that it could contain areas of interplay spaces and diaphragms, and would be strong enough to hold a building. It had to do not with structure, but with discovery of spaces in light. The truss was something which you made and then went to, to find out what it was like. I was looking for the spaces as though they were already naturally, nonconsciously made, from which I let hang a few strands, themes which would hold it all in place. It was almost like a child's drawing.

In light of what there is not, how can one dare to show a drawing that can't be made? Ronner showed to me. I thought it was my first study of the interior of the Dacca auditorium. I said I didn't have any such idea, but it looked so much like it that I cringed. I said, *I don't know what it is, I don't know what it is.* He said, *I suspect it's the Kansas City Tower.* He's looking for the first thoughts, the intuitive beginning. Knowledge hadn't anything to do with it. The more I saw it, the more I recognized it as being the drawing I made. It's really a monster. It has no right to be, except that the drawing is absolutely charming.

There is a wide difference between the professional and the architect.

The architect is a person.

The professional is not a person.

There are a few of us like myself who didn't accept the word, *Service*—it doesn't feel right. Still, I am a man who tries to serve the client. If you're an artist doing a painting, you're not offering your service. If you're sculpting, you're not offering your service. If you're writing, you're not offering service. The profession of architecture must not be considered less of an art than the others, so why should I be called a servant?

Why am I not giving an offering?

The distinction should be made between the architect who is bound in the profession, but is not in any way bound to that which holds the profession. He feels the camaraderie of his fellow people. I feel the camaraderie whenever I meet a group of architects. I seek their company to know what others feel, never thinking that I have the pride of being in the profession.

They are people who are reacting in their own way to an assignment to express, called architectural commission. The urge to express lies behind it. How full is this expression? In what way do you feel this is the motive or drive which makes you make a building.

Sher-E-Bangalanager
Dacca, Bangladesh
1962-74

It's (Dacca is) very ragged. There are many things that were done very poorly. The interior is like the exterior except it seems shabbier because the light doesn't get to it. When it's finished, I have designs I want to do with it, with the kind of tapestries I want there. There are places where I need a tapestry because it cannot stand the way it is. A great rug on the floor will make the walls look as though they were there a thousand years. They have a virility that is like the memory of a giant.

I visited the land again in the height of the monsoon, and I realized how thorough the hardship is during those times when almost half the land is innundated.

I was given two thousand additional acres of land. I saw the monsoon acreage. Most of it was low land with some established parks.

I toured the land and saw what happened during time of war. They are very different people. They hold the state first, religion second. What held the East and West together was supposedly the religious agreement, but when the East was freed from the West, they considered the country first.

I had a thought which divided building architecture from land architecture.

I took over the role of land architect, and I sold them the idea of roads which were bridges. These bridges were brick bridges with arched areas. During the dry season, you can walk under them, or grow under them if you like. They should be made as a kind of rock which was given to them after the monsoon. I was thinking of building houses on them, even above the street of the bridge.

I don't know if you'd call this a premise. It isn't really a premise.

It's not an idea unless it works. There's no such thing as an idea that fails.

A word has to be something which is not so sophisticated as it is homespun. This is the character of commonality.

Don't disinvite commonality by wrapping it up in a ball of sophistication with a scanty meaning behind it.

The distinction must be made eventually. I've made the distinction: The hall is a worthy thing in a school, whereas the corridor degenerates into a place to walk through. It loses its light, and it isn't worthy.

What is being learned should not be learned as a subject. It should be learned as a revelation, something revealing, something that has a concern element in it.

Out of the will to learn comes the concern. As soon as it is a concern, it's not graded. It cannot be graded, because the concern has become an individual concern.

One could be praised for having that kind of mind, and others who don't have that kind of mind have to wait until the time when their mind is able to receive it in its own way.

I am a perfect example because during school days I felt that maybe, if I made a drawing, they'd understand me. Maybe if I won a prize in drawing, they'd respect me. During Latin I was relying on my drawing. Many a time, I'm sure, I was passed only because I could draw. And I wanted to tell people about the drawing, so they could get their minds off the grade.

You have the beginnings of understanding only within yourself.

I have never read a program or a book whose content I didn't have to repeat so that people would understand what book I read. I'd say, *What book was that?* and they'd tell me, and I'd say, *They didn't say that.* Sure enough, when I read it again, it *would* say that. You translate into your own terms.

When I talked to the painter who painted a picture five hundred years ago, I asked him, *How would you like to have a bulb sitting there looking at your picture?* He'd first of all say, *What is it?* because he doesn't know, so how could it be right? The stuff is still the same stuff, and the light is still the same light.

How can you honor a man for what he did by putting it in the light of a bulb, which has no mood whatsoever? It is just flat as a hat—flatter than that.

You can give all the arguments in the world, all the statistics in the world, all the lighting curves in the world. All these things just brush off me. I laugh about it.

The window is a natural lighting fixture because it distributes the light and metes it out, all the things which are different from man. It's a device, a little locomotive. No motor is involved. It's simply a chosen shape—a design to allow in the natural light which would be good and not injurious.

I was wrong at one stage where I used the shape as a connector. I used it because I was orienting the thing a certain way out of respect for the trees. That is where love overdoes it. I regard a tree with such importance, as though it were an old man who must be respected.

That happened once before in the psychiatric hospital which I did. I tortured that building for a tree. And then, because it didn't have much life anyway, it fell during construction.

Kelly developed the right curve. I made a line; I thought it should be something which throws the light. Then I was thinking it should be made of some transparent material so that you could see through it. That was the problem I gave to Kelly. He, very much the material man, thought of it as perforated metal. When I saw the perforated metal, I could see right through it to the building across the way, and I said, *That's it*. The right kind of pinpoints of holes gave the image, which was grayer the less holes you had. They were like multiple eyes.

Much must be given to Rick Brown, (and a hell of a lot to Komendant). He recognized the inherent weakness in the thinness of the shell. He was thinking of firming the edges of the ends, not allowing it to go wild, which it can do. He is definitely fabrics-minded because he recognized its weaknesses, its strengths, all in one shot. His ambition was immediately aroused. It can be aroused very easily, to a point where he becomes jealous of the world. He said, *This can span a hundred and fifty feet! This can be done!* He made this pronouncement in the style of the triple negative. I liked his ambitions. He whittled it down to a hundred, and I didn't ask for anything more than a hundred.

It was the kind of spirit in which one could feel confident and know something would be done.

From a Conversation with William Jordy

I began to work with metal mouldings on the medical center, which is now torn down. I'm glad it's torn down. Though technically this thing worked out beautifully, I was not experienced enough with the potentiality of it.

I was looking for an answer to the window which, when made of stock members, did not please me. I also thought it was technologically false because you were trying to make it look like a familiar moulding which would be applied more to wood than it would be to metal. Wood is complete, it's full. If you make a hollow column in metal, it must be a container. It's completed and it's right. But when you're dealing with nothing on the inside, you're suspicious of the metal that's helping in on the interior which you don't want to show, or it is a limitation of another material.

The openness of this metal moulding is an insect-inspired thing. It's made the way an insect is made: terrifically light, but tenacious, able to hold so much. That's what I thought when I compared a Roman bridge with a stone bridge; one was elephantine and the other was insectine.

I am a man who doesn't rely on knowledge whatsoever, because I always distort it badly. I think I am hearing something but actually it is something totally different. It's a response only to what I can see, or convey, to express. The expressiveness immediately comes to my mind.

Can the material express itself?

It's what takes me away from steel construction, which has to be fireproofed. The steel is lost, and the steel's beauty is completely a servant. Steel doesn't deserve it because it's a marvelous material.

Stainless steel doesn't have to be painted, and concrete looks terrific against it. One enhances the other. Anything painted against concrete humiliates both materials.

The painted looks wrong and the concrete looks wrong.

A very sharp edge and shadow joint against concrete, even if the concrete is at fault, tells you the limits of the concrete, the limits of the steel.

Not the limitations, but bringing it down to the limit.

You shouldn't care if it comes out in a faulty manner. That is in accordance with what you expect from it technologically.

You must accept it for what it is and look at it even humorously.

What can save it is something against it which proudly says, *What you can't do, I can do.*

Kimbell Art Museum
Fort Worth, TX
1966-72

Mellon Center For
British Art & Studios
New Haven, CT
1969-74

The Kimbell Museum and the Mellon Museum are completely different in their conceptions. In Fort Worth, all the gallery is on one floor. Therefore it can consistently get its light from the top. The walls are free and still can get natural light. The walls are just as important, and natural light is essential.

When the sun is not out, the mood is the mood of the day, and the paintings live day after day in a different way. That was appreciated by Mr. Mellon when he saw it on a dull morning and he had to get close to the painting to see it. And he made the remark that when he gets up in the morning and looks at the things around him, he also has to get close to them because it isn't a museum. And that gave him the sense of a house.

Every building is a house, regardless of whether it is a Senate, or whether it is just a house.

It is the room that's important when you're in it. The whole building means nothing compared to the room you're in. And, if you consider that a plan is a society of rooms in whatever may be their duty and in what way they supplement the duty of others, then the plan begins to be something, the spirit of which you can convey to others.

It touches everybody.

It doesn't become a mysterious manipulation on the part of the architect to make things work.

He has a superduty to give life to a miracle, that being the realization that the room is the beginning of architecture.

A room is expected to have a completeness.

It has decided inspirational qualities.

You want to deserve being there.

It gives you a duty born in every one of us, to teach the other man. You are elevated by it, so it is an offering from which you are the greatest gainer.

Kimbell Art Museum
Fort Worth, TX
1966-72

The rooms in Fort Worth are a hundred feet long. They're not so much rooms as they are a series of halls with low and high spaces, the low spaces being somewhat servant to the larger spaces.

In the low spaces you can have enclosures. I was even thinking in terms of a little tearoom, or a closet, just to serve the larger vaulted areas. They could still be a kind of interim between the two walls. But as time goes on, these areas could be where paintings are stored so they can bring out of storage other paintings that relate to things around. Directors want to do this when they have a teaching attitude. They want the things around them. Even books on the subject can be stored there.

The natural light comes directly through ten-foot slits in the vaults. Below them are what I call natural light fixtures which send light on the vaults, and from the vaults you get the light in the room.

The light is brilliant in Texas. It's a silvery, nice light.

I also used the same fixture to bring electrical power, to give light at night—supplemental light or any emphasis you may want to put on a painting.

The natural light that enters this room is no more injurious than artificial light. And you don't have to employ artificial light except for emphasis on the inside. In most cases that I've seen it, the artificial light wasn't on at all.

The fixture is made on an aluminum frame. It is a very thin aluminum, perforated so you can see right through it. I wanted to give you the sense that you could see through it because the main thing was not to get any contrast. If this were solid, you'd feel the contrast between where the light is not and where the light is, and it would give you a feeling of heaviness.

Contrast is not friendly to the eye. It's the cause of glare.

The changing dimension of the slits at the ends of the vaults are caused by the fact that the end pieces are semicircular and the vaults become wider as they go down. The vaults need power at the top. It's contrary to what you would expect. It is light at the sides and heavier at the top. At first it was hard for us to get used to it, but this is Komendant's fearlessness. It's not even a matter of fear. He knows the figure, and the figure gives him the shape. Something other than this gives me the shape. This unfamiliar thing of the thinness and the thickness there—to contrast it, not to follow it, I made the end walls purposely semi-circular, to emphasize the fact that this is a little and that's much. Just to give honor to the engineering, and not to disguise it. I think its effect is rather captivating.

It sets up a sense of wonder.

The vault doesn't have the ability to know its duty is to be straight at its bottom points. It has a tendency to break away slightly from the purity of the cycloid. So there is a thickening at that point to say: *Now, hold your line*. And that's what it does. It's holding the line. The stabilizer is also being used to enclose a six-foot space across which is the separation between the building. Otherwise you have no way of supporting a six-foot span except from end to end of the six-foot distance.

If you thought of it as being a leaf instead of a structure, then it has all of the freedom of not having to enclose anything. Not needing glass. Not doing anything at all. It would be irregular, just like a leaf, but it would span and it wouldn't fall. That's the nature of a vault.

To discipline it as an enclosure, one must add that which is not purely necessary for the vault itself to stabilize its dimensions. If it were just holding hay, it would be fine. If it were an enclosure in a park, you wouldn't have to do anything to it. But because it meets other requirements like having a marriage of materials, then it's necessary to do something.

There's a continuous slit in which the wall does not touch the vault. It goes freely from place to place. From a hundred feet to a hundred feet. That was done to show how it was made, just like a wonderful cabinet. If you look inside, you see all the dovetailing. It's completely evident, not disguised.

I was influenced by the old buildings to make a distinction between ornament and decoration, and I found that the joint is the beginning of ornament. Where two things come together you want to celebrate the two coming together. Ornament is adornment of the event of two materials coming together. Decoration is just application, decor, adding something.

The capability of the cycloid vault itself determined the dimension of these slits. The fact that it could span and be its own beam had to be given the fullest celebration of its nature, given its internal desire to tell you all about itself. To decide to make it less would have shortchanged it.

Komendant advised that we could go as much as a hundred and fifty feet. For a moment we said, *Why not?* But then we felt maybe we'd better leave good enough alone. There's where our intuition came into play, and we passed judgement on the whole damned thing. We also felt it might negate how good the twenty-foot dimension was. It would look narrower, and we didn't want that.

You look for the appropriateness, and that's what causes you to make it a hundred feet.

We also liked the idea of having three sections. The central section centers the east side, and the break which it gave us offered expression to the expansion joint which would be necessary with great distance. One expansion joint gave us no entrance, so we chose three sections with two expansion joints. A hundred feet is a very good expansion joint dimension.

It came together as a marriage between aesthetic sensitivities and engineering.

If you honor engineering, you begin to honor the other aspects of architecture as well. With Komendant you can do this because he has an innate sense of the nature of something. When he says *no* to something, it never becomes *yes*. The engineer who says, *Tell me what you want and I'll give it to you* is useless. The one who says, *I can do it this way, too* is another useless engineer.

A painting is made in natural light.

We are born in natural light.

Regardless of all the warnings about natural light, I felt that you were being given only an ersatz of light with artificial light.

Mellon Center for
British Art and Studies
New Haven, CT
1969-74

This was brought out so very well when we were making the mock-up in Mellon. We were insisting on the same idea where it was possible. And that was only on the upper levels of Mellon. Below also were paintings that were being shown. They were always related to natural light but not necessarily by having the light above.

Mellon is conceived as twenty-by-twenty rooms, some coming together. Where the partitions are left out, the columns are twenty by twenty. The columns are a kind of room-making discipline, by having them inducing the sense of the room even though the partition is not there, the column being that which tells you where the wall was left out and the column took its place.

In a sense it is where the walls parted and the column became.

I had a prior scheme for Mellon in which I put the mechanical outside. But it didn't work because it proved to be too expensive. I wanted it of the same metal as the exterior, matte stainless steel, pewter-like in character. There wasn't so much readiness on the part of the engineer to see the validity of this. But later it proved to be valid, though it may have cost a dime more. There was instrumental beauty in the realization that there was a high discipline, not a grab bag of all kinds of things put into a loosely conceived box.

At no point was I able to gather all my forces because Mellon was much more complex than Fort Worth.

Fort Worth had fundamental opportunity. All the spaces of the gallery were on one level, and the operation was on the other. We could have had the gallery on several floors, but it just happened to be my frame of mind at the moment, and I was interested in the more unsophisticated but tenacious qualities. Also the land was more free in the confines of the site.

At Mellon the land was restricted and the requirements of the space were more, so I had to do something other than have it all on the floor. There were so many pressures—Yale's tax problems and how it could meet the city's demand for buildings on sites which are commercial and being interrupted by non-commercial uses—that the idea of a store was good. Also the students were instrumental in seeing that the street's continuity, the urban character of the street, not be lost.

In the Mellon Center, because I could not put these instruments outside, I placed them in the center of the space. And there I call it the Franklin stove. It's the same material as the outside. The ducts come exposed through the space and feed the central area from two sides.

I would have used three instead of two, because the duct system should not have to stretch its arm to feed another area without feeding the passage it goes through.

The mechanism must be completely serving both aesthetically and physically.

It must be there just like a tree, its branches and its leaves, without borrowing one branch from another tree.

This I was not able to accomplish. But I must find this opportunity. It must come with all the complexities seen as a single order. Often the problem isn't so much in your mind as it is in the conditions that offer themselves.

It isn't something that you worked and worked on to force into place, because it just doesn't work. You make something artificial.

The idea was to get as much light from the central space as possible, so that the two sides of the peripheral spaces would have a light source on both sides. I allowed the amount of window that each space needed on the periphery to be dictated by the interior space.

The shield for the sun blocks out the north light. Richard Kelly worked on this. It looks like an angry crab. It looks awful. It has these domes which give even light on the walls. North light is used for art studios because it's a fixed light. But is also has the most injurious rays. Baffles prevent the glare. The light that comes through here is less injurious than the light that comes through the fixtures in Fort Worth.

In pouring concrete I use a wood form, which actually becomes better the more you use it. Where the one form meets the other, I have allowed the concrete to bleed out by making a cut in the plywood which doesn't quite penetrate the first layer of plywood. When the concrete pours, there isn't a resistance to the flow outward at the joint. Trying to make it stronger and stronger by keeping the wood together makes insufficient accuracy in the alignment, and I came to the realization that if you could allow it to bleed out some, you would then have no trauma at the joint, no honeycombing. And this proved to be right.

Salk Institute
La Jolla, CA
1959-65

Courage? No, it's just a feeling about a thing.

It's being the concrete for a moment and seeing what it wants to be.

This was laughed at, of course, but we believed in it. We allowed the whole basement of Salk, which was quite extensive, to be experimental ground for all the concrete. We had a competition between the Fuller Company and ourselves. I'd had somebody there, Fred Langford. Langford is a man who, when he sets to work on something he believes in, never gives in. He became a thorn in the side of the company, but they had to concede. Salk was there to help us, because he has a good sense of choice.

Not only was it a hell of a sight better looking, but it lent itself very well to the saving of money and repairs. We allowed all the imperfections to exist, regardless of some instances where honeycombing did appear.

We allowed nobody to touch the concrete. It wasn't necessary to touch it, anyway. Even the honeycombing, where it came, looked very good because it looked like concrete.

Then I realized that travertine does beautifully with concrete because it is also an irregular kind of stone. It has unpredictable elements in it like concrete. The use of the two materials gave it a monolithic character. There couldn't have been a better realization of material. Contrasting material would have been very bad.

Originally I thought of slate for floors. And it would have been slate if we hadn't had a better bargain on travertine coming as ballast to California. Slate, coming from Italy, was more expensive. By chance, the travertine came and proved to be by far the better material. That was a good break.

The other leading material in it was good. I used teak for the window frames in the studies, which were holding glass and holding shutters for the modulation screens pocketed in the walls.

The color of the teak is being gradually erased by the salt of the air. Again, very sympathetic. I didn't like its tobacco juice color at the beginning, but everything else carried so well that I didn't worry too much about it. Now it's becoming white.

I used polished stainless steel for all the windows in the laboratories.

I used lead for scuppers, for the path of water. I also used lead to seal the screw-tie openings, so that there is no bleeding of the rust and the steel which is left in the screw-tie opening.

Kimbell Art Museum
Fort Worth, TX
1966-72

In Fort Worth I used the same combination as in Salk: travertine and concrete.

There are no columns in the building other than the columns that hold the vaults on the ground floor of the gallery. Below there are extra columns to hold the span. But on the periphery of the building, I avoided columns, other than the ones above, by using enclosed walls as beams. Prestressed beams from column to column. These remain concrete on the exterior.

There are some walls which do not answer to the column discipline. These walls were not used as beams, but simply as fills. This happens especially at the ends of the vaults. The ends of the vaults are enclosures in concrete which are not used as a structural material. Therefore they were divided from the structure itself. They are in concrete to avoid wrecking due to the weather conditions of Texas, which include high winds and tornados.

I could not have anything that touched the vault. Therefore I had to have a stiff wall which held itself up by its own ability. I deliberated at one point to make it of a block material covered with travertine. I didn't want to invest fine concrete work in a fill-in wall. It didn't seem right to me.

It was difficult to give the purest expression to this wall since it was an unwanted wall, anyway. So it was covered with travertine.

The walls that were there as the drama of the structure were left in concrete. They were a hundred foot walls as beams. Only a sliver of light separated the cycloid from that wall.

This also freed all the areas below the columns. The column was such an important element of a vault that it was not to be helped by any other column in the building.

William Jordy

From a Conversation with David Rothstein and Jim Hatch
Autumn 1973

I am actually more of a builder than I am a designer. I know it.

In terms of material I could make a building in which the materials sing out. It looks like a stupid old thing, but then that material becomes something unusual because of the builder's attitude.

If you think of a designer in the true sense, that's exactly what I am. But a designer in the typical sense means nothing but somebody who decides on the color of the marble in the lobby of a hotel. It's all window-dressing the exterior.

A man said to me once, *Just make me a nice outside.* Exterior decoration.

I say I'm a builder. I feel terribly proud of that.

Contributed by David Rothstein, Architect
Stockbridge, Massachusetts

What was has always been.
What is has always been.
What will be has always been.

His work is in this continuum where all styles blend, confirming the unmeasurable truth which a work of art reveals. In his hands every medium touches its limit, revealing its nature, and is given radiance through his free classical inclinations by his choice of mass, shape, line and color.

Roosevelt Memorial
New York, NY 1973-84

Painter, Sculptor, Craftsman and Teacher, also I discovered the Architect in him. This became clear working with him on my newest commission, the memorial to Franklin Delano Roosevelt. His ready suggestions about the required sculpture, as the ideas unfolded, offered new attitudes and, even more, a grasp of wholeness which influenced the overall concepts of the design.

About Art

That moment when the eyes opened. *Beauty* the Light!
Could it be so if Joy had not inspired sight?
Joy, the medium impelling creation over trials of infinite pulses from Nature's touch to the marvel of seeing
has, is, will be *the birth of beauty*
the sense of the prevailing harmony at once felt.
Art—the first word.

Annual Report Text, Fleisher Art Memorial
Philadelphia, Pennsylvania
4 December 1973

When I was in my early teens, I went to the Graphic Sketch Club. I walked from 7th and Poplar to 8th and Catherine. I was given an easel, paper and charcoal in the life class. All I could hear was the swishing of the strokes and the soft and privately directed voice of the critic. It was a meeting availability, a place full of offerings.

One Saturday morning I came early. No one seemed to be around. The room to the right of the entrance was open. I walked in to see the work of the masters of the school on the walls. Someday I hoped I would be selected too. I noticed that the piano in the room was open. I had been playing at home on an ancient, large piano given to me, which was also my bed. My instrument had the sound of little bells. When I touched the keys of the school piano, angels filled the room. I sat down to play the Second Hungarian Rhapsody, not the way it was written since I could not read. When I left the room, I found several people had been listening. They asked that I play the next day at a concert which the Symphony Club was giving in this room. I tried everything to refuse but I had to agree. Sunday I played the same piece but faintly as I had played it the day before. (Luckily, I was the first to play.) Mr. Fleisher offered me a scholarship to study composition (not piano). When I told the good news to J. Liberty Todd, a Quaker and Director of the School of Industrial Art, he was flabbergasted, *No, you must not accept. Nothing but Art!* he said. My mother was heartbroken. My father agreed with him.

At Central High School, William Gray, teacher of art, gave talks on Architecture. I was to be a painter but he touched the very core of my expressive desires. How circumstantial, but how wonderful is the light thrown upon the threshold when the door is opened.

The Samuel S. Fleisher Art Memorial,
administered by the Philadelphia Museum of Art

Key Lecture, Symposium on the Education and Training of Architects
Tel Aviv, Israel
20 December 1973

It was great to hear the remarks of Mr. Zevi and Mr. Kuhn, for which I particularly have an affinity. They didn't know what to do, but they sure felt the feelings one does have when architecture comes into our consciousness and sensed that it is a something which always was, even before it became. I'd like to repeat what I think—that what is has always been, and what will be always was, and so on—because we don't derive it from any kind of successive buildup of comprehension. There is the comprehension already locked in, otherwise, it would never have been received to begin with. You never would have had it if it weren't true to man's nature. That's true of other aspects of man's doings and expressions. We live to express, and it seems there is no other reasons for living, really, but to express.

I had to think this out for myself. What I'm going to say is nothing that I've read. I was surprised to hear about form and shape in exactly the same terms as I came to, myself, without reading about it. I remember nothing really. I still don't know the size of a brick, and I'm amazed that I touch a switch and the electricity goes on, and still I can practice architecture. It certainly wasn't the knowing part of it that makes a difference. That is the most distrustful part, by the way, because it comes from knowledge, which is, of course, incomplete. And it comes to you in that way that makes knowledge, which is distrustful to relate to others, more distrustful because it enters your singularity and then it becomes privately wrong. The only thing that could come out of it of any value would be in what way a person's singularity is revealed. That is the most precious thing one can give to somebody else because that revelation has such qualities of commonality that the other man derives it where he couldn't otherwise get it. The sharing of one's knowledge and singularity conjures up another man's qualities of singularity, which he could not discover in any book. It's always discovered through another singularity. And so it is, when a work is done, that the work actually teaches tremendously. It teaches by example, or rather I would say by deed, and that, of course, is the powerful force of Le Corbusier, Frank Lloyd Wright, and Michelangelo. They taught that way. They did not teach in a school. They taught by their work.

School, however, has a place, without question, and I don't know how I'm going to frame it in some orderly way, except that I feel that school has a decided place because the spirit, or the inspiration, to learn is such a powerful inspiration that it is a nondeniable thing. I think it comes from the way we were made because the odyssey of our making has ingrained in us the intuitive, and this had to answer to all the laws of nature. Otherwise we wouldn't be. No single law made us. It is always the total harmony of the laws, or you might say, order itself. This sense of order, which a great scientist always seeks, he derives from his knowing enough to feel, for he feels order, though he doesn't know it. He doesn't know other laws, but he feels the joy of having felt them sweep over him through what little he knows. Order is felt, not known. Every time it is felt, and not known.

In order to teach myself, I teach; and when it rubs off, the student gets it. Then I thought about Zevi's remark about beginning all over again, and I couldn't think of anything that is a more inspiring thing to say, and a more hopeful thing to say, than this as an approach to any subject. Anything of interest a person has must start with the person and not start where somebody else left off.

The examples of architecture, or rather so-called architecture, just fill the atmosphere with a pollution that cannot be considered such a thing as architecture. It is the practice of architecture, it is the profession, but it is not architecture. And design is not art, but design is important. I want to say it, but must in a different way, because my sense of shape and form is the same as Mr. Kuhn mentioned. (I almost thought that I had nothing to say after he had spoken.) Form is the nature, is the realization of the inseparable parts. If you take one part away, you destroy the whole thing. And design, that which has presence in the mind in a sense of form, puts it into presence through nature—through consulting nature—because nature is the maker of everything. Nature is the giver of presences.

Then I thought, *What would be a harking back, starting from the beginning?* I should like to say that when I read history, and I'm particularly interested in English history, which fascinates me. Though it's a bloody history, it still has this quality of a search. However, every time I start to read Volume I, I linger on Chapter One, and I re-read it and re-read it and always feel something else in it. Of course my idea is probably to read Volume Zero, or Volume Minus-One, if I could only live so long as to read Minus-Two, just to peer into this terrific thing—man, who has this great capacity for putting things into being that nature cannot put into being.

Man wants nature because of his impelling forces of wanting to express, and his need to express the expressible. To express is really the soul of the soul. And the instrument we have for expressing is a marvelous instrument. We know it's marvelous when we hear Richter play the piano. That is really where the architect wants to show himself as well. Only such expression can satisfy the one who is really thinking. The right title *architect* belongs to he who has conveyed marvelous emergences that seem to elicit *yes* from every man—and no denial. Certainly we are not going to imitate what was done, but we can learn enormously from what has been done.

Tradition is a kind of golden dust that falls; if you put your fingers through it, there is a crystallization out of all circumstances which brought it about and made it be. If you put your fingers through it, I think you can give the powers of anticipation, because in what has been accepted before by man as a place to live, a place to be, a place to talk, to learn, there must be considered a miracle, and nothing short of it. You don't discard it. You don't burn the books. You look at them until you put holes with your eyes through them. They are marvelous examples. And anything that is too close to you now can be or may prove to be only good for a very few examples.

A singularity is the beautiful facet of all humanity. The more people you have, the more facets you will see. When I hear people complaining because there are three and a half people per acre, I wonder what they are talking about. I wonder about the social scientists who try to mete out how many children people should have. All those things may be good economy for those who are living, but what of those who are in limbo, those who are not living who *can* live? If the world gets overcrowded, that's part of the nature of things, that's part of the truth of things. Planned economy, planned socio-living—all these things are meaningless to me.

The sense of commonality, of human agreement, should be in every plan that is made.

I think of an indescribable void from which stems man. In the indefinable condition of silence, there's no word, there's just the spirit rising to seed an instrument upon which the soul can be played.

Nature will give you anything provided you obey its laws. Through the laws of nature one senses the rules that man gives. Rules are made to be broken.

When you realize a higher realization than the rules you employed before, it means you have come to a wonderful moment in man's presence. As a rule, it's supplanted by another rule.

A rule has its most magnificent moment when the time for change comes and modification of this rule is made.

Law never changes.

Law is nature's way, nature's unconscious way.

There is no chaos in nature. The Greeks said it, a long time ago. Their minds were not cluttered, because they had no books. They realized that nature's laws were irrefutable. Nature is only in its play of the laws, changing its attitude, changing its position into new and constant play of equilibria. Everything is always in balance, except the next moment is not in the same balance as now.

We think that is chaos, but it isn't chaos. Anything can happen, no matter what it is, provided the laws are in play. You are surprised by it and you are troubled by it—that only means that you have to learn more.

Chaos exists in man's mind, but not in nature.

Every expressive aspect of man is a grip on the will to live.

Nobody wants to go.

The body fails and thoughts of going become easier. But the desire to live forever is predominant. Man won't rest until he is able to complete that fairy tale.

If I were to choose another profession and feel elated to be able to enter it, it would be to write the new fairy tales. That's what motivates us, the incredible.

There is a well-known architect—I don't want to say he's famous, because that accolade belongs to time—I was bemoaning to him the ideas about planning cities. I wanted to build a city in no time flat. I had theories which seemed to bring more profit to others than myself. I had drawings which could not be brought into fruition. He told me a very loving thing, that often the things that you are unable to put into being are more powerful in that stage than they are when put into being.

The purity lies in the incompletion.

I don't believe a man does what he wants when he does something. He defends, like I do, to the last brick what is put up. And I honestly do. I believe forever in this lousy block. But when it's finished, it tells you of your inadequacies, which you defended to the very end.

Contributed by Carl W. Hauser, Jr.

Then thinking again about sources—somehow Volume Zero minus one and so on and so forth—I reflected on what I try to think of as silence. Silence is a sort of wordless aura of joy to desire *to be to express,* and nature seems to be his brother who exists merely to produce the material for the making of things. And I thought, *What is material but light which has become exhausted?* The mountains are exhausted light, spent light. The streams are exhausted light. The air is exhausted light, and we are made from exhausted light. If we think of the desire to be, to express, as having presence by the grace of light, and if we know that from light, one can find a way to express, to bring about, to make manifest, to put into presence, then there is a natural tendency in us, in our intuition, to move towards light to find the means that makes expression possible. Also, because they are two brothers, light moves to desire as well, and they meet at a threshold, and the meeting of that threshold is inspiration. Each person is a singularity. The threshold is also a singularity because the threshold is a something. It is in the person, and each one is not like any other.

Inspiration is the moment when the desire to express meets the possible. When a boy sees a beautiful painting, it might just say, *I will be a painting.* And through the painting, he realizes the prerogative of a painter as compared to the prerogative of the architect. The painter can paint the skies black in the daytime. He can paint dogs that can't run and birds that can't fly and make doors smaller than people. The architect must use round wheels unlike the sculptor, who can use square wheels to express the futility of war. He must use round wheels. He's got to make doors bigger than people, and he knows the sky isn't black in the daytime. All these arbiters sit in the realm of art, but art is the only language of man. Everything serves art, the scientist, in what he discovers, the nature of nature. In the end, all must serve art.

There is the power to make gold from the unmeasurable qualities of science, and there is the power to write, which is measurable. There is the measurable and the unmeasurable. The writer goes a long way holding very close to him the unmeasurable qualities, never allowing even the first word until it is the most worthy. And just at the door, you might say the entrance to light, he surrenders and must express. That means he must use a word but how careful his words are. He knows the words well, and these he gets by traveling a long, long time to the moment when he has exhausted the unmeasurable and finally settles on a word. The scientist too holds to the unmeasurable very, very closely, waiting for light to come to him, or, you might say, the names to come to him. He knows the longer he waits, the more objective he will be. He will know and gather more for the character of that which is measurable. However, as soon as he expressed what he did, he must express his research in terms of art even though all the language is scientific. Einstein travels, just like the poet does, a long, long time before he gives up the unmeasurable qualities, because he won't settle for merely knowing isolated things. He wants to know everything. Thus he goes a long distance in another sense because he needs only a smidgen of knowledge to be able to reconstruct the universe; but he thinks in terms of order and not information.

The schools are just replete with information which is very temporal; if you don't have a head for it, you forget it. Who ever learned anything that's not a part of himself? Nobody. I studied physics, and I sat next to a man who took the same notes. When I took notes, I didn't hear the physicist. My friend could hear the physicist and take notes. Whose notes do you think I copied? His, of course, to pass the examination, because I couldn't even read my writing. If the teacher had said to me, *Look, Kahn, I know you're never going to be a physicist,* he'd have been dead right. If he had said, *You must listen to physics because you're going to be an architect,* I could not have agreed with him more. I read his books now really avidly, not understanding but feeling somehow the character of them very, very much.

It worried me very much to think in terms of science and light, because my thinking might be so very inconsistent with another man's, the other singularity. I think, also, that teaching is really singularity to singularity, but instructing is something else. A teacher fights knowledge because he knows that it's different in everyone that receives it; information you can get from a book isn't worth repeating. You just refer to the book. There is no other sphere. When looking through the nature of things, when redefining things for myself (because I don't remember things), I make images which seem really to be information. When I was designing the theatre for Court Lane, I thought that possibly the theatre with its auditorium and the stage was like the violin, that it was an instrument, that it was absolutely essential that a whisper could be heard. I decided then that all the rest of the theatre was a violin case, and the theatre was a violin. I held to this religiously. Initially, I had limited information about acoustics, and my first shapes would never have worked. (You must listen to those who know the appropriate shapes of acoustics.) There were many things I had to learn. I won't even go into it. My original sketches, however, never failed to go away from the research into works that have been done because there isn't a man alive who did something who thinks he is finished with it. I am sure that Beethoven died thinking he did nothing because it was the yet not said, the yet not made, which he was looking for, not the way he, at the moment, expressed something

Now, I wish to tell you what I feel when I enter the classroom. To me the class is a check. I really couldn't practice without it. I consider the students sort of pure in their way, and I consider myself as having to answer to that purity. As I said, I teach myself, and what rubs off the student gets.

I thought of the simplest thing, and this was the room. The room in no way exists in nature. The room is so marvelous that its size, its dimension, its walls, its windows, its light—*its* light, not just light—have an effect on what you say and what you do. If there was just one other person in the room besides yourself, I am sure that what you would say would be generative. You have no witnesses. There is nothing to show off for, and somehow you can be generative. Let a third person enter that room, and I'm sure he'll resort to your lines, to what you said before. You change an event to a performance. Just so sensitive is a room. I think a plan is a society of rooms, each one having been lived in.

The person, who senses architecture as a great expressive need and thinks nothing of the profession except in what way he can be in a society of others like himself, cannot really build a school with twenty classrooms the same size looking the same way when he realizes that every room has a different response, a different ring to it, a different tonality, a different colour. If light comes from the west, the colour is not the same as it is when light comes from the east. One actually gets a green room naturally, or a yellow room, or a red room, depending on how the sun is positioned. Maybe it isn't distinctively painted red, but the sense that it must be so, even if you can't see it, is also necessary to inject. Where do you get this knowledge? From books? You get it merely from your inside. Training is helping another trust the marvelous, singular qualities that exist inside of himself. If that is so, the spaces, the rooms, in talking to each other, would become vested with qualities demanding you to make them in a way you would not have been able to do had you only thought of those rooms as a mere name, a mere checklist you set out to supply, whereby every room is accounted for. The names are on the sheet; therefore, it must be a good plan because everything works.

While connecting the classrooms in a kind of thought, you may say the *hall*, and not the *corridor*. You think of the corridor then as a sort of sneaky passage from place to place whereby the teacher will not be seen when she doesn't wish to be seen. The usual solution of pipes in the ceiling and lockers in the corridor just morally couldn't be used. If a hall would have to be a place which looks to the garden, it would probably be desirable to be in the hall because it happens to be a place for one student to meet another. Who would ask what the teacher said? It would be one of the boys to the other boy. And the other boy might say, *He didn't say that. Well, what did he say?* He said, *This and this. Oh, now I understand.* It becomes indelible when one boy of the same age tells the other one without fear or concern that he will be marked or judged. In such an atmosphere, school becomes the place where it is good to learn.

I threw away an entire set of drawings, for I came to the realization that there is a laboratory of the pipes and a laboratory for the experiment. When I got that clear in my mind, the ceiling of the pipe space was just as high as the laboratory space. It was more in its nature, and it was recognized as such because the plan was covered everywhere. It's the kind of thing which you may call a language such as Bruno Zevi is looking for, although I cannot be so presumptuous as to say that I know this language. I do not, but somehow out of the discussion with those who are interested, the natural sense of offering that a person has emerges. When he offers, that's what he really does the best. I know when a dish fell in Mozart's kitchen and it cracked and the maid shrieked because she was surprised, Mozart came in and said (and this is a purely invented story), *Oh, dissonance.* And dissonance entered music as an offering. He didn't own dissonance. It wasn't his creation. It was his realization somehow, within the intuitive. He had to offer only his own version of it, and he offered that as if it belonged to him. So too there are principles, and there are realizations that do not belong to you at all. You can only claim you expressed it. The more transcendent that expression is, the more it can influence by simply being inspiring. That is a great gratification indeed. However, when such a work is copied (the way it looks), it is death to the imitator because the work belongs to the originator. There is no credit in composing like Mozart.

Let us consider the nature of house as being different from *a house,* and being different from home, for home can only exist when people are in it. They are the creators of *home.* You don't build a home. You build a house. At best, if you build a house, there comes out of it a sense of a way of life, a reflection of a way of life which inspires your own way of living. The greater the way of life, the more free is the way of living. Form and shape are so very important. When I was working in Dacca, I realized that possibly, if I made a round window in brick, that I'd satisfy some earthquake conditions. Such a window would force these upward and to the side, and would have equal consideration with the forces that come down from above. Later in a book, which I got in England at Foley's, on the works of Leonardo, I saw the very same drawing there, and the title of it was *as a remedy for earthquake construction.* Students have seen this, and they copy the shapes, but they don't copy the realization of form which happened to correspond to the shape in this case. The form is the recognition of the realization about what could be the nature, or what is done when earthquake construction is considered. The engineer, in the same way, has to train himself to realize that what he must do is not merely to satisfy the structural conditions, but to determine the appropriateness of what he is doing. That's very seldom found. Of course there are conceptual engineers. We really do need them, and engineers must be trained as conceptual.

In speaking of city planning, urban design, architectural design, I think there should be no distinction between urban design and architectural design. The two are strictly architecture. If you divide them, you kill architecture. I'd rather kill twenty-five notions about urban design, but I'd never touch one little hair of architecture. That has proven itself quite conclusively to stand quite high in the estimation of the products of man's mind. I believe that urban design, if it's used, and taught and distinguished from architecture, becomes merely a marketplace item. It's another title you can put on which would impress city authorities very much because after all we are dealing with the city. They say this man must be good because he took urban design. City design is not design, except as it is framed as an instruction. This could be design. It doesn't have anything to do with shapes that are being made or forms that are thought out. I think form has very much to do with city planning, the very nature of things, and it could be a very great study. Instead, it is just information you see planners assemble. Most of these that are done on planning are trivial because they do not give you a sense of the wholeness of a nature which people have made, by the force of their natural inclinations, to come together, to meet. One of the deep inspirations of man is to meet and to learn, and I defy you to find others. They are all modifications of the same.

Third World Congress,
Association of Engineers and
Architects in Israel

From Lecture and Walking Tour,
Fort Wayne Art Center Dedication
Fort Wayne, Indiana
1974

This is the first time I've seen this building.

I've stayed away from it as much as I can.

What I've seen tells me many things about how I should present my work, which doesn't come off quite as well as I expect. To look at it, it seems entirely too much like I know what I'm talking about, when that's not so.

You are dealing with the unmeasurable, and if you didn't say a darn thing, it would be much clearer than saying anything. The quality must be unmeasurable; otherwise, it's valueless.

I hold distinction between desire and need.

We live by reason of desire.

Need is just so many bananas. It's disgraceful not to give the need. It's the duty of every individual to see that those who are alive are supplied their needs. No duty of government is more important than making duck soup of need. Making need is an absolute right of anyone in this world.

That country which does not foster the greatness in our feelings of desire is a country that is still not up to its fullest capacity.

I believe in the fairy tale.

I believe in the wish of the fairy tale as the beginning of science.

You wish you could fly, especially when you are being attacked by ruffians. That's not possible in certain ages because things don't come together in quite that way, but the wish is still there. It comes about because anything man can think about is the realm of reality.

Reality is the dream. Reality is the fairy tale.

The true reality is the fairy tale, not the everyday course of things, which is only circumstantially living the fairy tale, full of disappointments, full of less than what you'd expect. That's not man at all. Experience is purely incidental. The unattainable, the yet not made, yet not said, is what motivates man.

Art is the giver of a light.

When you hear the familiar strains of the Fifth Symphony, it is like a relative entering the room whom you haven't seen in a long time, and you realize for the first time that his eyes are blue.

Seeing something again is an important aspect of art. You don't ever see all at one time. You could see it indefinitely, and there would always be something you haven't seen, because art is a product of the intuitive—the most powerful instrument within us. The intuitive is the most accurate sense we have.

Science can never reach it.

Knowledge can never reach it.

The beautiful thing that the intuitive gives is a sense of commonality, a sense of human agreement which is agreement without example. Something can be produced for the first time, and somehow it has a quality of having always been there. That is the quality of human agreement.

Louis Kahn Defends—Interview, Indian Institute of Management
Ahmedabad, India
31 May 1974

A work of art is religion.

Architecture is an art, the technology merely supports it.

Sometimes there is a revelation. One realizes that this is how it should be, that by design this was meant to happen, but one hasn't the technology to achieve it. It is there, but beyond one's grasp.

However, it is this desire, this realization, that matters. Da Vinci dreamt of flying—that's what is important, not that he couldn't do it.

A realization is like a fairy tale. It is what man desires and reaches out to but cannot get.

It is this desire, not want, that elevates man.

That's why I have always loved the fairy tales, the *Arabian Nights*, things Oriental. When I got the contract for Ahmedabad, my first in this subcontinent—Dacca followed close on its heels—the first thing I did was to read the *Arabian Nights*.

It was difficult building here. I knew I wanted to build in brick, because brick is natural, not like concrete, and also for the sake of economy.

Economy is not at all the same thing as finance.

I had to learn how to lay brick from scratch. The people here couldn't lay bricks the way they should be. They just put one brick on top of another and sloshed the cement on. Why hide the beauty of open brickwork?

I asked the brick what it wanted, and it said *I want an arch,* so I gave it an arch.

But then I had to teach the bricklayers that an arch was really an arch and not just any curve between two points. I wanted the first arches ever built here to be left as they were, a little playground for children.

If there is a realization, and it takes shape into an idea, it cannot ever be prevented from taking a concrete form. Then it might be criticized.

You can criticize a man, but you cannot judge him.

If a man does something and is prepared to die by it, he is right.

An interview by an Indian Team

Institute of Management
Ahmedabad, India
1962-74

I'd like to know what you want to hear—not about management, for I don't know anything about management.

Sir, could you tell us how long you have been an architect?

Recognition came late. I did not start late. A man is late when his last job is still poor.

Could you tell us something about those holes?

I know what you are all thinking about. I can imagine how it's going to be from now on.

What are the holes for?

To make accurate spitting possible.

Why are they so big? Could not smaller ones do as well?

How big is big? You are looking at an interpretation of a building within a building. This is a porch you are looking into. There is a building for communing with nature, and another building inside. Everybody is crazy in his own way.

Don't you think you could have built these dormitories cheaper?

It is not correct to measure costs as the sum of items.

Cost should be measured by the values the architect puts on his creations.

For me cost is relevant only to the extent that if a banana cost one rupee, half a banana should cost half a rupee. How can you omit the value of the artist's dedication, of his giving himself wholly to the work? Cost should be subservient to character. It seems to me that Indians are more American than Americans.

Why is there no interconnection between the rooms? Can't you
have a double bedroom and an adjoining study, to be shared
by two students, thus having bed-study combinations?

It was considered much better to have single rooms rather than double rooms. It has been proven almost exclusively in all dormitory arrangements that single rooms are better. Two men in a room could lead to peculiarities. You may get stuck with a guy you don't like in a double room. The interconnection idea is a nice one for a hotel, but not for a dormitory. Two in a room only increases the intensity of fights; after all, if you only have one in a room, you can fight only with yourself. The authorities are to be praised for avoiding the temptation to economize by having two in a room.

So you have used some psychological insights?

Yes, this is the only measure to use.

Did you use the bricks to create an austere atmosphere? It is
so monotonous. We have so much brick all around us. Why
don't you hang some pictures?

Why don't you hang some pictures?

Why is one wall plastered and whitewashed, whereas all the
others are left bare?

That one wall is plastered because it is very thin. If a brick wall is very thin, the sides would be irregular. We have made one side regular and the other side, which is very irregular, has been plastered. Basically, the plastering has been done because a thin brick wall can't be made regular on both sides.

Why is the staircase round? Couldn't it have been like an
ordinary staircase?

An ordinary staircase would have broken into the space too much. A circular staircase is much more compact. It needs less stairs, less landings, and takes up less space. It is also cheaper.

Why have you raised some hostels by fourteen feet, and dug
holes elsewhere? Why did all this mud transfer take place?

This is only a way of making different levels. It is good to have as many levels as possible. Originally we wanted many more levels, but it was too costly so we reduced it. These levels add greatly to the beauty of the structure. You will thus have sunken gardens lower than the dormitories so that the students can go down and create all the hell they want without disturbing anybody else.

Why did you not have a complex of apartments, with
apartments of various sizes so that people could take the ones
they needed? I am referring to the faculty houses.

Every family should have a separate house and a garden.

But why do you have these connecting walls?

For privacy.

But sir, these walls have no effect. The other guys can look over the wall into our balcony.

Well, then, consider it a good idea for promoting friendship.

But the houses still could have been separate units without the walls.

No, you can't really separate the houses without these walls. If there is no wall, your dog may walk into the next house.

Why do all the houses face the same way?

The houses are all oriented to the wind. You are supposed to get the wind at all times of the year. Of course, the wind blows off your papers, but that doesn't matter.

Why don't you have any windows on the side walls of the houses?

A brick construction depends not on what's open, but on what's closed. Fundamentally, a brick construction is closed, and then openings are made into it. It is not like concrete in which one can have holes everywhere by putting a bit of steel here and there.

I have never seen a campus with a pond in it. Why is it there?

Don't you like it?

It is quite beautiful, but it is deep and so it is dangerous.

I agree, but I want it as a separation between the houses and the school. At present, the separation is very little. But when a pond comes, there will be a real separation because people don't walk on water these days. The separation is both physical and psychological. And since the pond covers a fairly large area it will cover the space. Moreover, it will help reduce the dust. There's too much of it all over the place.

There will be no bridges. It will be an inconvenience, but it is good. You must have something in life to care about. Only then do you live a full life.

Won't this reduce faculty-student interaction?

I think of the interaction as mostly consisting of fist fights. Simply walking past and saying *Hello, Professor* is no interaction. When the pond is there, you will think twice before going to a professor.

I would like to have a walk around with you. You should point out these complaints to me. By sitting here and talking it is not easy for you to communicate those difficulties, and it is not easy for me to understand.

Contributed by
Balkrishna V. Doshi

When you make a building, you make a life. It talks to you.

I like the idea that, just because money is available, you don't have to be ostentatious. I agree with that totally. If I were a millionaire, I would build a house very modestly.

It's silly to think that you want to preserve wood—except for termites. Natural woods as it grays is so marvelous. I think a yellow house and green leaves looks awful, but a gray house and green leaves looks absolutely marvelous. We have to ask nature to help us out.

I don't think lighting the outside—lighting trees and things of that nature. I think it's very artificial, I think it's very wrong. I think there should be actual shutters on the upper level so that you can adjust the light and the glare, especially in the winter. These would project into the room, giving the room a lot of interest. Below, I thought there should be a curtain so you don't see yourself at all. At night you close the curtain and you actually feel encased in the room. It would look very good. I would feel cozier inside. The shutters would not be louvered, just panels of wood. It would be a wood window instead of glass. Glass is very imposing.

Reprinted from *Interior Design Magazine*

One day, as a small boy, I was copying the portrait of Napoleon. His left eye was giving me trouble. Already I had erased the drawing of it several times. My father leaned over and lovingly corrected my work. I threw the paper and pencil across the room, saying "now it is your drawing, not mine." Two cannot make a single drawing. I am sure the most skillful imitation can be detected by the originator. The sheer delight in the act of drawing has its way in the drawing and that also is a quality that the imitator can't imitate. The personal abstraction, the rapport between subject and the thought also are unimitatable.

In the presence of Albi, I felt the belief in the choice of its architectural elements, and what exhilaration and patience were combined to begin it and work towards its completion. I drew Albi from the bottom up as though I were building it. I felt the exhilaration. The patience it took to build, one didn't need, for I drew it without bothering about corrections or correct proportions. I wanted only to capture the excitement in the mind of the architect.

As notations in music reveal structure and composition for hearing, the plan is the score that reveals the structure and the composition of spaces in natural light.

The plan expresses the limits of Form. Form, then, as a harmony of systems, is the generator of the chosen design. The plan is the revelation of the Form.

To an architect the whole world exists in his realm of architecture...when he passes a tree he does not see it as a botanist but relates it to his realm. He would draw this tree as he imagined it grew because he thinks of constructing. All the activities of man are in his realm, relating themselves to his own activity.

A few years ago I visited Carcassonne. From the moment I entered the gates, I began to write with drawing, the images which I learned about now presenting themselves to me like realized dreams. I began studiously to memorize in line the proportions and the living details of these great buildings. I spent the whole day in the courts, on the ramparts, and in the towers, diminishing my care about the proper proportions and exact details. At the close of the day I was inventing shapes and placing buildings in different relationships than they were.

The editors chose several sketches of mood and development of a few projects rather than isolated drawings of a greater number of projects. Such a decision appeals to the architect who starts, like the writer and the painter, with a blank piece of paper upon which he imprints the gradual steps in the development of something he wants to make exist. The sketch book of painter, sculptor or architect should differ. The painter sketches to paint, the sculptor draws to carve, and the architect draws to build.

Reflect on the Pantheon which is recognized as one of the greatest of buildings. Its greatness has many facets. It is the realization of a conviction that a building could be dedicated to all religions and that this ritual free space can be given expression. It presents a belief of a great man which led to its design as a non directional domed space. If architecture may be expressed as a world within a world, then this building expresses it well, even refining it, by placing the oculus, the only window, in the center of the dome.

This building had no precedents; its motivation was clear and full of belief. The force of its "wanting to be" inspired a design equal to its desires in form.

Today, building needs an atmosphere of belief for the architect to work in. Belief can come from recognizing that new institutions want to emerge and be given expression in space. New beliefs come with new institutions that need to be expressed as new spaces and new relationships. The architectural realizations sensitive to the institutions' particular form would set a new precedent, a new beginning. I do not believe that beauty can be deliberately created. Beauty evolves out of a will to be that may have its first expression in the archaic. Compare Paestum with the Parthenon. Archaic Paestum is the beginning. It is the time when the walls parted and the columns became and when music entered architecture. Paestum inspired the Parthenon. The Parthenon is considered more beautiful, but Paestum is still more beautiful to me. It presents a beginning within which is contained all the wonder that may follow in its wake. The column as a rhythm of enclosure and opening and the feeling of entering through them to the spaces they envelop is an architectural spirit, a religion which still prevails in our architecture today.

A space can never reach its place in architecture without natural light.

Artificial light is the light of night expressed in positioned chandeliers not to be compared with the unpredictable play of natural light.

The places of entrance, the galleries that radiate from them, the intimate entrances to the spaces of the institution form an independent architecture of connection. This architecture is of equal importance to the major spaces though these spaces are designed only for movement and must therefore be designed to be bathed in natural light. This Architecture of Connection cannot appear in the program of areas—it is what the architect offers the client in his search for architectural balance and direction.

The client asks for areas, the architect must give him spaces; the client has in mind corridors, the architect finds reason for galleries; the client gives the architect a budget, the architect must think in terms of economy; the client speaks of a lobby, the architect brings it to the dignity of a place of entrance.

Architecture deals with spaces, the thoughtful and meaningful making of spaces. The architectural space is one where the structure is apparent in the space itself. A long span is a great effort that should not be dissipated by division within it. The art of architecture has wonderful examples of spaces within spaces, but without deception. A wall dividing a domed space would negate the entire spirit of the dome.

The structure is a design in light. The vault, the dome, the arch, the column are structures related to the character of light. Natural light gives mood to space by the nuances of light in the time of the day and the seasons of the year as it enters and modifies the space.

In Gothic times, architects build in solid stones. Now we can build with hollow stones. The spaces defined by the members of a structure are as important as the members. Theses spaces range in scale from the voids of an insulation panel, voids for air, lighting and heat to circulate, to spaces big enough to walk through or live in. The desire to express voids positively in the design of structure is evidenced by the growing interest and work in the development of space frames. The forms being experimented with come from a closer knowledge of nature and the outgrowth of the constant search for order. Design habits leading to the concealment of structure have no place in this implied order. Such habits retard the development of an art. I believe that in architecture, as in all art, the artist instinctively keeps the marks which reveal how a thing was done. The feeling that our present day architecture needs embellishment stems in part from our tendency to fair joints out of sight, to conceal how parts are put together. Structures should be devised which can harbor the mechanical needs of rooms and spaces. Ceilings with structure furred in tend to erase scale. If we were to train ourselves to draw as we build, from the bottom up, when we do, stopping our pencil to make a mark at the joints of pouring or erecting, ornament would grow out of our love for the expression of method. It follows that it would become intolerable to hide the source of lighting and unwanted ducts, conduits and pipe lines by pasting acoustical material over structure. The sense of structure of the building and how the spaces are served would be lost. The desire to express how it is done would filter through the entire society of building, to architect, engineer, builder and craftsman.

To begin is the time of belief in form.

Design is the maker that serves this belief.

To build is action from a sense of order.

When the work is completed the beginning must be felt.

Form is the realization of inseparable characteristics.

Form has no existence in material, shape or dimension.

A design is but a single spark out of form;

It is of material and has shape and dimension.

It is hard to talk about a work when it is done.

You feel its incompleteness.

I recall the beginning as Belief.

It is the time of realization of Form.

It is feeling as religion, and thought as philosophy.

Then there is no material no shape no dimension.

And then I recall the adventure of design when dream inspired.

Form must answer to the laws of order so as to be.

One feels the work of another in transcendence—in an aura of commonness and in the Belief.

My medical research building at the University of Pennsylvania incorporates this realization that science laboratories are essentially studios and that the air to be breathed must be separated from stale, waste air. The normal plan for laboratories places the work areas along one side of a central corridor, the other side of which houses the stairs, elevators, animal quarters, ducts and other facilities. In such a corridor there is mixed together with the air you breathe the outflow of contaminated, dangerous air. The only distinction between one man's work space and that of another is the difference in numbers on their doors. For the University, I designed three studio towers in which each man may work in his own bailiwick. Each studio in these towers has its own escape sub-tower and exhaust sub-tower for the release of isotope air, germ-infected air and noxious gases. A central building around which the three major towers cluster serves as the area for facilities, usually to be found on the opposite side of the corridor in the normal plan. This central building has nostrils for the intake of fresh air located far from the exhaust sub-towers for vitiated air. This design, the result of consideration of the unique uses to be made of its spaces and their service requirements, expresses the character of the research laboratory.

From what I have said I do not mean to imply a system of thought and work leading to realization from form to design. Design could just as well lead to realizations in form. This interplay is the constant excitement of architecture.

One day waiting for a friend, I watched the crane lifting heavy members at the Medical Building at the University. On previous days, watching its movement, I resented its presence—a red painted monster, out of scale with the buildings and the members it was lifting into place. It imposed its image on every progress photograph but because I had to hang around it, it gave me a chance to reflect on its meaning, and I realized that the design of a building could have a direct bearing on how capable is the crane. I thought of columns a few hundred feet away from each other carrying great spans. No longer did they appear as columns really but as stations, a composite grouping of service rooms composed of large prefabricated and intricate parts joining dramatically to each other. Truly the joints of each fabricated part became strong and visible from a distance. It reminded me that joint is the beginning of ornament. Now the column formed a space itself designed to serve the greater space. Because the members were so big, weighing even more than the crane before could carry, I imagined that I would demand bigger cranes and forget resentment. Now the joints waited to be emphasized with insertions of sculptured gold accents. The levels within the column were covered with marble. The members forming the sinews for its strength were carefully articulated to express its work. Small pieces coming together could not give rise to such thoughts...suddenly the crane became a friend.

Then I thought of the enclosure. Structures of old combined the roof and the wall with the same material. Now the column and the beam has become so capable through the science of concrete and steel that there is no rhythmic relationship to the enclosure. The enclosure, therefore, is on its own. It is even conceivable that one could build a stone building in the Renaissance manner to encircle the structure. This building could contain the rooms needed to serve the great interior. If we think in terms of the materials of today, then it is enclosed in a curtain of glass. And to emphasize the miracle of glass, the mullions would also be of glass. I did not want to accept the enormous tenacity of steel in so minor a role as to divide one piece of glass from another. When I thought it over, however, I realized the whole thing was pretty flimsy but then a thin, little man with a high voice said to me "You need help. May I introduce myself. I am Mr. Stainless Steel. I can teach you how to reinforce glass and glass mullions with these miracle strands using them only where they can brace the glass without shading their powers." Now I learned another lesson, that each material has its design position in architecture. So I reflected on the crane and its influence in thoughts about design.

Nature makes its designs through the tenets of order.

Nature does not know how beautiful the sunset is.

Nature is of non-conscious existence.

Rule is conscious. Law is non-conscious.

I have learned that a good question is greater than the most brilliant answer. This is a question of the measurable and the unmeasurable. Nature, physical Nature, is measurable. Feeling and dream have no measure, have no language, and everyone's dream is singular. A man is always greater than his works because he can never fully express his aspirations. To express oneself in music or architecture, one must employ the measurable means of composition or design. The first line on paper is already a measure of what cannot be expressed fully. The first line on paper is less.

Turn to feeling and away from thought. In feeling is the psyche. Thought is both feeling and the presence of order. And order, the molder of all existence, has of itself no will to exist, no Existence Will. I choose the word "order" instead of "knowledge" because personal knowledge is too little with which to express thought abstractly. This Existence Will is in the psyche. All that we desire to create has its beginning in feeling alone. This is true for the scientist; it is true for the artist.

But to rely entirely on feeling and to ignore thought would mean to make nothing. When personal feeling transforms itself into religion (not a religion but the essence of religion) and thought becomes philosophy, the mind then opens to realizations—realization, let us say, of what the Existence Will of any particular architectural vision of spaces may be. Realization of this nature is the merging of feeling and thought when the mind is in closest rapport with the psyche, the source of what a thing wants to be. It is the beginning form. Form encompasses a harmony of systems, a sense of order, and that which characterizes one existence from another.

Form has no shape or dimensions. For example, "spoon" stands for a form having two inseparable parts, the handle and the bowl, whereas "a spoon" implies a specific design made of silver or wood, big or little, shallow or deep.

Form is *what*. Design is *how*. Form is impersonal, but design belongs to the designer. Design is prescribed by circumstances—how much money there is available, the site, the client, the extent of skill and knowledge. Form has nothing to do with such conditions. In architecture, it is a harmony of spaces good for a certain activity of man.

Reflect, then, on the abstract characteristics of "house," as contrasted with "a house" or "home." "House" stands for the abstract concept of spaces good to live in. "House" is thus a form in mind, without shape or dimension. "A house," on the other hand, is a conditioned interpretation of living space. This is design. In my opinion, the greatness of an architect depends more on his power to realize that which is "house" than on his ability to design "a house"— something prescribed by circumstances. "Home" is the house and its occupants. It becomes different with each occupant. The client for whom a house is designed states the areas he needs. The architect creates spaces out of these required areas. Such a house, created for a particular family, must, if its design is to reflect trueness to form, have the character of being good for another family

As a problem in architecture, consider a chapel of a University. Is it a space divided for denominations of set ritual or is it a single space for inspired ritual?

In search of form for such a chapel, its concept may come from how you think about its undefined nature. To invent a circumstance, let us imagine the feelings of a student of architecture after an inspiring criticism. Full of dedication to his art, he passes the chapel and winks at it, he doesn't go in, he winks at it. This is inspired ritual.

The chapel has a central space which for the moment we won't describe, around it is an ambulatory for those who don't want to enter. Outside the ambulatory is an arcade for those not in the ambulatory; the arcade overlooks a garden for those not in the arcade. The garden has a wall for those who don't enter and merely wink at the chapel.

Schools began with a man under a tree, a man who did not know he was a teacher, discussing his realizations with a few others who did not know they were students. The students reflected on the exchanges between them and on how good it was to be in the presence of this man. They wished their sons, also, to listen to such a man. Soon, the needed spaces were erected and the first schools came into existence. The establishment of schools was inevitable because they are part of the desires of man.

Our vast systems of education, now vested in institutions, stem from these little schools, but the spirit of their beginning is now forgotten. The rooms required by our institutions of learning are stereotyped and uninspiring. To be sure, the uniform classrooms required by the Institute, the locker-lined corridors and other so-called functional areas and devices, are arranged in neat packages by the architect who follows the area requirements and the budgetary limits established by the school authorities. But such schools, though good to look at, are shallow as architecture because they do not reflect the spirit of the man under the tree. Nevertheless, had the beginning not been in harmony with the nature of man, there would have been no beginning to the entire system of schools. The Existence Will of *school* was there even before the circumstances of the man under the tree.

That is why it is good for the mind to go back to the beginning—because the beginning of any established human activity is its most wonderful moment. For in that moment lies the whole of its spirit and resourcefulness, from which for present needs we must constantly draw our inspiration. We can make our institutions great by giving them, in the architecture we offer them, our sense of this inspiration.

Reflect for a moment on the meaning of "school" as contrasted with "a school" or institution. The Institution is the authority from which we receive the special requirements for a school. A school, or a specific design, is what the Institution expects from us. But "school"—the spirit school, the essence of the Existence Will—is what the architect should convey through the medium of his design. It is here that the architect is distinguished from the mere designer.

The actual classrooms in such a school should not follow the usual soldier-like dimensional similarity but should invoke use through their spatial variety, for one of the most wonderful aspects of the spirit of the man under the tree is his recognition of the singularity of every man. A teacher or student is not the same with a few, in an intimate room with a fireplace, as in a large, high room with many others. And must the cafeteria be in the basement, even if it is not in use so much of the time? Is not the relaxing moment of the meal also a part of learning?

A realization of what particularizes the domain of spaces ideal for *school* would make the designing of an institution of learning challenge the architect and awaken in him an awareness of what *school wants to be,* which is the same as saying an awareness of the form: school.

Giotto was a great painter. Because he was an artist he painted the skies black for the daytime and he painted birds that couldn't fly and dogs that couldn't run, and he made men bigger than doorways. A painter has this prerogative. He does not have to answer to the problems of gravity, or represent images as we know them in real life. As a painter he expresses a reaction to Nature, and he teaches us through his eyes and reactions about the nature of man. Again, a sculptor is one who modifies space with objects expressive of his reactions to Nature.

Architecture nevertheless has limits. When we touch the invisible walls of its limits, then we know more about what is contained by them. A painter can paint square wheels on a cannon to express the futility of war. A sculptor can carve the same square wheels. But an architect must use round wheels. Though painting and sculpture play a beautiful role in the realm of architecture, just as architecture plays a beautiful role in the realms of painting and sculpture, they do not have the same discipline. One may say that architecture is the thoughtful making of spaces. It is not the filling of areas prescribed by a client. It is the creating of spaces that evoke a feeling for appropriate use.

A great building must, in my opinion, begin with the unmeasurable and go through the measurable in the process of design, but must again in the end be unmeasurable. The design, the making of things, is a measurable act. In fact at this point you are like physical nature itself, because in physical nature everything is measurable—even that which is yet unmeasured, like the most distant stars which we may assume will eventually be measured.

What is unmeasurable is the psychic spirit. The psyche is expressed by feeling, and also by thought, and I believe it will always remain unmeasurable. I sense that the psychic Existence Will calls on Nature to make that which it wants to be. I think a rose wants to be a rose. Man, created by Existence Will, came into being through the laws of Nature and evolution. But the results are always less than the spirit of existence.

In the same way, to accomplish a building you must start in the unmeasurable and go through the measurable. You must follow the laws, but in the end, when the building becomes part of living, it must evoke unmeasurable qualities. The design phase involving quantities of brick, methods of construction and engineering is over, and the spirit of the guiding's existence takes over.

The motor car has completely upset the form of the city. I feel the time has come to make a distinction between the viaduct architecture of the car and the architecture of man's activities. The tendency of designers to combine the two architectures in a simple design has confused the direction of planning and technology.

Viaduct architecture enters the city from outlying areas. It must now be more carefully planned and, even at great expense, must be more strategically placed with respect to the city center. Viaduct architecture would include the street which, in the center of a city, wants to be a building —a building with room beneath for city piping services so that traffic interruption will not be necessary when these services need repair. This viaduct architecture would encompass an entirely new concept of street movement. It would make a distinction between the stop-and-go movement of the bus and the go-movement of the car. The area-framing expressways would be like rivers. These rivers would need harbors, and the interim streets would be like canals, which need docks. The terminal buildings of this viaduct architecture would be the harbors—like gigantic gateways expressing the form of the Architecture of Stopping. These terminals would have garages in their cores, hotels and department stores around the periphery, and shopping centers on their street floors.

Such a strategic positioning around the city center would present an ideal protection against the destruction of the city by the motor car. In a sense, the conflict between the car and the city is a war, and planning for the new growth of cities is not to be regarded complacently but as an act of emergency. A distinction between the two architectures—the architecture of the viaduct and the architecture of man's activities—could produce a logic of growth and a sound positioning of enterprise.

The city is made up of institutions—that which has been established and is supportable by all men. Education, government, the home are such institutions. When an architect begins his work, the building he is about to design must present itself as belonging to an institution. Even before satisfying the client's specific needs, the force of the institution in society should be the background of his architectural decisions.

I cannot predict the architecture of the future. We can only work within the laws we comprehend now. The architecture will be based on new rules as the system of laws becomes more and more part of a new comprehension of physical order and the nature of man. There is power in man to surpass even his own physical limits. For instance, a man, I'm sure, wants to fly like a bird which he now can, and swim like a fish and run like a deer. You might say that the clover-leaf is the cheeta. He is jealous of the cheeta and the car is invented. The car gave use to its own needs and now is the clover-leaf. What we need instead of the opportunistic corrections of the city is to sense the new physical order which the car demands; we need an architecture of movement or a viaduct architecture. This architecture would give a more positive imagery to the modern city and make it the point of departure for other buildings related to it.

Many of the following interviews are by Richard Saul Wurman

Gabriele Aggugini

I met Professor Louis I. Kahn for the first time in November, 1968. Some time before a contract for the supply of an air conditioning system to be erected in Dacca (now Bangladesh) had been awarded to my company, Marelli Aerotechinica of Milan.

A team from Marelli, which I belonged to, was in charge of the project of such a system. A meeting was arranged in Philadelphia in order to discuss that project with both the architect and the consulting engineer according to a contract clause.

After that meeting, I met Professor Kahn again in Venice where his project of a new auditorium was exhibited, and also in Dacca in 1970.

Too much time has passed and unfortunately, I don't remember his words exactly. However, his spiritual sense of the architecture is still in my mind.

During the meeting in Philadelphia, many problems came up and efforts were made in order to match the technical project and the architect's requirements.

Our design had dealt, in the usual way, with the air distribution system of the libraries included in the National Assembly building. I mean that we had aimed at achieving the best air motion and a very low noise level in the occupied area.

I realized, however, that the Professor's idea on this subject was quite different.

The air, he said, *should enter the libraries like a gust of wind in the blue sky!*

I think everybody present was shocked by his statement, being that they understood that it was impossible to carry it out in practice.

He probably realized our perplexity and clarified his purpose: He explained that the air ducts for the libraries would have to be manufacturered in a trapezium shape. The trapezium, however, would have no upper side so that it would act as an air channel running through the rooms near the ceiling and detached one or two inches from it. The slot between the duct edges and ceiling would provide room air supply.

This arrangement was discussed extensively with Professor Kahn, but no solution was achieved because we didn't find any technical support to fulfill his proposal. Diamond-shaped ducts were accepted in place of the former proposal.

In spite of this, something struck our minds. The Professor's speech was actually impressive and made us think of a new world, a world in which there are no technical borders and which belongs to the children's fantasy rather than to the spoiled and frustrated present mankind.

The Professor's feeling still reminds me of the ancient Greek mythology where man used to live very close to nature and nature was alive in man's mind.

In my opinion, Kahn's architecture aimed at revaluing man, giving him a new room to live and to realize himself.

I think his purpose was not to create just a reading room, but a place where readers could study as if they were in intimate contact with nature.

I deem that the statement of Professor Kahn contained a great idea: to give back to man his human sense and to remind him of the nature he belongs to, even in such an industrialized and polluted world.

He wanted air ducts as well as other servant elements to be involved in this picture; his architecture is intended to be employed for the benefit of man as a human being and not as a subject.

When I saw him last, an adverse political situation had affected the development of Dacca National Assembly, at that time under construction. He was determined to bring his job to a completion, and said, *Men pass, while buildings will remain forever.*

He will also live in his architecture eternally, which his soul has moved into.

Bernard J. Alpers

I knew Lou for many years and was in intimate contact with him on many occasions. There was a good deal of the imp in him. In our younger days, Lou would sit at the piano while I put a copy of the *Saturday Evening Post* before him. The assembled group would then sing the headlines as we turned page after page to the accompaniment of whatever came into his head. This capacity of losing himself in the gaiety of the moment was characteristic of him to his last days.

Joseph Amisano

I had not seen Louis since 1940 when some other students and I visited his office and found him most solicitous to our break-in, as he patiently showed us the work of the office. It was my first visit to an architect's office, and I was struck by its institutionless quality, and Louis' exuberance contrasted sharply with the matter-of-fact architects with whom I had come in contact at school.

It wasn't until that Sunday in 1951 that we met again at the American Academy in Rome. These were the years before the Fiat onslaught, the country not yet recovered from the bombings and deprivations of war. The streets late at night revealed the Renaissance as it was: fore-squared to the coarse stone streets, facaded undulating, sculptured, made live by flickering overhead lights swaying in the wind. It was the effects of the light that preoccupied Louis and fascinated him: the deliberateness of the detailed forms, some carved like deep wounds with shadows deepening into reaches that promised forbidding secrets. The streets were mystically quiet, and Louis would lean away from a scene and then rapidly walk up to a building and touch it, like a friend.

The message of light repeated itself time and time again in his mind, each time with greater intensity, and many of his drawings of that period were drawn as shadows without line. At Delphi, Louis went out into brilliant moonlight and portrayed the Temple as a series of cloaked figures, extending their long shadows down the mountain slope. Rome may very well have been the psyche for many later buildings. Certainly Kujarats' penetrating voids extend from what fascinated Louis during those formative Roman nights.

Louis spent most of the days wandering in Rome and its museums, feasting on the Italian scene. He once remarked that the nocturnal Renaissance still life became animate when daylight and the Italian people took over the scene. When he gradually conceded that either the Academy was a hopeless educational experiment, or its people simply wanted to be left alone, the time seemed right for a trip, and on a late fall day, Louis, Spero Daltas, my wife and I took off for Greece and Egypt.

To qualify for reduced fares on the Egyptian airlines, Louis—with eminent propriety—signed on as a qualified student. We had the necessary papers to notify *whom it may concern* that as students we were to be given such courtesies as were customary for academicians. I doubt that Louis was better off financially than most of his charges: except for Daltas, we were all dependent on a monthly stipend and Louis as our charge d'affaires saw that we lived within it.

We left Rome by way of Foggia and then went on to Athens, but intermediate stops were necessary, because the pride of the Egyptian airlines was a cloth-covered Ford Tri-Motor in which we flew silently in an attitude of prayer, the tension finally relieved when the wheels touched Greece.

For the most part, Athens was anticlimactic for Louis. It was too new. He preferred the continuity of Rome to the Greek antiquities buried in a 19th-Century environment, but he did enjoy the Placka where the modern Greek was enjoying his new political freedom.

Louis was all cranked up to go on to Delphi and Parnassus, sites of the human struggle where democracy and tyranny once stared each other down. So we took off, via Corinth, by bus.

Louis' outwardly robust appearance belied a fragile body that, on that trip, nearly came apart because of the antics of a Kamikaze driver who took the turns through those war-ravaged roads, missing oncoming vehicles over Bailey bridges by the thickness of this paint. As one S curve followed another, Louis vowed that when we got to Delphi, he would demand of the Oracle to see to it that the driver spend eternity riding his bus around Purgatory. By the time we got there, whatever stamina he started out with was gone and we damn near had to carry him to his room!

My wife offered Louis aspirin and her seal coat, because the hotel was without heat or hot water, but he gallantly refused, preferring to die in silence between the frozen dampness of bed sheets.

The goats awakened us, their bleating and the bells echoing in the foothills of Parnassus. Louis was already on the terrace, sheltered from the wind; the sun was shining and he was reborn. After tea and hard toast, we were off to see the sights. My wife and I headed for the temple, Daltas in another direction, and—as often happened—Louis wandered off on his own. We could see him in the distance with his thoughts, paper and Conte, musing the immediate scene. By mid-morning the sun had warmed us. Louis returned and picked a dramatic spot for lunch overlooking the valley. Throughout this part of the trip, these lunches were happy picnics, always winding up with us stretched out, letting the sun and the Retsina wine do their work.

The rest of that day was spent sketching and looking. By late afternoon, the sun disappeared and it was time to get back. After a brief rest, we were on the terrace ready for a dinner that consisted of half of an anemic chicken divided among the four of us (the other half was reserved for the next day). On the third day, Louis discovered two small children battling each other with a dried cod, and he brought us the possibility of having cod as an alternative, but the proprietor didn't consider dried cod a fit fare for Americans. Louis convinced him that he should make an exception in this case. It was prepared by the gods and Louis could not resist the Retsina in spite of his delicate stomach. It put him in a gay mood. He and the proprietor, the son of Pericles, carried on the most animated conversation, with a good deal of toasting and hand shaking—a bewildering scene since neither spoke the other's language.

Daltas, the Greek emissary, was supposed to see us through these barriers. Instead, Louis carried the day eyeball to eyeball, expounding the theme of Greek stoicism, Greek women, Greek songs and even the disastrous wine.

He was a consumer protagonist for a better world. He used the words *people* and *architecture* interchangeably.

It was a delight to watch this man, enraptured by life, his voice rising in pitch as an idea came to light and he chased the idea-forming images to make certain that in your mind's eye, it was crystal clear.

He never tired of exploring new ground. We often disagreed, but we were his admiring audience, and could have gone on all night. Each of us who knew this complex man remembers him differently. I, for one, remember him as a loving man. I remember Louis urging me to settle in Philadelphia; he'd get me the clients, he said, putting his hand on my arm.

As it worked out, I should have stayed another year. I should have left when Louis did, because without him to sketch with, I bought a camera, and have pitifully little to show for it.

Nadar Ardalan

Lou [at the time of his death] was engaged in Persia on a work of great scale—perhaps it might well have been the last important new work before his untimely demise. The project was a new city center for Teheran, but as Lou saw it, the project was a new Teheran. His sketches and thoughts remain and, together with Kenzo Tange, with whom a collaborative effort had been commenced, we hope to manifest some of the thoughts to the degree that we are able.

The death of Lou was a particularly great loss for the unfolding of contemporary architecture in the Orient, and especially that of Persia. In the embers of the traditions of these ancient lands, Lou sensed a validity of his own personal intuitions. In return, he provided a confirmation to those who sought for an identity in these same ashen fires.

Louise Badgley

I was working for Lou a short time when he had to go to Rochester regarding the First Unitarian Church. Never having traveled by train, I knew nothing about the accommodations. I reserved a roomette for him, which proved a disaster. His comment to me: *I may be only 5'6", but even a midget couldn't dangle his feet in one of those.* I got the message.

Lou was going on an overseas trip and it was my responsibility to get everything in order. My first duty—the correct passport. On arriving at work the following Monday morning, I received a phone call from Mrs. Kahn telling me Lou had arrived in New York, boarded his plane only to find he had his old, cancelled passport. The other one was still in the files. Mrs. Kahn had to go to the files on a Sunday, retrieve the valid passport, be driven out to the airport, book a flight to New York, so she could hand Lou the passport. She told the stewardess her plight and the airlines very generously offered to do the necessary for Mrs. Kahn and hand-deliver it to Lou at Kennedy. I was in a state of shock; I wrote Lou a letter of apology and resignation, not knowing the vagaries of overseas mail. (Length of time of delivery was possibly five days, if at all.) Lou came back ten days later, and I met him, of all places, watching the parade of Easter finery in Rittenhouse Square. I mumbled some sort of lame excuse to him, asked if he got my letter of resignation, and he replied, *Even baseball players get three strikes. I can't let you go yet because I want to see if you can top this one.* That's all there was to it.

And would you believe, it was nearly eight years later, when I nearly got that third strike. I was leaving the office, having been recently (then) married and going to go overseas. We were all working towards getting Lou off to India. He was due to leave the evening of the 4th of August. I was looking over all the papers the new secretary and I had assembled for him as our part of the trip, and he had no visa for India. Funds in the office were pretty low, so I had to give the secretary my own money to go to New York and get the visa (after many frantic pleading telephone calls to the Indian Consulate to bail me out of this dilemma) and get her back to the office before Lou's departure time from Philadelphia. Of course, he never knew about that one.

We had just received a telephone call from Miss Katherine McBride while in the Twentieth Street office, informing Lou that she would like to visit him and chat about the possibility of new dormitories at Bryn Mawr. Lou was pleased but his next reaction was, *We must clean up these dirty areas, and you must help.* For the next several hours, Lou and several other people in the office and I were literally on our hands and knees, scrubbing the woodwork in his office, dusting off the books in the bookcase, running around like field mice trying to make a silk purse out of that sow's ear of an office. President McBride's comment was, *Your floors smell deliciously like pine oil. I hope you didn't clean just because I was coming.* Bless her.

When I returned to the States for the first time (1971), Lou and Esther insisted they take Doug, Davy and me to lunch. Doug couldn't make it because of business reasons, and I pleaded with the Kahns to have sandwiches sent into Lou's office. We would put Davy on the floor with crayons and paper, and I could enjoy myself. Davy had not acquired table manners as such and Doug and I rarely took him out to eat with us (Davy was just past two). Lou and Esther insisted we go to Bookbinder's, which was close by. What a distaster! Davy proceeded to take the oyster crackers on the table and start pitching them like baseballs at the waitresses, at the wall, every which way. Lou got so tickled by Davy's behavior that he, too started throwing them. Esther and I were mortified, but there was no stopping them for a moment. Then, Davy was eating a tunafish sandwich, and Lou a chicken salad. Davy reached across the table and took part of Lou's sandwich, so Lou reached back and took the other half of Davy's. It was a riot, trying to figure out which of the two was the more mischievous. Esther tells it a different way, that Lou was the one who was embarrassed, but about two months after the incident, my daughter Linda came to the Project for Friends Select, and Lou took her down to the fourth floor and enthralled the fourth floor staff with all the details of that luncheon date.

As you know, I used to charette with the boys to get the work out, ready, what have you. One night, Henry Wilcots and I were running the specs through the Bruning machine for the Adele R. Levy Memorial project. We had about one hundred sheets of their specs to run off, and we were literally all night doing it. Then, of course, came the collating and binding, etc. and the transmittals. In the meantime, Lou and the men were preparing the drawings, and others were preparing the models which we had to present to the Art Commission in New York at 10 am the next morning. Henry and I finished up just as morning was breaking (say about 5:45 am). Lou came to my desk and asked me if I were tired, and I said I was. With that, he handed me a five dollar bill, told me to go home, take a shower, change my clothes, and be back by 7 am, so I could go to New York with Neil Thompson to make the presentation to the Commissioner of Parks. I couldn't believe it. Without our

knowing it, Lou had called them and told them his Project Manager (Neil) and his Office Manager (me) were chosen by him to make the presentation and they would have nothing to worry about. How Neil and I ever made it up there (he also had worked all night) is a story in itself, but we did, and it was one charette I remembered for years to come, believe me. Along with the twenty-four-hour duty we had put in, I burned the inside of my nostrils so severely that I was never again allowed to use the Bruning machine (by my doctor, that is.)

I remember well, naturally, Lou coming back from the Masters Class trying so hard to tell me the off-color jokes he had heard that day, and always forgetting the punch line. Then, in true LIK spirit, he would make up a new punch line as he went along. Lou telling a joke was an experience.

Lou had an affinity for never having any cash on him. On many occasions when Lou would come back from school and I would be there waiting for him, as you men always were, too, he would say, *Louise, how much cash do you have on you?* I'd have maybe five or ten, depending on what day of the week it was. He would borrow it, and then sign the petty cash voucher with my name, instead of his. Trying to get it back from him or the bookkeeper was something else again. He did it to me so often, I finally got angry with him one time, walked over to the window with a bunch of petty cash slips and proceeded to forge his name, using an old one as a guide. With that his face beamed, and he never again used that ploy on me. He didn't realize how easy it was to forge a signature until he watched me do it, so you can be sure he was honest after that.

Many times, Lou's flights would be early morning ones, and if it were raining hard, actually foggy, or snowing, or some bad weather signs, he would call me at home and tell me about it. Usually, I would have to get on the phone immediately and try to make other arrangements, which were not all that easy since he had the tickets with him and they would want the numbers, etc. for transferring. One morning, I just could not get him on a flight because they were all booked solid and the agents weren't impressed with Lou's name enough to bump somebody. When I called him back to tell him I couldn't get him a flight, he got so angry, he hung up on me. When I got to work that morning, the word was that he had called a particular airline, told them he was Vincent Kling and that he had to be in such a place by such a time and his private plane was down, could they accommodate him? How in the world he fooled them when he got to the airport we never found out, but they did take him and he got to where he was going.

Among my myriad chores was dressing Lou and getting him to special functions on time. By dressing, I mean, taking his things out of the suitcase so the wrinkles would be out by dressing time, hanging the things in his men's room, and sort of lining things up in an order for him since his bathroom was particularly small. On these occasions, he would keep popping out of the room asking my help on this and that, and putting the studs in. One time we lost a stud, and here he was, half in and out of a tuxedo, on his knees on these filthy floors trying to find the shirt stud. We couldn't find it, so we had to put in an emergency call to Esther to bring another pair from home. After they left, I got down on all fours and finally found the darned thing, but the picture of Lou scrounging around like a puppy dog on the floor never left my mind, and to this day, as I walk in that area, I can still picture him, popping in and out of that room trying to get ready for those special events.

Our Christmas parties were always very quiet, special occasions, the food and drink were modest but plentiful, and my area was the party place. Everything would be cleared off to make ready for the festivities. On one of these party days, Lou asked me to go around to the William Penn Shop with him and get the makings of a party. He would go from counter to counter, picking up this and that, all sorts of cheeses, breads, breads, fruits, and so on. Our arms were full of the goodies, and we went to the cashier to be checked out. Lou paid for everything, and handed all the bags to me for carrying. Lou had such a long stride in walking, and with this overweight on me, naturally I had to walk slower. Lou turned around and looked back at me, nearly twenty paces behind him, and said, *Now you know how I feel when you send me on trips loaded down and unable to keep up with the mainstream,* the message being to give him a modicum of things to take with him and send the rest ahead—but the vagaries of our office didn't always permit this. And many times after that, he chided me about the Christmas lesson.

Lou always needled me about my untidy desk. Since my desk and its immediate areas were in a sense the hub of outgoing things, it was never easy to keep it uncluttered. Innumerable times I would come in to work and find little nasty-nice notes from Lou about my *clutter,* which was not always my fault.

Lou was being interviewed by *LIFE* magazine in conjunction with the Salk project, and one of the story editors sat down with me and asked if I could give some insight into Lou as a person. Lou happened to be within earshot and I allowed as how I had many little notes from Mr. Kahn which I would gladly share with *LIFE* someday. Lou never left me a note again, complaining about things, that is. I had many notes, but he managed to leave out the nitpicking, as it were.

One last item, but certainly there are too many more and memory does not always serve me.

When Dr. Salk visited us on Twentieth Street, it was a memorable moment for all of us, these two very famous men under one roof for a common cause, the Salk Institute's beginnings, and though I knew little of what went on in Lou's office, when it was time for Dr. Salk to leave, there was Lou at the window to his office, waving goodbye to Dr. Salk getting into a cab. It was a gesture which showed the little boy side of Lou which was always there, but not always let out for the world to see.

Jakob Bakema
The first time I met Louis I. Kahn was in Otterlo (1959) where a group of young architects decided to meet more among themselves (Team X) and less in the wider circle of CIAM (International Congress for Modern Architecture).

Knowledge is a servant of thought and thought is a satellite of feeling.
It is for the architect to derive from the very nature of things what a thing wants to be.

Then, visiting the Robie House in Chicago with some students in 1962, we approached a door just hearing inside a hoarse voice: *This really is a door even making welcome being closed and giving protection being opened.* Then the door opened and Louis I. Kahn stepped out and we said welcome to each other, meeting again after three years. In the evening of that day, he gave a talk about his Salk Institute project...*how pipes and containers have to be honored by having their own space from where they can give their service to places for people to stay...*

We had many meetings at the Penn School of Architecture (1967) as we fought to have accepted in the school *Planning by architecture and architecture by planning.*

Later on we met at the Mediterranean coast judging projects and still later in Jerusalem where Teddy Kolleck talked about the evolution of his city: *One should only build on a hill if by this the potential hill-being becomes realized.*

So we were many times meeting at problem places or simply by having food and talk together in his private workshop, looking at his India projects: *Look, Jacob, here the wall will be of no brick; it will be there by light, it will be a window.*
Culture is the smile of necessity.

My wife and I went the day before his funeral to Bryn Mawr, seeing there the dormitories. At a first meeting after his death with students in Kahn's studio, I was asked to say something: *Louis I. Kahn could make the inside of a building become like a silhouette in outer space.*

When he was talking, his face became for me a kind of vibration of the man, being part of existence, and his work was a kind of materialization of this vibration. I shall remember Louis I. Kahn's face as *a gentle smile of necessity and intensive desire for culture.*

Luis Barragan
I have remembered very much our master and friend Louis Kahn, because you know quite well the admiration and gratefulness that I have had for his teachings and for the distinguished occasion he granted me by inviting me to be a minor advisor in architecture on landscaping at Salk Laboratories.

I find myself unable to add something new to whatever has been told about such a great personality, but I only have to say that his presence and conversations were and must be in the future for me an example to love life and trust in the same, and, of course, his remarkable teachings in Architecture and Urbanism.

With exceptional generosity, Louis Kahn used to transmit his wisdom to all those who used to listen to him, great knowledge based upon his vast experience and benignity.

The enthusiasm and serenity with which he used to see life were contagious.

I had to regret that due to my bad understanding of English, I could not understand well what he told me in our conversations. However, his own presence and some of his phrases made such an impression on me that I wished I could know his psychological points of view, not only in respect to architecture but on human problems, too.

Lou called me once on the telephone and a year went by without him calling again. He was congratulating me for I had published some books about gardens. He told me, *Those fountains you made are something very virile. I am interested in working together in some project.*

Something strange happened to me. I am not a studious man. When Lou called me on the phone, I didn't know who Louis Kahn was. Louis K...a...h...n? I was astonished at my ignorance. He was very surprised about this matter, but in spite of it said, "I am taking a trip. I will call you when I get back."

One day Lou called me on the phone, and he also wrote: *When can we make an appointment to speak about the Salk Institute? I have a program for you, so that you can design the gardens for the Salk Institute.*

I am going to repeat the same story he tells:

The appointment was at a hotel in La Jolla in San Diego. We had breakfast together and then we went to see the site. On the site they had already started to plant some orange trees; they were very small. I told him (because the original scheme of Lou Kahn was the two buildings and a garden with trees, a group of trees, groups of trees, gardens), *I am a landscape architect.* I told him at first sight, *Only one thing: not one leaf or botanic place. Did you understand me? In terms of botany, don't put one leaf, nor plant, nor one flower, nor dirt. Absolutely nothing.* And I told him, *A plaza [here] will unite the two buildings and at the end, you will see the line of the sea.* He told me without thinking, *All right, I prefer that.* He told me, *We will decide in ten minutes when Dr. Salk comes by; he will decide what should be done.*

After ten minutes Dr. Salk came and I explained the same thing, and Dr. Salk answered the same thing: *It shall have a plaza.*

Lou was thinking and stated a very important thing, that the surface is a facade that rises to the sky and unites the two as if everything else had been hollowed out. It must have an expression.

I know what I'll do. Let's think that we must consider the canals for drainage that will go to the end to a fountain that it has over there. That pattern of the canals is what must resolve the facades, that it must make sense and be beautiful at the same time. Then he thought about the material, and he went to Mexico to look at materials. He came, I don't remember to what city, he wanted a lilac stone. Do you know the lilac color? It's pink and blue: lilac. But he called to see if they could send it. He could buy that material but it would take them a year or two to make it. It was impossible. But what he had already solved was that drainage for the plaza. Very small channels but very well defined, that would collect the rain water and would bring it to a fountain that was just as you went down. Have you seen it? Even though the fountain had been designed without needing the channels. Then he thought, *The pattern of those channels is what is important, the material.*

Shall we leave the stone, or shall we have a channel made out of sheet metal? He was hesitant, uncertain, and what I could say was: *Yes, with that channel with the same stone.* I don't know if he liked me telling him that.

Later on he sent me a photograph. It had a very beautiful material, travertine. That plaza turned out something very beautiful to see. A very well done thing that made the design worthy.

And Lou Kahn in general, independently from architecture and the conversation that I had with him about the project, he was for me, a great philosopher. Unfortunately, I haven't been able to keep up with English. Some things that are not architecture, things that belong to life, human life and all that were extremely interesting to me, but I didn't keep them in my mind nor did I write them down. That was during the interviews and I was very sorry not to be able to speak English so that I could understand the philosophy and Lou Kahn's conversations of universal and human content.

One thing. Lou Kahn liked to speak, to be listened to, and so, what would satisfy me was to listen to him speak even though I understood very little. There wasn't a kind of dialogue. He liked to speak and I, not speaking English, liked to listen and try to understand.

He seemed to have the joy of living, enthusiasm about everything without any bitterness, and was very interested in his projects, in humanity, in everything.

Henry Berg

I met Lou when I was Assistant Director of the Paul Mellon Center at Yale University. I used to go to Philadelphia about once a week to see Lou's drawings in the early stages of the design. I remember about the third or fourth week I had to go down alone and I was terrified at the prospect of that long lunch at Bookbinder's where I'd have nothing intelligent to say to a man who I already revered as a great genius. We were seated at the table and I began babbling about an article that I had read a number of years before in *Architectural Forum* which discussed the prevalence of committees as clients and their inability to come to specific instructions to guide an architect and I asked Lou for his reaction. It was the only architectural tidbit that I could summon up in my embarrassment. Lou looked at me and said, *I don't want a client who knows exactly what it is he wants. That man doesn't need an architect. I want a client who knows what he aspires to.*

I remember a dinner that we had after the completion of one of the early design stages at Mellon Center at Morey's in New Haven. Paul Mellon was there and Lou was at his right hand. Obviously he had been working all night to get the presentation finished and he was in an expansive mood. He spoke about the poverty of his youth and how as a poor student or, I should say, a struggling student, he used to go off with some of his friends for oysters and beer when the beers were a nickel and the oysters were less. And he talked at great length about how he had to struggle through those early years and the implication was clear: *And here I am sitting next to Paul Mellon, one of the wealthiest men in the world, and building a building for him. He's come to me, Lou Kahn.* And within a few minutes the conversation shifted from him and Paul Mellon was speaking about some of his own reminiscences. Lou was fast asleep.

Richard Bleier

A few of us went to see Mr. Kahn in Philadelphia with some thoughts about [a problem we were having]. Somewhere in the discussion, fearful of getting his back up, as unobtrusively and gingerly as possible, I asked Mr. Kahn perhaps could he see a way to compress to a two-floor building by combining the second and third floors. He explored the idea somewhat, and to get to specifics, I said, *Now, Mr. Kahn, in your idea of bringing the sanctuary down to the second floor.* But he cut in on me emphatically saying, *It wasn't my idea; it was your idea; and it's a good idea!* Pride of ownership didn't interfere.

Mr. Singer, our builder, and I arrived in Kahn's Philadelphia office for our appointment early one weekday, and Mr. Kahn had just returned from East Pakistan. As we met, I complimented him on the just published November 15, 1970 *New York Times Magazine* article about him by Susan Braudy. He said he hadn't read it. (Breathes there a man with soul so dead, with a 12-page article in the *New York Times*—and he hasn't read it?) So I went on to say that I thought Miss Braudy really conveyed his personality well in the article, but I felt she has made him appear very inflexible—and I said that I didn't find him inflexible. He parried the compliment, I think, by saying one must have his standards.

Eventually, we got down to discussing our project and I had four main points to take up which needed to be decided and on which our Committee had instructed me to try to win Mr. Kahn over. We discussed and battled over these points all day, spending over an hour on each. Finally, when all points were settled and we were about to leave, Mr. Kahn said, *You came here with four points and we are going to handle each one as you asked—not so inflexible, eh?*

One time Mr. Singer, the builder, and I came to Philadelphia with our rabbi. We had already known that Mr. Kahn had his own ideas about the design of the Ark that holds the Torah or biblical scrolls, even though the design of the Ark and other furnishings were not in Kahn's contract with the congregation. So the rabbi explained that he appreciated Mr. Kahn's thoughts and that perhaps someday we could afford to execute his design for the Ark, but meanwhile we would bring our Ark from the old Temple as a temporary expedient. To which Mr. Kahn replied, *Rabbi, I have found there is nothing so permanent as something temporary.* Pow!

Marion Tournon-Branly

For the architect who still believes in the importance of spirituality in art, Louis Kahn remains among the last witnesses of the Sacred in architecture. None of his creations leaves one indifferent.

I will talk about several meetings I had with him.

The first took place in the studio of my father, the architect Paul Tournon. G.H. Pingusson and Jean Faugeron brought Louis Kahn to a party where artists and students had gathered. On the same day, *L'architecture d'Aujourd hui* had given a reception to which all the architects were invited. I had very much regretted not being able to go to it. How pleased I was to see arrive this man whose architecture I loved so much. He very quickly showed lively enjoyment of the ambience of the studio, and laughing, said to me, *Some young people at last. I feel so much better.* He was leaving the next day, but having met Madame August Perret, we offered to take him to the apartment of the precursor of reinforced concrete before his flight.

My sister, who is a painter, myself, and the architect Pierre Devinoy, another student of Perret's, went to pick Louis Kahn up at his hotel to take him to 51 Rue Raymond. It was a meeting none of us will forget, and Lou was still talking of it long after. Perret was wonderful. We spent time going over each detail of the apartment. We talked of Auguste and at the end, she was so happy with this provocative presence that she offered to have him listen to the tunes that she had written herself and played on the piano for her husband. She was then 80. There was so much freshness and spontaneity in those few hours.

When it was time to leave, one of my students arrived with a big bunch of lilacs from his garden. *How does it feel when a woman offers you flowers?* I asked.

It's already happened to me in India, where it's a custom of hospitality. I like it.

This was the last memory, this happy smile. I had given him the beautiful book on Vauban, which we had all signed. He loved students; it was a great joy to him.

I will not speak of the immense sadness I felt with his death. The studio was silent. I felt that each one of my students was suffering and trying to make the pain lighter. One of them gave me three beautiful drawings he had made of Lou. They stay on my desk as the essential presence of a believer in architecture, in this epoch of doubt, often without hope.

Howard Carlisle

I first became acquainted with Lou Kahn through his monumental works through pictures of those edifices because I am intensely interested in architecture myself, but only from the layman's point of view. I remember vividly how awed I was one day about ten years ago as I was passing the Barclay and I saw the renowned Lou Kahn walking toward me. I reacted like a child seeing a movie star and I immediately asked for his autograph. He did not know, of course, and I did not mention it at that time, that I was currently the assistant principal of his high school.

It was not until June 1973 that I had the opportunity to spend some time with Mr. Kahn, when I invited him to speak at a luncheon in honor of our seniors who were being awarded service commendations for their work at the school. It was on the spur of the moment that I picked up the telephone and called to ask whether he would honor us with his presence as a distinguished alumnus of Central High School. I did not have to bypass a half dozen secretaries to speak to him personally, and he readily accepted. The day he spoke he charmed an audience of 350 parents, students and faculty by the beauty of his words and the aura of aesthetic immutability that surrounded him. My only regret is that I did not have the talk recorded for it was an essay in the beauty and form of life and architecture as he learned it at Central High School and the University of Pennsylvania and later practiced it in his own work.

A.J. Diamond

The Yale class was paying us a visit. The blackboard Lou used for our class was a small board on wheels. We told him of the Yale visit. *In that case, we'd better have two boards,* was his response. I couldn't find another blackboard, but discovered an old, battered upright piano. I wheeled this in and told Lou I couldn't find two blackboards, but said, *You have one blackboard and one piano.*

It was the best afternoon we spent with Lou. He alternated between the blackboard, with strong expressive scribbles, and the piano, with shy, serious fragments of Bach, and his self-conscious, humorous talk. The fact that there were some attractive women members of the Yale class didn't hurt. The class hardly broke between the afternoon session and the evening one at McGillin's Pub downtown.

At another time, Lou showed us on the blackboard how to draw symmetrical classical detail. He took two chalks, one in each hand, and with a springy step reached the top of the blackboard, and with both hands came down the blackboard with a perfect left and right profile of a Classical column capital, finishing with a flourished double scroll.

B.V. Doshi

A dream was made a distant moon ago here
Management as a science must be taught
And there's a high ideal to the work here
In Camelot....

...And of course, there was Merlin...a little old man with a thatch of snowy hair and wistful blue eyes named Louis Kahn. His world was the world of the fairies, gnomes and goblins whom he loved, and of magic....

Out of his magic came weird shapes—arches, holes, patterns of light and shade, a creation...a fairy tale.

Like a will-o'-the-wisp, he came and he disappeared before anyone even realized it. He was here to plan the dining area and the EDP complex and left us with those and with his wisdom.

A work of art is religion...architecture is an art, the technology merely supports it...sometimes, there is a *realization*—one realizes that this is how it should be, that by design this was meant to happen—but one hasn't the technology to achieve it....It is there, but beyond one's grasp. However, it is this desire, this *realization* that matters...Da Vinci dreamt of flying—that's what is important, not that he couldn't do it....In this, a realization is like a fairy tale—it is what man desires and reaches out to but cannot get; it is this desire, not want, that elevates man...that's why I have always loved the fairy tales, the Arabian nights...things oriental.

When I got the contract for Ahmedabad, my first in this subcontinent (Dacca followed close on its heels), the first thing I did was to read the Arabian Nights....

It was difficult building here—I knew I wanted to build in brick, brick is natural—not like mortar...and also for the sake of economy and believe me, that is not at all the same thing as Finance. I had to learn how to lay brick from scratch. The people here, they couldn't lay bricks the way they should be—they just put one brick on top of another and sloshed the cement on...why hide the beauty of open brickwork?...I asked the brick what it wanted and it said, *I want an arch,* so I gave it an arch....But then, I had to teach the bricklayers that an arch was really an arch and not just any curve between two points... these first arches—the first ever built here—I wanted them to be left as they were—a sort of a little playground for children....

If there is such a realization, and it takes shape into an idea, it cannot ever be prevented from taking a concrete form. It might be criticized, you can criticize a man...but you cannot judge him. If a man does something and is prepared to die by it, he is right....

We cannot judge you. Camelot cannot even criticize you—it was your magic that made the dream come true. But Merlin, why did you have to disappear?

He talked of many things. He was all the time talking about work as art. He talked about the spiritual aspects more than anything else. He talked about God and Buddha. He talked about the value of work in relation to the reward one gets. I suppose there were a lot of things there hovering in his mind. I have never seen Lou speaking ever at the dinner table about his financial difficulties. We were sitting together and it happened that he mentioned that he had a lot of bank notices and he would just throw them in the wastepaper basket. He wanted to not bother about them because to him work was more important. But I saw that it was really, really bothering him immensely. To give you an example, we were sitting in the garden that evening and he said, *You know, Doshi, I was in an airport waiting for a plane and I bought some small children's books, you know. One of those books was also written on Buddha.* He said—they were very nice books—children's illustrated books. And he said, *Look at the life of Buddha. He wanted to achieve something which was more important to him than anything he could get. He left his kingdom, he left his family, he left everything.* And he said, *Don't you see, I am also like Buddha. I have come to Ahmedabad. I am doing the Institute of Management and I am not even getting a farthing out of this job. And I'm still working. Maybe the reward is the work I'm getting. The reward is the appreciation I have of things that people have of me. And perhaps this is what I'm doing.* I said, *It is true, Lou, you are very much like Buddha, because I have never seen you thinking anything else but good things of people. Constructive attitudes. Trying to find the solution to a problem and making the world better.* And it is true. His project here is probably the best he could give us. And I know how it all happened. I met him in '62—no, first I met him in '58 in Philadelphia when I came on the Graham Fellowship. I was with him in the evening. I came to his office. He showed us his Richards Medical Center drawings—some other projects—the bathhouse. Then he wanted to see some of my works. I showed him the photographs and he liked the houses that I had done. He said, *These are the ones, which are very simple, primitive houses. Your modern building—you know, the City Hall—that structure is not so good because...it's all right, it can be accepted. But this one is—the houses are made with arches and the way they end up is very primitive, very direct, a very clear statement. And I hope you do it sometime, you know. Continue that work.*

And his work and more so, his generosity, was very affecting. He took us to dinner—me and my wife, two of our friends—and then we left.

In 1962, the Institute of Management was to be built and they were looking for some architects, and they agreed to my suggestion. I met Lou in '72 in Aspen and I told him about this. So on his behalf, I sent a telegram to the clients—that is the National Institute of Design and the Institute of Management. I had a very funny role to play, which is still there. I represented the clients and I represented Lou—in this process, we became very good friends. He came here. He thought he was to design the National Institute of Design. But it was really the Institute of Management which he had to design. It was difficult for him to change his ideas. He was always talking about architecture and design. And I was insisting that no, it was the Management we should talk about. So after four days, he became resigned to the fact and began to think of the Institute of Management. This kind of adaptability is very rare. People do get offended. He was not like that. He was humble and appreciative of the situation. When we proposed to him that we could not pay him any more money but his stay, to that also he agreed. I have not seen even architects in India who can agree to do work for the sake of work. Even Corbusier at a given time would say, *No, this must be given, otherwise I'm not free.* Lou somehow felt that if he could ever demonstrate what he could do, if anybody could give him a commission, he thought it was a sort of favor to both of them and he never liked to refuse that. It was almost like a gift and he returned it with double generosity. When he began work on this, he began to talk about the institutions; he talked about his project in Dacca, he talked about his project in Islamabad. And every time he talked about the people of India, I got more and more interested. Somehow he found there was a much closer affinity between him and the people of India. I really feel that he was more Eastern, he was more Indian than a lot of Indians are. I think he was in the wrong place. Maybe it was good; because of that he could realize many things. In India, perhaps, he would not have. But tempermentally, he was like a sage; he was like a yogi. Always thinking about things beyond, thinking about the spirit. I have not seen many architects who talk about the spirit. Maybe they can talk about the emotions. They can talk about the future. But they don't exactly talk about the main thing, the spirit of man, the feeling that the man has. And this kind of impression is not only mine. It was the impression of the Sarabhai, Kasturba Lalbaha, the old man, you know, who Lou Kahn respected immensely, and even the other people who Lou met. To give you an example, before we left—that is, during his last trip—to the airport, he wanted to leave on Friday, so he could reach Philadelphia on Saturday. But Kasturba was not here and he said, *I must see Kasturba and Sarabhai and I don't mind leaving on Saturday; I'll reach home on Sunday.* So we managed it. It looked that he was tired. He was anxious to go home, but he stayed on. So on Saturday afternoon we met Kasturba. We went to his house, he had some tea. *I'll come back in May; I'll bring these drawings, and I'd love to do some work.* Because the plan was to be an extension complex of the Management Development Center and the kitchen and dining block for the Institute of Management were just beginning. He had made some sketches and the sketches had to be modified, which he did. He just made very rough drawings. It's impossible to do drawings in two days or four days of two such large schemes, costing not less than like seven or eight million rupees. Only two buildings, but big ones. So he said, *I've made sketches and everything is looking fine.* He explained the scheme to Kasturba and we chatted. Kasturba told him, *You will bring for me cashew nuts from there, from Teheran, when you come?* And Kahn said, *Of course I will bring for you not only one box, I will bring for you two boxes, Kasturba. If you like something, I must do it for you.* This is the kind of relationship he had developed with people. He felt that everyone to him was very close. He loved everyone, he respected everyone. It's very rare how very few people will ever have a kind of feeling towards other human beings. I think Lou loved everything. To him, everything was alive. It was brick, mortar, stone, wood—I think everything was speaking to him. You can feel it when he talked to things, when he looked at things. When he wanted to make it tender or strong, he always tried to do as if they were all alive. This is a very rare phenomenon. Corbusier, I knew, was like that. Lou expressed it in his behavior. Perhaps Corbusier was more introverted in this aspect and Lou was not—I don't know. When I told Kasturba about Lou's demise, his heart failure, I have never seen Kasturba with his eyes full of water. He felt very sad. He said, *Every time Lou comes, we always have lunch with him. And how we missed this time lunch?* He said, *I know I was away, but why?* He said, *Anyway, it was good that at least he came just to tell us goodbye.* That kind of relation with a client—I don't know whether it exists in other places. But Lou had developed a bond; he had developed a feeling beyond professional relationship.

Whenever he came to the Institute of Management, the students would look at him from a distance, the faculty would look at him. They allowed him to do whatever he liked, you know. He was coming years and years. In the early years, he used to come a couple of times a year. In the last two years, he didn't come. He came only the last time. So very few had known him. Some who knew him liked him; some knew him from his buildings. They all said that it was very strange that this could have happened to this man who they thought was a yogi, because things like this should not happen to a yogi.

He was interviewed by students. Sometimes he was asked questions which I'm sure anybody else would have been very upset. But he took it in the great and tried to answer them. One thing I admired about Lou was that whenever he had no answers, he would keep quiet.

The last time that he was here—he always liked my children, in particular the youngest one, Marisha. He thought she was the most remarkable because she had the talent of Picasso. He liked to think this. So this time, we said, *We'll show you all there is that she did.* And mind you, more than 40 to 50 minutes, he is going through each drawing, watching them carefully, satisfying himself of every intricacy that she was drawing. And then once he explained why this was good and why this was not good. In fact to me, it was a revelation. I had never felt that this man saw so well and in such detail. Because I learned how to see things—hope I can do that some day. It was very unusual to see this man who has two projects to design, but he could change his mood—get involved with something else, totally absorbed.

He was going to work with Tange and he had done the scheme which Tange had very much liked. And he felt that this was the first time that not only he had the job, but he also may make a little money.

People were shocked to hear about the amount of debts that he had. All that was for architecture and nothing else.

When I came to Philadelphia about '67 or '66, Corbusier had just died in Paris. And I passed through Paris and came to Philadelphia to teach. It must be, what, the 5th of September or so? I went to his office. He was sitting there sad, depressed. He had a bottle of aquavit and gave me a little drink. And then after a few moments of silence, he said, *So, you've heard* I said, *Yes, I was in Paris.* He was very sad. And I said, *I've said that we would arrange a meeting with Lou Kahn with Corbusier, but somehow it was not destined.* He said, *Yes, I know.* He said, *You know, Doshi, every time I build a work, I always feel that this work is for somebody to see. If this is printed and if the copy goes to Le Corbusier's hands, what will he think of me? He's the only man for whom I do the work, because otherwise, to whom shall I show?*

In the early years in '64 and '65, when Lou used to come here for ten days, twelve days, even two weeks, we used to have a very good time. We used to go out in the evenings. We used to have parties at different places. And he used to tell us a lot of jokes, sometimes even dirty jokes. He was a great storyteller. He told us many jokes and we used to really laugh. He used to enjoy listening to jokes. In the recent times, the last two or three years, four years, this had decreased. Also because he was more busy with a lot of things, he had to do a lot more things, you know, he had to accomplish. Recently, at the Iran Convocation, there was an exhibition of some photographs of Lou in the early times—'62, '63—and I was looking at those photographs. Except for the slim body—slightly thinner body, there was hardly any change in the last ten or twelve years in Lou. I looked much younger. I look now perhaps a little older, but Lou particularly looked the same. And that's why it was very difficult to think that this person could ever get old. It is a natural belief. And, in fact, some people said—that day he was standing there—the people asked me my age. *I don't know why they ask age,* he said, *because what is age? Isn't it the mental age that counts?* And he said, *In India, people are always concerned about age.* It was really a strange remark, but true. He never felt old. He was always so involved with things—the dreams, the children's stories—but every moment he was full of life, full of vigor.

Before Lou left, we had a long talk about art and he described many ways; but I had not made any notes from that. So after his death, I was thinking of writing for myself what he said and this is what I wrote in my diary:

To become, one must allow one's beliefs to attempt the incredible so that in the process of discovery, the fountain of joy and the spirit of light remain endless. That's what becomes art as it expresses life's memorable events.

I wrote this so that I can remember not only Lou but what I had discussed with him. Like to allow one's own beliefs is what I told him, and he was very happy. I thought that if one really continued this way, it would be much nicer. At this moment, I have nothing else to add.

Elliot Gould Fisk
As a boy still in knickerbockers in his early years in Philadelphia, he helped the family and paid his way by playing the piano at matinees of a movie house. He also ran a newspaper route in the heart of the city, where he managed, by expense of uncommon energy and effort, to complete his deliveries at dusk and before he had to sprint home for a late-ish family supper.

One afternoon, distributing his evening paper to the box office of the Philadelphia Academy of Music, he discovered to his total delight that, on the stage, before the dimly flood-lit velvet curtains, in preparation for that evening's concert, a magnificent ebony Chickering grand piano had been rolled into place, center stage. Fascinated by the warm glow and the silent splendor of the moment, he laid aside his bundle of newspapers in their leather strap and, entranced by the grace of the noble instrument awaiting its virtuoso, he stole on tiptoe up onto the stage. Within seconds and almost without a thought as to what he was doing, he was caught up passionately and rhythmically in the pianistic fireworks of Liszt's Hungarian Rhapsodies. Finished with a sigh, he had not yet left the bench to resume his late round when he was aware that someone in the dark at the back of the auditorium was heartily applauding in hopes to encourage him to go on. But, young Lou was both startled and a little alarmed, so that, as he dashed for the exit, he ran almost head on into the burly overcoat of an elderly gentleman, who, placing his hands on his shoulders, said, *Boy, you have talents and a musical sense that befit a genius! Do you want to become a concert pianist in your own right? Because you readily can, for I can arrange that you have full scholarship either at Curtis or Juilliard.... Here is my card. After you have thought about this and discussed it with your family, come to my office and I will arrange everything for you.*

Lou already knew what he wanted to make of his life, so that he never talked of the opportunity at home. He continued at the movie piano, until he mastered the massive banks and pedals of theatre organ, his performance at which, supplemented by the returns from the newspaper route, drew increasing attention to his promise and, in due time, won himself his first scholarship at the University of Pennsylvania.

Vicenzo Fontana
Louis Kahn went to Venice in 1971 and 1972 to give some lectures and to work with students at the Universita Internazionale dell'Arte, directed by Prof. Giuseppe Mazzariol.

I met Kahn in both these times. The first time I took him and his wife to the Lido for a dinner with Mazzariol and his wife. After dinner I went back to Venice with the Kahns, walking from the vaporetto's stop of S. Zaccaria in Riva Schiavoni, to the Albergo dell'Angelo where they had a room. When we arrived at the Ponte della Canonica, in the back of S. Marco, a drunk man, who was singing very loudly, fell down on the steps of the bridge and hurt his face. The blood was dropping from his nose and his mouth, so Kahn, like the good Samaritan, rushed up to hold him and with his handkerchief cleaned the man's face. But he could not stand up by himself, so we waited about twenty minutes until some people, it was late in the night, went to call the family of this man. His wife and his son came after a while and reproved and beat him; finally they took him home.

The second time was in February or March 1972. Venice was cold, rainy and windy and Kahn was complaining about bad weather. He told me that such a city on water had to be built in a warmer climate, not in the North of Italy. I was walking with him near the Venice Theatre to see an opera by Britten and he observed the side of the church of S. Fantin by Sansovino.

He very much loved the proportions of the nude stone wall and he said that this was a very great architecture. He told me that he was now using unpolished stainless steel in the Fort Worth Museum that had the beauty of lead, and asked me if I could find some big jars of terracotta for the porches of the Museum. I sent him many addresses of workshops near Florence where he could find them.

Nick Gianopolis

The story that's always amused me is not only the story but the manner in which he used stories to illustrate points of view to people. A few years ago there was a client that Lou didn't have the utmost confidence in. He felt the guy, the people were a bit shady and frequently in his meetings he would tell stories to I think let his clients know that they weren't manipulating him the way they thought they were.

Was this Baltimore?

Yes. And I recall one day having a meeting down at the 20th Street office where he tells the story of....

It couldn't have been 20th Street if it was Baltimore.

No, I mean the 15th Street office. When he told the story of two young friendly competitive men who grew up in the same little town of Russia or Poland as the case may be. And they were always competing and vying with each other. They were just friends/enemies all their lives. They finally reached a stage in their position in society and professions where they finally were no longer friends. They were now enemies. And they challenged each other to a duel. So they had selected pistols, the place of the duel, the day, the time. The day arrived. One man went to the forest. He was waiting. It was before sunup in the morning. Time went on. Around ten or eleven o'clock in the morning they heard hoofbeats of a horse. A horse and young boy coming down over the hill and everybody was curious. The young boy had a piece of paper. He handed the piece of paper to the seconds, the seconds handed it to the man and he ripped it open and here was this note from his friend saying, Abe, you shoot first, I'll be a little late. And he said this with such a smile, such glee, you know, this client who was on the other side of the table was absolutely silent. I thought this was pretty neat, you know. He made his points. He made his point that they weren't going to pull anything over on him.

Oh, our first association with Lou was very interesting. I met Lou in the fall of 1950 when I came to Philadelphia.

Where from?

From Center County, upstate. A classmate of mine, David Zipperfunnel, that you probably know, had done some work for Lou, I think on a part-time basis when he was with Pearlheim and Wenger, and so he took men over to introduce me to Lou shortly after I had come to the city and the fellow I had come to work for, his name was Major Gravell, who was one of the, I'm convinced finest old engineers in this city. He died in...,

How do you spell his name?

Gravell, G-R-A-V-E-L-L. William H. Gravell. His nickname was Major from World War I. It turned out that Gravell was an old friend and at that time just before Gravell's death, Lou had been talking to him about the Yale Art Gallery and going with Annie Tyng up to see Gravell at his place in, I guess, Mt. Airy. And Lou was struggling in developing this tetrahedronal floor system and apparently Fiester, his engineer, was a little bit reluctant to go that way, and Gravell was encouraging him. He felt that it was a possibility that this could somehow develop.

And there really wasn't the tool of analysis available at that time to do it, but yet he was encouraging. Shortly thereafter Gravell passed away and the firm of Keast & Hood was formed and it wasn't more than a week or two after we had formulated this group, the Keast & Hood firm, that we received a call from Lou asking us to come over and talk with him. And so we went one afternoon, Ray Hood, Dan Debona, Tom Litig and myself.

Same old group.

Same old group over on 20th Street and Lou was telling us that he had been to see Gravell, which we had known. Gravell had never really told us how he was encouraging Lou and Lou was almost at an impasse wondering could he really develop this or not, this system of construction. And Fiester was apparently still not encouraging about it, not to the degree Gravell was. And so it was at that meeting I think where the system came together where through our discussions with Lou, we said to him, *Lou, if you just simply consider one side of these, one direction of these tetrahedrons being a solid, canted joist, a series of canted joists, being braced by the inner planes of the tetrahedrons, why then you have a system.* But Lou said, *No, I want to have the sense of the void all around. Let me talk to Fiester.* Because apparently the School felt there was a little holding back. I think he was committed to get this job, the design completed so they could go out for bids. Well, apparently he talked to Fiester the next day when he went up to Yale and Fiester said, *Oh, yes, by all means we can do it this way,* and the first thing you know it was designed and they got Matt Comber to build a test panel of the thing and the thing worked very well and that was the end of that. But that was really the first time we had really done anything with Lou and it wasn't more than ah, it seems like a few months went by and he had the Trenton Bathhouses, the first time there. And he called up and said, *Bring the gang over.* He wanted somebody to talk to.

Oh, yes. He only worked by talking to people.

That's right. And so in a couple of sessions we had agreed that....

That was his real turning point, building that.

I think it was.

That little teeny twirp of a building.

That's right. In a couple of sessions, we had something that he felt he wanted to do and we felt that yes, you have it here and we'll do a few numbers for you and it worked out very simply and it was a very crystallized approach towards a very minimal structure and in a maxiumum amount of space and it worked. So then that was the beginning, I think, of our associations with him. That was also the beginning of our association with Bob Venturi, because Bob was spending time with him at the time of the Washington Competition, and that's where...

The Library Building.

Right.

It looked like a pyramid.

That's right, a ziggurat.

I was a student at Penn then and published that in the Pennsylvania Triangle. You know, that little magazine at Penn. The engineering and architectural magazine.

I vaguely remember.

And I published that there as a student. That was like 1965-66.

Yes, it would be that period. Just before Bob went to Rome and so on the Washington, then there was another one. There was the Fermi Competition shortly after that.

The Fermi Corporation was that very low slab thing that he did. It hardly looked like anything. Yeah, I remember that. I haven't thought of that building in so long. I don't think there's any drawings of that around. I've never seen any drawings of that in any of his...

If anybody would know, Tim Vreeland would know, because Tim handled the job.

I was just thinking. I was in his office. I came in one night and helped charette as a student.

I charetted on the Washington job and also on the Fermi. Komendant came in on the Fermi thing and he had not, ah, Komendant had not done any work for Lou but he had been in promoting the Lakewood precasting that he was a member of, ah, the firm. And Lou had said to me, *Well, do you think we can trust the fellow, his engineering judgements and so on?* And I said, *Well, from just what little I know of him from the meetings we've had, he certainly impresses all of us. He speaks at a technical level that's beyond our experience or our background.* And he said, *Well, let's call him down and maybe he'll help us on the Fermi.* So Komendant came in and did a few thumbnail computations, the kind that are necessary for submission, and I said to Lou after that, I said, *Look, I think he's got something here,* and he said, *Would you mind working with him?* and I said, *No, I'm sure we can arrange something,* which we did. But this began a long period of involvement. Actually, before that we had done the AF of L building, which was demolished recently.

I have a couple of rolls of film of that coming down.

That building was, ah, well, I want to say something about that building. We worked very very hard on that building and that was the first time, to our knowledge, there was ever a continuous poured-in-place Varrendale System done anywhere in this country or anywhere else. Technically, we thought it quite an accomplishment and Lou liked that part, but he disliked what was done to him in changing the exterior. Whenever he had, ah, he had designed it around brick, with brick panels and then the union went and substituted the granite later after making and redesigning the building to begin with.

The window detailing on that building is incredibly beautiful.

Oh, yeah. A fine building, a fine building.

I wanted to buy one of the windows, but just couldn't get it. It was too complicated.

Well, it was interesting, this is an aside, that shortly after that he wanted to show, Komendant tried to promote the matter of Varrendale construction and Lou took Komendant and one of the fellows from Lakewood, an old fella, up and showed them the building and.

Showed them what building?

AF of L. Because he wanted to show them, ah, that he had done a whole Varrendale building and Komendant came back to the office after—I happened to have gone later—and the fellow that told me told that Komendant did not like the building. Komendant did not like the Varrendale. He said, *That's not the way you use Varrendale,* which amused the hell out of us, to say the least. But, ah, and then Lou once said to me, *What's wrong with that building?* And I said, *There's nothing wrong with the building, Lou.* How you deal with personalities.

Did you ever work with Anne Tyng on anything? She is still around.

Yeah, Ann, we had, Ann was always involved in the conceptualizing of a number of the projects that Lou was doing, and I don't think, well, I don't think there was a building per se that was, that you could say was Ann's building. She was influential.

With the exception maybe of the one that went up like that.

Well, yeah, and yes we had talked on that one. There was never any real engineering done on the city hall twisted tetrahedronal, as well as the synagogue up in the north in one of the suburbs.

Oh, the triangular one.

Yes. That also kind of grew out of a tetrahedronal concept. But yes we had worked with Ann. As a matter of fact, one house which Ann had done which she is now doing additions to is the Shapiro House up in Gladwyne. It was two little squares and apparently she had recently just designed an extension of the house in the same kind of squares, you know, with perametal wood frame roofs, I guess. Was Ann there during the Trenton Community Center? I think she was in and around.

I think she was sort of in and around then.

I don't really recall.

Sure she was, because she was still heavily into Bryn Mawr.

Well, that followed. Bryn Mawr followed.

It was later, so she was...

That's right, but, yes, we've worked off and on with Ann over the years while she's been with Lou and after she had left Lou we still worked with her and helped her. Tom in particular helped her with her house. Apparently she had gone to City Hall, and they said *Well, that's all very interesting, but you better have some engineering on it.* So Tom told her how to...

Did you ever have any funny trips or experiences with Lou?

Oh, yes, lots of them. No, once he got away from the office he was great. He could relax, and I remember once going up to New York on the development of the Olivetti project, you know, when they were going through the throes of getting a budget and a scheme together. There was Lou and Duncan, Euwell and maybe Langford, I'm not sure.

Which one, Fran?

Yeah, it may have been Fran. And some of the people from Barclay White's office, who were the builders, and we had gone to the meeting. The meeting was rather short, it was a hot day, we didn't want to wait in the station and there was a little, outside of Penn Station there was a little bar about a block or two away and there was a baseball game being played and we just wanted to have a glass of beer and the question was would the ballgame be over before we caught the train or not. And they had a television set up in back of the bar and everybody's getting itchy about missing the train and it was like about three minutes from train time and finally the game was over and Lou said, *Let's go.* And we ran. It must have been about a block and a half and we made the train. He was really colorful. He really used to get enthused. And other times, like on Saturday, he would call up very insistent in the morning that I come into the office and...

Did he call you at home?

Oh, yes. Constantly.

Constantly.

Saturday night, Sunday. After a while you learned how to cope with it, but it was awhile before you learned that the reason he wanted you in before noontime into his office was because he was going to sneak out to a football game in the afternoon and he wanted to get his licks in before that. Because inevitably he'd keep you there till about 1:30 and then he'd say, *Excuse me, I have someplace to go.* Well, you know, by the time two o'clock or two-thirty would come around and you'd finally wind everything down and everybody was hungry and we'd all say, *Let's go to lunch. By the way, where's Lou? Oh, well, he's out to Franklin Field, or he's out to watch Drexel.* But he was gone. That was Lou. There was another time we had. There was a matter of different points of view in the development of, on the design of the hostels in Dacca, where the Pakistani Government had submitted design criteria, one of which was a requirement for meeting certain seismic requirements. And Lou initially wanted to do these buildings in reinforced concrete below buildings and then later on he elected to do them in brick, once he felt there was the competency to do brick work the way he wanted it. And, too, he was convinced by the PWD people that it would make work and politically it was expeditious to make work for a large bulk of people there in Dacca. But we felt that to design for the seismic conditions that they were setting as criteria would require going to the reinforced type of masonry which is common here to California, you know, two of brick, grouted core, and we had talked....

What kind of core?

Grouted core.

Oh, grouted core, right.

And the brick would be like four, three, four. Like a three-inch grout core, it's actually concrete, like gravel concrete. So there we had also reviewed this at great length with Charlie Etter from the University at Villanova. Dr. Etter from the Civil Engineering Department who also felt this and he really set the method of analysis for the AF of L building, you know, the continuous ground-built girders. Charlie built the whole analytical approach to that and he was a very close friend of ours.

I've never heard his name before.

Well, Charlie has always kind of been on the outside.

How do you spell his name?

E-T-T-E-R. And Charlie has been a consultant to us and has been ever since then. He was an old employee of Gravell back in the late 1940s and early 1950s before he got his doctorate at MIT, so Charlie concurred with our concern that we should design with the reinforced core, but Lou just found it hard to accept and I recall on one of the trips we took down to Dacca, we were going to take the information the first drawings and details for reinforcement of the masonry, and Lou was taking it with some apprehension because he didn't believe in it, but he could not be convinced. We could not convince him. Somehow he felt that he had selected masonry and there was enough in the physical characteristics of the masonry, in the shapes of the openings he was doing that it didn't need the steel in the gravity core. Well, Olmer and I were going to take this trip with him. There was a mixup on the plane schedule going out of Kennedy in New York and he was able to take an earlier plane than we were because he was then going to go via Great Britain, stop and see somebody, and then meet us in Dacca.

Probably to buy some ties.

Possibly, who knows, or an old book or something. So it was very amusing. He was going through the gate where the ticket had been taken, turning around and saying to me, *Whatever you do, you can't talk to PWD about that reinforced masonry until I get there.* And what he was going to do, he was going to try and counter whatever we were going to say, and, well, it turns out that we got to Dacca a couple of days before he did and by the second day we were there, they knew the purpose of our being there and we were holding back the drawings and they were a little perturbed, *well, look, you're here and supposed to be doing something for us but you haven't shown us the drawings and we know you're bringing drawings on reinforcing the masonry.* The work has got to start. They're putting the foundations in. So finally they prevailed on us to show them the drawings and felt it wasn't so bad. It wasn't as bad as Lou had been concerned about.

Was Lou worried that they wouldn't do it because it was too fancy, or what?

No. It was against his principles. Against the principle of introducing steel into masonry. This was a job where he was going through the evolution and crystallizing of his belief that the material utilized in the building should be capable of making its own openings. And it took us a while to understand that.

So what happened?

So anyway, there ensued thereafter this give-and-take period of a year or two where the Pakistanis wanted to cut the amount of reinforcement in the core or like we had bars, a bar every 24″ vertically, they wanted to do it every 48″ and Lou kept saying, *Well, you really don't need it. Cut it down to 48″.* And we never really knew how much was going in there and then eventually when Harry Pombaum—Harry had worked for us and when we withdrew from the project, we turned over everything we had to Harry, because Lou wanted somebody to continue the project—and on the first trip that Harry took when we went over there, we went walking up the street and he said, *My God, reinforcing walking on centers. What's going on here?* And he said, *Well, Professor Kahn said it's all right.* So he said, *Do it according to the drawings.* So eventually it went back to the core reinforcement. But you know, there's always this give-and-take between us. It was always that way. That was the colorful thing. The other thing that was terrific about Lou was the people in his office were always so concerned and frightened of him that when they had a job under construction they were really driving the builder right to the wall with having the work done as precisely as shown on the drawings, and then Lou would come by unannounced and he would look at the contractor's deviations and say, *Gosh, that's terrific.* When Millcreek Housing Project was being built, the second bays with the row houses, there was a matter of the way the thickness of the joint, bedding joint was varying and varying—it was supposed to be a 3/8″ joint. In some cases it was up to 5/8″. But there were a couple of old Italian brick masons there and they had this grapevine joint. Well, the way they used the tool was just terrific, just didn't look wrong, and the brick was not that precise. It had a little bit of a soft edge to it that here was this big meeting where Lou was going to come out and everybody was hoping he'd read the riot act to them—and he loved it. The old story is, how can you win?

How did you sense the office work?

Oh, well, he was the mainstay of the whole office. Oh, I've got another story to tell you. A story that most people never knew, you know. On the Millcreek housing project, that's what brings it to mind, they had some precast forms ready, and the precaster is up near Bethlehem or Easton or thereabouts. I don't even know if the firm's in business anymore, but they were going to make the precast Iver House hoods and lids, and they called and said they had the forms ready and had a couple of samples made and would we go see them? So Marie, Lou, and I drove up one day. I just had my little Saab, my little three-cylinder Saab for a few weeks, and Lou thought it was a pretty neat toy. And so it was a hot day and we arrived up there around noon time and saw what we had to see and I had asked Lou if he had ever driven on River Road down on the Delaware to New Hope and so on, and he said that no, he hadn't, not for years and let's go that way because the highway was too hot. There was no shade. This was in June and it was a terribly hot day. So on the way back, as we approached New Hope, I said to Lou, *Have you ever visited George Nakashima?* And he said, *No, I've never met the man,* and he said, *I like some of the things he does,* and he was just starting Salk. He was just getting into Salk then and he said, *I have some ideas about using wood. It may not be a bad idea to meet him.* So I stopped along the side of the road in a service station and called Nagashima, who has pretty stringent rules about people visiting there, and I said to George, *I'm up this way with Lou. Do you mind if we stop by and have an occasion to meet each other?* And George said, *Oh, by all means. Have him stop in.* And so we stopped in shortly thereafter and it was really great the way they greeted each other, you know, very correct and polite and George drove Lou around on his golf cart that he uses and showed him what he had and Lou was amazed at the selection. So Lou was amazed to see the selection of wood that Nakashima has collected and was curing it these various stages. And it was a very very nice little visit lasting no more than a half hour or forty-five minutes and Lou asked him a couple of questions about wood and how it weathers on the exterior and so on. Nakashima confirmed I think Lou's query that teak was by far the best wood to use and eventually he did use teak. Lou was wondering whether he should use epitong and a few of these other woods, and Nakashima said that the most dimensional, the most serviceable wood was the teak. As we were leaving and they were bidding adieus, Lou went over and shook Nakashima's hand and he said, *Mr. Nagasaki, it was a pleasure to have met you.* And Nakashima just grinned from ear to ear. And Lou said, *Oh, I missed that one, didn't I?*

I mean, he obviously wasn't the same as most people you meet.

How about those times when we went over to talk to him about the money he owed us and he'd get us in the room up front and he'd kind of sit there with his hands on the table and he'd say, *I know why you are here.*

And he'd talk about everything else.

And he'd say that things weren't going too bad for him. Then he'd go over and lift up this old piece of cloth he had and bring out a piece of bread, the glasses and he would know why you were there but he'd just talk about all the prospects of things that were to happen in the future. He was a professional optimist. But he would never commit himself to doing anything about the thing that you were there to talk about. But with all of that you still came away from the meeting not ready to beat him over the head or something like that, but accepting him for

what he was. It's, ah, he had a way of dealing with people and I suspect some of the problems with jobs from time to time were because he would attempt to think that he could outguess how someone was going to react to something. Some of the things that he did from time to time I'm sure were geared not to what he wanted, but to how he thought the person he was talking to was going to react to. He was a showman. Some of what he said was geared, ah, part of any ability to speak or to convey messages or thoughts is geared to gearing yourself to your audience. And he was very conscious of who he was talking to and tailored I think what he had to say to the group that he was talking to.

When did you first meet him?

Well, I guess it was when we were still out at 2031 Chestnut Street. And that would have been back in the mid-fifties or early fifties. The early fifties. We were over when he was down on 20th Street.

This is maybe not a very important question, but I was just thinking of it. But I know when he died I was so shocked. Was everybody taken aback by it? I mean, he wasn't so young, but I was so shocked. I couldn't believe it. I sort of felt he would live forever, you know, one of those kind of people.

He seemed to be very durable. You didn't think of him as, ah, he had so much vitality, so much energy and we would know that when he was getting ready for a trip that he'd be in the office all sorts of hours. He did not behave, he did not act like a man who was ill or likely to be ill. He seemed to hold up well under a rather rigorous schedule. Yes, I guess the thought had crossed my mind, you know, well, what if something happens to Lou. I know we talked about it, because Lou owed us money and the question of how hard do you press and what do you do and so forth and I guess you know, had there been any thought that Lou's presence was in a limited time, certainly we would have behaved differently than we did.

A number of years ago when my wife and I were in Cape Cod for a short vacation, on the way back we stopped at Yale to see the Art Gallery. And, as chance would have it, while we were having lunch in some small restaurant near the campus, there was Lou with a group of faculty and students. He spotted us and said oh, what are you doing here and how long will you be here, and we told him that we were on our way back to Philadelphia that afternoon. And he said, *Well, could you wait a little while and then take me home?* Well, we naturally left about eight o'clock instead of five, but on the way back he was reminiscing about the days he had spent in Europe shortly after finishing at the University in the mid-to-late 1920s, and how he remembered on numerous occasions having to bail Ed Stone out because Ed Stone would receive a check on a monthly basis and towards the end of the month the money would be gone and Lou would take him to a little local cafe nearby where he had an arrangement with the proprietor whereby Lou would play the piano so that he could buy Ed Stone's supper.

I never heard that story.

And I never heard the story repeated. Lou once told the story that there was some kind of gathering going on in Yale in the winter, and it turned out during the lecture or after the lecture when they came out to the street all the cars were snowed in because of the heavy snows and so he and another gentleman that he didn't know at that time proceeded to help motorists get their cars out of the ditch by pushing them. And Lou thought this was just great, you know, putting his shoulder to the cars and pushing them.

That macho thing with him.

That's right. So then, I guess after one or two cars had been pushed out, why he turned around and introduced himself to the fellow next to him, and apparently it was Charles Addams, the cartoonist. And so then Lou proceeds to tell him how much he enjoys his cartoons.

A. Gulgonen

Kahn was always ready to start once more. That is why he was young, up-to-date, without trying to be avant-garde, original and the latest.

The critics and architects who write about him, classifying his works, usually misunderstood them; and the young architects who thought he was not the latest, they were deceived themselves.

Last year, during his last visit to Belgium and France, we were together in Bouges, in Bruxelles and in Paris. We had long walks, many visits and long evenings talking on different subjects, such as the sense of belonging to a place, memory and symphony, the joints of the brick wall.

In Paris, he was invited to give a conference to an audience of engineers, administrators and architects. It was by invitation and many people in key positions were invited. Many students who knew that he was in Paris also came, but because they didn't have invitations, they were asked to listen and see him on a giant screen in another hall where the conference was diffused simultaneously with the utilization of the latest techniques of communication. Lou didn't like the idea and the students refused sharply to go to another hall, and wanted to be with him. At the end, there was a place made for them to stand, and everybody was happy.

The conference itself was very exciting and was a surprise and even a shock for many successful businessmen who came to listen to a world-famous American architect and to pass a nice time. He might even flirt with them, as other famous architects do, knowing that they always look for big names in their grand operations.

He started his talk attacking the way the problems are solved in Paris in a very realistic way, with great consciousness of their actuality and importance, and the roles of architects facing them. In a rather young spirit guided neither by historicism nor speculation, he sharply criticized the way the mistakes of American cities are repeated. The expressways in the city: *this time along the Seine.* The problem of pollution: *all the miracle of a river has disappeared.* And the speculative nature of the developments: *like the missing tooth,* and the mediocracy *in the country of LeCorbusier whom I consider as my teacher;* and lack of sensibility to cultural values and their architectural expressions. Although he accused them responsible of *this second oldest profession of the world,* he was never pessimistic. He encouraged the opportunities given to the younger architects. When he condemned the Tower of Monparnasse, it was because he *couldn't see any trace of the French engineering genius of Perret, Eiffel.*

Then he showed his works proudly, nobly.

Ann Miller Haigh

He had a way of zeroing in on a word of great precision for meaning to describe or explain something. (And if such a word didn't exist, he'd invent one.)

He also enjoyed silliness at times. I remember the marvelous silly fun we had rehearsing him for his visit with newly-elected Mayor Rizzo. Lou, optimistic, idealistic as usual, was going to plead the case of the Art Commission's ideas for the City on a person-to-person basis with the Mayor. I was trying to convince him that the effort was futile and said that he didn't even speak the same language as Rizzo, which I said was comprised mainly of obscenities and vulgarities. Whereupon Lou proceeded to practice cursing. He dredged up every blue expletive he could think of until we were immobilized with laughter. It wasn't the same, however, without the South Philadelphia accent—and nothing, of course, came of the meeting.

Lou loved music so much that he could even respond to the limited potential of two spoons clacked together. At one all-day Art Commission meeting at Vince Kling's farm near Reading, to take a break from the heavy discussion, we took a sort of bluegrass et al break, with everyone singing and playing various instruments: guitar, banjo, autoharp. Lou, after bemoaning the fact that his instrument—organ/piano—was not portable, picked up two kitchen spoons and joined in the jam.

I love Lou. Working for him for three and one-half years on the AC was an incredible learning and feeling experience. Art Commission meetings, with the former commission (Bob Engman, Ian McHarg, Vince Kling, Jack Wolgin, Matt McClosky, Bonnie Winterstein, Charles Madden and Bill Costello—a rather mad and interesting group) seemed to turn him on, and he was most often brilliant. And he was beautiful—always showing the greatest respect for the personal integrity of artists and architects—even when he knew they were hacks.

Often he was very difficult to work with. Expediency and pragmatism were two things he was loath to accomodate. We would spend hours on the telephone composing letters to explain AC actions or, most especially, to communicate Lou's hope for a project, a planning attitude, a principle. A letter in progress might run to three or four legal pad-sized pages before Lou would inevitably say: *No, no, forget all that. Let's just say simply this...*and the communication would be reduced to one paragraph of four sentences.

Lou had a great involvement with words. He felt that if ideas and feelings could be adequately communicated on a level of mutual respect, attitudes could be changed. He had a poet's sensitivity to words. I remember one AC review of a piece of playground sculpture entitled by the artist, *Whale.* Lou, among others, highly praised the sculptor and the AC gave the work unanimous approval. *But,* Lou said, *don't call it* Whale. *It's not a whale...call it Fish if you want.* And he quickly sketched the snout of a whale on a piece of paper and pushed it over to me. *This,* he said, *is a whale.* That (pointing to the sculpture model) *is* not *a whale.*

Bits and pieces of things Lou said keep coming back to me—incisive and beautiful things—which often, in the context of a municipal design review board meeting, sounded bizarre to and shocked the nearly rigid representatives of various city departments, developers or/and even some of the architects. The classic comment Lou made, after a presentation involving specifications and dollars ad infinitum in a hard facts, big business manner, was: *But it* (the building) *doesn't sing.* Another comment, which the newspapers quoted in such a way as to make it sound silly, was one of the truest evaluations of current road advertising I've ever heard: The AC had been given the design of the *Message Tower* at Veteran's Stadium to review and all the big guns had been called out by the Administration and by the sign-handlers to persuade the AC that this single structure—tied as it was to the financial package of the computerized scoreboard—was absolutely essential to the life of the city, equated in some mad way with the success of the stadium. Lou listened patiently to the lengthy presentation and to the comments following and then said quietly: *This should not be built. It will take the stars out of the sky.* Every time I drive past that brontosaurian structure, I wish somebody up there had listened to Lou.

Larry Halprin

I had some very strange experiences with Lou, actually. (All of this, in a sense, has not got very much to do with how I felt about him.) The first experience was a very strange and unpleasant one. He called me one day—or was it Jonas Salk? I don't remember which one. I became close friends with Jonas afterwards and good friends with Lou as a result of this, or rather, in spite of it. They said they wanted me to come down and work with Lou on the landscaping gardens for the Salk Institute. I went down.

At first I was a little concerned because I knew Lou was a very good architect and a very strong one. I said, *What am I going to do down there?* They said, *We'd like you to work with Lou.* I wanted to know exactly what I was going to do. They said, *We've had some very unfortunate experiences with someone else who wasn't very good who designed the garden and Lou said you and Barragan are the only two people in the world he could work with and he's talked with Barragan, but that doesn't seem to be working. Would you come down?* I said, *Are you sure that Lou is accepting the fact that I'm coming?* They said, *He looks forward to it very much.* Finally I said, *OK, I'm coming down.*

I went down and we talked at length about the idea and he said he had talked at length with Barragan about paving the courtyard and that didn't seem right because it would be too glary and too harsh. I said I'd make a pass at it. I designed something which, whether it was right, wrong or indifferent, was not unreasonable, but it was quite soft. I had some stones in the courtyard, as I remember it, and grass running between the joints. It wasn't all paved because I thought there would be a tremendous glare in the courtyard and I did a number of things outside.

To make a long story short, people liked it very much but then five days later Lou called and said he wasn't sure about it. He had liked it in the beginning. Then he called and suggested we meet again out there. He came back to the same thing about the paved space. Gradually it bore on me that Lou wasn't really interested in anything I was saying at all. He was being very polite. He really wanted to be verified, a verification for what *he* was trying to do. I was never quite clear; I wasn't even that unwilling to do what he wanted to do as long as it was right, which I didn't think it was.

I found, really after a bit, that he wanted me to validate what he was trying to do and it was silly for me to be spending the energy on it that I was. I was taking it seriously. I thought it was...I'd seen other things of Lou's that I thought were better than the Salk Center. I didn't think it was the greatest thing he had ever done and I especially think that paving that courtyard was the wrong thing to do.

I've never brought myself to go down there [since it was finished], but they tell me that people find that courtyard not good because it's terribly glaring and not pleasant and the whole idea was the courtyard was the common living room for the whole thing. I didn't feel that was the right thing to do, but even if it was, I felt the energy I was pouring into it on the creative level wasn't justified because he just wanted me to validate what he was doing. So I just left. I didn't quit, I didn't do anything, I just never appeared again.

I think there was a certain amount of tension about it, because I felt I had been had. If he had been honest with me and said, *I really want to design this myself and would like your help and tell me what materials to use, etc....*

The next time I saw Lou was in Jerusalem on the Advisory Council. I remember the first time we saw each other. Have you ever seen two dogs who kind of circle around each other? The first meeting was kind of like that, but then I think by common consent we embraced and it was a release of tension. From then on we were very cordial. He used to go out of his way to talk to me. I don't think there was anything personal. Every time we were on that commission together we talked. He asked me very often to share his meetings with him. From then on it was pleasant and very friendly. I don't remember if we ever got into a very intricate dialogue after that. I got over it and I think he did also. I had respect for that.

I don't think he could function on any committee, because it wasn't his game. Some people are extremely good on committees and some are not.

When I dealt with Lou it was like going backward in time, as if my daddy had—and Lou was older than I by fifteen or twenty years—as if somebody had waggled their finger at me, which I had become accustomed to. Here I was being put in a position which I had struggled successfully to get out of. I felt I was finally at a point where I could deal with a person like Lou, but it didn't work. Therefore, I was upset emotionally, professionally and personally on a level that he probably never understood. Maybe I should have told him.

That's interesting because I've never really talked about it. It affected me psychologically in a profound way which Lou did not understand, which I never revealed until this moment. I feel much better talking about it.

If it was going to be done, I feel better that Lou did it rather than some schmuck.

W.S. Huff
8 November 1959
A Sunday breakfast with Lou.

Another discussion. The subjects are those that presently occupy his mind and ones that I encourage myself. These same things I try to say, but often I do not find the words (even my repetition of Lou's words here lacks the magic of the moment of his saying them—on the other hand, I have made my own additions and, of course, present them according to the extent of my own understanding).

Thus, the discussion of the state of consciousness, a principle characteristic of life; of thought and feeling, the two parts of consciousness; and of love, the most important aspect of feeling.

He spoke of the rare meeting of two people who have immediate and mutual understanding. At this moment the human is overcome by the feeling of the "everness" of this relationship—the "everness" of it before, as well as after, the instant of its happening. His being becomes intensely vibrant, most exhilarated, most exciting and meaningful. And in this moment the human spirit is in (what Lou calls) "silent combat."

There is no thinking, nothing rational, in the consciousness of this state of feeling. In fact, this aspect of being is completely out of the control of thought.

The experience is most beautiful, most life-stirring; it is an awakening to the understanding of the very nature of man's soul; and with it comes the wonderment and humble gratitude that this certain realization should have been given himself.

(One result of such an experience is a desire to want to give oneself spiritually as well as materially—also to learn a greater love for all of man.)

None of these things are new discoveries, but they are realizations that every man must go through himself if he is to achieve a recognization of his oneness with the universe.

R. Julius
When he came to Aspen in 1972 and spoke at the conference, afterwards we found ourselves walking along with him and we reminded him that we met him in London when he was over there earlier and he remembered. He told us he was extremely excited because he'd just come back from London where he'd been awarded a medal by the Queen. He pulled it out of his pocket there and said, *Your Queen gave me this yesterday.* We thought it was really rather sweet that he'd been carrying it around with him all day, in and out of the tents and the conference.

Esther Kahn
Some of the notebooks have little poetries in them and things that he hadn't written before. Of course, they are all piecemeal and they are not...The last thing he wrote was the forward for Scarpa's book.

He labored over that—it was so hard for him.

I know he labored. I used to get so provoked with him. He'd say, *I've got to go back,* and I'd say, *Well, why, Lou?* [He'd say,] *I've got to write.* The thoughts just flew when he spoke, but writing was difficult. So many a time, he would bring his writing, he would take everything off this table—the lights are very good in this room, and he loved this room anyway—and he would go upstairs and watch his favorite television programs.

Which ones did he like best?

He loved Westerns. Oh, he loved Westerns. He liked Bonanza and he liked any Wild West real good western. And he liked detective stories. He got sort of interested in detective stories, but he used to say, *You're the detective story expert, I can't figure out what is happening,* and I would say, *Oh, it's so-and-so did so-and-so, and he's the villain,* and it was always true and he would say, *How did you know?* Then he would go to bed and around 3 am, he would come down here and write for a couple of hours, but he didn't do it often enough. He had to be surrounded by his books if he wanted to look something up. He felt very comfortable in the crowded, informal, almost dreary atmosphere of his office. He loved the informality of that and yet he had the same thing here, but in bad weather when he was going back to writing, he would write here.

I was trying to remember the other day an incident that you would have never known. It was so typical of Lou and I don't know what made me think about his clothes. He was terribly fussy about his clothes and I sort of get disturbed when they describe him as a little man in baggy pants. I never thought his pants were baggy—they were made by Brooks Brothers, and they had to be just right, and just the right color. But he hated to shop, hated to take the time to shop, except for neckties.

Didn't he used to go to Princeton for neckties?

Well, when he was there. And he had those black bowties—they were a soft wool and the first time he had them made was before Jackie Kennedy was coming to the office, and he put on one of these black ties, askew on purpose, and he would sometimes spend a half hour—I always waited down here until he left. And he'd be upstairs and I'd hear walking back and forth, back and forth, probably changing ties twenty times that didn't suit him, and then coming down with those little black bowties.

Yes, ties and books, too, I remember.

Oh, books. Yes, well an awful lot of books. Old books, and he didn't care what the cover was like, he didn't care about the cover.

I knew Lou when. And when I met Lou, some of the people—and I'm not meaning the real people—some of the people wouldn't have looked at him twice, you know. He was an insecure young man just starting out, and the minute we met, I knew there was something very, very special about Lou. And I say there were only two people in this world who knew what Lou was going to amount to way back in 1927 when I met him, and that was my father, who Lou idolized, who was a great man and died quite young, and myself. And that is true. Oh, his mother thought he was great, I mean she would go to such heights such as when my daughter first started to play the flute she came to Philadelphia and Susie was just starting, maybe at nine years old, to play the flute—and she said, *Better than Kincaid.* Well, that wasn't me with Lou. That was a mother with Lou. But not me—I knew what Lou was, I knew what Lou was going to be from the minute we met. He had that certain—oh, I don't know—whether it was the excitement I felt when I was with him or what. And I didn't know about the field of art. Music, yes, but not graphics—the graphic arts. The dance, the theater—my father was a great devotee of the theater and I can remember as a child, our greatest joy was Saturday afternoons going to matinees and I saw all the plays from up and down, because Daddy would take us. So I knew the theater and the dance and music, but I didn't know the graphic arts. I learned those from Lou, as little as I know about them. But he loved to talk, and our first date, that's what (well, it wasn't our date, I mean the first time I met him) the attraction was, he was talking and I just couldn't stop listening, and that was it. And that was it for both of us, really.

But I want to go back and tell you about the clothes. I was thinking of these two very ridiculous incidents—maybe even three. Lou was the talker, speaker, lecturer—I don't know what you want to call it—of the Alumni Chapter of the University of Pennsylvania School of Architects. They have their May dinner and he was going to be their guest speaker. And he was being honored. I can't remember whether the Richards Building was completed, or just up, and the meeting started in the plaza of the Richards Building. I had been with a friend who was a graduate—not of architecture, but the School of Design—which is long gone from Penn, but was a very excellent school—and she had come only to this because Lou was going to be there. And I had said, *Lou's going to Japan the next day: I'm worried sick. He hasn't anything to wear. He's wearing the only suit he has to travel in.* And somebody asked Lou a question about the building and Lou took his beautiful broad hand and a piece of charcoal out of his pocket and made designs on it, showed it to everybody, then he took his hand and wiped it right down on the one and only suit he had to take to Japan. I thought I would die. But she reminded me of that. She said, *I'll never forget the way he did that.* Well, that was so typical—just so typical. Those things didn't matter to him, although as I say, he was terribly fussy about his clothes—his shirts, everything—but actually in a way, they didn't matter. They had to be right, but they didn't matter.

I don't know whether he ever told you this story, which I think is beautiful. It was before we moved into this house and he used to very frequently after we had dinner at the Art Alliance, not want to go back to the office. He would go to an all-night movie to relax. And after sleeping there maybe an hour or an hour and a half, he would go back to the office. He was walking on Market Street and he had his raincoat, in what state of disrepair I don't know, slung over his shoulder, and was walking along Market Street looking for an all-night movie, when a lady stopped him. She was an elderly lady, very shabbily but very beautifully dressed. Everything was mended, but in the finest of taste. She was obviously a very genteel lady that had come down in the world financially. And she said to him, *Young man, how can I get to so-and-so?* And he said, *Oh, madame, I'll take you.* So they marched along Market Street and I presume he must have talked to her. They got where she was going and he said, *Now here you are, this is where you are going,* and she opened her pocketbook, took out a quarter and handed it to him. And Lou very graciously took the quarter and put it in his pocket.

Lou did tell me that story. It's a terrific story. Lou told me that story and I thought I would never stop laughing. And he was so proud of himself with that story that, as you know, when he would start to laugh, it was just a sort of little snicker, and he would laugh and he could hardly get the rest of it out for laughing.

I had a letter from a student who said—it's a very long letter, I haven't answered it—something like six pages, an angry letter in parts. A letter that describes how he first worked for Lou and how he felt Lou encouraged his own ideas on everybody, which of course he did, because he couldn't have people designing things which weren't fit for him, and he said he tried three or four times—he signed up for the class, was accepted and then felt he couldn't really stand the strong personality of Lou, and then this year, he went into class. He said, *You know, it's amazing, he never even bothered to know our names—then he comes up to us, and puts his hands on our shoulders, and he looks into our eyes,* and he said, *What more do we need?* And he did have that. He didn't bother to remember names, because he couldn't remember names, and I had a couple of

funny experiences—one this summer and one last summer The phone rings and I answer it. And Lou says, *Esther, I have so-and-so and so-and-so in the office and he starts with this problem*—and then he says, *Can you tell me their names?* And last summer, the day before Labor Day and I can't ever forget it because we were having about 15 or 16 people for dinner on Labor Day and there was no place to get food on Sunday. And I had prepared all this food for these people and Lou calls and says, *I have a couple of people here from New York— they are friends of Sue's—and I think I'd better bring them home for supper.* Three people. I said, *Lou, it's really very bad because everything I have is for our party tomorrow. Why can't we take them out?* He says, *Oh, not the way they look, couldn't take them anywhere.* I said, *All right, I'll manage.* So he brings them home, doesn't introduce them. We had a rather difficult evening in one respect because they wouldn't eat white rice, they only wanted wild rice, but it worked out all right. And I had been led to assume that they were friends of Sue's. And I started talking. They had never heard of Sue. Lou got it in his head that they were Sue's friends and he brought them home for dinner.

Lou had some very bad faults. One of them was that he didn't know how to say *no.* That was his worst fault. He couldn't say no to anybody who came into the office, taking up his time—no matter who they were or how busy he was. Always took time. Three and four hours he would spend with some. He did not know how to say no; he simply could not say no. And another major fault he had was that he felt that if he didn't talk about it, the problem would go away. He didn't believe in talking things out. He really thought if you don't talk about it, the problem would disappear. And I think they were his two major faults. They got him into a lot of trouble. And he had difficulty making decisions. His mind was so fertile. But he would have one thing, and then two minutes later, he had an entirely different idea. Well, people couldn't understand that, but that's the way a creative artist is. I guess you've heard this expression: he said, *You can't chew pencils and spit ideas.* And people would say to him, thinking they were helping, *Well, why don't you get a business manager, why don't you do this or that?* He couldn't work that way. I always understood it, and I understood why.

You know, every time I see an article, an historical article about Lou, there's always a different story about the scarring of his face.

I'll tell you the story because I went with Lou, we were going to be married, and I never asked him. I knew it wasn't hereditary, so I didn't care. It was pretty bad, too, when I knew him. He was very thin, and even when I met him in 1927, his skin was really very bad and was hanging. And, in fact, some of my mother's friends couldn't understand how I could consider marrying a man like that. They thought it was terrible. You know, I was the pride and joy of the family.

Was he conscious of it?

Yes, he was very conscious of it. And I'll tell you a couple of stories about it. He always wore a hat. I have a wonderful picture of him the way he looked—Lou was the first Jew ever taken into the Architectural Honorary Society. Lou had sort of a blond color hair and he lost all the color while he was in Europe; his mother had been white when she was 35 and Lou turned gray long before that. Anyway, they lived in a little place that had, of course, just an open fireplace. Little children wore pinafores; the boys didn't wear trousers, they wore pinafores. And Lou could describe to the day he died the color of the coals, what a chemist would call *burning back.* They turned an unusual shade of blue and green—I guess they weren't getting enough oxygen. And Lou was fascinated by the color, and he wanted to save it—the color—and he put his hands in the fire and he picked out the coal, which was this gorgeous shade of blue-green, and he put it in his pinafore. And, of course, the pinafore went up in flames and he put his hands over his eyes; that's why he was scarred from his eyes down and the back of his hands was scarred. He saved his eyes. And for months they didn't know whether he would live.

How old was he?

Three. And that's the story, because one day, I don't know what, but I made some remark and he thought I was talking about his face, and I said no. He said you never asked me. I said, no, because I knew it wouldn't affect our children, so I didn't want to ask you. But he said, well, I'll tell you. Then he told me when he was a very small boy, they were poor when they came to this country, and he had very poor clothes and everything else and the children were very cruel and he used to wait and slide along the side of the brick walls and be the last one to class on time because the children always teased him so much about the way he looked. But he would always come home with those stars pasted on his shirt from his elbow down for his beautiful drawings. And the children began to realize that here was something special when Lou was six years old and could draw up on the blackboard gorgeous American flags for whatever day it was; children began to respect him and began not to subject him to such tortures. But Susie had a most unpleasant experience when she was about five or six years old. They were crazy about each other and she was going to Friends Select, and the bus would come pick her up at our house. And I was very fussy, I didn't want to let her stand there alone, because sometimes the bus would be late. We could stand on our porch and watch her, but nevertheless, always one of us walked across the street, because he didn't rush in to work quite as fast as he did in later years; sometimes we would go together. And one day he was getting ready to take her across the street, and she said, *Daddy, I wish you wouldn't come,* and he said, *Well, why, Susie? Well, I can wait by myself, and I'll just wait by myself.* So she went across the street, and Lou and I stood on the porch watching her. When she came home that afternoon for milk and cookies, I said, *Susie, why didn't you want your father to wait with you? Well,* she said, *yesterday when I got on the bus, two girls sitting in the back of the bus said, Her father's nothing but a monkey.* I said they are just ignorant foolish people. Because Lou used to jump around and dance and tell stories while they were waiting for the bus. They are jealous, because their fathers would never do that for them. And after that Lou went back to waiting for the bus with her. And I never told Lou why she didn't want him to wait for the bus. So he's had his heartaches about that, too, but as he grew older, his face became much more interesting looking, as if it were something outstanding and really not scarred. But he was pretty raw even when I met him for the first time. And one of the stories the rabbi told was absolutely correct. After we got married, Lou threw his hat away and never put it on again. The last time he ever wore a hat was when we got married. I was quite beautiful—you may not have thought it, but I was, and I guess he felt if it didn't bother me, it wouldn't bother anybody. So he had a pretty hard time of it.

He'd been feeling fine, didn't he, except for those crazy trips?

He was tired. He wouldn't admit to anybody that he was tired, but he was tired. The last few months, he even told Norman Rice he was tired. I thought he was tired, and I tried very hard not to interfere. But Lou would always have indigestion and he had very severe ulcers one time. Lou and I had gone to the Orchestra to hear an all-Bach concert with the Philadelphia Orchestra, and Lou said, *Esther, I am awfully sick,* and I said, *Let's leave.* We were sitting downstairs, and he said, *No, let's wait for intermission,* and at intermission, he absolutely just crawled up the aisle into a cab and, of course, I took him up to Jefferson. When we got to Jefferson, I told the resident on my service, who was a neurosurgeon, and he came down and thought Lou had a red hot gall bladder, so he called somebody, and Lou was in agony. After they admitted him, and there were all kinds of diagnoses, they said he had a gall bladder and he had to be operated on. And Lou said, *I'm not going to be operated on, I don't have a gall bladder.*

How old was Lou then?

Maybe 45, something like that. My chief had a long talk with him, and Lou said, *I want more X-rays.* And they took more X-rays and found out that he had a nice red hot ulcer—not a bleeding ulcer, but an ulcer, and I think this was just before he went to the Academy. And, of course, I stayed in the hospital all night; I called my mother and Sue was just a little girl, and I knew what an ulcer diet was like and I couldn't imagine Lou trying to live on what he called *fairy food* and that kind of stuff. And he had a very, very smart doctor—he was no psychiatrist, he was nothing, but just a very smart man. Everybody that came to the hospital brought Lou boxes of black cigars, and he had a pile of cigars alongside his bed. The doctor came in smoking a great big black cigar, blowing smoke all over everything and saying, *Lou, one thing you have to do—it would be a good idea if you cut out smoking.* If he had told him to stop smoking or he mustn't smoke, it would have been no good. And Lou looked at him and said, *Really?* and the doctor said, *Oh, yes, smoking aggravates the ulcer, and you've got a nasty one.* Lou took the boxes of cigars and threw them right in the wastebasket. And we went through hell for three months, but that's the way he stopped, and he never smoked again.

He used to smoke cigars?

Cigars, cigarillos, cigarettes, anything. Never smoked before breakfast, but after that, there was always something in his mouth. Always. He loved a good cigar when he could afford it.

Lou always had a tendency towards indigestion. That's why he wouldn't eat garlic, wouldn't eat spiced food. The last few months, I was very careful—everything was broiled, we never had anything with fat—but the last few months, he seemed to be troubled with a little indigestion, but he was going through such agonies, I didn't think anything of it. Now, he seemed perfectly well before he went away. On Friday night, we had a whole series of circumstances, like Lou visiting his family two weeks before he died, and some of his family from Westchester coming here to dinner to bring the book that Lou for two years never had the time to look at. And Lou seeing his grandfather and all these people, and knowing all their names, and the giggling and laughing. Well, the cousin told me that when Lou opened the door, because Lou came from school before they got here, and Len said to him, *How are you?* and Lou said, *I'm tired,* and that's not like Lou. So when Doshi called me on Tuesday, it was 3:30 in the morning, and that was the first indication we'd had that Lou had been on the Bombay plane. We couldn't find out. He said to me, *I don't understand where he is, Esther, because I have never in all the years I've known Lou seen him so well, so full of fun, so full of vitality to accomplish so much. He was absolutely perfectly well and happy, and he promised to come back in June and he promised that this time he would bring you with him.* He said, *I don't understand where he is.* But we have some very curious confirmations of people who saw Lou and said he was not alone in the men's room. This past Saturday, I got a letter from somebody I know at Penn from the Alumni Club, who said her brother was in the men's room when Lou was there, so I tried to get her on the phone. I finally got her on Monday, and she said it wasn't the brother that knows Lou, but another brother who lives in New Brunswick. I said I'd like to hear about it, and she said, *I'll have him call you.* So, in about ten minutes, he called me and said that he and his wife had been to the matinee of the theater on Saturday, and were going home to take the 8:30 train to New Brunswick, where they lived. He said it was 8:00 when they got to the station. He went down to the men's room and he saw a man. Now, Lou had gone in there at 10 minutes to 7, according to these young artists from Philadelphia who saw him go in there and waited for him—and he never came out. He saw Lou walking around with his jacket thrown over his shoulder, his shirt open, and no tie and so this New Brunswick man went over and said, *Is there anything I can do for you?* And Lou said, *Yes, I don't feel well, I have a pain. I think we should send the porter for a doctor.* And this New Brunswick man immediately got the attendant, and the attendant immediately left. And he said Lou did not look sick. He looked in complete control of himself, but he looked gray. Well, Susie very frequently said when she came home in the last six weeks that *Daddy lookes very tired, don't you think he looks pale?* He seemed in complete control; he was walking around. This man said if he felt he had been very ill, he would have stayed. *I went upstairs to tell my wife, and just then I saw the attendant come back with the police. And that was it.*

He ran into a bus sometime after his eye operation; and he had no peripheral vision. I think it was remarkable. You know Lou could read a clock without his glasses. Very frequently, when he was coming down for an apple or something, I would have to remind him to put on his glasses. But he did fabulous things for a person without a lens. And one day, I was waiting for him for his supper and he comes in. I said, *What's the matter?* and he said, *I got run over by a bus. I think my foot's broken.* It was at Fifteenth Street and he was going to buy paper, and I guess he didn't see the bus coming. And Lou put his hands out—you know how powerful Lou was; he loved being strong, he was very proud of it, he could break your arm

if he wanted to—so he put his hands out to try to push the bus away, and all that happened was the wheel went over his foot. I said, *Lou, you were right near the Graduate Hospital, why didn't you just go over there?* He said, *Because my feet were dirty and I want you to wash them first.* So I got a basin, soaked his feet, put fresh socks on, called a doctor friend who was at Graduate Hospital, said, *I'm bringing Lou over, I think he's got a broken foot.* Art called the Emergency Radiologist and of course they saw us right away and he had a broken toe, that was all, but a very badly bruised foot.

I want to tell you one story about something you wouldn't even know about Lou in the good old Depression days. And we were married, you know, in August, and in September, he walked out of Cret's office because he had no work. He was designing designs on the lintels in Cret's office and he just couldn't do it. He had to support his family. And I had my job; it paid very poorly, but I just loved it, and it had many advantages, as when we went to Jeff and when we moved to Jeff, in particular. Our group used to get together. We had practically no money. Everybody was in the same boat, but we used to have the best time. And one of the best times of all was singing the *Saturday Evening Post.* We would take a copy of the *Post,* which I had been a devotee of even though I knew it was ridiculous, ever since I was a small child. Daddy brought it home once, and I always got it after that. We would stick it up on the piano, and Lou would sit down and play the piano. And we would put an ad up and he would play appropriate music for the ad, and we would sing the ad, and then we would turn another page. And we would spend hours doing that with the *Saturday Evening Post.* We had the best time.

Esther Kahn

Lou liked nice clothes and he never had discovered Brooks Brothers until one day he and Oscar Stonorov were doing something or other and then they had to go to New York and Oscar went into Brooks Brothers and they both bought themselves white linen suits—real linen suits—and oh, that was the height of luxury for Lou and that's when Lou discovered Brooks Brothers, because he never bought any clothes anywhere after that except Brooks Brothers.

He had gotten this raincoat and the time when we had our apartment, our living quarters were on the third floor and I came into our study and I saw Lou stamping around. And I said what are you doing. And he said the raincoat looks too new, I'm dirtying it up. It was on the floor and he was beating it up with his feet so he could repair it. Oh, dear. And he tried ever since to buy a white linen suit but he simply couldn't get it. He wouldn't wear the clothes with stuff in it. He wanted the pure linen but he couldn't get it. We dyed the one brown because he got it so filthy, it had to be dyed. It couldn't be cleaned anymore or washed anymore. But he had such a love of ties. Everybody laughs when you say Lou had a tremendous collection of ties. They always saw him with his little black bow tie. He just loved neckties. I think that he had every color, shape and size of blue polka dot there was.

It's very curious how Lou did not believe in collecting. He didn't believe in possessions. He didn't like possessions. And that's why we do not have, everybody thinks we ought to have a tremendous collection of things from all the places he visited. The only thing he would buy is odd pieces of jewelry for me and a piece of silk or something like that, but he never bought statuary or brasses or anything. Rugs occasionally, a small rug; he liked rugs. He loved rugs. Of course what he liked the pocketbook didn't have. He brought a couple of rugs from Teheran but he never collected. He didn't want to own things, he didn't want to be owned by possessions. That's why he never wanted, never wanted a car, never wanted a house, never wanted anything to be owned. Maybe that's why he gave away his drawings. And yet if you asked him he wouldn't give you any.

Alan Kahn
Rhoda (Kahn) Kantor
Marvin Kantor
Ona (Kantor) Russell
Steven Kantor
Alexandra Tyng

AK: I could always respond to his inventiveness and his sensitivity. They impressed me the most. Of course he was a man of genius—not purely in terms of purely intellectual qualities, but in terms of the presence of the man—the way he would laugh, sometimes his little observations. He would describe somebody on the street in an interesting way. Once I asked him what he liked about this country or that country, and he described the country in an unusual way. He described England as a little door with a big man going through it, and France the opposite. That's clever as hell, but I like to believe he told it to me the first time out of his imagination. I thought it was a good example of how the man perceived things, how he could put a lot together in a small package. He had an economy in that sense.

The other thing I liked about him was his constant growth. The way he inspired people, and especially the way he inspired young people, made a greater contribution than what he had to say himself. The repercussions of his life will go on almost indefinitely.

RK: My perception of him is purely from a humanistic standpoint. I always found him to be a person who could communicate with people on all levels, and do so without a condescending attitude. I found that to be a wonderful quality in him, because he associated with many people from all over the world, and yet he gave everyone enough of himself that he made them feel as though they were important. There were occasions when, in family gatherings, he would talk to people who were of rather "low intellect," and yet he communicated with them very easily and never made them feel as though they were insignificant or less intellectual than he. There was one woman—I never quite knew if she was a relative or a friend of my grandparents, Lou's mother and father. Everyone called her *Fat Rosie.* She was an enormously rotund woman who was peasant-like in her manner and style. She would always question him about Europe. Although she had visited Europe maybe once in her life, she always spoke with great authority, and although Lou had been there on many trips he treated her as if she *were* an authority. He never made her feel insignificant, or as though something she were saying were not true or interesting.

He also loved a good joke. He loved to play the piano, although he did not play exceptionally well.

SK: The only thing I remember was when he and Uncle Alan played *Chopsticks* together.

RK: That was a memorable occasion.

MK: He would play piano like he was in a frenzy.

AK: Inspired.

RK: He was great when he had a couple of drinks in him. He was terrific.

OR: I remember seeing him over at Sarah's. Sarah had such a tiny little place. He always stayed there. And I remember the piano also. Everybody sitting around and playing. Very warm memories of that. Didn't Sarah live right next door to a factory? Grandpa Kahn and Grandma Kahn lived there and Sarah lived next door. I remember going there and eating, and they had walnuts and raisins. They were poor.

RK: They lived in a garage, actually. Uncle Lou could have stayed anywhere, but he always insisted on staying there.

AK: When he came for a visit everybody looked forward to his coming. It was a special event in the family. And not because of his eminence; he himself was nice to have around. He would touch base for a while and be off.

OR: Every time I saw him he had on a black suit and a white shirt.

MK: His tie was always askew.

RK: Did you ever see him when his tie was *not* askew?

AT: No, I never did. But then again it was a hand-tied bow. Actually, he was very particular about his clothes. He would only wear certain colors and the most expensive materials. He had his pants specially tailored and it would annoy him when people described his pants as baggy. There was even one comment that his shoes didn't match! People seemed to want to describe him in such a way that would make a real character out of him.

RK: They described him in one book as a birdlike man. A birdlike man!

AT: I didn't see him that way at all. I don't know how anyone else feels, being in the family and seeing him as another family member, but I never saw him as an old, old man with thick glasses. The eyes behind the glasses were much more a part of him.

RK: Maybe people saw him as an eccentric because when it came to architecture he spoke on a plane that was difficult to understand. But I never saw him as anything but an uncle.

OR: He was so sweet to me. I was very young when I remember seeing him, but I liked being around him. There was something really appealing about him.

AK: When I stayed at his house a couple of times, I would see him in his pyjamas watching Westerns at one o'clock in the morning. He used to like to do that, and it never quite fit in with how I understood him. The multifaceted parts of him were really interesting.

RK: As realistic as architecture is—you're dealing with space, but you're also dealing with materials that are real—there was a part of him that believed in mysticism. That story about the time he went to the guru was fascinating. He said he was frightened at how much information was given to him by the guru that never could have been known. The guru even volunteered to tell him when he would die, but he said he didn't want to know. He'd never been frightened before, but that scared him.

I remember when my father died. He came out for the funeral. At the funeral he broke down and cried, he was so saddened by it. Although they didn't see much of each other because they were separated by distance, they were very close, a close family.

AK: When his mother died, I called him and he came out. We had warned him that the end was coming very quickly. He arrived in the middle of the night, and she had just died. She died at home, and I was in attendance. He stood at the foot of the bed and looked at her for a long time, and he cried very bitterly for a period of time. After that he was perfectly himself. Throughout the ceremonies and everything else that had to be done he was really quite okay.

He was extremely close to her. She, more than anyone else, inspired in him a sense of the mystical aspect of life. He got that from her because she was very much in tune with that.

RK: She was very creative, too. She did beautiful things with her hands.

AK: I guess we've always talked about his parents as being most unusual people. If you asked me how, I don't know if I could tell you, except everybody would gravitate toward them because they had a specialness about them just in their manner, their way, their presence. Very much like he had. If you try to put it into words, it's pretty hard to do, but everybody seemed to know it. Even the most ordinary people—friends, neighbors—would have that same gravitation toward them.

Lou had that even with strangers. He was not a particularly impressive man to look at, and yet as soon as you came near him you would sense it. If I were the kind of person who believed in halo effects and all these energies people generate, and in people with wholeness inside them having a different kind of halo about them, he would be that kind of a guy.

I'm not talking about charisma alone. But he had it, even doing the most ordinary things, even the way he handled a pencil.

I stayed at his house one time. He loved grapefruit. We would eat grapefruit sitting across from each other, and I would be watching him eat that grapefruit. He'd eat the whole thing. He would approach the grapefruit almost like he was making a drawing. When he was all done, the thing would be absolutely perfect. I would try to copy this—I tried to copy him in every way—and I would always end up with the grapefruit all over the place. Not that the way he ate the grapefruit itself was so remarkable, but it fit with everything else he did.

The more I'm talking about that specialness, the further I'm getting from it, because as soon as you start defining it, already it's not the same thing.

The concepts he was talking about—*silence and light* and the *existence will*—I liked the ring of terms that he used—I liked the ring of them but I never could quite understand them. Once I asked him how he could be so sure about something which is unknown, unproven, and never thought of before. *The reason,* he said, *is that I know the order of things.* That sounded nice, but I didn't know what he meant by it. Now as I'm getting older and I'm learning about different things I understand better. I'm a generalist by nature. I don't know very much about any one thing.

AT: His mind worked pretty much that way. He wouldn't want to know too much about one thing or get too specialized. He wanted to bring things together.

AK: I think that's how you make new beginnings. I do it only because it's a more natural way for me to perceive things and live with things. He seemed to be a hell of a lot better at it.

There are scientists who are great measurers, and there are scientists who are great thinkers. Lou said one thing that I always appreciated. He was upset at a lot of scientists—and a lot of architects. He said, *We're getting to be a world of measurers, not a world of thinkers or doers.*

From a personal standpoint I feel stronger about his parents than I did about him. Of course they were my grandparents. But in Lou I saw much of what they inspired. And I know that much of how he ended up as a human being came from them. I'm not just talking about the genes. I'm talking about perception or a sensitivity to life, and these people had it.

RK: Especially Grandmom. Grandmom did imbue him with this kind of philosophy or whatever it was that he developed. I'm sure that part of it was genes and part of it was influence. She was a unique person. You might say she was angelic, almost, in her behavior and in her relationship to other people. And Uncle Lou certainly got the ability to communicate with the common man as well as with the upper echelon from her.

He was extremely respectful of his parents. I think he held them in awe.

AK: He would refer to them frequently, and even some things he wrote would refer back to them. It wasn't as if he left home and that was it.

He was like a continuum of them.

David Karp

During the early stages of the Hill Central Area projects [Hill Central Area Redevelopment, New Haven, Connecticut], Lou and I used to travel to New Haven for meetings with the Redevelopment Agency and the School Board.

We needed more money on one trip—I think because of extended meetings we realized we'd miss our plane and Lou decided to take a late train back rather than wait for a flight the next day. The Pennsylvania Railroad only recognized pure cash in those days. So I called the office and asked Jeanette to wire the money.

After the meetings we went to the Western Union office. The money had been wired, would Mr. Kahn please show some identification? Lou looked at me with a rather pained expression and said, *I don't carry any identification—I don't even have a wallet.* And that clerk refused to give us the money, totally unimpressed by argument, until Lou said, *Wait a minute,* reached into his pocket, and produced a letter. It was a letter he had received that morning from President-elect Nixon, a letter Nixon had addressed to prominent members of the arts community. Lou said he had spilled coffee on the letter and with apologies for the coffee stains, showed the letter to the clerk.

Well, she said, *if you have a letter from Mr. Nixon, you really must be Mr. Kahn.* And we all broke up with laughter.

Steve and Toby Korman
15 April 1974

SK: I said, *Lou, you can't. You're a quitter if you leave the art commission. The City needs you. And because we're losing a lot of good people, to lose you would be a mistake.* I said, It's a wrong thing to do. Now you're needed more than ever. So the question is you can quit, but what does that do for the City." He thought about it. And anyway, he went to see Rizzo. And Rizzo didn't really know who he was, but he had kind of heard his name. And they're sitting there and he says (they're kind of like going nowhere; just throwing words back and forth at each other) and all of a sudden, Lou got up, walked over to him and held him by the arm, and he said, "I squeezed him and I hurt him, I know". And he said, "Just remember one thing, Rizzo (he called him "Rizzo"), Any time I want, I can beat the hell out of you." And that impressed him. After that we got along beautifully, he said. And this was the way Lou was. I think what was interesting is that Lou loved that.

Something which is humorous. I told him it was an all-wood house. I talked to several people, including my father who had a tremendous respect for materials—50 years in it—I have a lot of respect for him. And we wanted to go to plaster and Dad said, "an all-wood house—just don't do it. It's a problem." Because Lou wanted to use the base the way we used the flush. He says, "you're breaking in everything." That would have been. He says, "Please, use a heavy dry wall, insulate it, do anything you want. Use the metal bead, anything you want, but do it this way."

I explained it to Lou and Lou said, "Well, what's drywall?" And I tried to explain it to him, and he said, "Well, I've never seen it." So I took him to Burt's (Korman) house. And I didn't say anything. And then I said, "Well, what do you think of this?" And he said, "Well, this is a good place...this is what I'm talking about." I said, "Lou, this is drywall." He loved it. He thought it was very enjoyable, very interesting.

The first time he came out to see the house. We had first started construction, and he hadn't seen it in about a month and a half; and I was very nervous. There were a few areas that we had moved ahead on and I wasn't sure about.

Were the foundations beautiful?

SK: I'll give you an idea—pre-stressed concrete all around the entire border, 1′ X 6″ done on the job manually. It took over a month and a half just to do that. At that point, the builder said, "It's the same story, I've gone through it before. Here it goes." And he was having a fit. But that time when Lou came down. I'll never forget this story. I was so scared. We decided to get him drunk. And we went out and we tried and we tried. And we were so drunk, we get him out here and we were plastered; we could hardly stand. He looked at the house and said, "Steve, you know we can't look at the house now. I can't see what I'm doing." He came all the way up and never got out of the car, because we were plastered. We got bombed out of our minds. I couldn't drive. He couldn't talk, he started to slur. Well, when he took his two spoons to cut his steak, we said, "Lou, they're spoons."

TK: He was incredible. But it has changed our lives; just being involved with this house. I feel a definite change. I'm so much more aware of architecture and what he philosophized about. It's opened up a lot of other areas....

SK: I don't think the house changed us as much as dealing with Lou. It's interesting, I notice that the only art I really like is people I know who painted. I really don't have any desire to own anything of a person I don't know. I like to be involved with the people. Maybe that's something special. You know you think of them. This house wouldn't mean much to me without Lou. And I was really involved. I mean no one can take away the hundreds of hours because that's something I had. And when I was going through it—it was, you know, every Saturday and Sunday, other people were playing tennis or golf, which I enjoy—I'd go down there. But I enjoyed it. You know, it was a special thing. And one humorous story, which is cute; when I walked in one day, it was a Thursday or Friday, and the Mayor of Jerusalem was there. And he said to the Mayor, "And, of course, you know Steve Korman." That just struck me. It wasn't, "Steve, of course you know the Mayor." And you felt like an idiot. He loved my grandfather. He used to love our stories about Pop because he really felt he was special. And I guess he saw the special way we related with him. Lou was very Jewish, very religious, and very hurt about the Jewish community. Not religious. That was a big thing to him. I think he almost sensed that people thought he wasn't and that bothered him. It almost was out of character the way he felt.

That's because they had not asked him to do any buildings for them. And actually it's a shame because they've done some nice monuments and spent the money for it, when they could have had a Lou Kahn.

Kisho N. Kurokawa

My first meeting with Professor Louis I. Kahn was at the World Design Conference, Tokyo in 1960. One night, I, as one of the prepatory committee of the Conference, asked to have a discussion through the night with Professor Kahn.

The year of 1960 was the beginning of Metabolism Group. Concept of *master space and servant space* was a most fresh stimulation for our theory. Also, his concept of *Realization-Form-Design* was very much similar to an Oriental philosophy or Buddhist philosophy. Philosophy of Buddhism takes a [more] serious view of invisible existence than [of] a thing itself.

The year of 1961, when I visited Professor Kahn in Philadelphia, he said that he would meet me at a coffee shop near his office at 7 am. In the early morning, drinking coffee and talking lasted for two hours and was terribly impressive.

Professor Kahn is one of the very special and few—a philosopher and a poet who, through an architecture, was able to talk of the philosophy of life.

Professor Louis I. Kahn is one of the very rare architects whose influence is so deep in contemporary Japanese architecture.

Bill Lacy

As great as his buildings are, I suspect that his true legacy will prove to be those whom he taught and his works, and the works of those whom they will teach, and on and on.

Dennis Lasdun

I remember one instance that sparked off a bloody great row in the Jerusalem Conference. They're reconstructing the old part of the city and we walked through a part of it which was clearly of some pride to Teddy Kolleck, but it was reconstructed in what Lou would call fake stone. I think everybody remembers that instant which sparked off a tremendous attack on the Jerusalem Plan including describing this reconstruction as so much *kitsch*. The thing he objected to was that stone to him was an honorable material which has certain properties, certain thicknesses that can be used, certain apertures that they make, but there was the whole question of the appropriateness of material for form and he would then make long pronouncements in the middle of this scene but he wouldn't be chatting, he wouldn't be talking to anybody. He wouldn't say, *Well, here, you shouldn't be doing this thing*. It would be a sermon about the nature of stone and how this was really not an honorable way of using an honorable material. I remember that very vividly. I think Teddy Kolleck was taken aback by the strength of the statements. He probably thought for a while that he could brush it aside, but in the end it stuck very hard and became a sort of rallying point. It happened to be that we detected something of a falseness of this, Lou did, in this stone and it rather set a tone for the rest of the conference.

G. Irving Latz II

I met him by accident and he did the building here [in Fort Wayne], in a way, by accident. I was head of the committee to select our architect. We had met and prepared a list for interviewing which did not include Lou. When I was talking to Philip Johnson in New York, it was he who, as he declined being considered for the job because he had too much work at the time, asked for the list we were considering and said that I didn't have the one architect who would be best. Such a recommendation from Johnson was enought to make me add the name of Kahn without prior committee approval. The only trouble with the Johnson recommendation was that the Kahn he was recommending was from Philadelphia and not from New York. Naturally, because I had not heard of Lou, I called a Kahn, architect, in New York! In our conversation he very modestly told me that although he would be interested in designing an arts complex in Fort Wayne, he felt the man I had in mind was *Lou* Kahn of Philadelphia. I mumbled a thanks and called Lou. The rest is, as they say, history.

He was, by the way, the only architect of the twenty we interviewed who was unequivocal in recommending a downtown location for the buildings. All the others hedged. This was interesting in view of the fact that we had a promise of twenty acres adjacent to the local university if we would put the building there. This would have represented quite a savings, but Lou said it must be in the heart of the city and convinced the Committee and subsequently the Board.

The arts seem always to be put in the position of proving their worth. Lou was often asked how he could justify the expense of the new building for the theater. After all, there were already several in Fort Wayne. Wouldn't it be better to build a hospital? He had two answers. His first ran like this: That is like telling me to choose between my right hand and my left hand. Both are necessary to my well-being and I can't make the decision except to say that I need both. His second was a humorous rejoiner that he would feel as thwarted if he wanted to hear a Beethoven symphony to have to go to the auditorium of the hospital, as he would to have an appendectomy performed in an auditorium.

Lou never seemed to care for anything of personal ostentation. His clothes, though adequate, were usually rumpled and when he stayed a period of time, he still carried only the meagerest of replacements. Even so, his carriage and way of walking was ramrod straight. To some, he even replied that everyone shows he has an interest in the arts merely in the way he carries himself! Whenever he left the house in the morning, he would take a sprig from one of the evergreen bushes he found around the house and put it in his buttonhole. He was always looking for and seeing beauty.

I met him at the airport one day to take him immediately to a meeting which was most important to the building. It seemed to me that he would do better if he had some background as to what the real problem was and to who would be at the meeting representing what particular viewpoints. He agreed and I started to talk in rather rapid fashion as we only had about fifteen minutes and I wanted to answer any questions he might have before we arrived at the meeting. I must have talked for about five minutes or so and then asked if he had any questions. He did. He wanted to know whether either my wife, who was with me, or myself had ever seen anything more beautiful than a certain cloud formation in the sky to our right front. He hadn't heard a word I had said; I couldn't compete with the beauty of the sky. Nevertheless he did just magnificently at the meeting, understanding immediately what the problem was and where and why everyone said what they did!

I am deeply moved when I think of Lou. He had a profound effect upon my wife and me and the people of Fort Wayne. To me, he was a philosopher who happened to use the medium of architecture to show his thinking. His building has had an effect in Fort Wayne and will have even greater impact over time. It has set a standard for achievement in our town and is being used in such a way that it is a solid building, sculptural in effect, without adornment. Not everyone likes it; not everyone understands it. I think it will be a monument to him and to the people of Fort Wayne long after we are all memories.

Robert LeRicolais & Norman Rice

NR: These meetings that Robert and Lou and I had in this room, nearly every Monday and Friday afternoon after the studio, were things that I think all three of us looked forward to very much because we just left the studio with all its difficulties and excitements, the tension and also the fact that in the studio, many things were brought to a point which might not otherwise have been brought to a point, just because certain things were brought up by a particular student's project. But I know that as much as I looked forward to these meetings—and I looked forward to them maybe even more. Maybe they were a kind of relief for him. Sometimes, he used to sleep in this chair where Robert is, and always would claim, *Don't worry about me, I hear everything you say,* which we doubted very much. But you know he had the ability often to—well, he was not only catnapper, but he had an ability to catch on very quickly as to what was going on. So he used to sleep here. And he looked forward to these things to such a degree that he often would delay keeping an appointment at the office with a client or something like this just to stay here.

Was he always the same to you? I mean, you've known him as long as anybody. Was Lou always the same? When he was younger, was there always the hint of what he was to become?

NR: Not when he was younger, no. No, not at all. Only in his, let us say, in his abilities. Or at least they weren't as visible. Only the abilities which he demonstrated even then. I mean, his great abilities to draw. He could always draw. He could draw anything.

How old were you both when you first knew each other?

NR: Well, I guess that we were about 10 or 11.

Was he always by himself?

NR: No, he was shy and I believe that was it. It was only in later years when his accomplishments made him renowned that I believe—and this may be a quack psychiatric analysis—I believe that he thought of his scarred face as a kind of distinction. It turned from something about which he was ashamed when he was a boy, because among boys, especially in our time, even a guy like me who wears glasses, in those days, was called *four eyes* or *pack eye* or something. Because people didn't...very few people wore glasses and certainly very few children wore them. But that was the culture, the street culture of the times. And I'm certain that even at the high school, at Central High, where the viewpoints were more gentle and genteel and intellectual, that he felt this. I'm sure that he did feel this, although I don't know of any incident where anyone in some crude or brutal way may have derided him because of this. I don't know of any incident. But he was known as a sort of nice kind of guy, always ready to do for you.

RL: I never saw him losing his cool, you know. He was always capable of controlling himself, and saying the right thing.

You've never seen him angry?

RL: No, no, Maybe he was, but he didn't show it too much. He always seemed to be in control.

NL: Yes, I would say this, certainly as often as I saw him during these last 13 years, I don't recall him being, let us say...

RL: Antagonistic towards someone. I admired this in him so much, you know. The fact that he could isolate his point of view and give the student a full chance to tell Lou his idea.

Lou belonged to what is known as myurgic. Myurgic, you know, the Socrates name of the art of making, of bringing a baby to the right....To express truths which are in himself and which he can formulate very easily, like a confessor in some way.

NR: Well, in this case he was like the great countryman of Robert's, Claude Bernard, the great physiologist, who along with other great statesmen said, *When you come across a student with talent, let him be. Don't try to impose too much of what you think you know on him. Just let him be.*

Was he aware of his lack of technical ability? Did he ever talk about or put himself down about that?

RL: That's a very interesting point. I think he was. But he had a great respect for science, but science was very poor for him. I think in respect for science, what he wanted was more to express than to explain. As soon as science could bring a way of expressing something, that was good. The other reason, I mean that was beyond him. He was not quite right to go through that.

NR: You see, Lou had as part of his nature, inherited—it was congenital—the sort of thing that Robert has just been talking about. Well, some call it great intuitive powers. I call them more than intuitive. It's really the power of the artist. In school, when he went through Central [High School] for example, he was always on the verge of being flunked.

In what subject?

NR: All subjects! I mean practically all subjects. As he would say himself; and he did say himself. Because the formal classroom atmosphere was not something to which he could acclimate himself easily. And I'm sure that in those years, and through all the years of this kind of academic craving, he was very uncomfortable and even very unhappy. And I believe that this gave him a kind of a prejudice towards what he would call information perhaps at its worst, or knowledge perhaps at its best. And yet he always would deride it. I think this may have been at the base of his feelings about city planners who believe so much in all the statistics and sociology and all the other things which they do, and which to him had no life-giving quality whatsoever.

RL: He constantly was within the world to express.

NR: As an artist, he would want to express, but he would not want to express with something which was already dead. And he realized that all of this stuff was dead already, and that you could not make anything expressive from it, let alone make anything which was alive from it.

I think that he began himself to understand that not everyone who may have had some fund of knowledge was some sort of penance. And he realized that you might have a kind of knowledge, which he didn't have, but that it might be used in a way or exercised in a way which was even artistic or you might call it intuitive. In his remarks very often even in the studio, he began to say this. Whereas I can recall when I first came to the studio, he would deride this altogether. So it indicated, at least to me, a development or let us say a change in his viewpoint. This would also apply to his view of the work that Robert was doing, I believe.

What is most attractive about Robert? To begin with, this is the most urbane man I know. And this urbanity which encompasses all of life, not just his work, but all of life and everything in it, is a thing which is attractive to all men who have any sense. And I'm certain that Lou, who did not have urbanity, liked that.

Did he ever visit you in Paris?

RL: Yes, for a short time, a very short period. He was always between two planes. He had a love for Paris which was absolutely unbelievable.

But you never sort of went around and showed him the town?

RL: No, we had no time for that. We had not time, always between two planes and that's it. It's the tragedy of life. You have desires, that was a very very favorite word of his, *desire.*

Towards the end, the last several months of his life, he talked a lot about joy. Did he talk to you about that? It seemed to be a recurring word in the last few months.

RL: That was some kind of, as you said, some kind of *leitmotif* coming back again. And I think that was one of his last words. I was with him and he said, *Robert, don't forget the almighty power of joy.*

NR: And I hope that this tape recorder has recorded that word which you used, *leitmotif*—the word which Wagner used so much. *Leitmotif.* And I was interested in that same thing because it was another expression of his which came more and more into being. I am not certain that I understood altogether what he had in his heart or in his mind the way he used it, but I can agree with it; even though I agree with it from what may be an entirely different viewpoint.

What did you talk about here? Did you talk about the studio or what?

NR: Everything under the sun.

RL: Only to be interrupted by the wives.

NR: Sure, Esther Kahn would call. Esther Rice would call.

This is where they knew they could get you.

Leo Lionni

[Leo Lionni, who was a friend of Lou's in the '40s remembers some of his metaphors—one in particular.] It was on design. Lou spoke of mosquito design, in which all structural elements are visibly declared (his examples were the Eames chair and the MG-TC) and elephant design where they are hidden in an all-covering sheath (Pinin Farina's Lancia Cisitalia).

Jack MacAllister

Did you know what he watched on television? His biggest thing was that he absolutely flipped over and he really got into women's roller derby. When we were in California, they had a lot of roller derby on television. I'd never seen one, and Lou was watching something and said, *Oh, it's 8 pm, do you have roller derbies on here at 8 o'clock?* And I said, *The what?* He said, *Women's roller derbies.* I said, *I don't know,* and we looked in the TV guide and there was one. And he watched these, and he really liked that, you know, these women knocking the hell out of each other, and skating around in circles, he loved it.

He loved football. I know he used to sneak off to Saturday football games at Penn all the time.

But women's roller derby...strange, and a slightly kinky thing to do.

Lou was teaching at Yale, which was really before he became internationally famous. This was 1953, 1954, something like that. I was an undergraduate, and I used to sneak off to the Architecture School in the afternoon to go to the library, and then I'd go upstairs and sit and listen to this funny little man. All I knew was that he was a teacher at the Architecture School. And Kahn, you know, used to stay very late always. He had no idea of the clock. And it was the first time that I ever saw a teacher who became a student at the same time he was teaching. It was very interesting, because the process—I understand it now, much later—he was teaching himself. You could watch it almost in the process as he was going. He would make a point, then he'd begin to erase it and make it again. I don't mean erase it literally; I mean erase it in his mind. And those sessions would go on until 6, 7, 8, 9 pm.

He was taking big jumps [at this time in his life]. It's also a time before he got to believe his own poems, which I found less satisfying. Somehow, it was when he was working on practical problems that the students were working on, and he was using those as teaching devices, as models. And he was trying to find in some ways like a blind man groping through a room.

The other story is an anecdote. Lou came to Virginia to judge a competition, out at the Virginia Museum. He stayed with my father. I didn't know this at the time. I didn't know this until I went and saw that he had written my father a letter. They had gotten on very well. And he stayed in a house—my father lives in a house that was done by a Beaux Arts architect named Barnabam, very great, one of the last great Beaux Arts neo-Georgian architects. He was an old man, exceptionally good. The kind that you found in the late 1920's. And when Lou came to the house—it has a very beautiful hallway with a curving stair coming down, and at the top of the stair, the bannister comes up the stair—the wooden bannister—as it resolves itself into a column, it takes three or four little meanders. And those meanders of the bannister are reflected in the floor below it, so that the cut-out of the stairway has the same meander that the bannister has. It's a whimsical notion. Anyway, Kahn walked up those steps. He got to the top of the stairs, and he saw that bannister, and he became—my father said he became exactly like a child. He walked along, kept running his hands along, kept his hands down the bannister in absolute wonder. Then he stopped and said, *Oh, this was a man who loved what he was doing. He was a great architect.* And for him to speak of a Beaux Arts architect who traditionally he should have thought was nothing, in a sense! And it was all because of that wonderful gesture. And that attention to tiny, tiny details sets him apart from all of the modern architects.

The (Salk) Institute used to pay Lou to come out for important meetings where there were terrible problems. They'd phone him and say he'd have to be out there right away, and he'd come out. I'd pick him up at the airport, and instead of going to the meeting, he would go to a bookstore downtown. He'd say he only wanted to spend half an hour there. It was an old bookstore, several stories high, which had mostly odd books like eleventh editions of the *Encyclopaedia Brittanica,* which was a sort of favorite of his, and we'd always miss the meetings, because Lou would be in there. He'd miss meetings or be two hours late. His whole schedule was set up for him to be at a meeting and instead of doing it, he'd get stuck in this old bookstore. And he'd buy half a dozen books in two or three hours. And if I dared to admire them, he'd give me half of them, so I always ended up with old books. He either paid in cash or he borrowed it from me. Then he'd give them to me anyway, so it didn't matter. He was really funny, though, the way he did that.

He hated staying with people. He really liked staying in hotels. He was very shy that way. You know the way some people are always staying with friends. He would always want to stay very independently. And it wasn't because he had anything going on; it was just because he...I think he probably had some old man's habits that he didn't want people to know of—you know, like getting up in the middle of the night, and that sort of thing. I suspected that, anyway. No, he always stayed in a hotel. He liked the La Valencia because he walked everywhere. And also the Del Charro, because of its kind of charm. It was an old stable remade.

We had worked for literally months in a concentrated way trying to solve the problem in the center courtyard, which Lou had always seen as a garden. Or perhaps everybody else had always seen it as a garden, and convinced Lou that's what it was. And every time he tried to come up with a design, it was corny, and he knew it. And he kept trying to find people who could help him make a garden.

He hired Larry Halprin and produced two or three designs which were not what we wanted. I'm not sure how much Halprin had to do with them, but they were just wrong, with evergreens against concrete walls and sort of foundation planning like for a house. And it went on and on and on like that and he kept arguing with Halprin about it, but nothing came of it, even though Jonas was very enamored of Halprin's intellect and they got along very well.

Then Lou went to a show at the Museum of Modern Art and saw Luis Barragan's work and came back and said he had found a terrific landscape architect. Of course, Barragan is not a landscape architect. He's an architect whose interest is in public spaces, but Lou thought he was a landscape architect, and so we managed a meeting with him where Barragan came to San Diego, and I picked him up. He met Lou and they talked for awhile at the Institute, which was all mud then. It was just absolutely unfinished. Both buildings were unfinished on either side of it. The court had been sitting empty for several months just waiting for Lou to come up with a solution. Lou had written to Luis and said, *I want you to come up and make me a garden.* So Luis walked into the courtyard with Jonas, Lou and myself—he looked up and down, his eyes lit up, and he smiled and looked at Lou and said, *Lou, this is not a garden; it's a plaza.* And Lou looked at him and slapped him on the back and he said, *That's it, Luis!* and everybody slapped everybody on the back and that was it.

[Barragan] talked about Giotto. He said, *The facade that's missing is the sky,* and there should be a bird in it like Giotto. And he saw all kinds of Giottoesque things. Barragan is very sparse; one bird in the sky is enough, two's probably too many. It was a day where the horizon was sharp on the edge of the whole center courtyard, and that really did it.

Then Lou asked me to go down and work with Barragan, with ideas about water, etc., which Luis really had the handle on. And I went down and spent a week with him and we did nothing except talk and walk and look at plazas in Mexico. I never came back with any drawings. It all finally came out of Lou. So, I'd say that Luis really was the one who just turned Lou's head—obviously the whole idea was there, and Luis was the catalyst.

But Luis absolutely fell in love with Lou. Absolutely thought he was incredible.

I went to Lou's office one Saturday morning when I was in my fourth year of architecture, seeing if I could get a part-time job because I needed money. It was about nine or ten o'clock in the morning, and Lou was working on the Washington University Library competition. And he said, *Sure, did you bring your pencil with you?* I said no, and he said, *That's all right, you can borrow one.* And he took me out to the drafting unit and gave me a board and asked me to work with him on the design of the Washington Library competition—the library for Washington University.

(I had him as a teacher for two years.) Lou sat me down and we worked together for three or four hours and he told me to do a whole bunch of drawings. It was like a study of the mechanical system: to do section, work out the structure, work out the column spacing, you know, all from charcoal sketches. So I started working them out and he said that the whole thing had to be done by Tuesday. You know, I looked at him, because what I had to do was like eleven drawings, plus work everything up. And anyway, nobody told me to leave and I didn't leave until Tuesday.

For a while he visited the Salk project with a certain frequency, and then his cataracts developed and they really got bad. Then he was in the hospital and had them operated on. He didn't come out againto La Jolla for about eight months. And then he'd come out, and he was just totally blind, I mean, when he first got his glasses. I guess it was the in-between period when he was being operated on that he used to come tpo the job very nervous because he knew what it was supposed to look like. And I'd have to walk him to the job and hold him by the hand. And he'd whisper in my ear, *Tell me when something's bad so that I can scream about it.* And so I'd walk up and say, *Lou, there's a really poorly laid concrete wall in front of you.* And Lou would stand there and wave his arms and say, *That's not acceptable! I won't accept that kind of concrete work!* And he couldn't see a damned thing. He couldn't see three feet in front of him. And I had to help him down curbs and everything. By the end of the job, he had his sight back.

It was all in his mind, not in his hand.

Did I ever tell you about the time he came to Del Mar after flying from India? I think he'd gone from Philadelphia to India through Europe. And it was very important that he be out here for a meeting. He arrived in Los Angeles and flew down here directly from India. In other words, he had gone around the world, except for the last connection between Los Angeles and Philadelphia. We had this funny little house in Del Mar built around a courtyard. And I arrived and brought him home about three or four in the afternoon. We had a little television in our bedroom, and the children were watching late-afternoon cartoons. Lou sat on the edge of the bed with us behind him and the television in front of him, and watched cartoons for about an hour, and then fell asleep and slowly fell backwards on the bed, and slept until morning.

I think Lou was only really effective as an architect when he had a very responsible and even difficult client. Lou could not design in a vacuum. He really needed a solid, constructive and critical client to do a good building.

You know the story of the roof [at Dacca]? The whole building was designed, and the roof wasn't designed. Then he went back and designed the roof and it was too heavy for the foundations that were already built. And then he went back to Komendant and the only thing that would work would be if it were a steel roof, which, you know, for Lou was like saying bar joists everywhere. I think it was resolved in stainless steel and cables.

You know what the form work was? It was cheap plywood covered with red checked tablecloths, plastic tablecloths, because that's all they could get. The cement is Russian. The reinforcing steel is Chinese—undeformed, just smooth bars. But the masonry's not bad.

Lou expressed one image, but I doubt that that's what he really thought of himself. He expressed himself often as a bumbler, you know, as being totally disinterested in any kind of gain out of a situation. And yet he would fight to the death for his own kind of gain.

To me, it was another way of being mercenary. It's not mercenary in looking for money out of a situation, but it was always to his advantage. So he would fight as hard as a Getty would fight for dollars; Lou would fight for his own position in a situation, which was often ideological, mostly, I think, because what he wanted to do was good. But often it wasn't; it was just to preserve his own position vis-a-vis other people. I mean, often times the idealism was lost out of his own ego, which was gigantic. I mean, it was just overpowering.

I don't think Lou was humble at all. And I don't even think of that as being derogatory. I think he knew he was goddamn good. And he was good at his skills, too, you know. He was good at drawing, at working out plans. The first year I worked for him, I had struggled over a plan for three or four weeks and couldn't get something to work. And Lou sat down in five minutes and solved it. And I said, *Lou, how do you do it?* And he said, *Well, I've been doing it for forty years—I should be pretty good at it,* which is humble in a way.

I didn't find humility in Lou. I found peasant charm. He had a kind of peasant quality about him, the way he would sit down and say that a boiled potato was the best meal he'd ever had, and really and truly enjoy simple things. I mean Lou didn't really like sophisticated personal things, as far as his own lifestyle. And in a way, that's humility. I mean, he didn't want to acquire things, he wasn't acquisitive, he didn't want to have a fancy house, and a lot of money and travel.

For instance, Philip Johnson. I remember the time Lou came back from visiting Johnson, and Johnson took him to the airport in his Mercedes gullwing. Lou had never seen one; he didn't know what it was. He asked him what kind of car it was, because, of course, Lou didn't drive and didn't know diddly about cars. Johnson said it was a Mercedes Benz. And Lou said, *Well, it's a very interesting car. How much does it cost?* And Johnson told him, and Lou couldn't believe him—it was something like $10,000 then. And Lou looked at us and said, *Do you know that you could buy five Volkswagens for that?* But you could pick him up in a very fancy car and he wouldn't know he was in a fancy car.

He loved it in California. We always talked about the light. In fact, about a month or six weeks ago, I got out the drawings of the meetinghouse and went through them. And the whole idea of having a wall outside which had holes in it and modifies light came to Lou, I think, the first time he came here because of the glare. Also, his eyes were hypersensitive at the time, so I think he overreacted tremendously because he was having his cataract problems. The glare can be a problem here, but it isn't overwhelming. But it led him to solutions of building problems which really I think are incredibly beautiful.

Lou never talked about more than his sister, his father, his mother—never more than five people.

Lou gave his father a board in the office and told him to go to work. His father came in from, I guess, Los Angeles. He was close to ninety. No, he was in his nineties actually. And Lou cleared a board off and sat him at the board and told him it was his and that he could work there and do anything he wanted to do.

He [the father] was taller and leaner, more like kind of a Dickens character. Stovepipe. Very scrawny, where Lou was always a little full. Lou was very proud of his strength, too.

On one New Year's Eve, I was about to leave the office. Everyone else had left and I was walking past Lou's office. He said, *Hey, Jack, come on in and have a drink with me for New Year's.* And he had an ice cold bottle of aquavit. He put it on the table between the two of us. He had some pumpernickel bread and some cheese, and we sat down and started talking. I was due home for dinner, too. Well, Lou and I drank the bottle. We both got absolutely loaded. Lou drank half; I didn't drink any more than half. He was still standing up, but pretty smashed. And we were talking and talking and talking. And I went home and Dina had dinner all ready. I made it just through about three minutes of dinner, and passed out at the table.

He had some very funny conventional notions about morality and ethics, at a time when those things were going through great upheavals in our society. As with modern music, Lou never tried to get on to it. You know, he never really tried to understand it. And he saw everything in very traditional terms that way. He wasn't a modern man in many ways. Like his total disinterest in any music that was written after 1900 really, which I always thought was very strange, that he wouldn't even listen to it. Like modern jazz, which at the period when I first worked for him, was very strong—the Modern Jazz Quartet and Brubeck and people like that. And everyone around him was listening to it, and Lou refused to. And all he'd talk about was Bach, which was funny. Also, modern painting.

I remember when Kennedy was running. He was in Pittsburgh and I've forgotten what time it was between his running and the election, but Lou didn't know anything about him. And Jack Kennedy called Lou from Pittsburgh, and he said he was very concerned about urban problems and he wanted to meet with Lou and find out what ideas he had and to see if something could be gained from talking to Lou, so he could formulate a policy. And Lou refused to do it. And I told him, *Lou, this guy is the great hope to a lot of people. You're crazy.* And Lou just said, *Well, I'm not political. I'm not going to go out and help some politician with his job,* which is really amazing. That was the kind of opportunity most architects seize upon and capitalize upon later. Jack Kennedy called him personally, pleading him to come to Pittsburgh or meet him in Harrisburg or do anything so they could sit down for a few hours and just talk about what was wrong with the cities, what could be done about it. Lou's ideas...he had read about Lou, people told him. He was very frank with Lou. Lou told me the whole conversation, and just told him that, *I don't know you. I'm not sophisticated in these fields. I'm going to have to know more. I want to know more and I want to talk to you, and I really want you to help me.* And Lou just said, *Well, I'm too busy. I'm not going to do it.*

He very much liked being honored, so there's no question about it. He and Aalto received degrees together and he was very proud of that. He was proud of very conventional kinds of awards, like those from the American Institute of Architects. He would never submit his work to the AIA for an award, where you have to prepare things and submit them. He wouldn't do it. And yet when they did honor him, he was proud as hell.

On Pine Street once, when we were living there, Lou used to come over a couple of nights a week, and Tim Vreeland used to come over, and occasionally Bob Venturi, and we would read plays. Lou loved Cat on a Hot Tin Roof, and always played Big Daddy, and would throw himself into it. We did it many times, and everybody would read a part. Lou just overdramatized the parts. He'd stand up and wave his arms, and really bellow out the part. Just totally get into it. And one night we were doing *Cat on a Hot Tin Roof* and we had a bassett hound puppy that was lying on the floor at Lou's feet. Lou was wearing pants with cuffs on them and the puppy was chewing down around his feet. And at the end of reading this play, which Lou was so engrossed in, he looked down and the puppy had chewed the cuffs off of both trouser legs, and Lou just looked and said, *Oh, my God, the cuffs of the trousers are gone.*

Jamine Mehta

I was just finishing my work on collecting material for the book and I was given a place in the office on the fourth floor photo room and I could go and lock myself. Most of the time I used to work in the evenings and weekends and I had a little radio that I used to keep with me to listen to music late at night. Generally I listened to classical music. People from the office told me that Lou didn't like radio, so I was very conscious of not having it very loud when he was around, and whenever he came to the fourth floor I would just jump up and turn off the radio. One Sunday afternoon I was working and there was nobody on the fourth floor and nobody on the fifth floor and Lou must have come in in the afternoon on the fifth floor. I didn't know and I was there listening to some beautiful baroque music kind of loud. He came down, he opened the door and he said hello in his sort of usual very cheery way. I jumped and turned off the radio and he said, *No, no, no, don't do that; don't worry.*

He went straight to the radio, took it up, turned it on again and started changing the dial. He knew exactly what he wanted. He was eager, like a child, to listen to the Penn-Princeton score and he held the radio right by his ear. He was the only one who could listen. He just listened to the score. He held it until the score came up and then turned it back to my station and said that's all he wanted. I was startled and I said I didn't think you liked the radio sound, I was worried that you might not like me having radio. *Oh, no, it's all right,* he said, and then he said, *Look, I'll make you a deal: I'll let you have your radio here if you let me come down and listen to scores whenever I want to.*

There is one serious moment that I remember and always will remember. He had asked in the beginning, when we sat down and decided what the book was going to be like. He wanted one thing to be clarified and that was the only demand he made specific. He made a lot of demands in terms of generally the kind of thing he wanted the book to convey, but this was a specific thing that he wanted clarified, that there is a difference between his sense of aesthetics which he called order and aesthetic as known generally. He said that it has always been misunderstood and he wanted us to clarify that and he wanted us to think about it. He wanted Aldo to make some notes and come back. Aldo was very busy and about a month or so later I put down some notes that I sort of thought interpreted his sense of order and I realized that if I presented it to him either he is going to like the idea or he is going to violently dislike it. But one idea was that it might make him think and I wanted some more elaboration on it. And he read the thing and didn't say a word for a long time. He objected to several of my notions and he sat down there quietly. For about five to ten minutes it was no word at all. And then he started saying things. I don't remember the exact words, but it was evident that he was deep within himself, that he was going through the terrain that even he had not explored. He had maybe subconsciously or unconsciously thought about things but never really verbalized it and he was struggling to verbalize that. It was like you can see on his face, it was unbelievable, something that cannot be put into words or cannot be described, but it struck me as a momentous opportunity for me to watch this man taking a deep sea dive into his own consciousness and struggling to find the right words. He said a few words, rejected them as not applying and then, after about twenty minutes of this kind of a struggle suddenly came out of it and said, *Well, it doesn't matter right now.* In other words, to verbalize it. And all the time I was expecting him to come out with the right kind of explanation and here he was coming back to me saying I'm not able to do it right now. It sort of made me come down to the ground, too. I was so proud of myself being a witness to that and then he made me realize that he was human after all. And there were several [moments] like this that I never really have tried to record but they are there and they are just an enjoyable thing.

One day he was showing me his sketchbook of Europe and there were various sketches, beautiful black and white sketches that he wanted somehow published and he was going through the drawings as if he was back in Venice and he was talking about the Piazza St. Marco. He was taking me to a guided tour and suddenly the phone rang, which I answered. It was Esther, reminding him that he has to be back because some guests are coming to dinner. And I keep the phone and I say, Lou, this is Esther. *Tell her I'm in Venice, she'll understand.* That's all.

We celebrated his birthday and this was during the class. I was at Master Class in February 1966. And we had just gone through one semester of work with him—the first semester in his class is always difficult; you don't know what to expect and most of us come from the usual kind of academic training, with the usual kind of professors, going through design problems, something like that and here you suddenly find yourself in an entirely new environment and you lose orientation for a while. We all felt that in the first semester we failed him. We were not able to come up to his expectation and he wasn't very satisfied with us, which turned out to be a wrong impression. Later on he told us—a long time later—that he remembered our class very much and that we were all struggling very hard but we, at that time, felt that we were not going through that. So we decided to do something to cheer him up. And somebody said, *Hey, his birthday is coming February 20. We said, Let's celebrate it and let's not tell him. And that happened to be a Friday, which was his studio day, so we just went out of our way and we had a jubilant celebration. We decorated the studio, somebody brought in 500 balloons, somebody rented a whole tank of helium and the whole studio was just full of colored balloons. Somebody brought in a huge Chinese kite, stuffed it up with balloons and let it fly in the air. I had brought this colorful Indian wall painting. The whole thing was turned into a fairyland and we had a big table in the middle with 65 candles on a huge cake, with orange letters on which somebody wrote, The Cake Wants To Be Eaten.* And lots of wines and apples and we were all there waiting for him to come in and he came in and opened the door and saw this thing and for a while he was just taken aback. He had a muffler; he took the muffler, put it in his hand and danced a little jig with it and we knew from now on it was going to be all right. He liked it. And he looked around and went straight to the wine bottle and poured wine for everybody.

We sat and talked and laughed a lot and everybody came by. By that time the whole school knew that Master Studio had a party going on and the whole thing was full of people. Perkins came in and we all had a good time. And then we thought we should give Lou some presents, birthday presents, but we couldn't come up with the appropriate thing to give him so I had a little card made on which we wrote, *To you we present our firm belief that architecture is possible.* I was reading Wright Brothers at that time and in one of the letters that Wilbur Wright wrote, I believe that flight is possible. I was taken by that, it was a beautiful sentiment. And we wanted to present that. But the spirit of the party was such that I was carried away and I said this to Lou: *Lou, since there are five Indians in*

a twenty-five student class, we are in the majority in terms of nationality. So we would like to celebrate this in an Indian way. And I sort of made up a little story that in India a child's birthday is celebrated and when the present is given the child is blindfolded and then he is given three wishes to guess what the present is and if none of the wishes are there, at least we get a feeling of what he wants next year. So we would like you to be blindfolded and wish. And he said OK, all right. So we blindfolded him and we gave him the card to touch and he said, *Is it a book of poetry?* and he said a few other things, but they all came out to be something of words, poetry. Then he opened the thing and read it and it was a time I really saw him moved. He was visibly moved by that. And he couldn't say a word and then suddenly he looked again and then ran back to the wine bottle and filled wine for everybody.

Moira Moser-Khalili

One of Louis Kahn's last trips abroad before his death was to Iran, where he and Kenzo Tange were preparing to design a 12,000-acre new town in the heart of the capital city of Teheran. During that visit in February, it was my pleasure to spend several hours with him in absorbed conversation. I came away inspired and happily impressed that the man was equal in stature to his buildings.

Now that he is gone, the memory of that meeting takes on added poignancy—not simply because he was one of this century's great architects, but because it was an opportunity to know a man with tremendous sparkle and contagious enthusiasm.

He spoke in epigrams of the sort that made you wish for a tape recorder. Many of his phrases were sharpened and polished with frequent use. Two of his favorites are particularly appropriate to Iran's arid desert culture and an indication of his philosophical affinity with this part of the world: *The sun never knew how great it was until it hit the side of a building* would have fit in well with sun-and-shadow oriented Persian architecture. *Ask bricks what they want to be and they'll say, 'Make us an arch'. Try to sell them a lintel and they'll still say, 'Make us an arch'.*

The charm of the man, though, was not so much his succinct phrases as his unassuming manner and intensity. Voluble and outgoing, he would come up to people with his hand outstretched and disarmingly say, Hello, I'm Louis Kahn, as if he were the grocer down the street, and you might just not remember his name. When he started to talk, his exuberant concentration transformed him so that you no longer saw the thick glasses and the terrible scars suffered in a fire when he was a child. He became radiant, the personification of mental animation, sitting hunched over with his hands clasped and building his words smoothly until he had constructed the perfect expression of an idea. Then sometimes he would stop to interject, *I just thought of this,* so that you could witness the man's act of creation in his speech.

He listened with an uncanny concentration as if every fold of his creative brain were attuned to your words. When he asked about the use of water in Iranian culture or the place of *strolling* in the society, I felt that I should answer him with every possible bit of information, reaming out my mind to yield grist for his creative mill. After he had asked me endless questions about Iran's culture as it is expressed in architecture and the use of spaces, out came the humility that marked his greatness. *When we've brought our plans to the place where we're proud of them ourselves,* he said, *it is architects like you—sensitive to Iran and its culture—that I'd like to give us their critical views.* It was a simple statement, not intended as a compliment, but I was honored.

And Kahn liked to claim that he himself had been made with a little Persian blood mixed into his Russian ancestry. Intuition and the *feel of a place* were important to him. It made sense, then, that he should say, with reference to Iran, *I've always had an affinity for the desert.*

We talked about the possibility of Iranian architects developing their own contemporary Iranian design idiom, and I described how Iranian architects who have studied abroad and returned argue with those who have been trained in Iran about which group is more sensitive to cultural roots. Kahn immediately pointed out that it is not a group or a school or a committee which leads the way. It must be one creative individual with the strength of leadership who can evoke in all a sense of *Yes, this is right.*

He said that what is constantly being sought through different design approaches is the *commonality* of architecture—that which all can accept as being a true and valid expression, even though it may be clothed in different forms. *The rules can be changed, but not the law, for it is only the rules that are made by man.* Kahn had made some beautiful rules in his lifetime.

When we said goodbye, he clasped my hand for several minutes as if the conversation were continuing through our fingertips. It was a long handshake. I didn't know it would be the last one.

Norman N. Rice

A year ago or so, Esther and Lou Kahn, and other friends, were at our home. While conversing with Lou and another man, I said that the funeral oration spoken by Pericles over the fallen Athenian soldiers was the greatest of all funeral orations. Louis aked me to read it to him; he was deeply moved by it. Let me read a few sentences from its beginnings:

Most of those who have stood in this place before me have commended the institution of the closing address. It is good, they have felt, that solemn words should be spoken over our fallen soldiers. I do not share this feeling. Acts deserve acts, not words, in their honor. Our sense of the merits of a number of our fellow citizens should not depend on the felicity of one man's speech. And those who have known and loved the dead may think these words scant justice to the memories they would hear honored.

When I was in the 6th grade and showed some talent in drawing, I was sent to a unique public school, long since gone, the Public Industrial Art School, established by a remarkable man with the unique name of J. Liberty Todd. There we were taught drawing and painting, modeling in clay, and woodcarving. There I first met and got to know Lou Kahn. He was an outstanding student in that school, renowned for his sketches of animals at the zoo.

Later, we were together during four years at the great Central High School in this city. I claim I was really educated at Central High and learned only my profession at the University of Pennsylvania. Lou claimed he passed the high standards and great faculty of Central only by the skin of his teeth; I told him his language showed the effects of four years of his youth spent with excellent teachers.

In those years, we and several other boys who wanted to draw and paint used to meet for sketching trips in the nearby countryside. (The countryside was more nearby then.) Also, in those years Lou won first prize several times in citywide contests in drawing. In our senior year, the head of the school's art department, William F. Gray, gave us a course in architectural history that included making drawings with ruling pen and India ink of famous buildings. Lou earned some much needed extra money in the somewhat illegitimate way of making drawings for untalented students; he said he masked his authorship by purposeful ink blots.

It was this course, and the wonderful teaching of William Gray, that inspired Louis to become an architect as they inspired me to do, and others before and after us. We then entered the School of Architecture at the University of Pennsylvania, and worked very hard for four years, often night and day, and gained the habit of working night and day that still persists. Lou worked till the end as if there were seventy-two hours in each day. In the senior year, we attained our heart's desire, to study in the atelier of Paul Philippe Cret, the bright star of the faculty, a great architect and teacher. When, many years later, Louis was chosen to hold the Paul Philippe Cret Professorship in Architecture and to teach at his alma mater, it affected him to the deepest.

One year after our graduation from Penn, John Molitor, the City Architect, was appointed architect of the Sesqui-Centennial Exposition of 1926. Lou was then working for Molitor, who appointed him chief of design. He quickly recruited his young architect friends and we became the team. Burning with our enthusiasms and with the ideals planted by our recent teachers, full of brash courage founded on naivete, we did the Exposition and its many buildings within one year's time. For that era, some of the buildings were very creditable. It was an exhilarating and encouraging experience for all of us, and especially for Lou.

After 13 years with Lou and Robert Le Ricolais in the unique, simultaneous teaching triumvirate of our postgraduate Studio at the University, I say that Lou Kahn was never a teacher in the conventional, didactic sense. He was an ardent missionary of architecture, and he loved being both of these. My preceptor, the renowned architect LeCorbusier, who was also a painter, once told me that he fought out his architectural battles in his paintings. I believe that the discussions in the Studio, with their give and take, helped Lou fight out and resolve many of his architectural battles.

He fascinated students by his poetic visions and the veritable flood of his images, the analogies with music, his evocation of primary essences. For the first time they saw the essential nature of a stairway, of a column and a beam, and a wall—and the differing natures of brick and concrete. He urged them not to become mere satisfiers of so-called building programs, mere problem solvers. Above all, he tried to inspire them, by his own example to become architects of the nature of a building as well as the architects of its plan and configuration. Of course, they were fascinated by discussions of his own works. The triumvirate was not always unanimous, as would be expected of three quite different men, and we voiced our differences, so that we, as well as the students learned from such free discussions.

Almost every Monday and Friday, late in the afternoon following Studio, Lou, Robert Le Ricolais and I went to Robert's apartment on Sansom Street. Over a drink or two, we talked of many things and ideas, as three comrades, frankly and openly. We discovered some important conclusions. For me, the Studio and these sessions have been a constant source of rejuvenation. Lou looked forward to those sessions, and often he would delay keeping an appointment so that we could be together a little longer.

Louis Kahn was in the tradition of architects and architecture that is not widely honored in our time, except by lip service. He was not acclimated to the marketplace where the avowed professional thrives best. He did not want the men of measured merriment to prevail. He believed that art and joy are for Life's sake. As Buckminster Fuller says, *God is a verb, not a noun.*

And now, let me paraphrase what I said nine years ago when LeCorbusier passed on:

Lou Kahn materially influences every architect. Not merely through his visible works of architecture, but by the principles he enunciated so beautifully. He influences us even if that influence is not consciously recognized or understood, or is denied. Human nature often induces the debtor to decry both the debt and the creditor, but this cannot diminish in the slightest degree the power and dimensions of Louis Kahn's genius.

In honoring him, it is not to honor a profession. In honoring him, it is not only to honor a man, singular as he was. In honoring him, it is for us to honor, and be dedicated to, the eternal art of architecture which men such as he comprehend with all their minds, which they sustain with wit and high courage, which they love with all consuming passion.

Thank you, comrade and friend of many years.

Moshe Safdie
On a sunny Sunday in the autumn of 1962, Lou Kahn was sitting with five assistants around a large wooden table in a Philadelphia deli, not far from his Walnut Street office. It had been a long weekend charette—one of many. This time we were working on the Indian Institute of Management in Ahmedabad, and Kahn, contrary to habit, joined us for a late lunch. We had been drawing sections and elevations of the enormous brick facades: large scale drawings indicating brick courses, concrete ties, great arches and circles, as Kahn evolved step by step with soft charcoal sketches the plans of the compound.

Something in the mood of the afternoon triggered an openness unusual amongst Kahn's assistants. Perhaps my recent arrival in the office, a hot-headed young graduate, the only one not from Kahn's classes at Penn, helped to fuel the discussion. "Don't you feel that making this an all-brick project in traditional brick construction is a romantic response to a world Indians are trying to break away from? Aren't they interested in new methods, new techniques, prefabrication, labor-saving devices? Have they not come to you because they feel you hold the key to a transformation of their present way?'

Kahn's response was about the beauty of handcrafted work, of Gandhi and the Cottage Revolution, the reaffirmation and the value of the crafts and how his building will help the Indians rediscover what they have. We persisted. I spoke of having seen women hand crushing rocks with hammers to make road gravel along the Delhi Punjab highway, and what a single rock crusher would have meant to them. But Kahn calmly restated his case.

Many years later in Ahmedabad, I met Doshi, Kahn's representative, (he also represented Le Corbusier in Chandigarh) who spoke of the surprise and initial disappointment when Kahn arrived with his drawings.

Several months later, Kahn was intensively at work on the capital of East Pakistan (now Bangladesh) in Dacca. The plan for the capital precinct emerged more axial and ceremonial than anything Kahn had done in the past. The building forms of the assembly building, the hospital and the secretariat were more exuberant and expressive with enormous interpenetrations of circles, flat arches, arcades and screen walls, relentlessly extending over thousands of feet. Was that the Kahn who only a few years earlier designed the Trenton Bath House, The Richards Medical Building and the Salk Institute?

For a moment we felt betrayed as Kahn came forward with a measure of sensuality and self-indulgence that we were unprepared for.

Now twenty years later, as students sit in their studios, Kahn somewhat forgotten, and work a design as they glance into an open book illustrating Hadrian's Villa, Borromini's oratory or Schinkel's great museum, or a magazine with neo-classical buildings, vintage '84, our concerns of then seem absurd. Who would have dreamt that within twenty years Kahn's fascination, search and inspiration from the architecture of yesterday would be replaced by the cartoonish mimicry. Or that his mastery of the materiality of building (in the nature of the materials). "I asked the brick wall, how should the window be?" And, "What does the building want to be?" Should [it] be replaced with a cardboard architecture of drywall, anonymous steel frames clad with stone and plaster, denying, camouflaging, the order of their construction?

We have come full circle. We speak of the virtue of labor intensive industries in the developing countries, the need to help them rediscover their own skills and crafts rather than impose imported technologies, thus reaffirming Kahn's intuition about Ahmedabad. We lament the architecture of our day, the architecture of stage sets, forms for effect, unfounded in construction and the purpose of building. We sense that has been engulfed by the world of styling and become surface decorations. It is concerned with the envelope, not the substance, silhouette, not the life within.

As time goes by, Kahn somehow stands apart as *the measure,* the standard, something to compare to, to evaluate by, to give sustenance. As the journals spin out page after page of trivia, we remember Kahn's words about the nature of school, a place for work, a room with light, and the making of a window.

When Le Corbusier died, Kahn said to an associate in sadness, who is there now to work for? Twenty years later I say, Lou Kahn we miss you.

Jonas Salk

I think he probably released in me something that was latent, of which I was not aware. This perhaps happens sometimes when two beings come together. We reaffirmed one another. When people used to ask me whether he was difficult to work with, it was always amusing to me. I always found it so pleasant and enjoyable. We could trade ideas. And it didn't make any difference whether he came up with the idea or I came up with the idea—the idea was born anyway. And all this blended together into a result. He amusingly used to say that sometimes he didn't know who the architect was. I had no difficulty with that, but he evidently must have had a much greater respect for the relationship in terms of acceptance, in terms of having an appreciation of my sincerity in respect to some ideas that we had been talking about. They were just intentions, hopes and aspirations, dreams if you like.

When I first met him, which was in mid-December of 1959, I stopped in Philadelphia on the way to New York from Pittsburgh. Some friends of mine—the Lowenthals in Pittsburgh—heard him speak at the Bicentennial at Carnegie Tech, which was in early September, 1959. I was not there at the time. And I had just come back from La Jolla where I had visited for the first time at the end of August. And they knew, I think, that I was going there and the reasons. When I came back, I spoke about the place, which I had visited in order to exclude it as a place for a serious institute. I imagined it to be something different than what I had thought to be an appropriate place, but I was urged to come there at least and see it. I went there specifically to rule it out. I had been resisting the trip for some time. When I got back, I obviously had been affected by what I saw and the Lowenthals, having heard Lou and having known me, said that we must meet each other. And I had a second visit to Los Angeles in November and this time realized that there was something serious happening.

I stopped to ask him how one chooses an architect. I spoke, I think, for fifteen or twenty minutes, about a number of things that he has quoted repeatedly since then, which I, of course, didn't appreciate myself, until seeing them back through the reflection of him, you might say. After which we went to the Richard Building [Richards Resarch Building, University of Pennsylvania], which was just under construction. And I went on to New York after that. I found being with him a very warm, stimulating experience. The kind of person he is—the poetic, mystical type—always warms my heart.

So that was in mid-December. I can't remember precisely what happened, but I visited La Jolla again in early January. I had him come out at the time of my next visit, which was the end of January. And then things began to move very quickly.

The beginning of working together, we never drew up a contract or made any formal arrangements. We spoke together. He needed some money, and I paid it out of an account that I had from the Institute. He worked at the things that were necessary, and it was that informal. Fortunately, there had been some money sent to me by people that was intended for me personally, but I had put it into a trust fund. So that was available.

At some later time, a contract was drawn up. I can't even remember when. And so the problem that I had questioned Lou about—how one chooses an architect—was never specifically answered. But I look back now and have decided that that was the way it should have been done. It was a stroke of good fortune that I'm sure I never would have succumbed if I had met anyone else except Lou. What would have been involved would be a great deal of hesitation and then I would have become very analytical about it.

Whenever we were together, we enjoyed being together, and we talked about all kinds of things, so that it was a characteristic outpouring. I don't know whether he said the things that he said to me to others. I'm sure that he did some, but I said things to him and talked to him with words that I had never used with anyone else. I believe the same thing was true of him. He was aware of this—we talked about this—simply because there was an affirmation, a feeling of safety and trust. And whatever was said was understood. He would speak in his language and I would speak in my language, but we understood each other. This sometimes happens when I speak to someone who speaks French, and I speak English, yet we understand each other. It was that kind of thing. And he would say something that I would then modify or qualify that had a mystical cosmologic aspect to it. And he'd ponder it and think about it and go back in thought. And that was the kind of play that went on. But we were never serious. We talked about serious things, but we never took them seriously. He was never heavy. It was always light when we would leave each other—at least for me. Instead of exhausted, I felt exhilarated, as if I had had a pleasurable experience.

In the end of March, 1962, we spent a weekend with our prospective builders, in order to choose one for the managing builder contract. Finally, after a whole weekend of presentation, I accepted the plans that then existed. And I must admit that I had interacted a good deal with Lou, but not to the extent that I did subsequently after the episode that occurred after the contract was signed that evening. I went outside alone. It was twilight. I tried to imagine how the buildings would look, and I must say, I suddenly became terribly unhappy. And prior to that, I had been looking at the plans and listening to Lou and rather letting things go. I was so preoccupied with other things that I didn't try to be as critical of what was emerging. We really were developing undifferentiated space, and I didn't worry too much about it, because it would be differentiated eventually, so I wanted to get something that could be built and we could get started with, as things were moving slowly.

That night, I didn't sleep very well, and the next morning, Lou and I had to go to San Francisco to meet with Basil O'Connor to report on our meeting with the managing builders. Well, I told Lou on the plane the next morning that I thought that we had to start over again, because I really was not very happy about the plans. And I sketched for him what I thought I didn't like, and also what I thought was needed. It had two very, very narrow—not gardens at all, but two alleys, and four buildings, and the laboratory portions were eighty feet wide. We hammered it out, and he was always very gracious about it. Finally the decision was made to change.

He was always very gracious in saying that this gave him an opportunity to build an even greater building.

I have no doubt [that he believed that].

We were both temperamentally the same. We're always looking ahead and going forward. And that which has already been done becomes very uninteresting, and if you see a better plan, you might even stop in the middle of what you are doing and go on to something else. So, we were very dangerous with each other in that respect. Nevertheless, at some points in time, I had to apply restraints which I knew affected both of us. But I think the building is...it makes my heart beat every time I come in. And when I show it to people who are appreciative, I get great satisfaction. I cannot tell you what I would do differently.

I would say the building is as close to perfection as anything possible.

Vincent Scully

I'm honored to be here. On the other hand, I'm not happy for obvious reasons. It is a difficult time to be on this platform. It's difficult also because it's hard to talk honestly about somebody like Lou. Like everyone who knew him, I loved him very much.

I suppose there were times, so long ago perhaps, when I didn't value some of his work as much as I might have. One has the feeling—I do—when someone like that goes, it's like a father going. Not in the sentimental sense, but in the sense that you feel you didn't value him enough really when he was there. You remember all the things which you had said, then it was too late, then it was over.

Men are much more interesting than gods. They suffer more. They have to be much more intelligent. They have to think and work and scheme all the time. And they are always in competition with other men; with their predecessors, with their students, and with their followers. And it's about some of that that I'd like to talk tonight. I hope that Mr. Kahn and I were friends from 1947 until his death, but I don't want to apostrophize it here in excessively personal terms. Instead, I'd like to do what may be a very bad thing to do at a time like this, but to assess him professionally from my own competence—the one I profess, at least, to have—as an historian. I think that there were five major historical truths about him. And I'd like to start by mentioning those. The first fundamental truth is that he survived. And he survived almost everything. And his survival is like his history of America. He survived fire and flood, immigration, the melting pot, Depression and war. And he survived into his early '50s without ever achieving any particular success at all. And he continued to grow inside throughout all those years, without public encouragement or reward. And this in a society where youth had always been the ideal.

Secondly, then, with enormous difficulty, and at an age when most of us are getting ready to topple over, he broke through the worn-out International Style model, and starting with the Yale Art Gallery of 1951, he began to create fresh architectural forms which were based upon a new assessment of reality. It seems to me that this is the most difficult thing that any human being can do. We all try to deal with reality through a model of its infinite complexity. We simplify it down through the areas that we can deal with. This, I guess, is called tradition. And to break those models, to start thinking...fresh, is the most enormous act that the human intellect can create. This, it seems to me, is what Lou did. His first great act was an act of destruction.

Then, thirdly, in breaking the old models, he released a generation of students that think and act upon their own. He also opened up, by breaking that model, their own paths—their own paths which had been separated from them by two generations of persuasive European influences. And those students of him are now an army. I think, myself, the best we have—Venturi, Giurgola, Moore, Millard, Robertson, Meyerson, Wurman, Stern and Clement—are only a few of them. By the later 1960s, some of them, along some lines, had gone beyond Kahn, but they could not have done so without him.

Then, fifth and last, he survived thereafter. He survived his own strong students. He survived thereafter into his 70s, long enough to unfold the whole of his force, and to put to use everything he had loved as a boy—and was probably seeking when he first entered Paul Cret's office in the 1920s. Rome, the Beaux Arts, the Noble Environment—it all poured out at last: Trajan's Market, Hadrian's Villa, Ostia Anticia, in the brick order, the arches, and the vast terraces of Dacca and Ahmedabad. And along with these came a whole new generation of students, some of whom revered him perhaps more than was entirely good, but to his enormous gratitude and joy. And then finally, returning alone to India in the sixth of such interminable journeys within a year, he died. And lay in his own kind of solitary state for two days, his thrown back, looking as those who found him said, victorious. Now, nobody can talk about Lou Kahn without a story or two, and I know there are many who are here who were privileged to spend much more time with him than I did; so perhaps I can tell two stories of a time when I was with him alone. That was when we were in the Soviet Union in 1965 on the Cultural Exchange program. One night in the middle of the summer, we were walking around the Kremlin and it was a beautiful long twilit Russian summer night. We were looking up at the towers. Whenever we went by, I pointed up to them and said, *They are, as you know, built by Romantic Italian architects in the Renaissance.* I said, *Look how they point.* Lou said, *Look how they bring the weight down.* Now, I was focusing, I think, on Venturi and the other—I think Lou called *semi-illogical architects.* Kahn was focusing upon what they were. And the essence of his architecture—solid, immobile, enduring—is, it seems to me, exactly that. Then later, we were in Leningrad, at the opening of a show of American architecture; and it was a disgracefully unprofessional exhibition, chosen to astound the Russians with the glitter and glamour of our material culture. And Kahn was asked by the Director of the exhibition to go along and describe it to the Lord Mayor of Leningrad and his entourage. And he refused. He said he wouldn't. He said it was a disgrace, and he wouldn't do such a thing. But he agreed to walk along with them and be there in case there was a question. So he did. And when they came to Kahn's church in Rochester, the Mayor of Leningrad said, *That doesn't look like a church.* Which, of course, from a Russian point of view, is absolutely true. And Kahn immediately replied, *That's why it was chosen for exhibition to the Soviet Union.* My interpreter was a terrible square and he did not interpret Kahn's remarks. But all the Russians laughed anyway.

And later, I remember, that night, I trailed around with him to Leningrad's white night—white night all night long in the middle of the summer—while he bought every rare book, and especially every architectural book that was available in that most glorious of northern cities, which after all, was situated only a very short distance from the Island of Osel on which he was born.

One is reminded over and over again of how Kahn at this time was willing to be what all the critics called *ugly*. And they did, over and over again, and condescended to him for this quality that he was willing to be ugly to be right, in a curious sense. He was cutting through in order to try to find the system. And as he did so, of course, the system began to come to life, with an integral structural and spatial character of its own. A great uncouth beast lumbering towards Bethlehem to be born. Now, that's clearly seen in his space frame skyscraper, in which now this bony structure dares to cast aside all the elegance of what Kahn called a *lady in a bronze petticoat, in bronze corsets*—which was the beautiful Seagram's building, to express the necessity to brace against diagonal collapse, to make a three-dimensionally stable structure or create a whole new form and a whole new kind of scale of space, in which the love of a connection, the love of a knuckle, the love of a capacity to add on to this as most of all this was a building in process which could go on and proliferate indefinitely. And at which the lover of that addition of the process means that fundamentally this is a kind of a frame for a whole new city in which living parts and functional units may be slid.

Alison and Peter Smithson

We tend to think of our architectural mentors quite often. Last week, thinking of Kahn, we wrote, "The most mysterious, the most charged of architectural forms are those which capture the empty air. The faery ring, Stonehenge, the standing columns of the temple whose cella walls have gone, the empty barn, the Kahn house of the square brick columns, the chimneys of the English Renaissance...such forms are double-acting, concentrating inwards, radiating buoyancy outwards. The power of the groups of columns through which one sees the sky, or the landscape beyond, as at Sunion or Selinunte town, is entirely different from that of the complete ring of columns as at Paestum or Segesta. We are aware at once of the mysterious empty air inside the ring. Unlike Kahn we may not hesitate to enter, but we know as we pass between the columns that we break into a solemn and mysterious place. That a barn—a roof on open columns—should be mysterious too? Is it that we think of it as a temple, or that we feel that something that when full is a block, a solid, a mass, then suddenly a void, then a void anticipating a mass, is a mysterious event? Or do we feel for the barn as we do for the renewal of a tree by the seasons? Perfect when in leaf and a mass in summer, perfect when veined air in winter. Especially perfect if we feel winter and emptiness as a cleansing, and spring as a renewal—a miracle every year. Maybe a barn is like that.

"But how do we see the Kahn brick-columned house-like-a-barn? (The de Vore House c 1955) Why did that seem so moving when it was first drawn (and not only to us)? Did we then feel it as temple, and temple as empty, and empty as barn, and barn as tree? The Kahn house of brick columns was a brutalist place for the intellect...not barn...not temple...free of the wheel of seasonal labour...free of gods or ritual. A frame in which a contemplative owner could camp out comfortably and appreciate nature, and by moving his screens see stars or moon as spectacle without himself becoming another's spectacle. Before this house design bricks had been unthinkable...and still were (even still are), but here and only here bricks became a brutalist tool."

At the same time last week, re-reading what we first wrote on Kahn in *Architects' Yearbook 9,* August 1960, "Any marginal disappointment with the actual completed buildings does not in any way diminish one's absolute faith in the importance and relevance of Louis Kahn's ideas—for architectural ideas have a validity of their own, irrespective of whether they are completely realized or not."

Also last week—strangely it now seems—at office tea, talking of how terrible was the most recent experience of the spanking-pace, non-ruminative, church-camp-style of American lecturing, someone said, "I once heard Kahn lecture..." and we were all off in happy reminiscence, considering quite a different phenomenon: for future generations we can only hope someone, somewhere, has Kahn on tape, talking informally to a group of students. No architect with a memory of a Kahn lecture can not be aware of another level, another pattern of architectural thinking.

Mrs. M. R. Nengnoi Suksri

I was known to Professor Kahn by the name of Tall Princess from Thailand, probably because of my long and unusual name to him. Before getting to know him, I was so impressed with his work starting with the Alfred Newton Richards Medical Center. That was why I applied to study for the Master's program at the University of Pennsylvania in the year 1950-60. After one year of study with him, I wish to write here that I was so honored to be one of Professor Kahn's students. He was not only the great architect of our time, but also the greatest teacher I'd ever met.

Charles H. Taylor, Jr.

Louis had just flown back from Russia, where he had been invited to talk to architecture students, initially at only a couple of institutes. He said he had stressed in his talks what a mistake it was to copy the shoddy design of bourgeois western buildings in their major construction, lacking any expression of joints and boundaries. Now if you look at your own log buildings and their beautifully articulated corners, he said, lacing his hand together, you will see how your own tradition has a special relevance for improvement of your architecture. Louis was well aware that he was pointing to an example from the rural heritage often scorned in the party line, but he also knew that the western comparison would hurt and he looked for help from national pride.

In the event, he was invited also to several other institutes in additional cities, which had been a part of his objective. I have always recalled this story as an example of Lou's special combination of tact and wit—how wisely he could use the biases and pride of his clients.

Stanley Tigerman

I was on my way to Bangladesh—I had been working on these projects there. I'd been there twenty times altogether. We had five polytechnics in five jungle towns from 1966. I thought, *They'll never get done.* It was incredible. Lou hated it.

I went to London and checked into Heathrow Airport. I was staying with a friend of mine, Roger Kunliff, Lord Kunliff, who used to be head of the Architectural Association—not the principle organization, but the professional organization. I'm at the airport and I see this old man, who looks like he has detached retinas, is really raggy and looks like a bum. It was Lou. I had seen him at Dacca two times before: he was a teacher of mine at Yale. He was on his way back to New York to die. I was on my way to Dacca. We had two hours together. We talked mostly about this friend of mine who got me into Bangladesh, Muzharul Islam, who later gave up architecture. He was the one responsible for Lou getting the capital (project). He was the Chief Architect of the Government of East Pakistan, before he went on his own. He was in my Masters Class at Yale. He was the one responsible for bringing Paul Rudolph and me over to Bangladesh in 1964, out of which Rudolph got the Architectural School and I ultimately got this project with this Polytechnic Institute.

Lou and I were sitting talking and he couldn't figure out why Islam had given up architecture. We were reminiscing. We had a nice talk. He seemed exhausted, depressed. He looked like hell. He was kind of beaten down. He looked just awful.

He was coming from Ahmedabad.

When I was at Yale, he was a teacher there and (Paul) Rudolph was kind of not nice to him. He knew that I was a friend of Paul's and as we were leaving, after I had said goodbye, he turned to go and he called me and said, *Tigerman, come here. I want to tell you something.* He said, *I know you are close to Paul, and I haven't seen him in such a long time. Tell him when you see him that I miss him and I think he is really a terrific architect.* I was really touched by that. Then we left.

I went to Dacca and four or five days later I read in the paper that he had died in this incredible way in New York. I changed my reservation and went back via New York. I thought that was such a touching story. I had breakfast with Paul at the Plaza and told him the story.

For me the experience was very touching because I realized that I was one of the last people that had seen Lou.

He had said all kinds of things. He was talking about Chicago, and how Mies had taught us all how to build, which he had told me before. He talked mostly about the state of Muzharul Islam, that he had done such a wonderful thing for Lou and then how he gave up architecture because of politics. Lou said, *There's so few things I know in life. I could never do anything but be an architect because that's all I know how to do.*

I was very touched by it. I knew it (was the end) even then, but I didn't realize (how important it was to me that) I had this conversation, which was the longest conversation I had ever had with him. We had had breakfast together in Dacca, he's been on juries of mine at Yale, I had seen him at the Museum of Modern Art in New York, maybe eight times before in my life. He was always very, very nice to me. (That last time) we were there maybe two hours having breakfast. He really looked awful. He was really beaten down. I think that high-rise project he lost in Kansas City affected him tremendously, the one SOM plucked out of Lou's hands.

David C. Tuttle

I became a member of the Rochester First Unitarian Church building committee in 1959, during the latter stages of plan preparation, and through the bidding and construction phases. As a civil engineer, I could feel that certain interests and exposures would then be put to use. They were, but I received much more than I bargained for. Lou's essential contribution to the design had already been made when I undertook any official duties with respect to the project. There was a particular paperwork session toward the end of the design, among Lou, one or two of his people, and the building committee (the business was largely conducted among the committee members of longer standing and Lou's lieutenants). Two attendees did not naturally or necessarily feel drawn to that exercise. These were Lou and myself, and we were sort of overlooked by the others for perhaps two hours, as we sat off in the corner of the large meeting room. Very early in the conversation, Lou set me to talking about *my* work, which at that time largely entailed the design of urban spaces and transportation facilities. In discussing a bridge crossing question, he put before me a fresh way of looking at the nature of design. His thesis was that a bridge *wants* to carry something from one side to the other of the feature spanned. If it is a stream, the structure must respect the stream and let it maintain its unity and function.

And if the direct economics of such an uninhibiting crossing are not feasible by traditional means, then a serious effort must be made to establish standards that *do* take account of the aesthetic imperatives of design, to find or develop production and construction measures that *do* make the appropriate design realistically implementable. I believe I have been guided ever since by these ideas in my professional work, and although my individual applications have been slight and unmeasurable, I (and I would think, he as well) have been gratified to see bridge standards evolve gradually toward allowing a semblance of these principles.

When in 1965 our church was obliged to expand or turn people away, a development brought about no less by the appeal of the building than by the attractiveness of the religious atmosphere, I found myself in charge of the new building committee and architect selection committee. History records that we again hired Louis Kahn and got the job done. In the demanding and rewarding process, my appreciation of this uncommon man was heightened. Ours was a small job set against the Olympian things he was trying to do at the time, but he took a very special interest and spent a prodigious amount of effort in reconciling our needs and our means. But it was done without compromising his aesthetic principles. I have had occasion to recall frequently an incident involving our discussion about working two small lavatories into a relationship to the classroom. To me, it seemed a simple matter of shrinking them to a size which would fit nicely into what seemed like more or less expandable space among some other facilities. To Lou, this would make the spaces *mean,* and even with respect to lavatories this would be less than the architect or the ultimate users would find acceptable. A rather extensive redesign had to be made, and a highly satisfactory solution was brought forth. I believe I have consciously or unconsciously been guided by this admonition throughout the ensuing years, and have, I believe, shunned *meanness* in designing spaces for human activity on an almost automatic basis.

After we had occupied the building for a time, a number of reports of nighttime prowlers and vandals came to the attention of the church board. Various strategies were proposed, and among those was the suggestion to install outside security lighting or building illumination.

I was requested to bring this suggestion to Lou and learn his thoughts. The substance of his response was not surprising. The words, however, were memorable. He said, *At night, the building wants to sleep.* We have let it do just that, and have undoubtedly averted unnecessary expense, bulb breakage and a fatigued building.

Joyously aware and infectiously buoyant, Louis Kahn raised the sights and spirits of this church community, as I'm sure you're hearing from the far reaches of his influence.

Alexandra Tyng

When I was in high school I would take my report card to Lou's office so he could sign it. Once I had a particularly good report card and I was very proud of it.

Lou glanced briefly over all the 1s (we got 1,2,3 instead of A,B,C), dismissing them as if to say, *I expected you to get them.* Then his eye riveted on my grade for art, a minor subject.

Why did you get a 2 in art? he demanded.

I explained that the teacher wasn't satisfied with one of my compositions, an abstract which I had very little interest in doing. I assured him my grade didn't really matter, but he insisted on going to the school and talking to the art teacher. I think she was impressed with what he said, because I always got 1s after that!

I thought it was rather silly of him to make such a big deal about my art grade, even though I was glad he cared that much.

Years later I was reading Lou's ideas that there should be schools of natural talent, that you learn nothing that is not part of you, and, most importantly, that works should be criticized in a positive way rather than be judged. I was impressed that Lou lived by his beliefs to that extent.

Lou gave me some wonderful presents, presents which influenced the course of my life and the development of my talents. He always chose the model with the finest workmanship. I knew even as a kid that his taste was exquisite. Sometimes, however, I was too young to appreciate his gifts fully. For instance, he gave me my oil paint set when I was about eight, and I didn't begin to paint with it until I was about fifteen.

Once my younger brother Nathaniel and I stopped by his office. Lou had just come back from a trip and he had presents for us. I was at the difficult age when I didn't trust anyone to buy anything for me. I wanted money, just money, so I could buy what I liked. My mother must have warned him of this, so with respect for my wishes he gave me a fifty dollar bill. Nathaniel's present was an old coin.

Nathaniel looked so dashed. You could tell he was thinking, *What good is this old coin?* He was seven or eight at the time and I'm sure fifty dollars looked like a fortune to him.

Lou sensed his feelings immediately. He explained that the coin was very rare, and worth a lot more than fifty dollars.

Of course, now *I* was jealous. If he could afford to buy Nathaniel a coin worth more than fifty dollars, then why couldn't he have given *me* more?

Nathaniel understood Lou's explanation, but I could tell he still would rather have had the money *now* even though he would be glad someday that he had the coin.

Nathaniel did collect coins for a long time. And I can't remember for the life of me what I spent the fifty dollars on. Lou didn't mean it as a lesson, but it was a good one.

Through those petty jealousies that siblings have, I think we both saw that Lou had given us presents with a tremendous amount of thought behind them.

Anne Griswold Tyng

Lou's scarred face, the result of his childhood accident with glowing coals, made him extremely shy. Although he had been called *scarface* at school, when I met him he was 44 and the scars were quite faint. In fact, I was hardly aware of them. What most impressed me about him was his intensity and vitality. I could immediately identify with his level of excitement and his dedication to the almost magical challenge of architecture.

Yet Lou's shyness still made him feel extremely insecure about giving a formal lecture. In 1951, I believe it was, he was invited to lecture by the Young Planners Group of Philadelphia, as we called ourselves. (In addition to myself, the group included Blanche Lemco Van Ginkle, now dean of the School of Architecture in Toronto; Martin Meyerson, recently president of the University of Pennsylvania; Louis Dolbeare and others.) I had been working with Lou on his traffic plan for Philadelphia, published later in the fall of 1953 in Yale's *Perspecta,* and thought it would be great if we could get him to present it in the Board Room of the PSFS building. We invited many Philadelphia planners and architects.

Lou still had great misgivings about giving a lecture. He told the story of his lecture on monumentality in the early 1940s. He had done a lot of research and had gotten some slides together. Since it was still during the Depression and Lou needed to earn some money, it was to be a paid attendance. Lou put on the first slide, and it was upside down. He was so undone he could not continue. Apologizing to the group and returning their money, he rushed from the room.

After reassuring him many times that I would double check the slides, Lou became more cheerful. He told the story of how Aalto had given lectures, knowing only one word of English, by simply standing up and pointing to the slides as they were being shown and saying, *Slidesees, slidesees.* Lou said with a grin that if Aalto could do that, he ought to be able to manage. He did manage—it was altogether a luminous event.

Lou, perhaps fortunately, never drove a car. He seemed to have no concept of what driving involved. When I drove him to a job to which neither of us had ever been and I would be trying to figure out how to get there, Lou would carry on the most intense conversation about the nature of space and what a building wanted to be, and expect complete attention with intelligent responses. Once when I made the mistake of telling him I was trying to find the way, he said masterfully, *Let's turn right here,* or *I think we should turn left*—without any idea of the directions. Not realizing that he had no logical reason for his directions, I obediently did as he suggested. We were very late for our appointment.

Once David Wisdom was driving Lou and me to the Container Corporation for a meeting when it began to snow. We came to a hill, and cars around us began to slip and slide. Lou said impatiently, *Let's pull ahead of that taxi!* When we, too, came to a standstill with the wheels spinning, Lou was sure we could get going again if he and I got out and pushed. By that time the storm was really setting in and we left the car by the side of the road, walking the rest of the way to our meeting. Coming home, we walked knee-deep in snow to the nearest railroad station, laughing with Lou about pulling ahead of the taxi.

The extraordinary level of dedication and persistence Lou had in his work had a powerful impact on all of us who worked in the office. He was sometimes aware of how demanding he was. When we were all exhausted in the middle of a charette, he would turn with a grin and say, *While you rest, do this.* When a client would call impatiently about a project, Lou would say, *You can't eat pencils and spit ideas.* More than once, when a contract for a job had been terminated, Lou would continue to work on it in the hope that he might persuade the client to continue. Once, in his exasperation with a building committee, he said, *They've just come out of the woods with their beards dragging on the ground behind them.*

Lou had a rare feeling for words. Perhaps it was because he did not go to school until he was seven years old—when a school-teacher neighbor informed his parents, recent immigrants, that he was already past the age when the law required children to go to school. Since he had always been drawing, images were more important than words, or perhaps words were, for Lou, images.

In putting his images of architecture into words, Lou was at first rather tentative. He would try out his word images on me. I can remember Lou's first realization of the distinction between the measurable and unmeasurable in architecture. The sound of the word *unmeasurable* sent me to a dictionary, wondering if such a word existed. There was *immeasurable,* which meant something quite different, and of course one could say *not measurable.* But at that time (and I looked in other dictionaries, too) *unmeasurable* was not listed. Yet there was obviously a need for such a word. Now in architectural circles, to speak of the measurable and unmeasurable is common usage.

In trying to explain his concept of the *nature of a space,* order, and design, Lou had a difficult time. He was not at all satisfied with his many different attempts to explain order. Finally, in exasperation, he said *Order is.* That had for me the quality of a revelation, especially after my conventional academic background in languages and grammar.

I can remember Lou's intensity and almost mischievous daring when he first came out with *Paestum was the time when the walls parted and the columns became. Became what?* was my immediate reaction, but almost simultaneously I sensed the vitality of the image of that event in architecture when the wall gave birth to columns.

Once, at lunch with Lou, he explained when an event occurred by saying, *That was when we lived at Twentieth and Walnut streets.* It took me a moment to realize that he was referring to the time when the office was at Twentieth and Walnut. In a sense, for Lou, his office was his home. He often said that his work had priority over any human relationship. He frequently napped on the hard oak bench in his office, and shared crackers, cheese, fruit and a bottle of wine or gin with those of us who were working late. Although some people in the office were stalwart about sticking to a nine-to-six schedule, there was also the *night shift* crowd to keep the drawing boards warm. Lou never seemed to leave the office.

Once, going up to the office in the elevator, George Howe admired Lou's crookedly tied straight-cut bow tie. Lou immediately took it off and gave it to him, while George, in response to his gesture, took off his tweedy four-in-hand and gave it to Lou. Although Lou admired the Ivy League men's look, he was never conforming or over-fastidious, but always had a natural, slightly tousled look. He was proud of his unusually broad muscular shoulders and the fact that his suit jackets never had padded shoulders. He told me that because of his build—broad shoulders and slim hips—the swimming coach at Penn had urged him to go out for swimming, but Lou claimed he never actually learned how to swim. In the old Bulletin Building and in the office on Spruce Street, where we had no air conditioning, he would work without a shirt with his shoulders in their full freckled glory.

In giving criticisms in the office and in his teaching, Lou never drew right on another person's drawing, always on tracing paper over the drawing. If anyone were insensitive or unconscious enough to break this rule, Lou would tell the story of Napoleon's eye. When as a small boy he made a drawing of a side view of Napoleon and was having trouble drawing his eye, his father very lovingly corrected the eye. Lou never forgot how he felt. He gave the drawing to his father, saying, *It's not my drawing anymore, it's your drawing.*

Marvin Verman

Lou was constantly changing the design of the Olivetti Factory in Harrisburg, Pennsylvania. The client was becoming exasperated, not being satisfied with Lou's previous design submissions. Therefore, at a meeting in New York, Lou brought a new one—in the form of a model—which he was eager to present. This model, however, remained in its box during the entire meeting and was never even discussed. At the end of the meeting, all the Olivetti executives left. Lou was alone with the box and the two architects from his office who acccompanied him. He looked at the box and said, *The dog was very good. It didn't bark at all.*

During a 1976 visit to Israel, Lou was asked to give a lecture at the Architects's and Engineer's House in Tel Aviv. It was a hypnotic experience for all who attended. There was only one light, over Lou's head, causing him to appear as a mystical figure in the darkened room. After the lecture, Bruno Zevi said to Lou, *I finally discovered you.* Lou answered: *That just shows how backward you are, Bruno.*

There was a period in the '60s when educational parks, combining numerous educational institutions in a common setting, were a topic of conversation among urban planners. Lou, when asked his opinion of educational parks, replied, *Do the trees talk?*

It was July 3rd and a new employee in Lou's office asked him if the office would be open on July 4th. Lou answered, *This office does not observe religious holiday.*

It was after midnight and I was driving Le Ricolais home. We were traveling down Walnut Street past Lou's office. The light was on, of course, and we both noticed it. Le Ricolais said, *While we sleep, he stands guard.*

Two days after Lou was buried, I went to Le Ricolais' apartment. I needed to talk to him for my grief was deep and I hoped he too wanted to talk. He did and we spent the afternoon exchanging thoughts and memories. That afternoon, Le Ricolais said, *Not many people can pass a life and say they met a man.*

Roy Vollmer

My first exposure to Louis I. Kahn was seeing a photograph of a project model. The impact of that image, that moment, told me who my teacher must be.

My first meeting with Louis I. Kahn was as a young student seeking summer employment. I had arrived early at his office and was nervously smoking a cigarette when he arrived and asked me to come in. There was no ash tray, and I did not know what to do with the long ash or the rest of my half-smoked butt. Seeing my dilemma, Kahn placed a simple slab of granite before me; then sensing my discomfort at soiling this beautiful piece of stone, he quipped that *the stone would not mind since it is being useful.* He then proceeded to expound upon the nature of stone, and it was a wonderful long time before he asked me what I came to see him about.

We used to mimic Lou because we really loved him. He was very loveable and very funny.

Most typically included forms were his voice, gestures, walk and other mannerisims, the way he fussed with his hair or eyeglasses, or the way he would get the phone buzzers all muddled and cut you off in the middle of a conversation. All such antics were mixed in with the profundities that he would often repeat, his praise or chiding, or a predictable kind of utterance or gesture that he was likely to make. Most were ended with a kind of jolly little *ho-ho* laugh.

Lou was never one to let the mundane realities of office practice divert his poetic sensibilities and philosophical attitude towards architecture.

One particular day, so typical of those *bad days at the office,* Lou was beseiged by so many telephone calls, letters, bills, visitors, and questions from his staff that he became upset. Suddenly, he turned to all within earshot and defiantly stated, *The office is the enemy of all thought!* and walked out the door. We looked at each other, repeated what he had just said, marvelled at his wisdom, and went home. We didn't see Lou for two whole days.

Lou had a tremendous insistence on his own originality and authorship. He just had to be the one to make the discovery about a thing and sometimes it was comical to watch him make it happen his way. This is not to say that Lou did not admit to drawing inspiration from the thoughts or expressions of others, but more than likely, when he was wrestling with a particular problem that seemed to be eluding him at the time, he would sometimes respond in some fairly unpredictable ways to some parallel thought or drawing you had just expressed. Sometimes he would pooh-pooh it and say, *No, no. That's not what it should be.* And sometimes he would praise it. He seldom would admit that it was an idea. Usually, he would excuse himself and disappear back into his office. Some time later, he would come back out into the drafting room. His face would light up like the child who has just discovered the cookie jar as he would sit down and recount in his own words his interpretation of that thought or drawing which you had, only a short time ago, tried to discuss with him. He would then unfold a truly marvelous tale about his new discovery.

Once, when I was back in Philadelphia for the day, I wanted to stop in the office just to say hello and possibly talk with Lou, if he were available. It was always a pleasant surprise when he was, and this day, I happened to be in luck. It was a Sunday and no one was in the office except Lou. He was in his private office and deep in thought when I entered. He looked up, smiled a cordial greeting, welcoming me to sit down, and started talking about spaces in light, and the meaning of spirit.

Each thought began to crystallize in his mind as he talked about it. He talked for two hours. After he was finished talking, he asked me what I thought of his idea. I replied (still a bit dazzled by his profound insight and lucid clarity) that it seemed just right. Lou looked at me and said, *Yes, it is pretty good, isn't it? I think I will present it.* I said goodbye as he started to draw profusely with the familiar charcoal on yellow tracing paper. The project was a proposal for the Memorial to Six Million Jews.

Once upon a charette, Lou looked up and asked, *Where's Tony?* (Tony had left the office about a month before.) When told this, Lou exclaimed, *Oh! No wonder I couldn't find him. I owe him some money!* He then immediately instructed Louise, his secretary, to send a check.

Colin St. John Wilson

I first met Lou when I came to the United States. It must have been 1960 at the invitation of Paul Rudolph to teach at Yale. And I went over to Philadelphia and met Tim Vreeland. He introduced me to Lou, and I showed him certain projects that we were working on then—which he already knew, actually, probably through Tim—the Oxford Library scheme in its earlier version and so on. And obviously one fell almost immediately under the personal spell. That's a silly expression, but I got some idea of the way his mind worked from articles in *Perspecta,* which had been brought over by somebody from Yale when we were working in the London County Council and which were left with us. So one had some idea of the way the man's mind worked and what kind of prejudices and what kind of fantasies he had. But, of course, actually speaking to him was very much to come under the spell of the way he talked and responded to what you were saying and then carried on from there. There was a kind of rhythm in it. And I keep on coming back to the word *spell* because it was that. One almost felt as if one was in the palm of his hand, sometimes, the way he was, and he always seemed to be enjoying it enormously. I think he got a lot from talking, from listening to himself. It was as if he was talking to somebody who might challenge what he was saying, making him think out loud things which he wouldn't have thought if he hadn't started that dialogue going.

He took me out to have a sandwich. I can remember the way he walked: funny stride, rather short figure but with a long stride, head down, looking unstoppable. And the most striking thing, or rather simultaneously with the way of talking and almost deliberately zapping you with that kind of spell, was his face, and one knows those images that you sometimes see where you cut someone's face in half and you reproduce and photograph it in two images. He had two faces more utterly different than anybody else would have two faces. One of them was quite angelic, I suspect. I always tended to think of him as if he were Father Zossimer from the Brothers Karamazov, the magically wise old sort of peasant priest. I can't attempt to recapture that without giving more thought to it but the sort of character that Father Zossimer was is something that seems to be a kind of kinship with Lou, who after all came from those parts, didn't he? He was born in Osel or somewhere. And very, very much, in a way, a Russian. He told stories of how his father took him to sauna baths as a kid. They used to start all night, you'd work your way up to the sauna. It was intolerably hot when you went in and you got accustomed to that level, so you climbed up a few steps and it was intolerably hot and so on, all the way up. And there's definitely a deep Russian streak in there, I think. And the other side of the face was that he could say some really cruel things even about people who one was sure he really respected and liked a lot. But he could suddenly flash out, you know. So he was sort of human, but it is unfair to expect that someone is going to be a magic man and a saint the whole bloody time. He was remarkably unbitchy, in architectural terms. I mean, the thing that was very good is, if he didn't like something, he just didn't say anything. It was a sort of disdain through silence rather than having to shoot it down.

Going back to the second occasion when I met him was in 1964 on the West Coast and Jack McAllister had asked me to call in, and I gave a talk at La Jolla, one of those funny club places overlooking a lake and Lou blew in and we had a little bit of clowning act because he'd come in, he'd left his drawings; we couldn't find his drawings. And he was doing a great act standing at the counter and leaning against it and the guy kept asking a question: what color were they and what did they have written on them? He kept giving these kind of funny, mad answers and then turning 'round to us and we would sort of provoke him on, and then finally the guy said, "How thick was the roll?" and old Lou says, "Thick as a woman's leg," and then he'd turn back around to us. He was really upstaging the whole sort of act. Oh, he was enjoying himself enormously.

I don't know if he ever found the drawings. That was Jack's worry, not mine. Another time, sitting out on Jack's terrace and drinking—Lionel Marks was with me then, too, because we'd driven over from Phoenix or somewhere—and I remember saying something to the effect that this is the way to drink because as your intake of the wine goes up, the light in the sky falls away and there's a kind of correspondence between these things. And Lou absolutely beamed at that. He said, *Now that's a great thought. Now that shows why you think well.*

I suppose that leads one to the thought that a great deal of his thinking was really around the kind of rhythm of natural things. And by that I mean particularly, one tends to always think of his building as being in daylight, and of his own kind of exasperation of the fact that, with the increasing sort of technological impact on the way you make an environment and so on, how the hell could you keep any of the heart in it that was there when all you were dealing with was natural light and natural seasonal temperatures. The fact that you could just switch it on or switch it off, I think, affronted him terribly. He made it perfectly clear that you can make a lot of fuss over the Richards Laboratory if you like but don't think I or anyone else can think that you can really make great architecture out of providing mechanical ducts for a laboratory. I mean, you can do a good job but the thing really operates at a much deeper level than that. So it was very typical that he would respond in that way.

I didn't see much of him for some time after that. Just the occasional quick call in Philadelphia.

I remember seeing his exhibition in New York. I think that the way that it was put across struck me exactly the way it would strike him, that it looked like a funeral, it looked like a farewell. It was very sort of dark and broody. I was absolutely fascinated by it. I think that some of his willfullness which was part of the kind of red-blooded thing didn't convince me in the way that time and time again I would say of Corbu: "That is absurd. But on the other hand, actually, it's right; it's bang on." With Lou I would simply say, "That's absurd and it's wonderful, but actually, it's not right." I mean, that's like sort of distinction between—I don't know what it is. It's something to do with a sense of tact, of and exactly balanced sort of judgement at the end of the day.

I recall, when he was in Cambridge, the talk he gave there. He talked then about how it was given to certain people at certain times to so maneuver themselves around in relationship to architecture that they saw it from a different angle. And I think that image of maneuvering around so that you get an alignment, sort of like imagining a kind of stellar system. If you look at it one way it won't happen; you move it around and suddenly zap, you've got a series of other things in line.

Peter Blake

It was a warm Sunday evening, in the summer of 1941, and several of us had driven out to some place in New Jersey, to look at a construction site. Now we were on our way back, and we were on Market Street, in Downtown Philadelphia.

There were four of us, I think: Lou, Willo von Moltke, Abel Sorenson, and myself. All of us were working in the office of Stonorov & Kahn at the time. We were driving in an open convertible and Abel said that what we needed was a few cold beers. Well, in those days Philadelphia was closed down tight on Sundays; and so, as we pulled up to a stop at a traffic light, I asked a guy in a car next to ours where you could get a drink in Philadelphia on a Sunday. *No problem,* he said. *Go to the 6th Ward Republican Club and tell them I sent you.* He gave me his card, and we took off for the address he'd given us—a small house just east of Broad Street, on Locust, I think. It was a one-story walkup, and we showed them the guy's card. It was about 6 p.m. and the place was quite empty. *Who are you?* the manager asked. *We're all Harvard men,* Lou said—which was a lie.

Anyway, we paid a dollar apiece, and converted to Republicanism. The Club was a rather dingy room, not more than 20 ft. by 30 ft., as I recall, and there was an old upright piano at one end, on a small platform. We ordered a round of beers, and Lou went over to the piano, sat down on the stool, and started to play Gershwin's Rhapsody in Blue, with enormous enthusiasm, energy and passion. The whole place began to shake—Lou had very large, very strong hands. He could crush your fingers in a handshake, and he could turn a piano into sawdust if he really tried. That night he was in great form. I don't know whether his repertoire on the piano extended far beyond Rhapsody in Blue, but he sure as hell knew it by heart.

After he'd been playing for a few minutes, the phone rang and the manager picked it up. *It's for the pianist,* he said. The hotel across the street was calling, and they said they had a hotel guest who seemed to be dying—could we tone it down a bit? Lou, who was very considerate of other people's feelings, immediately reduced his decibels substantially—but, being in the mood for music, he continued to play the Rhapsody in Blue, gently, almost secretly. The hotel called again: could the pianist reduce the volume just a little more? Lou cut back even further on the decibel count, but he kept looking out at the hotel entrance across the street, through the open window.

Suddenly he rose from the piano stool, and stretched his neck for a better look at the hotel entrance—never interrupting the quiet little Rhapsody, of course... An ambulance had drawn up in front of the hotel. Lou stopped, went over to the phone, and dialed the hotel. *How's your patient?* he asked. The answer must have satisfied him—for he hung up, walked back to the piano, and his fingers came crashing down on the keyboard, in a crescendo that shook the rafters.

We got the entire Rhapsody one more time that night, and I think I can hear it still...

Here is Lou, in his words, in his buildings, in his life. He was constantly searching—searching to bring out the best quality which was innate, but not a yet revealed. He was unconcerned with time—time was not a limited resource to be doled out. He was a man of joy—modest but strong, firm always open. He was concerned with the nature of materials, but never with materialism. He gave of himself with infinite generosity.

We were to have been at one of his magnificent buildings, the Richards Building, this morning, but for the rain; and Lou will live on through such great works such as the Richards Building. But his memory will also be perpetuated in other ways. The Governor, for example, wishes to name the Performing Arts Center in the Poconos which Lou designed, for him. And we of the University will honor him in an appropriate manner as well. But the way in which Lou will live most completely is through the lives of the many in this country and throughout the world who have been illuminated by him. And I speak not only of those who have studied with him in his classes, or studied with him in his office, but for the rest. Because he was and he is the teacher of us all.

Peter Shepard

How easy it is to say nothing but good about Lou. We all tend to say the same things because his purpose shone so clearly in his life and he expressed it so clearly in this buildings and in his teachings. Perhaps two or three things shine out above the rest. As Martin said, he was a pioneer all his life in the return to humanism. After that dry period when so many of us thought the fun had gone out of architecture, Lou brought it back. And it's worth noting that he was a man who was in a great tradition. He had a sense of the past as acute as his sense of the future. And this probably came from his early days with Paul Philip Cret and at the end of that great Ozark tradition, which was nothing if not fun. He was a modest man. Architects tend to be arrogant, and I think in his work, he was firm, decisive, but he was a modest man. And it's only been a week or two since I heard him say, *I would like to be judged by the buildings I am going to build, not the ones I've already done.* I felt at once that this was an untenable proposition for an architect and the architects of the world agreed with that. He had gold medals and praise from all corners of the globe for the buildings he had done, as well as for the promise of those he would do. But I knew him, as so many of the people here, mainly as a teacher. He was the spiritual father of the tradition of architecture at Penn and what a fortunate school it has been to have the undivided devotion of this man for the last 20 years. There's no way that we can conceive of replacing Lou Kahn. We will have to renew our tradition in other ways. But his effect will be an extremely lasting one, not only on this school, but on architecture generally. He had magic communication with the young. His language was idiosyncratic to the point where it exasperated the middle aged and the old, but was always lucid and compelling to the young. His gift of communicating—his own delight in architecture, was to my mind almost a divine gift. And it was curious how this element of being a prophet—perhaps a Jewish element, perhaps religious element—in the truest sense, make him talk of architecture in an immensely biblical and serious way, which I found very happy and I think all of his students understood. He used to talk long, but students used to crowd to hear him. I'll never forget the occasion in London when he came to talk—not when he got the Gold Medal—but long before that when he came to talk at the R.I.B.A., and we had known there was going to be a crowd, but we didn't know we were going to have to shut the bronze doors and call in the police to control the people outside who had come to hear him. We were that much out of touch with the younger generation at that time. But alongside this intensely serious attitude, there was a thing which I think we may be in danger of forgetting because here we are, those of us who loved him, sad because of his death. And at this time, it's difficult to remember what a fun-loving and life-enhancing man he was, because he was really fully human. And I remember when I used to be a visiting professor. I used to have an apartment on Sansom Street where Robert Le Ricolais used to live below me. And every Wednesday night, Norman Rice, Robert Le Ricolais, and Lou Kahn were there with gales of laughter telling all kinds of stories—not all of them proper, but all of them somehow connected with life. Lou's stories, however outrageous, always had a point connected with the handing on of life to the next generation, of the essential contradictions and beauty of life itself. Lastly, he was, above all other things, an ideal university man. And how rare it is to find someone who has devoted all his life to putting up buildings, and actually doing things in the world itself, who will give that kind of devotion within the walls of an academic institution. He simply said that the University is one of the most beautiful places to be in, and we were glad of that. May I end by quoting a poem of his. I feel that with my English accent that I won't be able to say it properly, so I will end, not with my words, but with his, and about teaching:

I have taught self-rewarding. School is my chapter. I write songs when I teach well, what I have done is never mentioned. Teaching is to represent the yet not said, the yet not made.

Jonas Salk

Out of the mind of a tiny whimsical man who happened by chance, great forms have come, great structures, great spaces that function. Some tell us the essence of the past, others—the creators, the discoverers and leaders—of an emergent future. The oneness surrounding it all is the mystery of his existence and in his creations. A mystery that will endure. For five decades, he prepared himself and didn't do what others wished they could do in five. Nobody sensed what he seemed to know about nature to reveal in form and in function eternal truths and beauty, each for verification of the other. From whence came his originality, his boldness, his courage? What or where was the source of his inspiration, of his judgment? There would be found the creative postules of nature itself. How does one capture and convey the Essence of Living Being? His words are those of a poet, his cadence that of a musician. He had the vision of an artist, the understanding of a philosopher, the knowledge of a metaphysician, the reason of a logician. When he caused to appear out of the invisible, the intangible plazas to see and to touch, the fruits of creation that continues without end, as if without beginning. What we see is not simply discovering what heretofore existed and a restatement of old perceptions. He brought into view a new reality. It is not without cause that our talks are of essence, of life, of continuous creation, because we speak of one touched by the divine spark—one marked to reveal that among men, some are possessed by a constructive and creative power to balance the power to destroy. The greatness of any age is in the works of those whose traces endure. We are gathered to pay homage and respect to a man whose imagination and whose work will have marked the time in which we lived. Our feelings of pride are mixed with feelings of regret that it will never be known how much or what more would have been expressed had life lingered until the capacity to create began to ebb. It is our good fortune to have known him, worked with him, loved him. Nothing need be said of what he has done.

Memorial Service
University of Pennsylvania

On behalf of his many colleagues and friends, those who will speak this morning in this service are: President Martin Meyerson; Dean Peter Shepard, School of Fine Arts; Dr. Jonas Salk, Director of the Salk Institute, La Jolla, California. The Memorial will begin with the Philart Quartet playing Beethoven's Cavatina from the Spring Quartet, Opus No. 130.

Martin Meyerson

Jeffrey Scott, writing early in this century in his remarkable book, *The Architecture of Humanism,* emphasized three values. Building on the principles of the Roman architect, Vetruvius, these were: commodity, or social utility; firmness of logic of a structure; and delight, or beauty. Nature unfortunately would seem to unite these qualities with extreme reluctance. But nature fortunately did synthesize these talents in Louis Kahn. Indeed, Scott's book title, the Architecture of Humanism, is a splendid description of Lou's entire career. Louis Kahn is one of a handful of great architects in the world this century. He was also a great teacher, and the two were inseparable. Here in this University which he loved, let us remember that he taught, he professed outside the class as much as inside it. He professed in his practice, so that the young from everywhere yearned to work with him. In his profession, perhaps only Walter Brookius was able to share the sublime culmination of being Master Teacher and Master Architect. I was 21 when I first met Lou, and I knew at once that I had encountered a great teacher. And all young people at all times knew this, and that is why I cannot accept from you that Lou was recognized late in his lifetime. He was recognized very early by the people he most wanted to reach, in the young, in the students. I have, ever since I first met him, marveled at his ability to inspire the young. His ability to teach was a capacity grounded in love. And late in life, he said the following: *I must reassess the time when a little boy who didn't know he was a student met a man who didn't know he was a teacher, and they met and cared for each other very much, and made an enclosure to get out of the rain, and that is a school — not merely something that a school board defines.* Now, for some, the written word and the spoken word are different, but not for Lou; and here are some of Lou's own words, some written and some spoken and recorded by others. He said:

It is not just enough to solve the problem. To review the spaces with new-found self-quality is a different question entirely.

I believe the greatest work of man is that part which does not belong to him alone. If he discovers the principle, only his design way of interpreting belongs to him alone. The discovery of oxygen does not belong to the discoverer.

I love beginnings, marvelous beginnings. I think beginning is that which confirms continuation. I revere learning because it is a fundamental inspiration. It isn't just something we do because we have a duty. It is born into us. The will to learn, the desire to learn is just one of the most, the greatest of inspirations.

Everything that you use is under scrutiny. There is nothing finished.

His works and their effect speak with blunt eloquence that can't otherwise be said. For him to be taken at the flood of the tide leaves us engulfed in sadness. As if drawn by some force, maybe to give expression to the meaning of the unmeasurable and measurable relationship, our paths crossed allowing each to help the other say and to reveal what would have otherwise been unknown. He will speak no more, but the dialogue will go on. He communicated what he comprehended. One could understand but never for him say what he alone could convey. Try however you can, imagine yourself in his presence, although the voice is mine, the words you will now hear are his:

Order is
Design is form-making in order
Form emerges out of a system of construction
Growth is a construction
In order is creative force
In design is the means — where with what when with how much
The nature of space reflects what it wants to be
  Is the auditorium a Stradivarius
    or is it an ear
  Is the auditorium a creative instrument
    keyed to Bach or Bartok
    played by conductor
    or is it a convention hall?
In the nature of space is the spirit and the will to exist
    in a certain way
  Design must closely follow that will
  Therefore a stripe painted horse is not a zebra.
  Before a railroad station is a building
  it wants to be a street
  it grows out of the needs of the street
    out of the order of movement
  a meeting of contours englazed.
Through the nature — why
Through the order — what
Through design — how
A Form emerges from the structural elements inherent in the form.
In design is the means — where with what when with how much
  Nervi grows an arch
  Fuller grows a dome
Mozart's compositions are designs
  They are exercises of order — intuitive
  Design encourages more designs
  Designs derive their imagery from order
  Imagery is the memory — the Form
  Style is an adopted order
The same order created the elephant and created man
  they are different designs
  begun from different aspirations
  shaped from different circumstances
Order does not imply Beauty
  The same order created the dwarf and Adonis
Design is not making Beauty
  Beauty emerges from selection
    affinities
    integration
    love
Art is a form making life in order — psychic
Order is intangible
  It is a level of consciousness
  forever becoming higher in level
  the higher the order the more diversity in design

Order supports integration
From what the space wants to be the unfamiliar may be
*   revealed to the architect.*
From order he will derive creative force and power of
* self-criticism*
to give form to this unfamiliar.
Beauty will evolve.

And so will Lou Kahn's creations, across time,
as the unfamiliar becomes familiar
revealing *the fullness of his symphonic composing*

And for all this
Thank you
Lou

The following pages are reproductions of the Notebooks of Louis I. Kahn

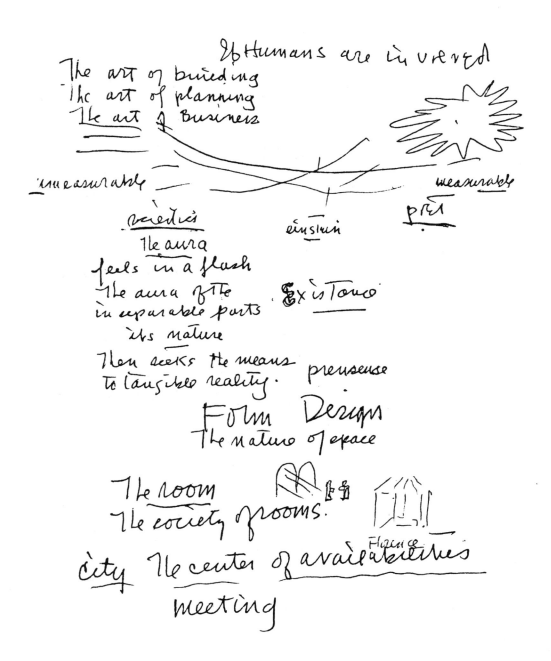

If Humans are involved

The art of building
The art of planning
The art of Business

immeasurable   measurable

sciences   einstein   psd

The aura
feels in a flash
The aura of the   Existence
inseparable parts
its nature

Then seeks the means   presence
to tangible reality.

Form   Design
The nature of space

The room
The society of rooms.

city   The center of availabilities

meeting

bulb - (basal plate = origin of roots + shoots)   cool, slow spring

Tunicate bulb = Daffodil + Tulip   stem

= laminate

greatest amt of food needed after   tunic   sheath of fleshy
                                     + leaves   scales +
unexpanded flowering   protection
flowering   shoot + next yrs leaves   storing food ar.
                                             center
(daffodils bulbs = poisonous to humans)

                                   * in axil of every
bulblets f. in axils of shoot leaves   leaf is a bud
                                       (veget. art.)
flower primordia initiated through temperature

aerial bulbets = bulbils
on stem (on lilies)   bulblet
                                 when independent =
                                 offset

Non-tunicate bulb

or Scale bulb   some
    Scaly   Lily bulb

easily damaged   every bulb = potential
must be kept continuously moist - never let dry out   plant

roots in mid-summer   principal root forms
can be produced on stem   on scale
above bulb

                          contractile roots

(Plant twice diameter of bulb = general rule)
Lilies plant deep except madonna lilies

~~contractile roots~~ If in doubt, plant more shallow than
                                                    deep
most bulbs require good drainage - otherwise disease
                                   from over damp conditions

vegetative stage - bulblet
Reproductive " - elong. of fl-shoot + flowers

FORMATION OF BULB

    single grow season → bulblet

tulip + iris bulblet disintegrates after flowering of flower

but new offsets form on base - takes a couple of years
if leave in ground - inferior to lifting + separating each year
+ nursing plants along - No variation in offspring that is vegetative in bulbs

Sep. 7 = First date in Sep. (latitude of Labrador but yield) 1 yr leaf new
11/14 cont Plant Propagation   2 yr " shoot
                                                                3rd "flowerbud"

| Rhizomes | German Iris   Lily of the valley
swollen underspr.   Spit   (not Jap Ins)   Fl. buds
stem w/ roots   Pachymorphous   Leptomorphs   PIPS
adventitious   (Gr. thick skinned)   (thin skinned)
    must
        large piece of tissue if   not fussy as to soil
        pachymorph (do not bleed)
        dip in ground charcoal(powdered)   Mesomorphs
        (+ bentite + sulpher) to seal
Virus problem in Iris : soak w/
Grays Iris solution.
Can separate anywhere of sure it has part
    of a root and an eye + enough food tissue
Easy to propagate - It runs over the place
after 3rd year   should be
likes LIME   separated, will not flower
                    return on spring (not Aug.)

* Most plants do not want alkalinity but some can survive in it
others cannot.

        Alkaline
diff. no   avaulable
elements   NEUTRAL   phosphorus gets
                        tied up if in excess
    5   alkalinity

        ACID
(FERNS - often crowns - split up)
        by spores cuttings
said - 1/2" Rhizome =
Specialized stem structure in which the main axis of plant =
grows horizontally just below or on surface of ground
mostly monocotyledons. ie. leptomorphic rhizome = bamboo

| Bulbs + Corms | Bulb = modified stem   leaves
                                                basal plate = stem
        leaf axil = bud or
If lift for sale   flower bud   daffodil
lifted when root is still   roots give only moisture not
active but needs cold period to initiate growth   food
        (6 weeks)
Force Daffodil bulb   if bring in with root, will it bud
    put in pot   is cold needed for flowering?
    cold 40° bakes   when leaf above soil then light cycle.
    to form roots

SOUTHEASTERN U.S.   I

F = FLORA   = aggregate, limits dictated by physiography
   Holarctic f = around the N hemisphere
N FAUNA   in this latitude we have holarctic f, interdigitate
Basins (belsona = sp) is where most significant plant events occur
   tend to homogenize flora + faunas

   Taxa = taxon
          groups (of differing composition)

* $F \left[\dfrac{taxa + taxa + etc.}{C.E.B.} \right] \times \dfrac{\text{genetic potential}}{\text{isolation (barriers)}} \rightarrow \begin{array}{c}\text{fill an}\\ \text{environment}\\ \text{niche}\end{array}$

       Rainfall, Temp.
C: Climatic, E = edaphic, B- biotic   Biome - Fauna + flora
C.E.B. complex or ecology   w/ different degrees of intensity, rates
   (cosmic radiation influences new speciation)

   C- minima = most important
Restrictions -   Soil: serpentine in N Calif. Coast ~ S Pa + Del. plants
(Tropics are a sanctuary of archaic times)
                          biota:
   Bio ta: { pollination (function) + hybridization
effect in plants (dispersion (in   )
                          reproduction)

Flora is like a megaorganism - many parts in balance - Macrocosm
                                                  GROWTH
       stink tissue a body
   (soma) — sp   semplasma a gonad } = organism
                                 plants WS = soma
                                       fi = sp

genetic potential - how much variability is intrinsic in the species
barriers restrict genetic potential:
         physiographic barrier

Epicenter of oaks in US = Mexican basin = 1 source (2nd) = Asia Alaska
      single, etroic lense - willow   down west coast
huts = limited dispersal range   in fingers → pockets
                          moving down Calif (b) rockies. cut off
                                              by Pleisto. glacier
Anemo/chory = wind dispersal)   Hydro/chory = water transport
      samaras, etc.   c)   most successful
Baro/chory = heavy fruit that rolls around (walnuts)   (ie coconut)
Bio/chory = distributed by animals   Ecesis = establish
                      (squirrels)   CEB can present Ecesis
Anthropo/chory = "   " man (Plantago major)
      (Vicariad = unintentional introduction)
       weeds.

2 Nov. B. Hort II   C. wilson Camellia - pink fl
                                   tricolor   *

Camellia japonica. Hardy here. northern limit
W. Ev. shiny. many cultivars

    Pink Snow   April or May in Pa. }
    Kumasaka   Feb or March in Va. }
    Paulette Goddard
    etc.

Camellia sasanqua - smaller shrub, narrower leaves
                          Blunt in apex   single fl.

    Flowers in November - "Crimson Buds"   (6' x 5' broad
                           "Cleopatra"   500 flowers
                           "maidens Blush"   D. Fogg's)
         slightly   "madam Butterfly
         curving
Do not plant broadleafco.
_____
shrub in full sunlight.
_____

Camellia chinensis - Tea or C. Sinensis   Native to India.
_____   Sikkim
    Flowers until Christmas - inconspicuous fl.
    broadleaf evergreen
    1st + 2nd leaf plucked at harvest time
    kept to 4 or 5' even if 400 yr old plant
    dried + fermented   must be protected against sun
Tea blooms - mid Oct on

    ┌──────────┐
    │ STEWARTIA │
    └──────────┘
        Earl of Bute who stand Kew Botanic Garden
      (10) spp - deciduous   2 in SE U.S.
                  rough flaky bark 8 in SE Asia
Fl cup-shaped - golden yellow stamens
Fr capsule - dehiscent along 5 lines

    Stewartia Koreana - more hardy
_____
Native: S. Ovata - Mountain camellia   N. Carolina
(or Pentagyna)   less hardy than oriental Tenn. Fla.
         5 styles separate   all others =

    S. malachodendron - Silky Camellia · SE U.S.
_____

Silence to Light
Light to Silence
   The Threshold at their meeting
     is the singularity
   is the generative touch of the inspirations
   is where the desire to express meets the possible
   is the sanctuary of ART
   The Treasury of the Shadows

The Pyramids ~~seem to want to~~ ~~are glad that~~ seems to say
~~So the~~ tell of motivations ~~that~~
and its meeting with Nature
in order to be

I sense
Silence as the aura of the desire to be to express '
Light as the aura 'to be to be '
Material as ' spent light '

(The mountains the streams the atmosphere
and we are of spent light)

Silence to Light
Light to Silence
~~The~~ The Threshold of their ~~meeting~~ crossing Their crossing
now The Threshold of their
singularity
is the Singularity
~~is the~~ ~~inspiration breath~~ of ~~the~~ Inspiration
(where the desire to express meets the possible)
is the Sanctuary of Art
is the Treasury of the Shadows

(Material casts a shadow the shadow belongs to light)

It is good to feel approval out of the un-measurable
of commonality — the ~~sense of~~ of human agreement —
the spontaneous of.
one can ~~one~~ ~~can sense~~ ~~Silence~~ ~~as desire~~
Sense Silence as the ~~breath~~ aura of desire to be to express

The Pyramids seem to say "Let me tell ~~you~~ of the
desire ~~that~~ motivating being and the meeting with
Nature in order to be"
one can sense ~~all~~ Nature as Light and all material
~~Material~~ as spent Light.

The mountains the streams the atmosphere and we are of
spent light.

Silence moves to Light
Light moves to Silence

Silence to Light
Light to Silence
~~Their paths~~ ~~lead~~ meet
The Thresholds of their meeting
is the singular
is the ~~inspiration~~ touch of inspiration   the un-measurable of the
is where ~~desire to express~~ meets the possible
The longest ~~path~~ ~~is~~ ~~the sanctuary of art~~ from Silence sustaining its desire to express
before crossing the path Light is ~~the~~ ~~to touch~~ the generator of poetry
The ~~longest~~   restraining its desire to express   what is manifest
Parting from Silence to feel Beauty, the total harmony of ~~all~~ ~~presences~~
~~to come to~~ ~~Silence~~ ~~to come to silence~~ allowing light to take its longest path
to silence is ~~its~~ is discovery in science.
not the best
Yet a Newton ~~needs~~ but a hint from ~~nature~~ Nature, the ~~approver of all presences~~
~~He moves after~~ lets not go of desire, ~~it get not said~~ the yet not made, the
~~the~~ disapproving his knowings in favor of a sense of order ~~out of~~
To sense ~~law~~ ~~as~~ as only a part of order

In the ten years since the printing of this book I have been given the opportunity to study ~~and design a number~~ reshape land and design new buildings and ~~buildings. which~~ This has taught me I have always. during that time prevailed ~~H Thought that~~ I was ~~able~~ to enjoy the experience of designing a number of buildings at the same time. ~~This had the effect~~ and got to thinking about what is common about ~~recognize the commoness of~~ buildings. ~~of bring into the nature It made~~ claim me to realize that Architecture began creation of the ~~well the room. and that the plan is the society of rooms.~~ It seems I found that Room is a unique identity in English. There is no word for it in French, Italian, or German. ~~To me, the room and its dimensions the the structure of a space in its particulars The structure A room may be but a room~~ the structure, ~~the first flight,~~ must be evident in the room itself. It is not a partitioned area. Its dimensions even respond to persons in it. and one does not say the same thing in a small room as in a large room. If you are in a room with only one other person you may say what you never said before, ~~and~~ if Another person entering in which owed have the effect of changing this event to feel moves ~~they say~~ are repeated.) so remote are the vectors of individuality. ~~what repeating~~ your lines. ~~So sensitive owned little room.~~ The plan is a society of rooms. ~~counsellable to regarded nature of The great chased to a plan~~ ~~spirit and~~ whose rooms decide ~~their names~~ to name ~~themselves.~~ I read saw it not to lead of real of interiors of rooms could name themselves after they are made. ~~When It issued to Vision~~ years ago I thought it important to know things. about ~~feel and the~~

Transfer in your way

A few notes ~~to amplify~~ ~~my~~ ~~short~~ ~~that~~ to add to my little talk before your committee on the Congress of the Institutions

The ~~buildings~~ ~~construction,~~

                                                                                    roman segmental or jack

~~I have visualized the~~ The buildings will be ~~made mostly~~ of brick ~~made~~ of brick construction ~~with~~ ~~use of a~~ making use of a arches for
                                                                                    a per   openings

~~in~~ ~~these cases~~ ~~of openings supported by~~ ~~very~~ and segmental and ~~and~~ ~~jack~~ arches ~~All steward~~ openings
                                                                    roman

Bridge building over ~~which~~ would be of a ~~composite~~ be ~~order of concrete and brick~~ with large span brick arches, aided by reinforcing.

                                                                                    architectural

The building indicated ~~are~~ in the model ~~are not~~ ~~in there~~ ~~so~~ are not in their final ~~form~~ ~~are~~ ~~in~~
~~regard~~ ~~to~~ ~~this~~ shapes. ~~The~~ The individual rooms and the relation of ~~these~~ rooms to each other ~~the~~

~~will be~~
~~will~~ ~~be revealed~~ ~~appropriate~~ when revealed ~~thru~~ by discussion ~~leading~~ ~~to~~ ~~be~~ ~~incorporated~~

of the elements of function will in spire the appropriate shapes or the ultimate material,
when the ~~in separable~~ ~~elements~~ on the function of spaces in keeping with the ~~proper~~ nature of the building
Discussion now bring out the needed

The buildings are visualized as of brick with to use of a variety of brick arches
The Architectural character is ~~to~~ ~~be considered~~ ~~diagrammatic~~ ~~in~~ is only ~~still~~ schematic
                                    as ~~it~~ indicated on the paper model
~~and you can't~~ When the ~~purposes~~ ~~and~~ purposes are established and the true spaces
defined ~~visualized~~ then the character of the buildings will be revealed, ~~then~~ in their building
                                    in their buildings the will   in their building

I believe ~~have learned~~ the first congress ~~to be held~~ ~~in~~ ~~the first~~ is Latin national ~~in 1826~~
        I conveyed the idea that the   will be it has already ~~occurred~~ as
I may also suggest, what I am sure to ~~be~~ of is considered obvious that as a National
Congress, the funds for its construction almost come from the Government,
is it unreasonable that as a National Congress the building could be (in an cost of the Government
and be the prime purpose of the ~~birthday~~ The birthday

~~I am developing th areas~~ ~~and~~ of spaces available
~~As~~ I am prepared to work on th areas of

The longest trace from Silence sustaining
the un measurable ~~of the desire to express~~ before
measurable, is permitted to
the means, ~~can~~ cross is the Threshold of Poetry

Parting from Silence restraining the desire to
Laws of nature,
express to grasp the ~~total harmony of order~~
~~enticing~~ the measures of extend its offerings ~~taking~~ by taking
~~allowing~~ light, ~~to take~~ the longest path to Silence
before crossing its trace and meeting at the threshold
is the Threshold 'Science'   toward

Yet a Newton, like the poet, needs but a hint
~~as~~
from Nature to sense the Universe He allows the
favoring
desire to express ~~to seek~~ the yet not expressed disapproving
of his knowing of Law ~~in favor of a sense of order~~.
the
~~in light~~ ~~seeking~~ only the
~~feeling~~
Total harmony of order.

What was has always been
what is has always been
what will be has always been.

His work ~~is of th confin woum~~ is in th continuum where all styles blend
~~to~~ confirm ~~~~ unmeasurable ~~qualities~~ truth which a work of art evokes. In his hands
~~~~ every media ~~is to left unfolding th~~ nature ~~its limit by the chosen shapes~~ mass,
Touches its limit)
and green radiance ~~~~ his choice ~~shape~~. line and
color
by his free classical inclinations

~~~~ Painter Sculptor ~~and~~ Craftsman and Teacher and working with him on th memorial to
~~~~ Roosevelt, discovered th architect in him. His suggest ~~~~ of ~~~~ He sculpture as the
ideas unfolded ~~~~ presented new appropriateness and even ~~~~ more influenced the
on all considerations of the design.

I wrote something about Art :

XX — XX

It is good ~~~~ about the feelings of an ~~~~ artist ~~~~ need th knowing
to want to express
if cannot be done ~~~~ How to express ~~~~ him. ~~~~ motivations
his expressions if ~~~~ feel does not belong to him. He ~~~~ what does not belong to him.

To Karel Mikolas

What was has always been
What is has always been
What will be has always been

His work is in this continuum where all styles blend, confirming
the unmeasurable truth which a work of art reveals. In his hands
every medium touches its limit, revealing its nature, and is given
radiance through his free classical inclinations by his choice of
mass, shape, line and color.

Painter, Sculptor, Craftsman and Teacher, also I discovered the
Architect in him. This became clear working with him on my newest commission, the Memorial to Franklin Delano Roosevelt. His
ready suggestions about the required sculpture, as the ideas unfolded, offered new attitudes and, even more, a grasp of wholeness
which influenced the overall concepts of the design.

About Art

That moment when the eyes opened. 'Beauty' the Light!
Could it be so if Joy had not inspired sight?
Joy, the medium impelling creation over trials of
infinite pulses from Nature's touch to the marvel of seeing
has, is, will be 'the birth of beauty'
the sense of the prevailing harmony at once felt.

Art-the first word.

Louis I. Kahn
November 1973

To Scarpa.

His details

~~Art is a work~~

In the ~~work~~ Scarpa

ornament, a celebration.

The joint ~~is~~ The ~~celebration~~ ~~inspiration~~ ~~tells~~ ~~the inspiration~~ ~~Form ornament~~ ?

In the detail is ~~to~~ ~~love~~ ~~for nature~~ ~~implant~~ adoration ~~regard~~ for nature

In the An element ~~is~~ ~~the dependence~~ ~~on the~~ ~~co-existence of~~ is inseparable depends on element

If the on the realization of the inseparable elements ~~is~~ ~~The~~ ~~realization~~ of Form lies Form

~~To the~~ Design connects nature ~~tells to~~ to give presence to the elements

~~The Art is to feel~~ ~~to~~ Form ~~tells~~ ~~manifest as the~~ ~~composed also~~ ~~symphony of the elements~~ :

Art is feel ~~also Art~~ ~~the~~ ~~Form~~ wholeness of Form, felt in Existance,

becomes manifest as a symphony of the elements.

~~for his name~~

To Scarpa

In the work of Scarpa

~~The inner substance~~
Beauty is the first sense
Then wonder
'Art is the first word'
Then the inner realization of 'Form', the whole ness of inseparable elements
Design talks to Nature to give presence to the elements
~~Art works Natures to hold the~~
~~Art makes the wholeness of Form felt~~
~~A work of art~~ Shapes which
Art is a work which has mastered ~~Nature~~ the means of Nature ~~to whole te~~
~~in making which manifest a~~
~~to bring a symphony~~ of the elements ~~to effect Form~~ admirable
~~te mind existence of Form.~~
~~Art is the first word.~~
~~Art is a work~~
~~A work~~

(first name inserted) Italies 'Carlo'

In the work of Scarpa

Beauty is the first sense
Art is the first word
Then wonder
Then the inner realization of 'Form', the wholeness of inseparable ~~part~~ elements
Design ~~talk~~ consults nature
To give presence to the elements   ness
A work of art makes manifest the whole 'Form' ~~nelae relationy~~ ~~for the~~ the symphony ~~of~~ ~~shapes~~
~~symphonic,~~ of the selected shapes of the elements ~~made manifest~~

In the elements
The joint ~~int~~ inspires ornament, its celebration
The detail is the adoration of nature,

Lou Kahn

In the work of Carlo Scarpa

    'Beauty'
    the first sense
    Art
    the first word
    Then Wonder
    Then the inner realization of 'Form'
    the sense of the wholeness of inseparable elements.
    Design consults Nature
    to give presence to the elements.
    A work of art makes manifest the wholeness of 'Form'
    the symphony of the selected shapes of the elements.

    In the elements
    the joint inspires ornament, its celebration.
    The detail is the adoration of Nature.

Louis I. Kahn

out sentimental and with the humor. brief —

Teacher — Architect

Biographical

People
Places
Events

European — American.
American.
Religion — a religion.
Bangladesh.
India.
Arabian Nights
Fairy Tales

Joy   matter

The American Revolution.
   The British enemy
   The British romantic history
   The Knights of the Round Table.

My mother's faith in America

My father's   200%   wasted talents.
   his un enterprising nature
   The store where he sold his wares
   for less than he paid for items to
   his friends.
   The little store that was constructed
   on $75.00 & — —

The story of the I jump. — recuperative inventiveness
Need to have people around me who cared — Jung aloud yule
in order to gather the — the sense of the tenents of an order
The story of the Public Industrial Art School.
   The story of musical tendencies.
   The drawings at an early age. Wanamaker.
                                    Academy of Fine Arts
The story of the High School course on Architecture William F. Gray

Influences — Implied. impressionistic. suggestive.
draw analogies from music. Tapestry of Florence.
Talk on the representation of leading to ———
the ——— reflection on the inevitable from the miracle of
beginning. Time alters the means by what is avail.
Then what was has always been. etc.

When sight became
~~Art~~ Beauty
Prevailing harmony at once felt
Yet not Knowledge yet not choice
what could have preceded
Joy ~~Joy~~
The Inspiration to see.
Then Joy feels Beauty
Art ~~Art~~
The first word.

Art is a work
a response to the desire to be to express
a response to the odyssey of our becoming
Recorded in the intuitive
From beauty to wonder to realization
~~to Realization~~ of Existance that wants to be
~~from existance~~ to Presence ~~a work~~
~~our~~ A work
From Nature's inspiration of to be to be

The nearer a work to Begining the more Transcendent.
~~The~~
The increddible ~~the revealing~~
of the unmesaurable
the in touchness with eternity

universal

9 January 1973

Ms. Carylin Walden
Grade 2
Child Garden Country Day School
Chesnut Street
Exeter, New Hampshire 03833

Dear Second Grade Class,

The drawings you sent me were all so lovely that I imagined before
I read the names on them, that is, the names of the artists, that
they came from Fairyland.   You see, I used to be just as
young as you all are. I believed in Fairies then. I believe in
Fairies now. That is why it was so easy for me to think that
these drawings came from the hands of Fairies.   One day I
spoke to a group of scientists and I made this remark, "The beginning of science comes from the wish in the Fairytale." You may be
surprised that these very fact-finding people that scientists are
believed also in what I said.   You see, older people keep
throughout their lives the preciousness and the eternal truth of
the sense of wonder.   I thank you, every one of you, for
reminding me of the joy of youth. I draw very well now and I made
drawings like yours when I was very young. I am therefore positive
that every one of you will be artists one day in one way or another.

Dear Carylin Walden.
I plan to give the school one of my
drawings of the Exeter Library
before the building was constructed

Louis I. Kahn
Louis I. Kahn

LIK/kac

Dear Esther!

This is Sunday mid night. We worked all day yesterday and to day preparing for our meeting in Ranalpindi, West Pakistan, with the Health Department in regard to the Ayub Hospital. Two new wings have been added to the original design. — Hd of Tropical Medicine and Cancer Research and Treatment both yukhed us, we beliere, are worried out now to the satisfaction of the doctors in charge,

To morrow we take up with the Joint Secretary of the Department of works the design and construction of two important roofs, — Hd of the National Assembly chamber and the Mosque. They want domes we don't indicate domes. There will be a hassle. Like a bad penny 'A touch of Islam' crops up periodically. This will now also be the case.

To day I walked in the garden adjoining the place we have our office. The plants are very unusual makes your head swim with the realisation how varied Nature can show itself. There is one plant the struck me particularly.

I will try to find the urge to write about what happens to morrow

I am definitely coming back on Saturday. My meeting in Ranalpindi late in the week almost resolve some of our matters. I will then fly to Karachi on my way home

love Lou

Just the ends have leaves about 7' high

always 1 2 3 start to leaf

year marks of previous blossoming.

When you see two plants in depth it is most handsome

from the city where the air port is located. From Rome
to Athens was the most exciting air ride I ever
experienced. I saw from the air Naples flying near
Vesuvius

from there we traveled the length of Italy with a fine view
of the many hill towns (Medieval) crossed at the boot
across the Adriatic to Greece which had the real
flavor of ancient Europe an unspoiled Italy. We
flew thru the mountain passes to avoid sniping from
the hills. The snow capped Carpathians were the most
majestic I have ever seen. We flew on over red
ports of the Greek historical areas and then approached Athens
by circuitous way (military reason), and saw for a
few fleeting moments the Acropolis.

Aegean Sea

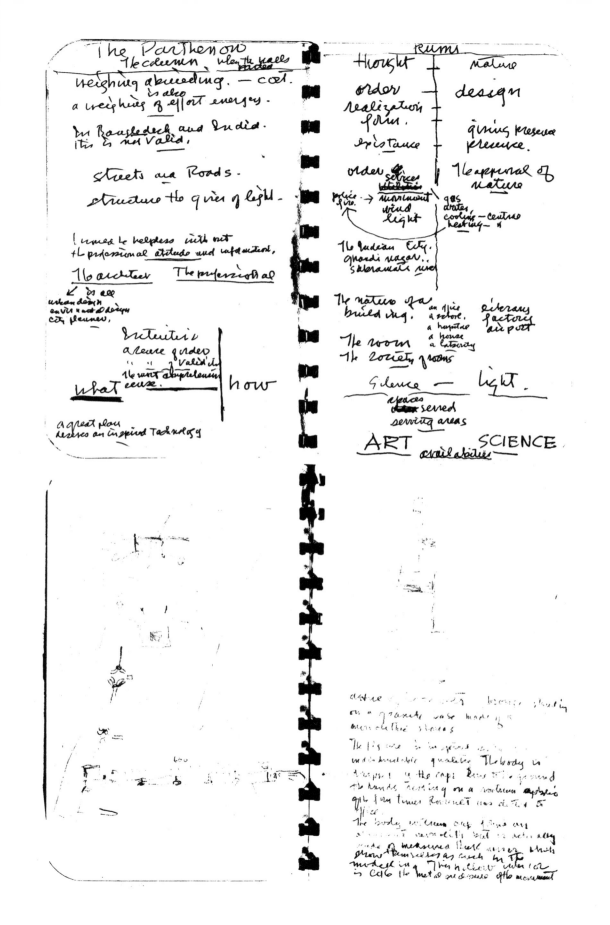

The Parthenon
The column when the walls ended
weighing a building — cost.
is also
a weighing of effort energies.

In Bangladesh and India
it is not valid.

streets and Roads.
structure the giver of light.

I mean to helpless without
the professional attitude and information.

The architect   The professional

It is all
urban design
environ and of design
city planner.

Intuition
a sense of order
"   "   of Validity
the want of comprehension
what cause. | how

a great plan
desires an inspired Technology

Rums

Thought		nature
order	—	design
realization form.		
existence	—	giving presence presence.
order services		The appraisal of nature
price live →	movement wind light	gas drains cooling — centre heating —

The Indian City.
ghandi nagar..
sakramati river

The nature of a building.   an office a school a hospital a house a laboratory   library factory airport

The room
The society of rooms

Silence — light.
spaces served
serving areas

ART   SCIENCE
availabilities

Human agreemen

There is en Monpartasse
tall buildings

From the standpoint of Human
Agreement the Mongart 200? I have
been walking on the time here taller
than the tall building

The Eiffel Tower is a tall structure
but does have people living in them,
Human agreement now except. This
as any isolated expression of French
would it accept the other one of adventure
I act like it.

Human agreement I assume would not
approve

This would not this tall building en
Monparnas have been the modification
of the French engineering in genius

of a tall building
in the wind.
as preserving the steps
of building in which the
lower columns were wide and
strong growing to the weight
the upper columns then
so weightless dancing
like fairies.
and the wind which tries
to up turn the building has
also in the architecture express
as a detail of bracing
against it.

This image would have
embossed every skyscraper
in the U.S or reversed have
been a french building

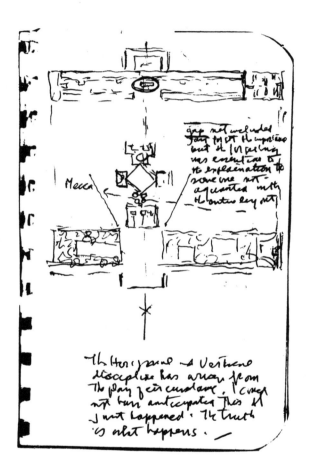

Mecca

The Horizontal and Vertical
discipline has arisen from
the play of circumstance. I could
not have anticipated this it
Just happened. The truth
is what happens.

Dalia

Silence

The aura of joy
to desire to be
to express

non material

Light

material is spent light
The mountains the streams
the atmosphere.

The Threshold.
The singularity
The Inspirations

(the beginning of Architecture)
The room   The classroom   The hall   The assembly
                                     (corridor)
                                     (The division of an area?)

(The light of the room)
The sun never knew
how great it was ---

The Plan
The society of rooms
The structure of the Rooms in Their light. (graphic).
(Structure is the giver of light)

Light and Room
Natural Light. (The modes) Artificial Light (static)

blue
yellow   Program (vs) Nature of the spaces.
red
green   house   the house The home. (a way of life) (a way of living)
                 School   The realm of spaces where it is good to learn
                 factory   The column is The enemies
                 Theatre —   Violin Violin case
                 airport —   The road building.

inseparable parts
                 The art gallery   The room of the painter sculptor   or arrangement
                 Shopping Center   Buying Center?   for interest.
Realization Form (not personal)
order-design (personal)
     shape

The Realization of a Form does not belong to the realizer (a person)
                                                (not a creation)
Design belongs to the creator
                                                It was there all the time
                                                Just waiting for its
                                                moment brought into light by
                                                It is in the nature. a person

I do not think that all schools of
Architecture need be the same
nor can They be the same
Their personel are not the same
  "   students have varied talents
The curriculum could suit both   with a Capital A
          But   and not with
The all should talk each other
as to nature of its study in what many ways They all teach (Architecture)

Let us suppose that the National Gallery were to build on its land a room. Its structure in its light evident within. Just dedicated, without reference to its use the marvel of ~~the~~ inspiration.

The room -- ~~The beginning~~ Stephen Douglas   → Baptistry of Florence

The society of rooms. The plan.

The academy of the ~~supreme~~ court.
    of the university   academy
The library as the place of the book
        price of the book
        The libraries of ~~the universe~~ ~~disciplines~~ of the disciplines
The STOA   a space for inspired USE — the teacher the student the measurement

Nature of the spaces

Science   and   light.

No aura of to be
to express.

The exerted   The price
Newton
Einstein field player

Matter material
The giver of all presences
to make manifest.

The profound ance of ~~all~~
you   touch   sight.   beauty total harmony
                      art the first word
                      art is a work.
    ?

— wonder — realization
Form —
    The inseparable parts
        Existence

Structure is the giver of light —

Natural Light

Form

Design
To presence

city plans   the orders
        aural abilities
        U.S.A.

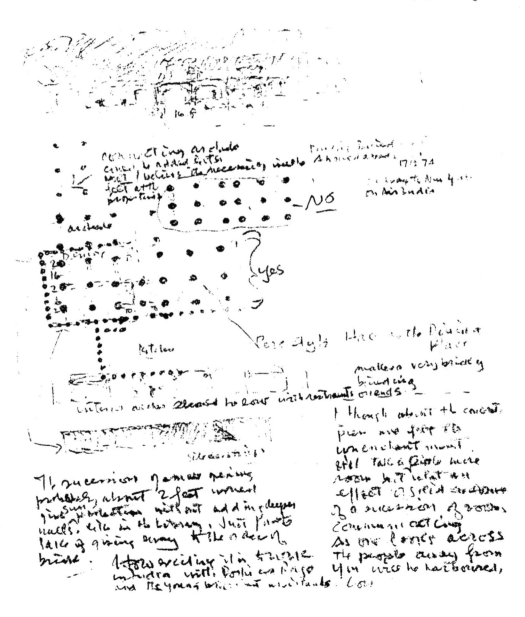

architecture —
true — .
orientation
Lot 9'
the nature of the space —
the room.
the plan as the society of rooms.

Conversational

I learnt things away

The letter. 10 years ago   what they represent now.
what used to be.   lots of work
what were the interests 10 years ago.
how used to do. not had to think of what was the way to
do.
Library at the window.
Yale building and had to think about

7← ———|——→ 10
turning point

oracle of delphi

I thought I had to know about things
which was good
                because
I learned that I did not
need to know things
              yet
it is more to the point.
to say that what you retain
is only what is already in you
and what if you forgotten was
a need to know.

make the memory
is delible by in reading
the etchings
tons of — — —
notly to do with what
you saw (storage)
doing to like one position
a revealing your nature.
is free of problem about avoiding problems
problem relates always to making
or not to what you make. The etcher is when best
a course directed by both in the work to its truest
from what you make the most precious account go now
presented as though which is his signal actual.
you them how to make they are the locus of possibility
also not — issues
But —It stands for things you it is not illustration

your nature
is
the
way built
to
respond to
work on
all its manifest
is the reason
that is is
The practice
men come
easily —

city Planning (is not design) It is the constant realization
urban design } of the nature 'city' as circumstances
Architectural design } Architecture reveal its nature

Architecture must become
The attempt of

The projects of building
Architecture ~~encompasses~~ urban design
It is essential to the emergence of architecture
The realm of spaces where it to-day
is good to learn
to live
to work
to recreate etc

meeting
learning

The services of the city

The car ~ The garage is part of the
the utilities design of the street
add central conditioning or road
(refrigeration) order of water.
Storage
The development of their Form
and design of ~~design of their~~
housing
The provision of the center and
other of the areas
Integration of The ring road
storage
shops.

Its measures
The character of its institutions
The character of its sectors
or
addresses
The memory stimulants
of its places and
their connections
(the art of its connections)
The courts of its entrances
The parks and garden
The streets
The roads.
The order of its water
The order of its sanitation
the order of movement
The order of air
The order of light.

The buildings
The Treasury of the space

The buildings
The entrances
The courts of gardens
The park

docks ways
to streets
prime streets

1

A city architect
is not like the
other.
The natural talents
have many niches
that fill the total
realm of architecture
It need thought
it need to honor
new realizations
new forms
new shapes
new shapes
as to its nature

Architecture
what the nature in form
how design
The crane. influences design
prefabrication "
The order of time "
The order of material "
The joint (The beginning of ornament) "
To free the spaces of gross services
placed in the
lands of the city

ghande nagar
sabramati river.

Stradegy of the   Of Places and People

When the "operational machinery" is upset it is
well not to think of corrective methods. They are too complicated
These corrective plans are subject to circumstance
and circumstances are unpredictable.

We cannot seek the Truth.
Because the Truth shows itself by what happens
weather you like it or not.   ✕

Needs are relative
needs deny give satisfaction from time to time
we live by our desires
Desire come from Joy.

The primordial ooz from which man rose
where miriad particles of Joy.
Joy emphatically empeeling itself to the manifestation of
                    Desire.   from TOUCH TO SIGHT
The Desire to express.   ART — is living and
out of the odessy of our making
which has its seat in our intuitions.
our most accurate sense.

                    NEED   India 2
Learning   Bangledesh. (DESIRE)
Meeting.

The measure of a country
The measure of a city   the (Institutions)
① Is the character and extent of availability
A boy walking the streets puts city

        what nature can make. It makes, now conciously

                    can come
From desire can come for An inspired
                              Technology
        The new plan comes deserves a 3
        out of desire (NOT NEED)

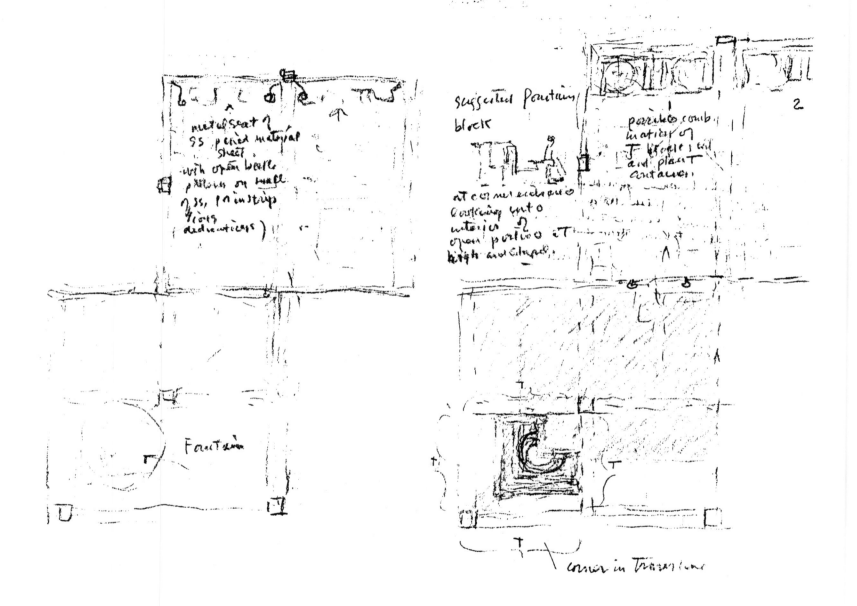

Suggestions in the place and
of conference, but of the
Yew Nosenery (suggested
by Zion) in the middle
of the Lower Court with
seating stone benches
around it.

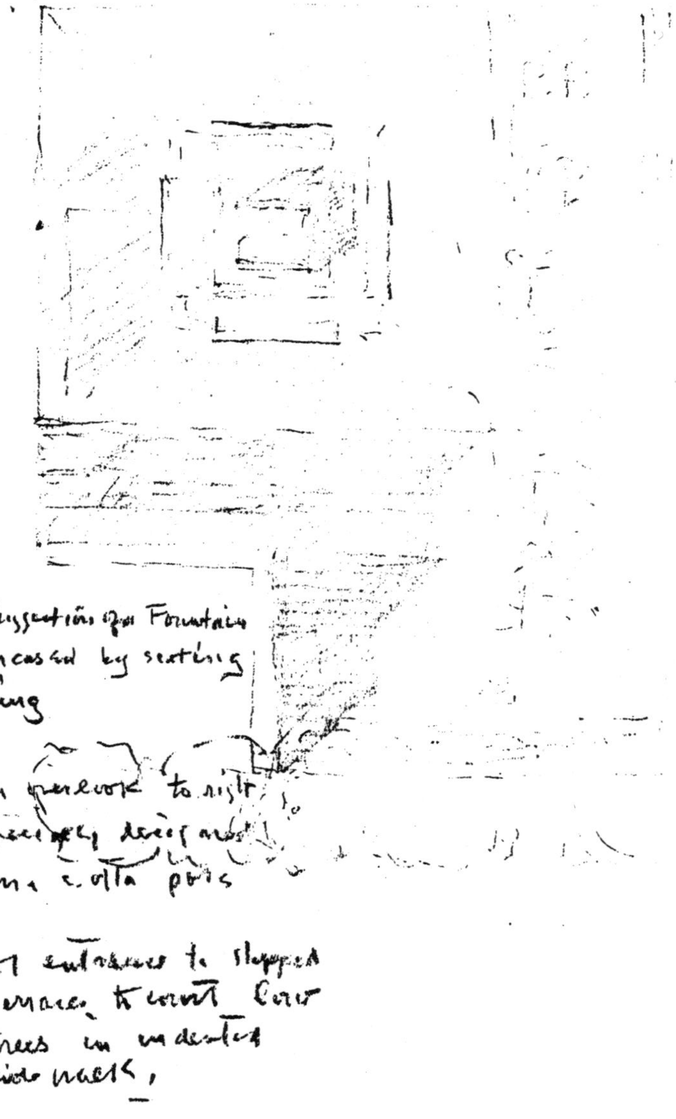

Suggestions for Fountain
encased by seating
ring

on overlook to right to
specially designed
terra cotta pots

At entrances to slopped
Terraces to count low
trees in understory
character,

Beauty — order — realization — form.

Form   ## Design.

Singularity   to   Singularity
The desire
who knows what he wants   The designer
                              who knows how to express
        motivation   motivation

The desire to express ←——————→ The maker of
                                   all presences
                    singularity

To express
The validity in Thought   The validity in nature
The un measurable   The measur able.

The sense of form
the in separable parts   design of the elements
    (the elements)   to be brought together
The nature of what is thought about   answerance—Form
                                   NATURE

what is known in presence is known   What is known in presence
thru the human sense of validity   put together in any other
The human sense of Form   arrangements is still merely
                                   design

THOUGHT   WORK
                                  motivation the sense
    motivation in a sense   of the laws of nature
    of existance   commanding or the singularity
                                  of the means to give
                                   present.

    Knowing   Knowledge

The art of design

What is yet not expresses
This will expectation which
each designer can express only in his
way. The locomotive though it is
                                conclusive

The enlargement from scaled drawing to full scale may be understood better by actual photographic enlargement of the small scale. The contours from accidentals are brought out & though not to be imitated still suggests the breaking up into smaller parts on the construction of the line. The single stroke at small scale becomes a constructed movement at full size. — Doing the mural at the Community Center at Trenton it was evident that the scale drawing was only directional and that the lines and fields had to be built up from the limits of the brush the medium and the surface and treated as a construction problem. The original idea of the discipline set by the existing 8 x 16 blocks still could hold however. The block actually is rough the scale drawing is smooth. The joints are not uniform the joints in the scale drawing are uniform. The transformation from drawing to an actual vertical wall — which cannot be tilted or laid flat as a drawings requires the use of a ladder and the jumping from it to view the work or back again. Many new experiences enter which are not present in making of drawing. The actual mural must reflect the labor different from that of making a drawing or painting. ~~Seeing the transformation from drawing~~ The struggle must be evident — felt by the observer. When one stops to consider the effect on our sense of a painting let us say 100' long painted to imitate the studio sketch. 100" long.

It is a question of scale. Scale may be defined as related to the labor and the instrument of labor is it the hand? the spray? the bull dozer a crane? Also it is related to the read ability of how it is done. We cannot expect the spray to simulate the action of the hand nor the hand to imitate the textures or uniformity of the spray. Nor can the hand paint a single line 10 feet long without re wetting the brush several times and perhaps modifys the color in so doing.

The house painter prides in disguising his brush marks and in the matching of colors uniformly.

The artist painter shows his brush strokes and considers each new brush stroke as a new color. (even though the same color is used).

Scale as the brush stroke

If the hand gets to be as big as a crane then the scale is equally as justifyable as the scale produced by the hand. These two scale must not resemble each other. Leger's immense mural (U.N.) from a 10" × 10" sketch emphows his back-scale.

Mies — Corbusier
who is prettier ?

Corbusier's work is eternal, visually provocative. Reason

Mies's work is usually perfect and logical. —— nice but many imitators of lesser stature

Corbusier cannot be imitated There is a hand and heart to deny needed in the work

Mies's work depending mainly on craft and proportion impersonal with indices is more easily imitated. But barren architects of ever increasing multitudes are always ready to make an easy touch. The "me too" boys will believe it belongs in the profession

Corbusier's imitators will try to make him prettier.

Corbusier does care about being beautiful. They think They are improving on Corbu They are only disclosing their barrenness.

Corbusier — Beethoven

Mies — Clementi.

We need a Bach in Architecture. Brunelleschi Bramante.
Who will it be ?

F. Ll. W

Wagner ? Floating down the Rhine in a cape on a barge on top of a staged concrete or flowers. This is now long ago that giant heart of gigantic courage and arrogance created from his environment the most wonderfully true architecture Amérique. Now he is influenced but won't admit it. Who ? Nobody specifically — Corbu ? oh yes [He hates him] Mies ? never ! [He doesn't mind him] The Box ? yes of course. The Triangle itself the T square too and the compass. They all come into it. Rhythm. Sex ? more than Corbu ! mind you ! more than Mies ? Asexual. Homosexual Non sexual of course. He's terrific that way.

The imitators of F. Ll. W are of a lower strata than those of Corbu. He is more arbitrary, personal, experimental or distainful of traditions. His democracy is a democracy of Kings. It used to a day to see a King with his tin lunch box going to work in his own personal factory where he alone is employed.

Mies is the master craftsman disciplined by a vision of classical Greek architecture. Corbusier is the master architect disciplined by the same vision but sensitive to his environment.

Mies's sensitivities with creating space reacts to imposed structural order with little inspiration drawn from what a building 'wants to be'.

Corbusier feels what a space 'wants to be', the order impatiently as he hurries to form. In Marseilles order was strong. Each gave rise to form. Ronchamp order is only dimly felt in form born of dream. Mies's order is not comprehensive enough to encompass acoustics light air piping straps stairs shafts various as being ruled and other services to space. His order of structure serves to frame the building but not harbor the servants of spaces.

Corbusier's order is aroused thru Corbusier as sculptor painter. The artist is thus thus in him. In the great musician – composer it is similarly there as deeply in touch and ready to make designs in sleep and awake with each touch a reflection of its creative ganglia.

Spaces under a span.

From L. Kahn

Compartmented Containers.

The spaces leave no impression how the space is made.
What is the meaning in the effort of span which
does not need to express that effort.

Compartmented Spaces.

Space made by a dome then divided by walls is
not the same space.

A span obstructed by partitions is like
every other note of a symphony played next door.

A room should be a constructed entity or an
ordered segment of a construction system.

Rooms divided off from a single larger space
must read as uncompleted spaces. As such the
larger structure should be sensed, if not seen
from end to end.

The fact that we are able to roof a wide space
may induce the compartmented ~~~~~ attitude
— The box with spaces in it. This attitude
matured in the drafting room (these spaces
comes from viewing the space from above at
small scale on a piece of paper on a board.

Misinterpretations of Mies's early drawings of
divisions in space.

The artist in architecture thinks in terms of the
spaces which he is creating. The means at his disposal
does not put him in touch with construction. The
spaces are therefore drafting room visions, 'sans suite'

Formalisms.

Buildings erected from contract drawings are
forced into formalisms - - -

June 7 '55

Craftsman – Artist
Mais (Johnson)
F.Ll.W.
Corbusier.

Anne is not satisfied unt.
the power expressed only by
form making ~~will the~~ not
derived from an order
of construction which is in
the architect inherent
in form, Ann claims that
~~if Corbusier or~~ had a growth
concept of structure as I
~~and she understands~~ ~~and be~~
be himself would not
be satisfied with his
work.

The last edition of the Sunday Times showed pictures of
Corbu's chapel at Ronchamp. Reactions differed widely. I fell
madly in love with it Mario feels the same as I do.
Dave thinks it arbitrary. Tim is not committed, Paul
just repeats my words of prior adding nothing, Dees says
it looks like hundreds of churches in Switzerland.
To me it is undeniably the work of an artist. An
artist able to retranslate a dream into the concrete
details of architecture, A dream full of the Known
unrestrained forms symbolic of religion to the
dreamer. The architect has accepts unafraid to
reconceive these symbolic forms even if they are
unfamiliar ~~of~~ to the forms which identify
his work. [To invent new symbols?]. To
adopt the old or rather for the artist to continue the
symbolism gives testimony to an energy still
felt of their power and truth, creates dynamics,
to interpret church (or religious place) by Mais Saarinen
Belluschi F.Ll.W. have all fallen flat on their behinds.
Compare their meticulous complications or puritanic
restraint or ~~impressionistic~~ no structural triangulations. with
Corbu's uninhibited embrace of 'church' around
him ~~its~~ absorption of its spiritual nourishment
(probably since childhood) unredeemed expressed by notions of
went contributes consistency of personal style. I believe the
artist is never career conscious. He is constantly
conscious of his art. yes!; not success nor the
existence of his compositions.

∿———∿

Corbu is the artist because he reacts, guided by
Can reaction to environment be so self centered
to command
design with glass boxes in Thule or Bagdad. [Can one
call himself artist at the time when to between
Corbu and Mais – two diametrically opposed personalities

The I mean me
I mean it both center, in
some respects I feel it because
I feel partly due to cross

The Palladian Plan

I have discovered what probably everyone else has found that a bay system is a room system. A room is a defined space. — defined by the way it is made. — by the way it gets a roof or ceiling and has its walls to separate it from the rest of the spaces ~~that is~~

In a system of bays not intended as rooms the rooms however do still exist though it may not have the walls to define it.

This brings up the familiar problem of division in a free space in which the structure is disregarded in the discipline

~~being~~ created without a consciousness of rooms ~~XXXXXXXXXXXXXXX~~ not intended ~~XXXX~~ ~~XXXX~~ ~~XXXXXXXX~~ from the beginning. The columns and beams are chosen as a matter of cost, or knowledge but not with architectural feeling.

An area ~~XXXXXXXXXXXX~~ constructed of let us say 16 square bays is actually composed of 16 rooms. With no partitions they are still 16 rooms

~~XXXXXXXXXXXXXXXXXXXXXXXXXXXXXXX~~
~~XXXXXXXXXXXXXXXXX~~

One room is a single spaned area or an area flanked by its supports.

To me that is a good discovery

The Palladian plan has that quality.
Johnson's plans have that quality in part
He is not so conscious of structure and therefore he fails in the "intrinsic". It looks Palladian only
Beauty is not skin deep. The eye is not the only judge.

Some one asked me how one may carry out the room idea in the complex problems of house
I point to the Da Vinci house which is studying

Labor day Thursday Janet Bloom, ?.
   facts and figures.
deadline for new Marshall — McLister
Fri — 7th   Fri Afternoon
   Layout conference.
~~Dear Ricks and Ilene~~ hasto let me or Cindy Tavar by noon
 this coming friday will be in offering again

In the ten years since the printing of ~~this~~ study book I have been given the opportunity to design and build new buildings, I was preveliged also to enjoy the experience of designing a number of buildings at the same Time. This is good, for one building tells the other of its nature leading to new realizations ~~of~~ of spaces, in composition
The principal ∧ of distinguishing the servant spaces from the spaces served which I thought about when designing the Trenton Bath House has ~~guided~~ been a constant ~~we~~ in the structure and character of spaces.

In the ~~but~~ ~~9th~~ 2nd book. I touched on ~~the~~ Thoughts about the affect of the intimate room and the large room on student and teacher ~~in the~~
I ~~very~~ feel that ~~many that~~ ~~read that~~ the room is the beginning of Architecture and the plan is the society of the Rooms. ~~Realization~~
~~While~~ In germany France and Italy I realized that 'Room' is not understood ~~in the same~~ as in English. ~~The was~~ So ~~beautiful~~ Beauty, a total harmony, is in ~~that~~ ~~not~~ the realizations of this word. If I were to speak in the Baptistry of Florence I ~~could not~~ ~~say~~ would be lead to say what I never said before. A room could be generative. This could happen, In a small room with just another person, A third person could disturb the vectors ~~the change~~ changing what ∧ could have been an event into a performance, and ~~renisteri~~ is a room.

What about Temple U.

someone had kissed
what I had long
expected.

premier Tone by Dart
all friends and each other alone
others.

It was a party
I felt any ... going with this
party ... expected myself
People were admiring people
I knew. Drawings I made
long ago were shown to me. I thought
long lost they were good better than
I thought I could do. Yet mine.
one an ink drawing with darks
of water color on a tinted very light
background.
Met Softie the night before in honor
of Carlos Tel Aviv

steel.   Insect
                Elephant.

stainless — unpolished —
coreten —
steel sophisticated shapes covered.
in surface reductions

tall
belted wings of steel with (concrete
                            (towers
                            (for
                            (escape)
                    sound control.

1 → The beauty of steel is its insect
like appearance and strength
covered as its insides is gone
meaningless.
Steel enclosure with belted wings
inside.

Bridge =
The free bar of the spaces between
the post supports.
The supports are becoming
farther apart.
The enclosure.
concrete is not possible not on steel
The expense of services. —

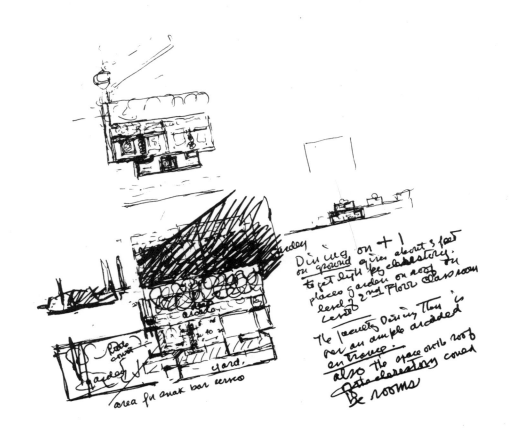

Dining on + 1
on ground gives about 3 feet
to get light [illegible] clerestory.
places garden on roof
level of 2nd Floor Classroom

The [illegible] Dining This is
for an ample arcaded
entrance.
also the space with roof
[illegible] clerestory could
be rooms

area for snack bar servic[e]

yard.

It seems to ... that the corresponding
of the hands be as through the
baton were transparent. The
hands could then be seen superposed
... in their position, but
these should be not like all these
drawings I know needs the sculptor

My remark that structure is the giver of light is thereby recalled in the march of columns in the great Temple.

light ~~light~~ no light .

no ~~light light~~ no ~~light~~ no light. is
The column is like the shine of the sun where the light is not.

the burnt figure. recognised as one i met
Clean up man to destroy erased wood - 3 inches long.
The beauty in blue seemed to constantly appear. easily detected at a distance.
The out fit tried on trousers placed them back when others try to conceal having taken them. As leaving figure meant this was fixed in guard whom they belonged to. the buttons marred the cloth.
Some security in a certain car... had other plans - left them with idea to go my own way. crossed again found them not having left and had to join them after all last night.
We were talking about the impropriety of breaking the capital in the light of desperate housing needs. some about the secretariate. Explains land use & inundated land which carried he built over. Filling lowlands in surmountable task. Density should be greater?
To stories as advocated who can climb these heights. they would have to sweat out heights as related to age. there cannot be elevators stored temporary houses to build.
Young people there at the lorry. this man's aide the doctor and his wife say need giving people said many things related to my relation with the authorities which were understood while wonder now since I cannot sleep (it is early morning) how wise I was stating to these people which if reported I am afraid would not rest well with me.
I wish I did not so much the determination to finish the capital.
The dream above was like a warning these strange innovated dream somehow is recognizably connected one would not be without the other. the also being bitters and one afraid of ones own folly which once lead to treachery intended to do good for the nation in I no way feeding an other primal fires for my destructive position yet heightening them to constructive criticism.

I ~~There of it~~

I ~~feel the Kinship~~

~~What I feel~~

One feels

~~Reflecting~~

~~As an Architect I can feel~~

That moment when the eyes opened 'Beauty', the 'Light'!
Could it ~~have~~ ~~hold~~ be so if Joy had not inspired sight?
Joy the medium ~~of~~ creation ~~unfeeling~~ ~~over~~ creation over infinite ~~stop~~ pulses from
~~team~~ touch to sight. What ~~a beautiful moment~~ in th was, is and will be
simple
~~the realization of Beau~~ 'the birth of Beauty' ~~felt~~ free of
Knowledge free of choice just the ~~sense~~ sense of it prevailing
harmony at once felt, ~~And Art is the Word.~~
~~Art is~~ Art — the first word. xx _____

inspired   presents it possible
~~Art to an Artist~~ the at the threshold where natures ~~wants~~ wants and Joy in creation
~~the~~ expression of ~~meeting~~ ~~the~~ of natures
A response ~~to~~ the Joy of creation in divining a desire to be to express ~~it in~~.
of inspiration

relate

miracles of around us, Veils the
~~the~~ Knowing ~~fades~~ ~~made~~ miracle. The miracle is blazing
~~Boredom~~ cast a shadow on